THE DAIRY BOOK OF

HOME COOKERY

The classic cookbook updated for today's cook

NEW EDITION 2012

Acknowledgements

Original recipes by Sonia Allison have been updated, tested and prepared for photography by the Milk Marketing Board and Eaglemoss Consumer Publications Ltd. New additions have been created by Eaglemoss Consumer Publications Ltd. All photographs by Steve Lee/Eaglemoss.

Managing Editor/Editor	Emily Anderson
Executive Editor	Nick Rowe
Copy Editor	Emma Callery
Designer	Graham Meigh
Photographer	Steve Lee
Food Stylist	Sara Lewis
Props Stylist	Jo Harris
Home Economists	Pat Alburey
	Kathryn Hawkins
	Lucy Knox
	Sue McMahon
	Kate Moseley
	Helen Mott
	Ruth Povey
	Lynne Riddle
	Jennie Shapter
Proof Reader	Aune Butt
Indexer	Christine Bernstein
Production Manager	Priti Kothary

First Edition 1968
Second Edition 1978
Third Edition 1992
Fourth Edition 2012

Eaglemoss Consumer Publications Ltd
Electra House, Electra Way, Crewe, Cheshire, CW1 6WZ
01270 270050 www.dairydiary.co.uk
First printed March 2011 © Eaglemoss Consumer Publications Ltd

ISBN-13: 978-0-9560894-3-4

123456789

THE DAIRY BOOK OF

HOME COOKERY

The classic cookbook updated for today's cook

Almost every British home you visit has a copy of the Dairy Book of Home Cookery. This really is the classic cook's companion that people cannot live without.

The Milk Marketing Board first published the book over forty years ago in 1968, this was followed by a metricated version in 1978 and another updated edition in 1992. Each edition proved extremely popular, selling over 1 million copies each. Yet, despite the passage of time with its changing fashion in British cookery and proliferation of TV chefs with their numerous recipe books, we still get daily requests for this original book. Many people have copies that are too tatty to decipher and others are keen to buy the book for children leaving home for the first time. To meet this demand we felt it was time to republish the book with some new 'classics' as well as old favourites

Since its last publication, many more ingredients are readily available in most supermarkets. This has been reflected in the recipe selection in this edition. Favourite original recipes have been included and there are also a number of new recipes that reflect the way cooking and eating habits have changed over recent years. Also, each recipe now has nutritional information per portion. This book is about easy, everyday cookery for all the family. It is a compendium of all those basic recipes invaluable in every kitchen.

Dairy cookbooks are renowned for their reliability and for their simple, attainable recipes. It is the original trustworthy cookbook, which has been updated for today's cook.

Contents

Cook's Information

Dry Weight Conversions

Recommended grams (g)	Imperial ounces (oz)
15	½
25	1
50	2
75	3
110	4 (¼lb)
150	5
175	6
200	7
225	8 (½lb)
250	9
275	10
300	11
350	12 (¾lb)
375	13
400	14
425	15
450	16 (1lb)
500	1lb 2oz
680	1½lb
750	1lb 10oz
900	2lb

These quantities are not exact, but they have been calculated to give proportionately correct measurements.

Liquid Conversions

Metric (ml)	Imperial (fl oz)	US cups
15	½	1 tbsp (level)
30	1	⅛
60	2	¼
90	3	⅜
125	4	½
150	5 (¼ pint)	⅔
175	6	¾
225	8	1
300	10 (½ pint)	1¼
350	12	1½
450	16	2
500	18	2¼
600	20 (1 pint)	2½
900	1½ pints	3¾
1 litre	1¾ pints	1 quart (4 cups)
1.25 litres	2 pints	1¼ quarts
1.5 litres	2½ pints	3 US pints
2 litres	3½ pints	2 quarts

568ml = 1 UK pint   (20fl oz)   16fl oz = 1 US pint

These quantities are not exact, but they have been calculated to give proportionately correct measurements.

Oven Temperatures

°C	(fan)	°F	Gas	Description
110	(90)	225	¼	cool
120/130	(100/110)	250	½	cool
140	(120)	275	1	very low
150	(130)	300	2	very low
160/170	(140/150)	325	3	low to moderate
180	(160)	350	4	moderate
190	(170)	375	5	moderately hot
200	(180)	400	6	hot
220	(200)	425	7	hot
230	(210)	450	8	hot
240	(220)	475	9	very hot

Guide to recommended equivalent settings, not exact conversions. Always refer to your cooker instruction book.

Suitable for Vegetarians

If you are cooking for a vegetarian, please ensure that any cheese, yogurt or pesto sauce you use is suitable for vegetarians. It should give this information on the jar or packet.

Spoon Measures

1 tablespoon	= 3 level teaspoons
1 level tablespoon	= 15ml
1 level teaspoon	= 5ml

If greater accuracy is not required:

1 rounded teaspoon	= 2 level teaspoons
1 heaped teaspoon	= 3 level teaspoons

or

1 level tablespoon

Recipe Notes

Cooking Times

Preparation and cooking times at the beginning of each recipe are approximate timings only. Where a second recipe is required, for example, pastry, these timings have not been added to the recipe in case you should choose to use the ready made alternative.

Cooking times may vary slightly depending on individual ovens. The oven and grill should be pre-heated to the specified temperature. Use the centre of the oven for baking.

For fan assisted ovens, adjust cooking times, in accordance with the manufacturer's handbook.

Symbols

❄ This symbol indicates that the recipe is suitable to freeze.

V This symbol indicates that the recipe is suitable for vegetarians, provided you are using a cheese, yogurt or pesto sauce that is suitable for vegetarians.

Measurements

For all recipes, ingredients are shown in metric and imperial measures. Follow either metric or imperial measures but do not mix them. Use measuring spoons to give accurate measurements. All spoon measurements are level. Abbreviations used are 'tsp' for teaspoon and 'tbsp' for tablespoon.

Sizes

Large eggs should be used unless otherwise stated.

All vegetables are taken as trimmed, washed and peeled where appropriate. Choose medium-sized fruit and vegetables, unless otherwise stated.

Weights are prepared weights.

Where a weight of an ingredient is expressed as 75g (3oz) rice, cooked, this means 75g (3oz) weighed raw, then cooked. If 75g (3oz) cooked rice this means 75g (3oz) weighed after cooking.

Alternative Ingredients

Wholemeal alternatives for flour, rice and pasta, can be used where desired. Extra liquid may be needed when using wholemeal flour as it may absorb more liquid.

When using wholemeal rice or pasta, follow the instructions on the packet.

Use whole, semi-skimmed or skimmed milk in a recipe. When heating skimmed milk in a saucepan, take care and use a moderate heat as it has a tendency to scorch if placed over a high heat.

Hard cheeses and yogurts with differing fat contents are also interchangeable.

Low fat spreads are usually unsuitable for frying and baking because of their high water content. Check their packaging as this should highlight their limitations.

Low sugar, low fat or low salt varieties of products such as jams, baked beans, sausages and mayonnaise are now available. These can be used in the recipes instead of the traditional products.

Nutritional Information

Each recipe shows the number of calories, fat and saturated fat per portion. The number of portions is shown at the top of each recipe.

Serves 2   Preparation 10 mins   Cooking 7 mins
Per portion 289 kcals, 11g fat (6.5g saturated)

Where there are portion variations, for example, serve 4-6, these figures are calculated on the higher number of portions. They are based on standard, not low fat foods and semi-skimmed milk.

At-Risk Groups

Certain at-risk groups, such as pregnant women, babies, sick or elderly people, should not be given raw or lightly cooked eggs, soft cheeses or cured meats. Recipes using nuts or nut oils should not be given to young children or to people with an allergic reaction to nuts.

Food Safety

Bacteria are all around us, although only a few types are harmful and cause illness. However, contaminated food which causes food poisoning quite often looks, tastes and smells perfectly normal.

It is therefore, important to know how to reduce the risk of food poisoning.

The three main ways to do this are:

- To protect food from contamination.

- To prevent bacteria in food from multiplying.

- To destroy bacteria present in the food by cooking/reheating thoroughly.

When Buying Food

Check the 'use by' or 'best before' date marks to ensure they are still current.

Use By Date
This is used on highly perishable foods. Eating food after this date could put your health at risk unless you have frozen or cooked it to increase its life.

Best Before Date
This indicates the time during which a food should remain in peak condition. It is used on foods that are not microbiologically highly perishable. If stored according to the manufacturer's instructions, the food should still be safe to eat after the date. However, its appearance and quality could have suffered, eg. biscuits could be 'soft'.

Best Before **End Date**
This is used on longer life food, eg. canned food. It is an indication of quality and is not used on highly perishable food. Do not buy damaged cans which have 'blown', that is where the ends are bulging.

Do not buy cracked eggs.

Buy frozen and chilled food last. Pack frozen and chilled food together and take them home as quickly as possible, particularly in warm weather. Do not leave them in a warm car or office or carry them around for too long. If left for just 1 hour, their temperature can rise and may encourage bacteria to grow.

If you cannot take food home immediately or you have a long journey home, especially during a hot summer, pack frozen and chilled foods in an insulated bag. This will keep it at the correct temperature. Put perishable foods in the refrigerator or freezer as soon as you get home.

Storing Food Safely at Home

Keep cupboards clean and wipe up any spillages immediately.

Avoid keeping dried foods in potentially damp cupboards, such as those above a steaming kettle.

Store packaged dry ingredients, such as flour, semolina, oatmeal, suet and nuts, in their original packets, in a cool, dry, airy cupboard. Once opened, transfer the packet to an airtight container, remembering to retain the date mark or noting down when the contents should be used.

Use cans and packets in rotation.

Store dried herbs and spices in wood, earthenware or dark-coloured glass away from the light so that they do not lose their colour or aroma.

Store dried fruit in an airtight container once opened as it will shrink in warm conditions.

Check flour, semolina and other cereal products for insect infestation and immediately throw away any affected foods.

Store root vegetables, such as potatoes and carrots, preferably unwashed, in a cool but frost-free, dry, dark, airy place. Do not store in polythene bags. If they must be kept in the refrigerator, keep in a paper bag or put in a polythene bag with absorbent kitchen paper around them to absorb moisture.

Refrigerator Storage

The best place to keep perishable foods, such as dairy products, meat, fish and cooked dishes containing these foods, is in a refrigerator.

Refrigeration does not kill bacteria, but slows down their growth. Keep the refrigerator at 0-5°C (32-41°F) as bacteria multiply quickly above 5°C.

Perishable foods should not be stored beyond their 'use by date', as the chance of bacteria multiplying is increased. It is therefore sensible to buy perishable foods frequently and in realistic quantities.

Perishable foods can often be frozen at home but this must be done when they are in peak condition, not just before the expiry of the 'use by' date.

Do not site the refrigerator next to a heat source such as the oven, dishwasher or central heating boiler as it will not work efficiently.

Do not overload the refrigerator. This will ensure it keeps cold at all times.

Defrost the refrigerator regularly unless it does this automatically. This helps it to keep cooler and use less energy.

Keep the refrigerator clean and wipe up spills immediately.

Do not leave the refrigerator door open as this warms the internal temperature.

Do not put warm food straight into the refrigerator. You should cool it quickly.

Cover all foods before putting in the refrigerator.

Organising Your Refrigerator

Put cooked meat and cooked dishes at the top, which is the coldest part, under the frozen food compartment if you have one.

Ensure that meat and poultry are wrapped so that they cannot contaminate other foods.

Put raw foods such as meat, poultry and fish and thawed foods in a dish, cover and store on the lowest shelf. Place underneath any cooked food so that juices cannot drip on to other food and pass on bacteria.

Put fruit, vegetables and salad ingredients at the bottom, preferably in the salad box.

Put milk, fruit juices, butter and eggs in the door.

Store raw foods separately from cooked foods to avoid cross contamination.

Do not store cooked foods for longer than 2 days.

Store eggs in the refrigerator.

Keep mushrooms in a paper bag and store in the salad box.

Once opened, store low sugar jams and sauces such as tomato ketchup in the refrigerator. If jams or marmalades grow mould or ferment, throw entire contents away.

Do not store opened canned foods in their can. Transfer to a container, cover and store in the refrigerator

The Kitchen Hygiene Guide

Keep the kitchen clean, crumb free and dry. As well as dishes and utensils, this includes the refrigerator, microwave oven, work surfaces, small appliances including their working parts such as blades and whisks, and the floor. When washing up, use hot water and detergent, rinse under very hot water and let it drip dry. Try not to use a tea-towel as this can harbour bacteria. A dishwasher is the most hygienic method of washing as it uses very hot water and also dries the dishes.

Change and wash tea-towels, towels, dishcloths, aprons and oven gloves often. Absorbent kitchen paper is a hygienic alternative for drying your hands, work surfaces, chopping boards and utensils.

Hang dishcloths and tea-towels to dry after use. Bacteria multiply rapidly in damp conditions.

Always wash your hands with soap and hot water before preparing food and after touching raw meats.

Wash your hands and utensils between preparing raw and cooked foods.

Clean and dry the work surface and chopping board before preparing food.

Use plastic polyboards in preference to wooden ones. If possible, have separate boards for raw meats, vegetables and cooked meat.

Do not prepare cooked food on a board just used for raw food and vice versa.

Always wash vegetables, salad ingredients and fruit before preparing them.

Do not allow pets on work surfaces and try to keep them out of the kitchen, especially when preparing food. Keep pet dishes and serving utensils separate from the family's dishes and utensils.

Good Cooking Guidelines

Make sure meat and poultry are thawed thoroughly before cooking.

Make sure large joints of meat and poultry are thoroughly cooked in the centre.

To ensure poultry is cooked, push a skewer into the thigh and if the juices run clear, the poultry is cooked.

Once thawed, do not refreeze raw food unless you have cooked it first.

Cooked, frozen then thawed food should not be refrozen.

Follow the recipe or manufacturer's instructions but always check food is piping hot throughout before serving. Ovens can vary. If the temperature in the centre of the food reaches 70°C for 2 minutes, most harmful bacteria are killed.

Do not keep meals warm. Keep them piping hot or cool quickly. If cooling large quantities, for example a casserole, stand the container in cold water, stir the food occasionally and change the water frequently. Once cool, cover and store in the refrigerator or freezer for serving later.

Do not reheat cooked dishes, whether prepared at home or purchased, more than once. Heat them until piping hot.

Vegetables

In the not so distant past, meat was a treat and our diet was based on vegetables. It didn't do us any harm: they taste good, most can be eaten raw or cooked, and are a valuable source of vitamins and fibre. Another plus for most of us is that vegetables are low in fat. They are available fresh and frozen. Their nutritional value falls rapidly if they are kept at room temperature, so buying frozen, or freezing them yourself, is a good option.

Choosing and Storing

It makes sense to buy what is in season locally: that way you'll get the freshest product at the lowest cost to the environment. Look for crispness and brightly coloured leaves.

Buy what you need and don't store vegetables for long. Most green and salad vegetables keep better in the fridge but tomatoes will lose flavour and texture. Root vegetables and squashes keep for weeks in a cold, dark place. Keep potatoes out of the light or they will turn green and start to germinate.

Types of Vegetable

Vegetables can be the first ingredient in the pan (many recipes start by frying onions) and the last, for example sprinkling on some mange tout as a garnish. There's a wealth of flavours, textures and colours to choose from.

How to Cook Vegetables

Peeling will remove dirt and germs, but don't cut too deep or you will remove valuable nutrients. Vegetables can be sliced thinly or into chunks or cubes, or grated. They can be cooked in many ways, from quick stir-frying to slower roasting. Their texture can be kept fairly fibrous or transformed into mash or purée. In most cases it is best to avoid overcooking as this loses nutrition and texture. If you favour steaming over boiling, then add 5–10 minutes to the boiling times given below.

Artichoke is used to describe two unrelated foods. The most widely available is the globe artichoke, which is the flower of a thistle. The fleshy part at the bottom of the leaf is eaten, as well as the heart (also sold canned or frozen). Jerusalem artichokes are the tubers from a plant in the sunflower family and are used as a root vegetable and in soup. Cooked whole, artichokes take 25–40 minutes to cook in boiling water. Artichoke hearts are much quicker: 10–15 minutes.

Asparagus is sold in bundles of spears, which are best cooked upright in a deep pan so that the tips steam while the stems cook. It is often served as a starter with melted butter or grated Parmesan. It can be steamed, grilled or boiled, each taking 5–10 minutes – snap off the tough ends of the stems first.

Aubergine is also known as eggplant and has shiny dark purple skin. It can be cut into slices to be grilled or fried, or the whole aubergine can be halved and the pieces baked. This vegetable is a mainstay of ratatouille and the Greek dish moussaka. Cook in boiling water for 10–15 minutes or bake at 200°C/400°F/Gas 6 for 30 minutes.

Bamboo shoots have a mild taste and are used to add a crunch to stir-fries and as a vegetable in some Asian recipes. They can be bought fresh from specialist stores but are more widely available (and easier to use) in cans. Add to a stir-fry towards the end as they simply need heating up.

Beetroot is sold raw or pre-cooked – either vacuum packed or preserved in vinegar. This red root can be part of a salad or a vegetable dish and is the main ingredient in Russian borscht soup. Cook unpeeled in boiling water for 30–60 minutes or bake at 180°C/350°F/Gas 4 for 60 minutes. Leave to cool and then remove the skin. Grate raw beetroot to add to salads.

Broad beans are best eaten young and tender – they become rather bitter as they age. Frozen varieties mean they are available all year round. Cook in boiling water for 5–15 minutes until just tender.

Broccoli is available in green or purple varieties and can be eaten raw or cooked quickly, for example to add colour and flavour to a stir-fry. Cut into florets and cook in boiling water for 5–10 minutes until just tender.

Brussels sprouts are a Christmas mainstay and have a delicate nutty flavour. When young, these miniature cabbages are also good shredded raw into salads. Cook in boiling water for 5–10 minutes until just tender, or halve and stir-fry for 3–4 minutes.

Cabbage is available as white, green and red. It can be shredded to make coleslaw, or lightly cooked – like other members of the cabbage family it contains sulphur, which releases a musty odour when the vegetable is overcooked. Shred and cook in boiling water for 5–10 minutes until just tender, or stir-fry for 3–4 minutes.

Carrots are a popular root vegetable that can be eaten raw when cut into batons to serve with dips or shredded in a salad. They can also be boiled or roasted and make delicious soup, often accompanied by coriander or orange. Peel and cook in boiling water for 15–20 minutes until just tender or roast at 180°C/350°F/Gas 4 for 30 40 minutes.

Cauliflower has a firm creamy head surrounded by vibrant green leaves. Its florets can be eaten raw or cooked and served with a sauce. Cut into florets and cook in boiling water for 10–15 minutes until just tender or bake at 180°C/350°F/Gas 4 for 20 minutes.

Celeriac is a large, knobbly root vegetable with a nutty flavour slightly sweeter than celery. It can be used instead of potatoes. Peel, chop and cook in boiling water for 15–20 minutes until tender or steam for a little longer.

Celery should have firm stalks with no sign of wilting. It is often used raw in salads and with crudités, added to soups and stews, or served as a hot vegetable.

Chicory leaves grow as a small, cream-coloured head. They taste bitter and are usually eaten raw as a salad. Chicory is also known as radicchio and Belgian endive.

Courgettes are miniature marrows available in yellow and (slightly stronger tasting) green varieties. They are a versatile vegetable but have high water content so they cook quickly. Slice and cook in boiling water for 5–10 minutes until just tender, or stir-fry or grill for 3–4 minutes.

Cucumber is most often served raw sliced into salads, but can be cooked and served in butter or made into a summer soup.

Fennel has an aniseed flavour and can be sliced to add a crunch to salads or cooked in various ways to serve as a warm vegetable. Trim and cook whole in boiling water for 20 minutes, or roast at 180°C/350°F/Gas 4 for 40–50 minutes.

French beans come in various forms of thin beans and are boiled or steamed and served warm or cold in salads. Trim and cook in boiling water for 5–10 minutes until just tender.

Garlic is a pungent bulb with a strong aroma and a real kick when eaten raw, but its flavour is sweetened by cooking. Peel and chop or crush for frying with onion, or keep cloves unpeeled and roast at 180°C/350°F/Gas 4 for 30–40 minutes.

Kale is a hardy relative of cabbage. It is cooked until soft and best served chopped or shredded, paired with game or in minestrone soup. Cut into shreds and cook in boiling water for 10–15 minutes until just tender.

Leeks have an onion-like aroma and flavour and acquire a sweet taste when cooked. They are frequently served in a white sauce or paired with other vegetables such as potatoes. Trim, slice and cook in boiling water for 10–15 minutes until just tender.

Lettuce is available in many forms and is usually served raw as the basis of a salad. If it goes limp, it can be refreshed by soaking in cold water for 10 minutes.

Mange tout are bright green flat pea pods that can be served as vegetables, cooked in stir-fries for 5 minutes or added raw to salads.

Marrow is a summer squash best eaten young. Cut in half lengthways and bake at 180°C/350°F/Gas 4 for 45–75 minutes, depending on its size.

Mushrooms, such as button, chestnut, oyster, porcini and shiitake, are available fresh and dried. Fresh mushrooms soak up liquids so are best added towards the end of cooking. Dried usually need soaking before being added to the pot, and have the advantages of being easy to store and carrying a big punch of flavour. Cook quickly by sautéing in butter, stir-frying, grilling or baking.

Okra is also known as gumbo, bhindi or ladies' fingers because of its long, thin shape. It is widely used around the world, often in stir-fries (just takes 3–5 minutes), although it can also be steamed, baked or stewed.

Onions are the first ingredient in the pan for many savoury dishes, but they can be overpowering. The mildest onions for cooking are the large Spanish onions, while red onions are so mild and sweet they are often added raw to salads and dips. Spring onions have more of a kick but are added raw in small quantities to dips and salads or cooked in stir fries. Peel and sauté for 3–5 minutes on a gentle heat to ensure they don't brown, or roast whole or as wedges at 200°C/400°F/Gas 6 for 50–60 minutes.

Peas have a lovely sweet flavour and are available frozen all year round and briefly fresh in their pods. Cook in boiling water with a little sugar and no salt (which toughens their skins) for 8–10 minutes until just tender, or add to a stir-fry for 2–3 minutes.

Potatoes are a staple food in many countries. New potatoes are firm and waxy and are best boiled. Older potatoes tend to be more floury so are good for mashing, roasting and baking. Larger varieties are sold as baking potatoes. Peel and cook in boiling water for 15–20 minutes until just tender, or roast at 180°C/350°F/Gas 4 for 40–60 minutes.

Runner beans are at their best when young as they tend to get rather stringy later in the season. Trim and cook in boiling water for 5–10 minutes until just tender

Shallots are very mild small onions that can replace their cousins in more subtle dishes. Trim, chop and sauté for 3–5 minutes to soften.

Spinach is popular as fresh young leaves in salads, while larger leaves should be boiled or sautéed just until they wilt. Frozen spinach is a good option all year round. Cook in boiling water for 2–5 minutes until just wilted.

Squashes are a family of vegetables that come in many varieties, such as pumpkin and butternut. Most have thick skins and hard flesh and make superb soup. Peel, cut into chunks and cook in boiling water for 10–15 minutes, or cut in half lengthways and bake at 180°C/350°F/Gas 4 for 40–60 minutes.

Sugar snap peas have crisp stringless pods and are widely available as an alternative to the similar mange tout. Cook in stir-fries for 5 minutes or add raw to salads.

Swedes have a strong flavour and are often added to casseroles or they can be mashed and served as an accompaniment instead of potato. Peel, cut into chunks and cook in boiling water for 15–20 minutes, or cut in half lengthways and bake at 180°C/350°F/Gas 4 for 40–60 minutes.

Sweet peppers are red, yellow, orange or green capsicums (they change colour as they mature) that can be eaten cooked or raw – although some people find them hard to digest in this state. They are a versatile addition to stews and stir-fries and can be grilled or parboiled, each in 2–5 minutes if deseeded and cut into strips. If you choose to stuff and bake them, allow 30 minutes cooking time.

Sweet potatoes are also called yams and are any orange-fleshed alternative to the potato. Peel, cut into chunks and cook in boiling water for 15–20 minutes, or roast at 180°C/350°F/Gas 4 for 40–60 minutes.

Sweetcorn is also known as corn on the cob, while its kernels share the name and are available frozen or tinned. They are a year-round addition to many dishes, rather like peas. Roast or barbecue the cobs for 8–15 minutes or cook in boiling water for 3–6 minutes.

Tomatoes are actually classed as a fruit but often used like a vegetable. They are available fresh all year round, although the tinned variety is convenient and easier to add to sauces. Raw, they freshen up salads and sandwiches. Fried, they are a mainstay of many Italian and other sauces. They can also be baked for 30 minutes in the oven at 180°C/350°F/Gas 4.

Turnips add flavour and richness to soups and casseroles. Peel, cut into chunks and cook in boiling water for 15–20 minutes, or roast at 180°C/350°F/Gas 4 for 40–60 minutes.

Organic Vegetables

Most vegetables are available in organic form, meaning they have been produced without artificial fertilisers, pesticides or fungicides. This means they cost more and may not look as uniform as other vegetables. Many people believe organic vegetables taste better. They should only need washing before use, unlike non-organic produce, which should be peeled to remove all traces of the chemicals that helped it grow.

Herbs

Herbs are leaves that add fragrance and flavour to savoury dishes and drinks. They are available fresh (in pots or packets), dried, frozen and puréed in a tube. Buy fresh herbs if possible and add them just before serving – heat dulls their flavour and colour.

Dry herbs are hardier and stronger: a teaspoon has the same effect as a tablespoon of fresh herbs. Store them somewhere cool and dark for up to six months, and add them earlier in the cooking process so that they absorb moisture and soften.

Popular Herbs and Blends

Basil has a pungent, warm smell and peppery flavour. It complements tomatoes well and is a mainstay of pesto sauce. Basil features in many Mediterranean dishes.

Bay leaves have a musty, slightly bitter flavour that blends well with other herbs (as in bouquet garni). Bay is usually used dried. It's often paired with red meat, in soups and stews and added to rice water.

Bouquet garni is a blend of bay, parsley and thyme, and is often added to soups and stews in a muslin bag that is removed before serving.

Chives have a mild onion taste and are used with potatoes, eggs, fish, in dips and as a garnish.

Coriander (cilandro) leaves look like flat-leaf parsley but have a lemony flavour that is used in Asian cooking.

Dill has aniseed-flavoured feathery fronds that are particularly used in Scandinavian fare. It is often paired with fish, potato or egg.

Fines herbs is a blend of parsley, tarragon, chervil and chives used in classic French dishes.

Lemongrass is fragrant and slightly sweet and is used in tropical dishes.

Marjoram is rather like oregano or thyme and is used with grills, tomatoes, poultry and fish.

Mint leaves have a sharp menthol flavour that overpowers other herbs so mint is mostly used on its own with foods such as potatoes, meat especially lamb, with chocolate and in drinks.

Oregano has a peppery fragrance and is used in Mediterranean dishes and pizza toppings.

Parsley is available curly or (more strongly flavoured) flat and goes well with many foods, especially fish and potatoes. It is often added as a garnish.

Rosemary is a woody herb with a smoky, pine-like taste, used in barbecues and with meat, especially lamb.

Sage is a strong-flavoured herb often paired with pork and in meat stuffings.

Tarragon has a strong aniseed taste and is used in classic French sauces and with poultry and fish.

Thyme has a lemon scent and can be used with many foods, particularly tomatoes and in soups and stews.

Spices

Seeds, fruits, flowers, pods, buds, bark, stalks and roots are some of the things that make spices. When cooked and ground up these strongly flavoured and fragranced powders can transform the taste of savoury and sweet foods. Spices do not keep their full flavour for long. For best results, get them whole to roast and grind yourself. This isn't always possible, though, and many spices are sold ground up. Buy in small quantities and store them in a cool, dark place.

How to Use

Most spices need to be cooked. They might be added to frying onions at the start of a recipe, or dry-roasted and added later on. The easiest way to roast spices is to bake them in a roasting tin for 8–10 minutes at 180°C/350°F/Gas 4. Spices are also used in marinades where they infuse flavour and add fragrance.

Spices and Spice Blends

Allspice has a hot, spicy smell and taste similar to cinnamon and is used with meats and in spice cakes.

Black pepper, also known as peppercorns, is the most commonly used spice with savoury dishes – although some people love it on strawberries.

Caraway seeds have an aniseed flavour and feature in seed cakes, biscuits and rye bread.

Cardamon is sold in pods that are crushed to reveal their little seeds. It is used in African, Middle Eastern and Indian cookery, including sweets and drinks.

Cayenne pepper is a chilli blend that adds heat and colour to many dishes.

Celery seeds have a warm bitter taste and a spicy aroma, so are used in small quantities with a variety of dishes, especially vegetarian recipes. Ground celery seeds mixed with salt are called celery salt.

Cinnamon, used in baking, with fruit, and Middle Eastern meat dishes.

Cloves are used in Christmas baking and many sweet and savoury dishes.

Coriander is used in African and Indian style dishes.

Cumin provides a characteristic curry flavour.

Fenugreek has a bittersweet taste and is common in Indian and Greek cuisine.

Ginger is used fresh or ground in savoury and sweet dishes.

Juniper berries have a piney aroma and are often used to complement the flavour of game.

Mace is the outer covering of the nutmeg kernel but it has a stronger taste. It is easiest to use ready ground. It is often used in milk dishes such as custards and cream sauces.

Mustard seeds have a hot, peppery flavour. They can be used whole or crushed in pickles and curries.

Nutmeg is used for Christmas dishes, egg custard and with spinach.

Paprika is a sweet, hot burnt-red spice used in Hungarian cookery and as a garnish.

Saffron is a delicate and expensive spice with a strong, bittersweet flavour and intense yellow colour.

Turmeric has an earthy, gingery taste and adds bright yellow colouring to Moroccan and Indian dishes.

Spice Blends

Spice blends make it very easy to add a refreshing 'hit' to your cooking. Popular choices include chilli powder (a mixture of dried chillies, garlic, oregano, cumin, ground coriander and cloves), Chinese five-spice, curry powder and mixed spice, which is used for baking.

Flavourings

Flavourings add or improve the taste of savoury and sweet food. The most common is salt. Some are added early on in cooking (for example alcohol, which needs to be heated to allow the actual alcohol to evaporate, leaving the taste), while others are added just before serving.

Types of Flavouring

Almond essence is available in synthetic or the (much better) real form made from bitter almonds and is used to reinforce the nuts' distinctive taste in baked food.

Anchovy essence is made from fish and is very salty. It is used sparingly to add a salty kick to sauces.

Beer can be added to meat casseroles, especially beef. It helps to tenderise the meat and adds a malty taste.

Chocolate is sold in many forms and can be used in sweet and savoury dishes – it goes surprisingly well with meat in some recipes. The simplest form for baking is cocoa powder. Chocolate is also available in chips and bars of dark bitter, plain, milk and white chocolate (which actually contains no cocoa solids at all). Good chocolate for cooking has about 70% cocoa solids. Carob is a low-fat, caffeine-free alternative to chocolate.

Cider is often used with pork and fish.

Coffee is often used to flavour ice creams and sweet fare. It is available bottled as concentrate, but it is just as easy to make your own strong brew using grounds or instant coffee granules.

Eau-de-vie spirits are distilled from fruit and used for flavouring desserts and drinks. Popular kinds include fraise (strawberries), kirsch (cherries) and poire William (pears).

Fortified wines, such as sherry, port, Madeira and Marsala, are used to add character to sauces and other dishes, especially Spanish and Italian fare.

Hoisin sauce is a sweet, thick sauce made from fermented soya beans, sugar, garlic and five spice. It is used to glaze pork or poultry or as a condiment.

Lemon juice adds a tangy hit to savoury dishes, especially fish, and desserts such as sorbets and mousses.

Liqueurs are sweetened alcoholic drinks from many sources, used for flavouring sweet dishes such as ice cream, sorbet and fruit salads.

Oyster sauce is both sweet and salty and used in oriental dishes.

Salt is the only rock we eat! Our bodies need it in small quantities and it enhances the flavour of many foods. It is bested added towards the end of the cooking process when its effect can be better judged. It is available as common table salt or in flakes and crystals of sea salt – best added sparingly for its texture. There are salt substitutes for those who want to reduce their sodium intake.

Too Much Salt

If you put too much salt into a stew, throw in a peeled, cut-up potato and remove it before serving. It will soak up some of the salt.

Soy sauce is made from soya beans and widely used in oriental cooking. It is available in dark brown or as more delicately flavoured light soy sauce.

Spirits such as rum, brandy and whisky are used as preservatives and to add flavour to sweet goods, such as fruit or chocolate cakes and Christmas pudding. Brandy can be added to some dishes just before serving and set alight to burn off the alcohol.

Tabasco is a hot sauce that can add a kick to many savoury dishes.

Tahini is a paste made from sesame seeds. It is widely used in Middle Eastern dishes and is a key ingredient in hummus dip.

Thai fish sauce has a strong taste and smell and is used like soy sauce in Asian dishes.

Vanilla extract is used with many sweet dishes, often paired with chocolate. It may be sold as essence or a natural extract.

Wine adds depth of flavour to casseroles, sauces and other dishes, and helps to tenderise meat. It is great for de-glazing after pan-frying or roasting. White wine has a lighter and subtler flavour than red.

Worcestershire sauce is a pungent sauce used to add depth of flavour to sauces, casseroles and cheese dishes.

Vinegar

Vinegar is made from fermented plant juices and is one of the earliest cooking ingredients. It is used as a condiment and in salad dressings. It is also a solvent, so is very good for cleaning!

Types of Vinegar

Balsamic vinegar is black and syrupy and makes a tasty salad dressing on its own or mixed with oil. It can also be used to add flavour to stews. Traditional balsamic vinegar is produced in a 12-year-long process in Modena, Italy and is very expensive. Many other (cheaper) varieties are available.

Cider vinegar is made from apple juice and is slightly sweeter than wine vinegar.

Distilled vinegar is colourless and often used for chutneys.

Malt vinegar is made from unhopped beer and is used for pickles, chutneys and as a condiment.

Raspberry vinegar is wine vinegar flavoured with fresh raspberries. It is sometimes added to gravy.

Red wine vinegar has quite a strong flavour and is used in salad dressings.

Rice wine vinegars come in Chinese and Japanese varieties and are best suited to cuisine from those countries.

Sherry vinegar has an intense, nutty flavour rather like mild balsamic vinegar and is particularly good in salad dressings.

White wine vinegar is milder than its red cousin and is used on its own in dressings and as a base for fruit and herb vinegars such as tarragon or raspberry vinegar.

Oils and Fats

Oils are liquid fats used for frying and in salad dressings. Solid fats are essential for baking. Oils and fats should be stored in a cool, dark place as otherwise they go off.

Types of Oil

Sunflower or **vegetable oils** are the best types for cooking because they are light, bland and can be heated to higher temperatures without burning. Other all-purpose oils are made from corn, groundnuts (peanuts) and grapeseed.

Nut oils, such as walnut and hazelnut, have a distinctive flavour and are mostly used for salad dressing and marinades.

Olive oil is made by crushing olives to extract their fruity, peppery flavour. Virgin and 'extra virgin' olive oils are higher quality because they are pure – standard olive oil is a blend. You can fry with olive oil at lower temperatures if you wish, but it is mainly combined with vinegar to make salad dressings. Good quality olive oil is also used as a dip for Italian breads such as ciabatta.

Sesame seed oils are strongly flavoured and feature in some recipes for Asian food.

Infusions

Oils infused with chillies, herbs or truffles are often used for salad dressings and marinades and might be added to specific recipes to add a layer of flavour.

Types of Solid Fats

Butter is made from cream, which has been further concentrated so that the final product is more than 80 per cent fat. It makes cakes and other sweet dishes rich and tender and is also used in savoury sauces. Unsalted butter is more creamy (and softer straight out of the fridge) and allows the cook to assess how much salt to add to a recipe more easily.

Lard is clarified pork fat used for deep frying and making pastry.

Margarine and **non-dairy spreads** are butter substitutes and have a variable fat and water content, but they don't have the same flavour. Most are made from soya, sunflower and olive oil and often include buttermilk.

Flavoured Butters

Highly flavoured butters add piquancy and flavour to grilled or fried meat and fish. Many different ingredients can be blended with butter to make excellent accompaniments.

After making, butters should be well chilled and can be cut into decorative shapes to serve at the table or on top of meat or fish.

A variety of flavoured butter recipes can be found on page 191.

Pulses

Pulses are beans, lentils and peas, which are the dried seeds of plants called legumes. They are sold dried (to be kept in airtight containers for up to a year) or pre-cooked in cans. They are a great store cupboard fallback to be used in dishes in their own right or to add nutrition and texture to stews and soups.

How to Cook

Dried pulses must be boiled to rehydrate them and kill off any toxins that might make them hard to digest. Apart from lentils and split peas, pulses should be soaked in cold water for at least 4 hours (overnight is fine) before cooking. Then boil them uncovered in fresh, unsalted water for at least 1 hour (check packets for details). Skim away any scum that comes to the surface. Pulses are often quite bland and absorb new flavours best when warm, so add seasoning or dressing as they cool unless you just tip them into a soup or stew.

Types of Beans

Some beans may need an additional 10 minutes vigorous boiling to destroy their toxins – check the packet.

Aduki beans are sweet and often used in salads and stuffings.

Black-eyed beans have a tiny black spot on the side and are often found in African and Caribbean cooking.

Butter beans are floury and good mashed into pâté or added to stews.

Cannellini beans are plump and white and used in rustic dishes like Tuscan bean soup.

Flageolet beans are pale green and have a delicate, fresh flavour that works well in salads and with rich meats.

Haricot beans are best-known as the base ingredient in baked beans and are good in stews and casseroles.

Pinto beans are sweet and used in minestrone soup and Mexican cooking.

Soy beans are a staple part of the diet in southeast Asia and are used in many ways, including to make soy sauce. They are bland so mix them with strong flavours.

Types of Lentil

Lentils include the grey-green French, or Puy, lentils, which have a rich, earthy taste and are good in salads, vegetarian dishes or with meat.

Red lentils go mushy when they cook so are best in soups.

Yellow and green lentils are used in soups and purées, such as dahl curry dishes.

Types of Pea

Chick peas are frequently boiled and mashed to form the basis for the Middle Eastern hummus dip.

Split peas are used for purées and soups.

Grains

Grains are edible grass seeds and are a key source of starchy carbohydrates that people have eaten for thousands of years. They are ground to make flour used in bread and baking, or added to thicken and provide nutrition to many dishes.

How to Cook

Whole grains should be rinsed before pouring into a pan of salted cold water and simmered. The cooking time varies depending on their shape, variety and age – check the packet. Many grains are sold pre-cooked and require much less preparation time.

Types of Grain

Barley is malted to make beer and whisky and is the source of malted drinks and flours. Husked, steamed and polished, it is also known as pearl barley, commonly added to thicken soups.

Buckwheat is actually from a plant related to rhubarb so is not technically a grain. Buckwheat replaces rice in Russian cooking, where it is known as kasha, and it is an important part of the diet of Japan. Buckwheat flour is used in the batter for the French savoury pancakes called galettes. In northern France and Belgium it is known as 'blé noir' – black wheat.

Bulgar wheat is made from steamed, dried and crushed wheat grains and has a light, nutty flavour. It is commonly used in Middle Eastern dishes such as tabbouleh salad.

Couscous is made from grains of semolina. It is a staple in North Africa where it is steamed and served with stew. It can also be used in salads. It is simply rehydrated by soaking in cold water for 20 minutes.

Cracked wheat is wheat kernels that have been cracked open. It can be used instead of bulgar wheat.

Oats are higher in protein than wheat and are available either as rolled oats or oatmeal. This nutritious cereal is used for porridge, oatcakes, flapjacks and to make a crispy coating for filleted fish.

Pearl barley see barley.

Polenta is an Italian form of cornmeal. When cold it is firm like hard cheese, but it softens when warmed. Polenta can be boiled into a sticky sort of porridge, or cut into wedges and grilled or fried.

Quinoa originates from South America and is sold in health food shops. It is prepared and eaten much like couscous.

Semolina is ground wheat grain. Medium ground, it is used in milk puddings and cakes. It is more finely ground into a flour to be made into pasta.

Gluten

Wheat grains contain gluten, the protein that makes dough elastic. However, some people find gluten hard to digest. Gluten-free grains include oats, rye, corn and buckwheat. For those people who are intolerant rather than allergic to gluten, spelt flour is widely available. Gluten-free flour and bread is now available in supermarkets.

Rice

Rice is the main food for about half the people in the world. Is it an excellent source of energy that goes well with many other foods or can be flavoured and eaten on its own.

How to Cook

The two main techniques are boiling and steaming. Soaking rice before cooking removes some starch and reduces its stickiness so the grains stay separated, but this is not always necessary or desired. The rice is boiled, either in plenty of water so that some will be poured away, or in just enough to be absorbed. Steamed rice is cooked in a steamer set over boiling water. Brown rice takes longer than the milled and polished white variety. Risotto rice is cooked in stock and forms part of the main dish.

Types of Rice

There are more than 100,000 varieties of rice. The most commonly used type is long-grain (Patna) rice, which can be white or brown. A well-known kind is basmati rice, often served with curry. There are also medium-grain and short-grain rices that have a softer texture. These are used for dishes such as risotto, paella, Sushi and rice pudding.

Did You Know?

Pudding rice is baked or simmered in sweetened milk.

Wild rice is actually thin, dark grains of grass, mixed with white rice.

Pasta and Noodles

Pasta means 'dough' and is made from wheat flour and water or sometimes eggs. Pasta is a satisfying meal usually served with a rich sauce. It is available dried, fresh and stuffed, and can be made at home with a machine. Pasta comes in many shapes designed to trap the sauce they are served with. Two basic groups are long pastas such as spaghetti, and short varieties such as penne.

How to Cook Pasta

Boil pasta in plenty of salted water, usually for 10–12 minutes (less for fresh pasta), but always check the packet. Salt may be needed because none is added when making pasta. Pasta absorbs water as it cooks, so will stick if there is not enough liquid – adding a drop of vegetable oil to the water can help prevent this from happening. When cooked, leave it to dry for a couple of minutes – it will absorb more of the sauce on the plate. Firm pasta is called 'al dente' and is easier to digest as it needs more chewing than soft pasta.

Types of Pasta

Conchiglie: ridged shells, great for chunky meat or thick cheese sauces.

Farfalle: bow-tie shapes that are often paired with creamy sauces.

Fusilli: spirals that make an excellent trap for meat and tomato sauces.

Gnocchi: small ovals of mashed potato and flour that cook in minutes.

Lasagne: flat sheets that can be coloured with spinach and are baked between layers of sauce. Some need soaking before cooking.

Macaroni: short narrow tubes often served with cheese or ham.

Penne: tubes used with thick sauces.

Rotelle: wheel-shaped and multi-coloured, so popular with children.

Spaghetti: long strands, often eaten with a spoon and fork.

Stuffed pastas: cook very quickly and are best served with simple sauces. Fresh works better than dried. Varieties include cannelloni (large tubes), ravioli (flat parcels filled with meat or vegetables) and tortellini (squares usually partnered with tomato sauce.

Tagliatelli: narrow strips served with fine-textured sauces.

Cold Pasta

Leftover cooked pasta is great in salads. Mix it with olive oil or an oil-based dressing to stop it sticking.

Noodles

Noodles are long thin strips of flour made from wheat, potatoes, rice or mung beans. They are a staple food in most parts of China and southeast Asia and are sold dried or fresh. Most are pre-cooked so they are boiled for a very short time to rehydrate, sometimes just by adding them to a stir-fry meal. Noodles can be eaten hot or cold.

Types of Noodle

Cellophane noodles (also known as bean thread or glass noodles) are made from mung beans and are transparent.

Egg noodles are wheat-based and can be added to soups or stir-fries.

Ramen is a Japanese wheat-based noodle often served with fish or meat broth.

Rice noodles cook in seconds and are sometimes deep fried, and used in soups and with sauces.

Milk and Cream

Dairy products such as milk and cream have been part of our diet for thousands of years.

Milk

Milk is available whole (with a fat content of 3.5%), and in various lower fat forms that still offer the same amount of valuable calcium, protein and minerals.

These are semi-skimmed milk (1.5-1.8% fat), 1% milk, and skimmed, which has a fat content of 0.3%. 1% fat milk still gives us the important nutritional benefits of milk, including calcium, protein, minerals and vitamins, but with half the fat of semi.

Milk is used in cooking to make white sauce (a mixture of butter, flour and milk), which has many variations such as Mornay sauce (used to make cauliflower cheese) and the richer bèchamel sauce.

Condensed milk is sweetened and thickened milk used in desserts such as cheesecakes and banoffee pie.

Evaporated milk is concentrated milk with water removed and can be used to add richness to savoury and sweet dishes.

Cream

Cream is the fatty portion of milk. It has a rich taste and smooth texture and is used in savoury and sweet recipes, or as a topping. Single cream is 18% fat and is used for pouring over desserts and coffee. It curdles if boiled.

Whipping cream has double the fat of single cream and can be heated or whisked to add air, increasing its volume. It is used to make ice cream.

Double cream is nearly half fat and is used for pouring and whipping.

Whipped cream is a foam of light, fluffy cream in a can, used as a topping on desserts and drinks.

Sour cream was once cream that had gone off, but is now made by adding bacteria to single cream. It adds a pleasant tang to dishes from Eastern Europe and other parts of the world and is used in dips, spreads, cakes, to enrich and thicken sauces, soufflés and some savoury dishes.

Other Milk Products

Crème fraîche is made from milk with added bacteria and has a slightly tangy taste. It can be used in sweet dishes or added to savoury sauces and will tolerate boiling.

Mascarpone is an Italian version of soured cream that is used in baking and dishes such as tiramisu. It is often referred to as cheese.

Yogurt is fermented milk that has thickened and gained a sharp flavour. It can be served as it is, or added to enrich curries (but it will curdle if boiled) or sweetened for desserts.

Greek yogurt is made from cow or sheep milk and has been strained, leaving a higher fat content.

Cheese

Cheese is one of our oldest foods – people have been making it for at least 8,000 years. It is made by warming milk, then leaving it to ripen. The milk can come from cows, goats, sheep and water buffalo and cheese is highly nutritious, being rich in calcium and protein. It is also high in fat and low-fat versions are available.

Cheese ranges enormously in taste from mild soft ones to pungent blue cheeses, such as Stilton. It is available pasteurised or raw, plain or flavoured. Cheese is eaten as a dish, melted into sauces or grated and used as a garnish.

Storing Cheese

Keep cheese in the fridge although it is best to have it at room temperature for a couple of hours before serving to release the flavour. It is best wrapped in waxed paper or foil rather than plastic, which holds in moisture and encourages bacterial growth.

Types of Cheese

There are more than 1,500 types of cheese in the world, ranging from fresh curd varieties, such as cottage cheese, to very hard cooked and pressed types, such as Parmesan. Here are some of the most popular and widely available choices in Britain.

Brie is a rich, creamy cheese with a white rind. It has a chalky texture that becomes runnier as it matures. Brie originated in France but is now also made elsewhere, including Britain. It melts well, so can be used for cooking.

Caerphilly is a crumbly cheese with a fresh acidic taste, which gets more creamy as it ages.

Camembert is a French soft cheese made from cow's milk. It has a delicate salty taste and can become pretty pungent as it ripens.

Cheddar originated in England but is now made around the world. It is a hard cheese with a slightly crumbly texture and a rich, nutty taste – although this varies as there are mild to extra mature variants on the market. It grates and melts well so is perfect for cooking.

Cheshire is one of Britain's oldest cheeses and has a dry texture with a mellow, slightly salty taste.

Cottage cheese is a snow-white, fresh lumpy cheese sold in pots that is popular with dieters because it is low in fat but high in protein. It is mild and slightly acidic: flavourings such as chives or pineapple are often mixed in to add interest.

Cream cheese is a soft, spreadable modern cheese made from milk and cream that has a mild, slightly acidic flavour. It is used in sandwiches and to make dips and a pâté, as well as for cheesecakes and baking. Flavoured and low-fat versions are available.

Danish blue, also known as Danablu or Marmora, is a semi-soft blue cheese with a salty bite that feels creamy in the mouth. It can be sliced, spread or crumbled.

Dolcelatte is a mild and creamy version of gorgonzola, made from richer milk. This Italian blue cheese has a sweet taste and is very soft.

Double Gloucester is a hard cow's milk cheese with a mellow, buttery and nutty character. Its name comes from the practice of making it from morning and evening milk.

Edam is a Dutch cheese that is ball-shaped and covered with red wax – or black for more mature versions. It has a sweet and nutty taste and cooks well.

Emmental is a Swiss cheese famous for the holes in its interior, produced during fermentation. It has a mild, fruity flavour and a firm, silky texture.

Feta is a crumbly white Greek cheese usually made from ewe's and goat's milk. It is preserved in oil or brine, which gives it a salty flavour – this can be reduced by soaking it in water for a few minutes. It is often crumbled into salads, but is also suitable for baking.

Fromage frais is a fresh, creamy and moist cheese sometimes blended with cream. It is served as a dessert and sometimes used in sauces and as a topping.

Goat's cheese is a group of cheeses made from goat's milk, available in soft and hard varieties in many shapes. It often has a slightly musty flavour and French versions are also known as chèvres. Goat's cheese is good to cook with.

Gorgonzola is an Italian blue cheese with bluish-green veins. It has a pungent and rich flavour and is eaten on its own or in salads and dips.

Gouda is named after its Dutch town of origin and is round with a yellow waxed rind.

It has an elastic texture and a mild, sweet flavour.

Gruyère is a Swiss cheese eaten on its own or used in dishes such as fondues and gratins – it is one of the world's great cooking cheeses because of its taste and the fact that it rarely goes stringy. It has complex flavours of fruit and nuts and is pitted with small holes.

Halloumi was originally from Cyprus and is similar to mozzarella, being quite milky and bland. It has a high melting point so it keeps its shape when grilled or fried.

Jarlsberg is a Norwegian cheese that has holes like Swiss Emmental but is sweeter and nuttier in taste. It is very popular in the USA.

Lancashire is a crumbly white cheese with a mild but tangy flavour. Its texture becomes firmer as it ages.

Manchego is a Spanish cheese made from ewe's milk. It is sold fresh or preserved in olive oil and has a sour and nutty flavour. Manchego grates well and is often used in cooking.

Mozzarella is an Italian fresh cheese made from water buffalo milk. It tastes like slightly sour milk and has an elastic, creamy texture. Mozzarella is a common pizza topping cheese, or is paired with tomatoes and basil in a salad.

Parmesan is a popular Italian hard cheese that is matured for up to two years to give it a tangy flavour and a hard, grainy texture. It is added to salads, pasta and soup among other dishes.

Red Leicester is a hard cheese with a distinctive orange colouring and a mild but rich taste.

Shropshire blue is a rich creamy blue cheese with a mellow flavour. It isn't made in Shropshire: it was created in Scotland in an attempt to imitate Stilton cheese.

Stilton is a richly flavoured blue-mould cheese with a crumbly texture. It has blue-green veins and a wrinkled rind, which is not eaten. Stilton is eaten on its own, or crumbled into salads, or added in hot and cold recipes.

Wensleydale is a delicate cheese with a crumbly and moist texture and a mild, slightly sour flavour. It is available white and, less commonly, as a blue-veined cheese.

Vegetarian Cheese

Some hard cheeses are made using an animal product called rennet, so are not suitable for vegetarians. However, vegetarian rennet is also now used, and many soft cheeses are made without this ingredient at all: check the packet.

Pregnancy

Pregnant women are advised not to eat soft cheeses and those made from unpasteurised milk because they may contain harmful listeria bacteria.

Fish and Shellfish

Fish is really good for us: it is high in protein and low in fat compared to meat. It is also easy to cook and very tasty, and with the growth in fish farming, many varieties are now available fresh all year round. It can be bought whole or in steaks or fillets, and can be fresh, frozen or canned. Some fish are also available smoked or cured, and thinly sliced to be eaten raw.

One way to classify fish is in two groups: white and oily. White fish include cod, haddock, hake, whiting and bream. Their flesh is white and low in calories, while their oil is all stored in the liver. In contrast, oily fish have fish oil between the flakes of their flesh, giving them a different flavour. Examples are mackerel, salmon, herring, trout, pilchards and fresh (not tinned) tuna. They contain vitamins A and D plus Omega 3 fatty acids, which have numerous health benefits.

Choosing Fish

Fresh fish doesn't smell 'fishy' (that's the smell of it going off), but there may be a whiff of the sea. The flesh should be firm and consistently coloured, and with whole fish the eyes should be bright and clear and the inside of the gills bright pink or red, not brown.

How to Cook

Fish cooks quickly – you can tell when it's done because the flesh starts to flake – and shouldn't be overcooked as it dries out. This will also happen if it is kept warm, so fish is best cooked just before serving.

Baked fillets usually take about 20 minutes at 180°C/350°F/Gas 4. Sealing fish in paper or foil before baking is called cooking 'en papillote' and helps to keep it moist.

Frozen fish needn't be thawed first – just add a couple of minutes to the cooking time.

Grilling or barbecuing takes 4–5 minutes on each side but less for delicate and oily fish. Brush with oil or butter first.

Microwaving takes 2–3 minutes.

Poaching keeps fish moist and if done with milk, softens the flavour of smoked fish. Typical poaching times are 4–8 minutes, depending on the thickness of the fish. Shallow frying times are 6–8 minutes and slightly less for deep frying.

Steaming cooks typical fillets in about 15 minutes.

Types of Fish

In addition to the most popular fish listed below, there are many other types of fish on the market. Some, such as coley and huss (rock salmon), are not as well flavoured, but they are great for adding to soups and pies.

Cod has dense white flesh and was once the mainstay of the fish and chip shop – although overfishing has led to other fish being offered too.

Haddock is from the same family as cod, but has a slightly sweeter taste. It is available smoked, which gives it a distinctive flavour.

Halibut is a white fish with a mild flavour that can be used instead of other flat fish, such as flounder and sole.

Herring is an oily fish that is sold salted, pickled or smoked, when it is known as kipper.

Mackerel has pale, firm flesh with an oily texture. It is sold raw or smoked, sometimes coated with pepper.

Pollock is abundant in the Atlantic and Pacific oceans (where it is known as Alaskan pollock). This firm white fish can be used in place of cod in recipes.

Plaice is a white, delicately flavoured fish.

Salmon is a very popular oily fish with orange/pink flesh that is cooked whole, or sold as fillets, or smoked and eaten raw.

Sardine is an oily fish with lots of tiny bones that cook with the flesh and are a good source of calcium. Pilchards are larger, older sardines.

Sea bass has a slightly sweet taste and is now available year round produced in fish farms.

Sole is used to describe several species of flatfish. It has a delicate, buttery sweet flavour and can be grilled, fried, baked or steamed.

Swordfish has a meaty taste and dense texture similar to pork.

Trout, available in several different forms, is an oily fish with a mild, subtle flavour.

Tuna has a dark, meaty flesh. It is also popular in tinned form.

Whitebait are tiny young sprat or herring, often coated in flour and deep fried to be eaten whole.

Shellfish

Shellfish are aquatic animals, usually with a shell outside the body. The two main types are crustaceans, such as prawns, lobsters and crabs, and molluscs, such as mussels, oysters, scallops and squid. Shellfish have a short shelf-life (longer if they are pre-cooked, like many prawns) as they deteriorate rapidly, but buying frozen is a useful option. They need only short, gentle cooking so, for example, prawns can be added to a fish stew a few minutes before serving to add colour and subtle flavouring.

Chicken and Other Poultry

Chicken meat is lean and tender, so it is easy to cook and without its skin has a lower saturated fat content than many red meats. It is sold frozen or fresh as an oven-ready bird with the innards removed, and in portions such as breasts, thighs, wings and drumsticks. Store in the bottom of the fridge.

Chicken Joints

Fillets are boned breast, often roasted or fried and served with a sauce. Chicken quarters, thighs, wings and drumsticks are easily roasted for a snack or as part of a meal. Other chicken products include chicken mince, crumb-coated pieces and goujons – thin strips suitable for quick frying.

How to Cook

Always defrost frozen chicken thoroughly then cook it as soon as possible. For an oven-ready chicken, remove the plastic wrapping and cover instead with greaseproof paper to let air circulate over the skin to lessen bacterial growth. You can add taste and reduce dryness by pushing butter and flavourings such as herbs or spices under the skin.

It is vital to baste chicken while it roasts or it will be too dry. Most chicken joints can also be grilled or barbecued. They don't always have much flavour so marinades and sauces will add interest. It is also important to cook chicken until the juices run clear to ensure any dangerous bacteria is destroyed. As with all meat, leave it to rest for up to 30 minutes before serving to improve moistness and let the flavour develop.

Types of Chicken

Corn-fed chicken gives the meat a yellowish colour and a deeper flavour.

Free-range chickens have more flavour than cheap chickens from battery farms because they can roam around and eat a variety of foods – a difference reflected in higher prices.

Oven-ready chickens are plucked and the giblets removed. They are sold in a range of sizes.

Poussins are young chickens that look lovely but have little flavour so are often stuffed or served with a highly flavoured sauce.

Other Poultry

Duck has a rich flavour and is higher in fat. It can be oven-roasted or pan-fried. It lends itself to rich or fruity sauces such as hoisin or plum.

Goose is also very fatty and is generally only available around Christmas.

Guinea fowl is smaller than the average chicken and its lean meat has a gamey flavour. It is best suited to oven pot-roasting, braising and stewing.

Turkey meat is even leaner than chicken. It is a Christmas staple, but is available all year round. Cook as with chicken. Roast turkey can be accompanied by various types of stuffing. See page 188.

Chicken Stock and Soup

Don't throw away the carcass or leftover bones: boil them for about an hour with vegetables such as onion, celery and carrots to make stock or soup. If you have the giblets, add them too.

Roasting Times: Poultry

	Oven temperature	Cooking time per 450g/1lb	Extra cooking time	Resting time
Chicken	200°C/400°F/Gas 6	20 min	30 min	15 min
Turkey (stuffed weight)				
small (under 6kg/13lb)	200°C/400°F/Gas 6	12 min	20 min	30 min
large	180°C/350°F/Gas 4	16 min		30 min
Duck	200°C/400°F/Gas 6 for 45 min then 180°C/350°F/Gas 4	35 min		15 min

Pork

There was a time when most families kept a pig, feeding it on scrap food and eventually eating every part of it. Its rich, tender meat is available fresh, cured, salted or smoked. Being quite fatty, it is full of favour, but must be trimmed properly to reduce its greasiness. In addition to cuts of meat, pork is also salted, cured and used in sausages. Versatile indeed!

How to Cook

Most cuts can be roasted, grilled, fried or braised. Lean cuts are best marinated to keep them moist. Pork is usually cooked until it is well done. Apples are a traditional accompaniment – perhaps apple sauce with roast pork, or braised pork in cider.

Pork Cuts

Belly of pork comes in thin, boneless strips that are usually slow-cooked to bring out its flavour. Cooking time is 1½–3 hours, depending on the recipe.

Fillet of pork, also called tenderloin, is sliced and fried or grilled, sometimes flattened into thin escalopes. Fry or grill for 4–5 minutes per side on high, then reduce the heat and continue to cook for an extra 5–7 minutes per side.

Leg meat is lean and best roasted. It is most commonly boned and rolled, then cut in half to make a roasting joint. For cooking times, see the table, below.

Loin of pork is a fine cut from the back, and sold whole or boned and rolled. It is often roasted with the skin on to form crackling. Or it can be divided into chops to be fried or grilled. For roasting times, see the table, below. Fry or grill chops for 4–5 minutes per side on high, then reduce the heat and continue to cook for an extra 5–7 minutes per side.

Spare-rib joint has a length of backbone along one side, which is often removed and the joint rolled for roasting.

Spare ribs come from the thick end of the belly and are mostly bone. They are often sold coated in sauce for roasting.

Bacon and Cured Pork

Bacon is pork that has been salted in brine and then left to mature. It is sold smoked or unsmoked in thin slices called rashers, thicker steaks (sometimes referred to as lardons) for frying or grilling, or boned and rolled as a ham or gammon joint. Cheap bacon often has a very high water content and is not good for frying.

Types of Bacon and Cured Pork

Back bacon is the best cut for grilling or frying.

Black Forest ham is dark and strongly flavoured.

Brunswick ham is a delicately flavoured German ham.

Pancetta is thin cut smoked pork belly bacon from Italy.

Gammon is pork preserved in salt, sugar and spices. This tender meat is sold as steaks or a joint. Joints may need soaking before cooking to remove some of the salt – check the packet or ask your butcher.

Parma ham is from Italy and has been dried and matured for two years, then sliced thinly and eaten raw.

Prosciutto crudo is sweet Italian dry-cured ham. It is very thinly sliced and eaten raw.

Salami is raw pork minced with fat,

Serrano ham is paper-thin, air-dried, salted ham from Spain that is eaten raw.

Streaky bacon is more fatty and can be added to stews and sauces.

York ham has been dry-salted and smoked to give a mild flavour.

Roasting Times: Pork

	Oven temperature	Cooking time per 450g/1lb	Extra cooking time	Resting time
Medium	180°C/350°F/Gas 4	30 min	30 min	15 min
Well done	180°C/350°F/Gas 4	35 min	35 min	15 min

Sausages

Sausages are made from raw minced pork or beef combined with breadcrumbs and herbs and packed into skins. They are sold fresh or frozen. Some sausages are cured by smoking, salting or drying and have a longer shelf life. Quality sausages have a meat content of about 70 per cent. Steer clear of those with a very low meat content figure – the legal minimum for pork sausages is only 42 per cent! Sausages are not just just a mainstay of the breakfast fry up: they can be barbecued, paired with beans in a casserole or cooked and chopped into a meaty stew.

Types of Sausage

Sausages are available with a huge variety of flavourings, such as apple and leeks.

Black pudding is made from pig's blood and can be poached, fried or baked.

Chorizo is a paprika-flavoured sausage that can be eaten as it is or added to stews.

Chipolata sausages are small, thin sausages usually served whole.

Cumberland sausages are sold as one long coil.

Frankfurters are pre-smoked and warmed to form the filling for a hot dog.

Lincolnshire sausages combine pork with parsley, sage and thyme, pepper and nutmeg.

Merguez is a short, spicy sausage from Algeria made with mutton or goat meat.

Salami is dry-cured sausage that is good in sandwiches or added to pizzas and stews.

Tolouse sausage is a fresh, coarse French sausage made from pork or chicken.

Lamb

Lamb is sweet-flavoured meat from sheep less than a year old. British lamb has the finest flavour, but New Zealand lamb can be cheaper. It is sold fresh and frozen, and smaller cuts generally taste the best – so it may be worth buying two small joints rather than one large one to cater for more people. Lamb meat darkens as it ages, becoming tougher and stronger flavoured. Lamb is popular in European and Middle Eastern cooking, especially in rich stews, kebabs and rice and curry dishes. Go for the leanest cuts, which should have firm, creamy-white fat.

How to Cook

Lamb is tender meat that can be roasted, grilled or fried, although tougher cuts, such as middle neck and knuckle, are best stewed. Cooked lamb is a brownish pink, but not bloody. The younger the meat, the paler it will look. The sweet taste of lamb is complemented by sharp flavours such as lemon, rosemary, garlic and mint.

Lamb Cuts

Best end of neck is sold as a rack of lamb: 7–9 cutlets in a row. It is also available as individual cutlets for grilling and hotpots. For cooking times, see the table, below.

Chump chops are usually sold cut up for grilling, but may be found whole, to roast. Grill for 3–4 minutes per side under a hot grill, then reduce the heat and continue to cook for an extra 3–6 minutes per side.

Knuckle of lamb is full of flavour and is best pot roasted or braised. Cooking time is 1½–2½ hours, depending on the recipe.

Leg of lamb is a roasting joint, sometimes sold boned. For cooking times, see the table, below.

Loin chops, cutlets and noisettes are grilled or fried rather like steak. Grill for 3–4 minutes per side under a hot grill, then reduce the heat and continue to cook for an extra 3–6 minutes per side.

Middle neck and scrag end are cheap, quite fatty and bony cuts suitable for slow cooking. Cooking time is 1½–2½ hours, depending on the recipe.

Minced lamb is the meat used in the traditional shepherd's pie, topped with mashed potato. Fry the mince for about 5 minutes to seal before transferring to an ovenproof container and adding other ingredients, depending on the recipe.

Shanks are best slow-cooked to tenderise the meat and release the flavour.

Shoulder of lamb is used in stews and roasts – when it might be boned to make carving easier. For roasting times, see the table, below. For stewing, allow at least 1½ hours.

Roasting Times: Lamb

	Oven temperature	Cooking time per 450g/1lb	Extra cooking time	Resting time
Medium	180°C/350°F/Gas 4	25 min	25 min	15 min
Well done	180°C/350°F/Gas 4	30 min	30 min	15 min

Beef

Beef is the king of meats. From the finest steak to the humble standby of mince, it offers taste and versatility. Most beef comes from bullocks – castrated male cattle whose flesh has plenty of muscle and a low proportion of fat. Good beef isn't necessarily the bright red colour seen in many supermarket packs: it should be a deep or dull red, showing it has been hung to increase its tenderness and flavour. It is sold fresh and frozen.

How to Cook

Beef, like other meats, should be fried at the start of the cooking process, or roasted at a high temperature. This browns the surface not to seal in juices (it doesn't), but to add flavour to the surface of the meat. All cooked meat, including beef, benefits from being rested in a warm place between cooking and serving. This allows it to finish cooking inside and the cooling means it retains more moisture so does not dry out as fast as if it was carved straight away.

Beef Cuts

Brisket is a fairly fatty cut from the lower shoulder. It is sold on the bone or boned and rolled. It is usually braised, boiled or pot-roasted and takes 1½–2½ hours, depending on the recipe. Brisket is traditionally used to make corned beef.

Braising steak is also known as chuck or blade steak and is quite lean. It is sold as steaks or in cubes and cooked slowly in stews (it takes 1½–2½ hours, depending on the recipe) – and is more tender than stewing steak.

Fillet, also known as tenderloin, should be succulent and tender. It is used as steaks and in dishes such as beef Wellington. For grilling fillet steaks, allow the following times on each side: 3–4 minutes (rare), 4–5 minutes (medium), 6–7 minutes (well done). Beef Wellington needs about 45 minutes cooking time.

Prime rib is a roasting joint, sold with or without its bone. For cooking times, see the table, below.

Rump is a prime cut that is cheaper than fillet or sirloin because it is not as tender, although it can actually offer more flavour. For grilling rump steaks, allow the following times on each side: 2½ minutes (rare), 4 minutes (medium), 6 minutes (well done).

Silverside is a roasting joint that requires regular basting to stop it drying out. For cooking times, see the table, below.

Sirloin comes from the back of the animal and is used for joints and steaks. For roasting times, see the table, below. For grilling sirloin steaks, allow the following times on each side: 2½ minutes (rare), 4 minutes (medium), 6 minutes (well done).

Stewing steak is from the tougher cuts such as leg and needs to be cooked slowly for 1½–2½ hours to make it tender.

Topside is a very lean roasting joint often sold wrapped in a layer of fat to keep it moist during cooking. For cooking times, see the table, below.

Minced Beef

Minced beef varies enormously in quality. The key is fat content: fatty mince is likely to produce greasy food. It is labelled lean, or steak mince, but many of these terms overlap: look for the stated fat content and go for the lowest figure you can afford.

Roasting Times: Beef

	Oven temperature	Cooking time per 450g/1lb	Extra cooking time	Resting time
Rare	180°C/350°F/Gas 4	20 min	20 min	15 min
Medium	180°C/350°F/Gas 4	25 min	25 min	15 min
Well done	180°C/350°F/Gas 4	30 min	30 min	15 min

Seasonal Food Diary

This list shows when fruits and vegetables are at their best.

January

Apple	Celeriac	Kale	Pear	Turnip
Beetroot	Celery	Leek	Potato	
Brussels sprouts	Chestnut	Onion	Rhubarb	
Carrot	Chicory	Orange	Squash	
Cauliflower	Dates	Parsnip	Swede	

February

Apple	Carrot	Kale	Potato	Turnip
Beetroot	Cauliflower	Leek	Rhubarb	
Brussels sprouts	Celeriac	Parsnip	Squash	
Cabbage	Chicory	Pear	Swede	

March

Beetroot	Cauliflower	Leek	Potatoes	Turnip
Blood orange	Chard	Lettuce	Rhubarb	
Brussels sprouts	Chicory	Parsnip	Spring onion	
Cabbage	Endive	Pear	Squash	

April

Apple	Endive	Radish	Spring greens	Watercress
Cauliflower	New potatoes	Rhubarb	Spring onion	
Chard	Peppers	Spinach	Turnip	

May

Apple	Broad bean	New potatoes	Rhubarb	Watercress
Asparagus	Cauliflower	Pea	Spinach	
Beetroot	Lettuce	Radish	Spring greens	

June

Apple	Cauliflower	Lettuce	Raspberry	Spring greens
Asparagus	Cherry	New potatoes	Redcurrant	Watercress
Blackcurrant	Cucumber	Peas	Strawberry	
Carrot	Gooseberry	Radish	Spinach	

July

Apricot	Cabbage	French beans	Radish	Strawberry
Aubergine	Carrot	Gooseberry	Raspberry	Watercress
Beetroot	Cherry	Lettuce	Redcurrant	
Blackcurrant	Courgette	Peach	Runner beans	
Blueberry	Cucumber	Peas	Spinach	
Broad beans	Fennel	Peppers	Spring onion	

August

Apricot	Broccoli	Fennel	Plum	Spinach
Aubergine	Cabbage	French beans	Potato	Spring onion
Beetroot	Carrot	Gooseberry	Radish	Strawberry
Blackberry	Cauliflower	Lettuce	Raspberry	Sweetcorn
Blackcurrant	Cherry	Peas	Redcurrant	Tomato
Blueberry	Courgette	Peach	Runner beans	Watercress
Broad beans	Cucumber	Peppers	Sloe	

September

Apple	Carrot	Greengage	Plum	Spring onion
Aubergine	Cauliflower	Kale	Potato	Strawberry
Beetroot	Courgette	Leek	Pumpkin	Sweetcorn
Blackberry	Cucumber	Lettuce	Raspberry	Tomato
Blueberry	Damson	Peas	Redcurrant	Watercress
Broad beans	Fennel	Peach	Runner beans	
Broccoli	Fig	Pear	Sloe	
Cabbage	French beans	Peppers	Spinach	

October

Apple	Brussels sprouts	Courgette	Pear	Runner beans
Aubergine	Cabbage	Cucumber	Plum	Sloe
Beetroot	Carrot	Fig	Potato	Swede
Blackberry	Celeriac	Kale	Pumpkin	Tomato
Blueberry	Celery	Leek	Quince	Turnip
Broccoli	Chestnut	Lettuce	Raspberry	

November

Apple	Cauliflower	Cranberry	Pear	Turnip
Beetroot	Celeriac	Kale	Potato	
Brussels sprouts	Celery	Leek	Pumpkin	
Cabbage	Chestnut	Lettuce	Quince	
Carrot	Clementine	Parsnip	Swede	

December

Apple	Cauliflower	Cranberry	Pear	Spinach
Beetroot	Celeriac	Kale	Potato	Squash
Brussels sprouts	Celery	Leek	Pumpkin	Swede
Cabbage	Chestnut	Lettuce	Quince	Turnip
Carrot	Clementine	Parsnip	Sloe	

Nutty Cheesy Twists

Nibbles

Buttered Savoury Almonds V

Serves 6–8 Preparation 10 mins
Per portion 202 kcals, 19g fat (2.9g saturated)

225g (8oz) blanched almonds
50g (2oz) butter
2 tsp olive oil
½ tsp salt
1 tsp paprika

Fry almonds gently in butter and oil for 3–4 minutes, turning often.
Drain on kitchen paper. Sprinkle with salt and paprika and serve hot or cold.

Variations

Devilled Brazils V

Follow recipe and method for Buttered Savoury Almonds. Use brazil nuts instead of almonds and add 1 tsp mustard powder along with the paprika.

Curried Walnuts V

Follow recipe and method for Buttered Savoury Almonds. Use walnuts instead of almonds and add 3 tsp curry powder instead of the paprika.

Spiced Pecans V

Follow recipe and method for Buttered Savoury Almonds. Use pecan nuts instead of almonds and replace paprika with ½ tsp cinnamon and ½ tsp cumin.

Stuffed Eggs V

Serves 4 Preparation 10 mins Cooking 10 mins
Per portion 284 kcals, 25g fat (8.3g saturated)

6 large eggs
110g (4oz) soft cheese
3 tbsp mayonnaise
Tabasco sauce
2 tbsp chopped chives
Paprika to garnish

Hard-boil eggs for 10 minutes. Remove shell and cut in half lengthways. Remove yolks and place in a bowl.
Mash egg yolks with cheese, mayonnaise and 1–2 drops of Tabasco sauce. Add chives.
Spoon mixture into egg whites then sprinkle with paprika.

Austrian Cheese Savouries V

Serves 6–8 Preparation 10 mins
Per portion 26 kcals, 2g fat (1.4g saturated)

75g (3oz) soft cheese
½ tsp paprika
¼ tsp caraway seeds
1 tsp finely chopped capers
½ tsp French mustard
2 tsp finely chopped chives
Savoury biscuits and capers to serve

Beat soft cheese until smooth and creamy.
Stir in other ingredients.
Mix, pile onto biscuits and top with capers.

Nutty Cheesy Twists

Makes 36 Preparation 10 mins Cooking 12 mins
Per twist 69 kcals, 6g fat (2.2g saturated)

375g packet ready-rolled puff pastry
1 egg, beaten
110g (4oz) Cheddar cheese, grated
25g (1oz) Parmesan cheese, grated
50g (2oz) walnuts, finely chopped
Salt and freshly ground black pepper

Lay pastry on a lightly covered surface and prick with a fork. Brush with egg.
Sprinkle with cheeses and nuts and season well. Press into pastry.
Cut in half lengthways then cut each into 2cm (¾in) strips. Twist strips gently.
Place on a greased baking sheet and bake at 200°C/400°F/Mark 6 for 10–12 minutes until puffed and golden brown.

Devils & Others on Horseback

Serves 6 Preparation 15 mins Cooking 10 mins
Per portion 105 kcals, 7g fat (1.9g saturated)

10–12 rashers rindless, smoked streaky bacon
8 cubes melon
8 large pimiento-stuffed olives
8 ready-to-eat prunes
8 pieces of sun-dried tomatoes in olive oil, drained
Olive oil

With the back of a knife stretch bacon out.
Cutting to fit, wrap a piece of bacon around each item, securing with a cocktail stick.
Place on a baking tray, brush with oil and bake at 220°C/425°F/Mark 7 for 7–10 minutes, until crisp and golden. Serve hot.

Salmon Roll Ups

Salmon Roll Ups

Serves 4   Preparation 15 mins plus chilling
Per portion 126 kcals, 8g fat (4.7g saturated)

110g (4oz) medium fat soft cheese
4 tbsp soured cream
2 spring onions, trimmed and finely chopped
Pinch of ground bay leaves
Freshly ground black pepper
110g (4oz) thinly sliced smoked salmon
Salad leaves to garnish

Mix together all ingredients except salmon.
Arrange salmon on cling film in a 20 x 15cm
(8 x 6in) rectangle. Spread mixture on top
and roll up (removing film as you roll). Chill.
Slice and serve garnished with leaves.

Salmon & Cheese Triangles

Makes 8   Preparation 40 mins   Cooking 10 mins
Per triangle 213 kcals, 12g fat (6.4g saturated)

110g (4oz) quark or low fat soft cheese
110g (4oz) Wensleydale cheese, grated
180g can skinless and boneless red salmon,
drained and flaked
1 tsp lemon juice
1 tbsp chopped parsley
8 sheets of filo pastry
50g (2oz) unsalted butter, melted

Mix together quark, cheese, salmon, lemon
juice and parsley.
Brush a sheet of filo pastry with butter, fold
in half lengthways, brush with butter.

Place a spoonful of filling in corner of pastry
and fold over repeatedly to make a triangle.
Repeat with remaining pastry and filling.
Place on a greased baking sheet and brush
with melted butter.
Bake at 200°C (400°F) Mark 6 for 10 minutes.
Serve hot.

Pigs in Blankets

Makes 8   Preparation 15 mins   Cooking 25 mins
Per 'pig' 358 kcals, 26g fat (12g saturated)

8 slices medium-sliced white bread, crusts
removed
110g (4oz) butter
3 tbsp tomato ketchup
1 tbsp wholegrain mustard
4 tbsp chopped parsley
8 pork sausages, skinned

Gently roll out each slice of bread with a
rolling pin.
Heat butter and tomato ketchup together
until melted.
Stir in mustard and parsley.
Brush butter mixture over one side of
each slice of bread then place a sausage
diagonally across each one.
Wrap up and secure with a cocktail stick.
Place on a baking tray, brush with remaining
butter mixture.
Bake at 220°C/425°F/Mark 7 for 20–25
minutes, until cooked and lightly browned.
Serve hot.

Dips

Avocado Dip   V

Serves 6   Preparation 15 mins
Per portion 78 kcals, 5g fat (0.6g saturated)

1 ripe avocado, peeled and stone removed
225g (8oz) quark or low fat soft cheese
Freshly ground pepper
2 garlic cloves, peeled and crushed
10 drops hot pepper sauce
1 tbsp fresh lime or lemon juice

Mash avocado flesh with quark or cheese.
Season to taste and stir in garlic, pepper
sauce and lime juice.
Cover and refrigerate or serve immediately.

Blue Cheese & Poppy Dip   V

Serves 4–6   Preparation 10 mins
Per portion 231 kcals, 20g fat (10.3g saturated)

150g (5oz) Blue Stilton cheese, crumbled
175g (6oz) cottage cheese
150ml (¼ pint) soured cream
2 tbsp mayonnaise
1 tbsp poppy seeds

Mix all ingredients together. Spoon into a
serving dish. Garnish with extra poppy seeds.

Curried Cream Cheese Dip   V

Serves 4–6   Preparation 10 mins
Per portion 287 kcals, 29g fat (13.6g saturated)

225g (8oz) cream cheese
4 tbsp mayonnaise
150g (5oz) natural yogurt
4 tsp curry powder
2 tsp finely grated onion
Salt and freshly ground black pepper

Beat cheese with mayonnaise and yogurt.
Stir in curry powder and onion. Season to
taste. Spoon into a serving bowl.

Raita   V

Serves 4   Preparation 5 mins
Per portion 35 kcals, 1g fat (0.7g saturated)

150g pot natural yogurt
½ cucumber, grated
2 tbsp chopped mint

Combine all ingredients, then chill.

Hummous   V

Serves 8   Preparation 10 mins
Per portion 100 kcals, 6g fat (1.1g saturated)

410g can chickpeas, drained
Juice of 1 lemon
3 cloves garlic, peeled and crushed
½ tsp ground cumin
½ tsp ground coriander
Pinch of salt
150g (5oz) natural yogurt
3 tbsp crunchy peanut butter
1 tbsp olive oil
Chopped coriander to garnish

Place chickpeas, lemon juice and garlic in a
food processor and whizz to a coarse paste.
Stir in cumin, ground coriander, salt, yogurt
and peanut butter.
Chill until ready to serve. Drizzle with oil and
sprinkle with coriander.

Guacamole   V

Serves 6   Preparation 10 mins plus chilling
Per portion 150 kcals, 15g fat (2.2g saturated)

3 ripe avocados, stoned
3 tbsp lime juice
6 spring onions, trimmed and finely chopped
1 chilli, deseeded and finely chopped
1 tbsp sun dried tomato paste
2 tbsp soured cream
3 tbsp chopped coriander

Mash avocado with lime juice.
Add all remaining ingredients and mix well.
Chill for an hour.

Salsa

Serves 4   Preparation 10 mins plus chilling
Per portion 52 kcals, 2g fat (0.3g saturated)

2 anchovy fillets, mashed
1 red onion, peeled and finely chopped
2 garlic cloves, peeled and crushed
400g can chopped tomatoes
1 tsp chilli sauce
1 tbsp chopped basil
1 tbsp chopped coriander
1 tbsp chopped flat leaf parsley
1 tbsp balsamic vinegar
2 tsp olive oil

In a large bowl combine all ingredients. Chill
for a minimum of 6 hours.

Soups

Iced Cucumber Soup V

Serves 4–6 Preparation 10 mins plus chilling
Per portion 69 kcals, 3g fat (1.4g saturated)

1 large cucumber
275g (10oz) natural yogurt
½ small green pepper, deseeded and diced
1 garlic clove, peeled and crushed
2 tbsp wine vinegar
1 tbsp chopped chives
Salt and freshly ground black pepper
300ml (½ pint) milk
2 tbsp chopped parsley to garnish

Grate cucumber on a medium grater. Transfer to a bowl and stir in yogurt, green pepper, garlic, vinegar and chives. Season to taste. Chill thoroughly.
Just before serving stir in milk. Ladle into soup bowls and sprinkle each with parsley.

Cream of Potato Soup ❄ V

Serves 4 Preparation 15 mins Cooking 40 mins
Per portion 188 kcals, 7g fat (4.1g saturated)

450g (1lb) potatoes, peeled and diced
1 large onion, peeled and thinly sliced
2 celery sticks, sliced
25g (1oz) butter
Salt and freshly ground black pepper
300ml (½ pint) milk
3 tbsp double cream (optional) to serve
2 tbsp chopped parsley to garnish

In a saucepan fry vegetables gently in butter for 10 minutes without browning.
Add 450ml (¾ pint) water and season to taste. Bring to the boil, cover and simmer gently for 25 minutes.
Liquidise, return to pan and stir in milk. Bring to the boil, stirring, and simmer for 5 minutes.
Ladle into warm bowls. Whirl on fresh cream if using and sprinkle with parsley.

Variations

Cream of Cauliflower Soup ❄ V

Follow recipe and method for Cream of Potato Soup. Use 450g (1lb) cauliflower (small florets) instead of potatoes. Add a large pinch of nutmeg with seasoning.

Cream of Celery Soup ❄ V

Follow recipe and method for Cream of Potato Soup. Use a large head of celery, sliced, instead of potatoes. After liquidising, press through a sieve to remove stringy bits. Stir in 3 tbsp double cream just before serving.

Creamy Carrot Soup ❄ V

Serves 4 Preparation 20 mins Cooking 40 mins
Per portion 236 kcals, 10g fat (6.1g saturated)

25g (1oz) butter
225g (8oz) carrots, peeled and sliced
1 large potato, peeled and cubed
1 onion, peeled and sliced
600ml (1 pint) milk
25g (1oz) rice
Large pinch of ground nutmeg
Salt and freshly ground black pepper
2 tsp lemon juice
3 tbsp single cream

Melt butter and fry vegetables gently for 5 minutes without browning.
Add 600ml (1 pint) water, milk, rice, nutmeg and seasoning. Bring to the boil, cover and simmer gently for 30 minutes or until rice is cooked.
Stir in lemon juice and cream.
Reheat gently and ladle into warm bowls.

Broccoli & Apple Soup ❄ V

Serves 4 Preparation 5 mins Cooking 25 mins
Per portion 117 kcals, 5g fat (0.4g saturated)

1 tbsp olive oil
1 red onion, peeled and chopped
2 dessert apples, peeled, cored and chopped
750ml (1¼ pints) vegetable stock
1 large head broccoli, roughly chopped
Freshly ground black pepper
6 tbsp low fat natural fromage frais

Heat oil in a large saucepan and add onion and apples.
Cover and cook over a low heat for 5 minutes, stirring occasionally.
Pour in vegetable stock and add broccoli.
Bring to the boil, cover and simmer for 15 minutes.
Season with pepper and add fromage frais.
Liquidise, and then return to pan and reheat if neccessary.

Tomato Soup

Leek & Sweetcorn Soup   V

Serves 4   Preparation 20 mins   Cooking 25 mins
Per portion 266 kcals, 13g fat (7.2g saturated)

25g (1oz) butter
450g (1lb) leeks, washed and sliced
1 onion, peeled and sliced
2 celery sticks, sliced
198g can sweetcorn, drained
450ml (¾ pint) vegetable stock
25g (1oz) cornflour
450ml (¾ pint) milk
50g (2oz) Double Gloucester cheese, grated

Melt butter and fry leeks, onion and celery until soft.
Add sweetcorn and stock and bring to the boil.
Cover and simmer for 10–15 minutes.
Blend cornflour with milk, add to soup and stir until thickened. Simmer for 5 minutes.
Remove from heat and stir in half of the cheese.
Serve topped with remaining cheese.

Tomato Soup   ❄ V

Serves 4   Preparation 5 mins   Cooking 25 mins
Per portion 97 kcals, 5g fat (3.3g saturated)

1 onion, peeled and finely chopped
3 celery sticks and leaves, finely chopped
25g (1oz) butter
1 litre (1¾ pint) tomato juice
1 bay leaf
3 cloves
Small bunch of fresh basil
1 tbsp chopped parsley
1 tbsp lemon juice
Salt and freshly ground black pepper

In a saucepan fry onion and celery in butter for 7 minutes without browning.
Pour in tomato juice and add bay leaf, cloves, basil and parsley. Bring to the boil, lower heat, cover and simmer gently for 15 minutes.
Remove and discard bay leaf and cloves. Add lemon juice and season to taste. Reheat for 1 or 2 minutes if necessary.

Pumpkin Soup   V

Serves 4 Preparation 10 mins Cooking 40 mins
Per portion 164 kcals, 9g fat (5.2g saturated)

25g (1oz) butter
1 onion, peeled and chopped
1 carrot, peeled and chopped
350g (12oz) pumpkin, peeled and roughly chopped
750ml (1¼ pints) milk
Salt and freshly ground black pepper
150g (5oz) natural yogurt to serve
Dried pumpkin seeds to garnish, optional

Melt butter and gently fry onion and carrot for 5 minutes, until softened.
Add pumpkin and milk and season to taste.
Bring gently to boil.
Cover and simmer gently for 30 minutes.
Liquidise, then serve hot swirled with natural yogurt and garnished with dried pumpkin seeds, if using.

Cheese & Vegetable Soup   V

Serves 4 Preparation 15 mins Cooking 40 mins
Per portion 271 kcals, 17g fat (10.1g saturated)

4 carrots, peeled and finely diced
2 onions, peeled and finely chopped
2 celery sticks, finely chopped
25g (1oz) plain flour
300ml (½ pint) milk
110g (4oz) Cheddar cheese, grated
25g (1oz) butter
Salt and freshly ground black pepper
1 tbsp chopped parsley to garnish, optional

Put carrots, onions and celery into a saucepan with 300ml (½ pint) water.
Bring to the boil.
Cover and simmer for 20–30 minutes or until vegetables are tender.
Pour in 150ml (¼ pint) water.
Blend flour to a smooth paste with milk and add to vegetables.
Cook, stirring, until soup boils, then simmer for 5 minutes.
Remove from heat, add 75g (3oz) grated cheese and butter. Stir until both have melted.
Season to taste and ladle into warm bowls. Sprinkle with remaining cheese and chopped parsley, if using.

Carrot & Mint Soup   V

Serves 4 Preparation 15 mins Cooking 25 mins
Per portion 209 kcals, 9g fat (5.1g saturated)

25g (1oz) butter
680g (1½lb) carrots, peeled and sliced
1 onion, peeled and chopped
600ml (1 pint) vegetable stock
600ml (1 pint) milk
2 tbsp chopped mint
Salt and freshly ground black pepper
Natural yogurt to serve
Fresh mint sprigs to garnish

Melt butter, add carrots and onion and cook for 5 minutes.
Add stock and milk, cover and simmer gently for 15–20 minutes until vegetables are soft.
Purée until smooth. Add chopped mint and seasoning.
Serve hot or well chilled, garnished with natural yogurt and fresh mint.

Courgette & Cumin Soup   ❄ V

Serves 4 Preparation 15 mins Cooking 25 mins
Per portion 153 kcals, 8g fat (4.1g saturated)

25g (1oz) butter
1 onion, peeled and chopped
1 garlic clove, crushed
2 tsp ground cumin
150g (5oz) potatoes, peeled and cubed
350g (12oz) courgettes, thickly sliced
450ml (¾ pint) vegetable stock
300ml (½ pint) milk
Freshly ground black pepper
Thinly sliced courgettes to garnish

Melt butter and fry onion and garlic for 5 minutes until soft.
Add cumin. Stir in potatoes and courgettes. Cook gently for 2 minutes.
Add stock, milk and pepper and bring to the boil. Cover and simmer for 15 minutes until vegetables are soft.
Purée the soup. Serve hot or cold, garnished with sliced courgettes.

Cumin

Ground cumin is the powdered, dried, seed-like fruits from the *Cuminum cyminum* plant, a member of the parsley family. It has a curry flavour.

Watercress Soup

Watercress Soup ❄

Serves 4   Preparation 10 mins   Cooking 20 mins
Per portion 147 kcals, 8g fat (4.4g saturated)

2 x 75g bags of watercress, chopped
1 onion, peeled and chopped
1 potato (about 175g/6oz), peeled and diced
25g (1oz) butter
450ml (¾ pint) milk
300ml (½ pint) chicken stock
Salt and freshly ground black pepper
4 tbsp double cream (optional), to serve

In a saucepan fry vegetables gently in butter for 5 minutes without browning.
Add milk and stock. Bring to the boil, stirring continuously, cover and simmer for 10–15 minutes.
Liquidise and return to pan. Season to taste and reheat.
Ladle into warm bowls and whirl with cream if using.

Variation

Lettuce Soup ❄

Follow recipe and method for watercress soup. Use 1 large lettuce, shredded instead of watercress.

Cream of Lentil Soup ❄

Serves 4   Preparation 15 mins   Cooking 1 hr 10 mins
Per portion 338 kcals, 16g fat (9.3g saturated)

1 large carrot, peeled and thinly sliced
1 large onion, peeled and thinly sliced
1 celery stick, thinly sliced
½ small turnip, peeled and finely diced
1 potato, peeled and finely diced
25g (1oz) butter
110g (4oz) split red lentils
Handful of parsley
600ml (1 pint) milk
300ml (½ pint) chicken stock
Pinch of ground nutmeg
Salt and freshly ground black pepper
150ml (¼ pint) single cream
1 tbsp chopped parsley to garnish

In a saucepan fry vegetables gently in butter for 7–10 minutes.
Add lentils, parsley, milk and stock. Bring to the boil, lower heat, cover and simmer gently for 1 hour.
Liquidise and return to pan. Add nutmeg and season to taste.
Reheat gently.
Stir in cream and ladle into warm bowls. Sprinkle each with parsley.

Minestrone Soup

Leek & Stilton Soup V

Serves 4   Preparation 20 mins   Cooking 30 mins
Per portion 278 kcals, 18g fat (11g saturated)

25g (1oz) butter
1 onion, peeled and chopped
175g (6oz) leeks, washed and sliced
25g (1oz) plain flour
450ml (¾ pint) vegetable stock
1 bouquet garni
450ml (¾ pint) milk
110g (4oz) Blue Stilton cheese, crumbled
Freshly ground black pepper
75g (3oz) natural yogurt

Melt butter in a saucepan.
Add onion and leeks and fry for 5 minutes until soft.
Stir in flour and stock then heat, whisking continuously, until soup thickens.
Add bouquet garni and simmer over a low heat for 20 minutes.
Cool slightly, remove bouquet garni and liquidise soup.
Return to pan, add milk and heat until almost boiling.
Remove from heat. Add cheese, pepper and yogurt and stir until cheese has melted.
Serve hot or chilled.

Minestrone Soup ❄ V

Serves 4   Preparation 15 mins   Cooking 45 mins
Per portion 145 kcals, 2g fat (0.1g saturated)

1 leek, washed and sliced
1 large onion, peeled and thinly sliced
1 carrot, peeled and sliced
2 large celery sticks, sliced
175g (6oz) white or green cabbage, shredded
225g (8oz) frozen green beans
400g can chopped tomatoes
410g can haricot beans, drained
2 tbsp chopped parsley
1 tsp dried basil
Salt and freshly ground black pepper
1 tsp caster sugar
900ml (1½ pints) vegetable stock
50g (2oz) macaroni
75g (3oz) Cheddar cheese, grated, to serve

Put vegetables in a large saucepan with tomatoes, drained haricot beans, herbs, seasoning, sugar and stock.
Bring to the boil, cover and simmer for 30 minutes.
Add macaroni and simmer for 10 minutes or until cooked.
Ladle into warm bowls and sprinkle each with cheese.

Vegetable Broth ❄ V

Serves 4   Preparation 15 mins   Cooking 1 hr 40 mins
Per portion 139 kcals, 7g fat (3.3g saturated)

25g (1oz) butter
1 carrot, peeled and diced
1 small parsnip, peeled and diced
½ small turnip, peeled and diced
1 onion, peeled and chopped
2 large celery sticks, chopped
1 large leek, washed and finely sliced
900ml (1½ pints) vegetable stock
2 tbsp pearl barley
Salt and freshly ground black pepper
1 tbsp chopped parsley to garnish

Melt butter in a saucepan. Add vegetables, cover and fry gently for 7 minutes without browning.
Pour in stock, add barley and season to taste. Bring to the boil.
Lower heat, cover and simmer gently for 1½ hours.
Ladle into warm bowls and sprinkle each with parsley.

Vichyssoise Soup ❄

Serves 4–6   Preparation 15 mins   Cooking 40 mins plus chilling   Per portion 217 kcals, 18g fat (9.7g saturated)

25g (1oz) butter
2 leeks, washed and sliced
1 small onion, peeled and chopped
350g (12oz) potatoes, peeled and thinly sliced
600ml (1 pint) chicken stock
Salt and freshly ground black pepper
1 blade of mace
150ml (¼ pint) double cream
2 tbsp chopped chives or finely chopped watercress to garnish

Melt butter in a large saucepan.
Fry leeks and onion gently for 7–10 mins without browning.
Add potatoes, stock, seasoning and mace. Bring to the boil.
Lower the heat, cover and simmer gently for 20–30 mins or until vegetables are tender.
Remove and discard mace. Liquidise and chill thoroughly.
Just before serving, stir in cream.
Pour into bowls and sprinkle each with chives or watercress.

Variations

Leek & Potato Soup ❄

Follow recipe and method for Vichyssoise Soup but serve hot not cold.

French Onion Soup ❄

Serves 4   Preparation 15 mins   Cooking 1 hr
Per portion 231 kcals, 13g fat (8g saturated)

350g (12oz) onions, peeled and thinly sliced
40g (1½oz) butter
900ml (1½ pints) beef stock
Salt and freshly ground black pepper
2 tsp dry sherry (optional)
4 slices French bread, each 2.5cm (1in) thick
50g (2oz) Cheddar cheese, grated

In a saucepan fry onions gently in butter until golden.
Pour in stock and season to taste. Bring to the boil, lower heat, cover and simmer for 45 minutes.
Add sherry to soup. Sprinkle bread with cheese and brown under a hot grill.
Ladle soup into warm bowls and top with a cheese toast.

Spicy Lentil Soup ❄

Serves 4   Preparation 15 mins   Cooking 20 mins
Per portion 267kcals, 7g fat (3.1g saturated)

15g (½oz) butter
1 onion, peeled and chopped
1 garlic clove, peeled and crushed
1 tsp ground ginger
2 tsp ground cumin
1 green pepper, deseeded and chopped
1 red pepper, deseeded and chopped
1 bay leaf
175g (6oz) split red lentils
600ml (1 pint) chicken stock
450ml (¾ pint) milk

Melt butter in a non-stick pan, add onion and cook until soft.
Add garlic, ground ginger and ground cumin and fry for 1 minute, stirring.
Stir in peppers, bay leaf, lentils and stock.
Bring to the boil, cover and simmer for 15 minutes or until lentils are cooked.
Remove and discard bay leaf.
Stir in milk and reheat without boiling.

Sweetcorn Soup ❋

Serves 4   Preparation 20 mins   Cooking 30 mins
Per portion 263 kcals, 8g fat (4g saturated)

15g (½ oz) butter
1 rasher streaky bacon, chopped
1 onion, peeled and finely chopped
2 large potatoes, peeled and sliced
2 celery sticks, sliced
300ml (½ pint) chicken stock
Salt and freshly ground black pepper
198g can sweetcorn, drained
50g (2oz) cooked peeled prawns (optional)
1 tbsp cornflour
600ml (1 pint) milk

Melt butter in a large saucepan.
Fry bacon and onion until soft.
Add potatoes, celery, stock and seasoning and simmer for 15–20 minutes until vegetables are soft.
Add sweetcorn and prawns, if using.
Blend cornflour with milk and add to soup.
Bring to the boil and simmer for 5 minutes.
Liquidise soup and reheat gently.

Chunky Fish Soup ❋

Serves 4   Preparation 30 mins   Cooking 25 mins
Per portion 199 kcals, 7g fat (3.5g saturated)

25g (1oz) butter
1 large onion, peeled and chopped
2 garlic cloves, peeled and crushed
2 leeks, washed and sliced
450ml (¾ pint) fish stock
400g can chopped tomatoes
1 bay leaf
1 bouquet garni
350g (12oz) assorted fish fillets, skinned and cut into bite-size pieces
110g (4oz) cooked peeled prawns
Salt and freshly ground pepper

Melt butter in a large saucepan and fry onion, garlic and leeks for 5 mins.
Add stock, chopped tomatoes, bay leaf and bouquet garni. Bring to the boil and cook for 10 mins.
Add fish, bring back to the boil and simmer for 5 mins.
Stir in prawns and cook for 2 mins.
Remove bay leaf and bouquet garni. Season to taste.

Prawn & Corn Chowder

Serves 4   Preparation 10 mins   Cooking 20 mins
Per portion 376 kcals, 14g fat (7.7g saturated)

1 large onion, peeled and finely chopped
15g (½oz) butter
450g (1lb) potatoes, peeled and diced
300ml (½ pint) stock
Salt and freshly ground black pepper
175g (6oz) cooked peeled prawns
198g can sweetcorn, drained
600ml (1 pint) milk
75g (3oz) Cheddar cheese, grated

Fry onion in butter until soft.
Add potatoes and stock and season to taste.
Bring to the boil, cover and simmer gently for 10–15 minutes, until potatoes are cooked.
Add prawns, sweetcorn and milk. Reheat, remove from heat and stir in cheese.

Mulligatawny Soup ❋

Serves 4   Preparation 25 mins   Cooking 55 mins
Per portion 192 kcals, 12g fat (6.7g saturated)

1 large onion, peeled and thinly sliced
1 small carrot, peeled and finely diced
1 large celery stick, finely chopped
50g (2oz) butter
25g (1oz) plain flour
2 tsp curry powder
900ml (1½ pints) vegetable stock
1 large cooking apple, peeled, cored and diced
2 tsp lemon juice
25g (1oz) cooked rice (about 15g (½oz) uncooked)
25g (1oz) cooked chicken meat, finely chopped
Salt and freshly ground black pepper
4 tbsp single cream (optional), to serve

In a saucepan fry vegetables gently in butter for 7 minutes without browning.
Stir in flour and curry powder. Cook for 2 minutes then blend in stock. Cook stirring, until soup comes to the boil and thickens slightly. Lower heat, cover and simmer very gently for 30 minutes, stirring occasionally.
Add apple, lemon juice, rice and chicken to soup. Season to taste. Simmer for a further 15 minutes.
Remove from heat. Ladle into 4 warm bowls. Whirl on fresh cream to serve if using.

Chicken & Sweetcorn Soup

Chicken Soup ❄

Serves 4   Preparation 10 mins   Cooking 40 mins
Per portion 211 kcals, 10g fat (3.2g saturated)

1 chicken carcass
1 onion, peeled and chopped
1 bay leaf
1 clove
900ml (1½ pints) milk
1 chicken stock cube
1 tbsp cornflour
¼ tsp ground nutmeg
110g (4oz) cooked chicken meat, chopped
Salt and freshly ground black pepper
25g (1oz) toasted, flaked almonds to garnish

Break up carcass and put into a saucepan.
Add onion, bay leaf, clove, milk and stock
cube dissolved in 4 tbsp boiling water.
Bring to the boil then simmer for 20 minutes.
Strain and return liquid to pan. Blend
cornflour to a smooth paste with 4 tbsp
water and add to soup. Cook, stirring, until
soup boils and thickens slightly.
Add nutmeg and chicken, and season to
taste. Cover and simmer for 15 minutes.
Ladle into warm bowls and sprinkle each
with almonds.

Variation

Turkey Soup ❄

Follow recipe and method for Chicken Soup.
Use a turkey carcass and cooked turkey meat
in place of chicken.

Chicken & Sweetcorn Soup

Serves 4   Preparation 10 mins   Cooking 15 mins
Per portion 304 kcals, 10g fat (3.7g saturated)

15g (½oz) butter
1 bunch spring onions, trimmed and sliced
418g can creamed sweetcorn
110g (4oz) frozen sweetcorn
175g (6oz) cooked chicken meat, shredded
750ml (1¼ pints) chicken stock
1 egg, beaten

Melt butter in a large saucepan.
Fry spring onions for 30 seconds.
Add creamed and frozen sweetcorn, chicken
and stock.
Bring to the boil, cover and simmer for 5
minutes.
Bring almost to the boil, add beaten egg
slowly, while gently stirring soup, to form
egg threads. Cook until egg has set – do not
boil.

Starters

Blushing Fruit Starter V

Serves 4 Preparation 25 mins
Per portion 120 kcals, 7g fat (0.8g saturated)

1 ripe avocado, peeled, stoned and sliced
Juice of 1 lemon
½ cantaloupe melon, peeled, deseeded and cut into chunks
1 pink grapefruit, peeled and segmented
1 paw paw, peeled, deseeded and sliced
Frisée lettuce

Dip avocado into lemon juice.
Mix fruits together gently.
Arrange frisée lettuce on individual plates and spoon fruit mixture on top.

Stilton & Grape Avocados V

Serves 4 Preparation 20 mins
Per portion 341 kcals, 30g fat (9.7g saturated)

2 ripe avocados, peeled, stoned and sliced
Juice of ½ lemon
110g (4oz) Blue Stilton cheese, crumbled
75g (3oz) black seedless grapes, halved
Freshly ground black pepper
3 tbsp soured cream
25g (1oz) toasted breadcrumbs

Dip avocado in lemon juice.
In a bowl mix Stilton, grapes, pepper and soured cream with avocado.
Spoon back into avocado shells, then sprinkle with breadcrumbs.

Bruschetta V

Serves 4 Preparation 10 mins Cooking 3 mins
Per portion 281 kcals, 14g fat (1.9g saturated)

4 ripe plum tomatoes
2 tbsp chopped basil
8 slices ciabatta bread
1 clove garlic, peeled and halved
Olive oil
Salt and freshly ground black pepper

Cover tomatoes with boiling water and leave for 1 minute.
Remove skins and chop. Mix with basil.
Toast bread on both sides, then rub one side of each with garlic. Top with tomato, drizzle with olive oil and season to taste.

Roast Peppers & Goat's Cheese

Serves 4 Preparation 5 mins Cooking 25 mins
Per portion 270 kcals, 20g fat (6.7g saturated)

4 red peppers, halved and deseeded
2 red onions, peeled and finely sliced
1 tbsp chopped thyme
4 tbsp olive oil
2 tsp caster sugar
Salt and freshly ground black pepper
200g (7oz) goat's cheese, thinly sliced
1 tbsp lemon juice

Place peppers, cut sides up, in a roasting tin and pile onions in centres.
Scatter with the thyme, olive oil and caster sugar and season.
Bake at 230°C/450°F/Mark 8 for 20 minutes or until peppers have softened.
Place cheese slices over onions and drizzle with lemon juice.
Bake for a further 5 minutes until cheese is melting.

Stuffed Mushrooms ❄ V

Serves 4 Preparation 25 mins Cooking 30 mins
Per portion 520 kcals, 32g fat (19.3g saturated)

8 large flat mushrooms, wiped
110g (4oz) garlic butter
8 spring onions, trimmed and sliced
½ red pepper, deseeded and finely chopped
110g (4oz) canned sweetcorn, drained
175g (6oz) breadcrumbs
110g (4oz) Cheddar cheese, grated
Fresh parsley to garnish

Remove stalks from mushrooms. Reserve caps and chop stalks.
Melt 50g (2oz) garlic butter in a non-stick saucepan and fry chopped mushroom stalks, spring onions and pepper until soft.
Remove from heat and stir in sweetcorn, breadcrumbs and half the cheese. Mix well.
Spread remaining butter over rounded sides of reserved mushroom caps. Put butter side down, in ovenproof dish.
Spoon filling into mushrooms and sprinkle with remaining cheese.
Bake at 180°C (350°F) Mark 4 for 20-25 minutes.
Serve hot, garnished with parsley.

Potted Mushrooms

Potted Mushrooms   V

Serves 4 Preparation 30 mins Cooking 25 mins
Per portion 225 kcals, 18g fat (10.6g saturated)

15g (½oz) butter
1 small onion, peeled and finely chopped
225g (8oz) button mushrooms, wiped and sliced
1 egg, beaten
4 tbsp single cream
2 tbsp natural yogurt
½ tsp dried thyme
110g (4oz) Blue Stilton cheese, crumbled
Fresh thyme to garnish (optional)

Melt butter in a saucepan and lightly cook onion and mushrooms.
Beat together egg, cream, yogurt and thyme.
Divide vegetables and cheese between 4 ramekin dishes. Pour in egg mixture.
Place dishes in a baking tin containing enough hot water to come halfway up sides of dishes. Bake at 180°C (350°F) Mark 4 for 20 minutes or until set.
Garnish with fresh thyme if using.

Garlic Bread   ❄ V

Makes 2 x 30cm (12in) loaves
Preparation 15 mins Cooking 15 mins
Per slice 44 kcals, 2g fat (1.2g saturated)

110g (4oz) butter
3 garlic cloves, peeled and crushed
1 tbsp chopped parsley
2 x 30cm (12in) French sticks

Blend together butter, garlic and parsley.
Make cuts down the loaves at 1.5cm (½in) intervals almost to the base.
Spread butter over each side of the bread slices. Wrap loaves in aluminium foil.
Cook at 200°C (400°F) Mark 6 for 15 minutes, opening up foil after 10 minutes.
Serve cut into slices.

Variation

Cheese & Garlic Bread   ❄ V

Follow recipe and method for Garlic Bread. Mix 110g (4oz) grated Double Gloucester cheese with butter.

Onion Bhajis

Onion Bhajis

Serves 4   Preparation 15 mins   Cooking 6 mins
Per portion 258 kcals, 21g fat (2.7g saturated)

Vegetable oil, for deep frying
1 egg, beaten
1 tsp lemon juice
50g (2oz) plain flour
¼ tsp turmeric
¼ tsp cumin
¼ tsp ground coriander
¼ tsp chilli powder
1 red onion, peeled and finely sliced
2 spring onions, trimmed and finely sliced
1 onion, peeled and finely sliced

Heat enough oil to deep fat fry.
Mix egg with lemon juice and 2 tbsp water.
Whisk in flour and spices to a smooth paste.
Add sliced onions and coat in the paste.
Drop tablespoons of mixture into hot oil and
fry for 2-3 minutes until golden.

V Fried Whitebait

Serves 4   Preparation 5 mins   Cooking 10 mins
Per portion 462 kcals, 42g fat (5.5g saturated)

450g (1lb) whitebait
50g (2oz) plain flour
Salt and freshly ground black pepper
Sunflower oil for frying

Carefully rinse and dry whitebait.
Season flour well with salt and pepper and
coat whitebait.
Half-fill a deep pan with oil and heat until
temperature is 180°C (350°F) or until a cube
of day-old bread browns in 30 seconds.
Fry whitebait in batches for 2-3 minutes,
until crisp.
Drain on kitchen paper.
Arrange on 4 individual plates and serve
immediately.

Mushroom & Stilton Mousses

Serves 6 Preparation 30 mins Cooking 2 mins plus chilling   Per portion 283 kcals, 25g fat (9.6g saturated)

175g (6oz) mushrooms, chopped
175g (6oz) Blue Stilton cheese, crumbled
6 tbsp mayonnaise
150g (5oz) natural yogurt
2 tbsp chopped parsley
¼ tsp cayenne pepper
½oz powdered gelatine
Salt and freshly ground black pepper
2 egg whites
Watercress to garnish

Mix together mushrooms, cheese, mayonnaise, yogurt, parsley and cayenne pepper.
Place 3 tbsp of cold water in a small bowl and sprinkle in gelatine. Leave to stand for 10 minutes.
Stand bowl over a pan of hot water and gently heat until dissolved. Leave to cool.
Fold gelatine into mushroom and cheese mixture and season to taste.
Whisk egg whites until stiff and fold into mushroom mixture.
Spoon into 6 ramekin dishes and chill. Garnish with watercress.

Salmon Mousse

Serves 6 Preparation 20 mins Cooking 2 mins plus chilling   Per portion 533 kcals, 54g fat (15g saturated)

1 sachet gelatine
180g can skinless and boneless red salmon, drained
2 eggs, hard-boiled, shelled and chopped
5 spring onions, trimmed and finely chopped
275g (10oz) mayonnaise
Salt and freshly ground black pepper
150ml (¼ pint) double cream, softly whipped

Sprinkle gelatine over 3 tbsp water in a small bowl. Leave to stand for 10 minutes.
Stand bowl over a pan of hot water and gently heat until dissolved. Leave to cool.
Mix together salmon, chopped hard-boiled eggs, spring onions and mayonnaise. Season to taste.
Stir gelatine into salmon mixture.
Fold in cream.
Spoon into 6 small dishes and chill until set.

Smoked Mackerel Pâté

Serves 6 Preparation 20 mins
Per portion 208 kcals, 17g fat (5.2g saturated)

275g (10oz) smoked mackerel fillets
Grated rind and juice of ½ lemon
Salt and freshly ground black pepper
225g (8oz) fromage frais
2 tsp chopped fresh tarragon
Lemon slices to garnish

Remove skin and bones from mackerel, flake flesh and mash in a bowl.
Add lemon rind and juice, seasoning, fromage frais and tarragon.
Mix well, then transfer to individual serving dishes.
Garnish with a slice of lemon.

Leicester Fish Pâté

Serves 4 Preparation 25 mins plus chilling
Per portion 303 kcals, 21g fat (12g saturated)

185g can tuna, drained
200g (7oz) Red Leicester cheese, grated
2 tsp lemon juice
150g (5oz) natural yogurt
2 tbsp chopped parsley
Freshly ground black pepper

Place tuna in a bowl and mash with a fork.
Add cheese and lemon juice and mash together.
Add yogurt, chopped parsley and season to taste. Mix well.
Spoon mixture into 4 ramekin dishes and chill.

Pâtés

Originating from France, pâté is a cooked smooth or coarse paste. It is usually made from meat or fish and has evolved from a Medieval dish. This dish was more like a pasty, with meat and vegetables encased in pastry.

Today, in France and Belgium pâté may still be baked in a crust and is known as pâté en croûte.

Pâté can be served with crunchy vegetables, toast, Melba Toast, crispbread, French bread, or crusty bread. For meat pâtés see page 53.

Prawn Cocktail

Serves 4 Preparation 15 mins
Per portion 147 kcals, 7g fat (1.5g saturated)

½ iceberg lettuce, washed and dried
2 tbsp mayonnaise
4 tbsp natural yogurt
3 tbsp tomato ketchup
2 tsp Worcestershire sauce
2 tsp horseradish sauce
2 tbsp lemon juice
225g (8oz) cooked peeled prawns

Shred lettuce and use to half-fill 4 large wine glasses.
Combine mayonnaise with natural yogurt, tomato ketchup, Worcestershire sauce, horseradish sauce and lemon juice.
Add prawns and mix well. Chill lightly.
Spoon equal amounts into glasses.

Curried Egg & Prawn Cocktail

Serves 4 Preparation 25 mins plus chilling
Per portion 147 kcals, 7g fat (1.5g saturated)

½ iceberg lettuce, washed and dried
3 tbsp mayonnaise
4 tbsp natural yogurt
2 tsp curry powder
4 tbsp chutney
2 tbsp lemon juice
1 tbsp sultanas
110g (4oz) cooked peeled prawns
2 eggs, hard-boiled, shelled and chopped

Shred lettuce and use to half-fill 4 large wine glasses.
In a bowl, combine mayonnaise with natural yogurt, curry powder, chutney and juice.
Stir in sultanas, prawns and eggs. Mix well and chill lightly.
Spoon equal amounts into glasses to serve.

Avocados with Shellfish

Serves 4 Preparation 15 mins
Per portion 287 kcals, 24g fat (1.8g saturated)

2 ripe avocados
Lemon juice
175g (6oz) cooked peeled prawns or crab meat
8 tbsp Thousand Island Dressing (page 62)
Lemon slices to garnish

Cut avocados in half lengthways and remove stones. Brush avocado flesh with lemon juice to prevent discoloration.
Fill cavities with shellfish and spoon over the dressing.
Garnish with slices of lemon.

Sesame Prawn Toasts

Serves 4 Preparation 10 mins Cooking 10 mins
Per portion 469 kcals, 39g fat (4.9g saturated)

Vegetable oil, for frying
200g (7oz) raw peeled prawns
1 egg white
2 tsp light soy sauce
2cm (¾in) piece ginger, peeled and grated
1 garlic clove, peeled and crushed
2 spring onions, trimmed and finely chopped
4 slices white bread, crusts removed
3 tbsp sesame seeds

Heat enough oil in a wok or large saucepan to deep fry.
Place prawns, egg white, soy sauce, ginger and garlic in a food processor and whizz to a smooth paste.
Stir in spring onions.
Thickly spread paste onto bread and cut each into 4 triangles.
Sprinkle generously with sesame seeds. Press into paste.
Fry in batches for 2–3 mins until crisp and golden.
Drain on kitchen paper and serve immediately.

Prosciutto Ham with Peach

Serves 4 Preparation 5 mins
Per portion 109 kcals, 8g fat (1.7g saturated)

6 slices Prosciutto crudo ham
2 peaches, halved, stoned and sliced
25g (1oz) rocket
2 tbsp extra-virgin olive oil
Juice of 1 small lime
Freshly ground black pepper

Cut each slice of ham in half lengthways and arrange on individual plates.
Top with peach slices and rocket.
Drizzle with olive oil and lime juice.
Season with black pepper and serve immediately.

French Country Pâté

Quick Liver Pâté ❋

Serves 4-6   Preparation 15 mins   Cooking 10 mins
Per portion 205 kcals, 8g fat (4.4g saturated)

450g (1lb) chicken livers
25g (1oz) butter
1 onion, peeled and finely chopped
2 garlic cloves, peeled and crushed
10 drops hot pepper sauce
¼ tsp ground bay leaves
½ tsp tomato purée
4 tbsp natural yogurt
110g (4oz) quark or low fat soft cheese
2 tbsp sherry

Remove and discard stringy parts of livers.
Roughly chop remainder.
Melt butter in a non-stick pan, add livers,
onion and garlic and cook, stirring, until
livers are cooked.
Cool, then place in a blender or food
processor with remaining ingredients. Purée
until smooth.
Place in a serving dish, cover and chill.

French Country Pâté ❋

Serves 6-8   Preparation 30 mins   Cooking 1 hr
Per portion 226 kcals, 10g fat (3.5g saturated)

175g (6oz) pig's liver, sliced
1 small onion, peeled and quartered
2 garlic cloves, peeled
110g (4oz) smoked bacon, chopped
110g (4oz) minced pork
110 g (4oz) breadcrumbs
1 tbsp chopped parsley
2 eggs, beaten
150ml (¼ pint) milk
Salt and freshly ground black pepper
3 bay leaves

Place liver, onion and garlic in a food
processor and process until finely chopped.
Turn into a bowl and add remaining
ingredients except bay leaves.
Pack mixture into a well-greased, base-lined
900g (2lb) loaf tin, place bay leaves on top
and cover with foil.
Bake at 170°C (325°F) Mark 3 for 1 hour.
Leave in tin or dish overnight.
Turn out. Serve cold.

Salads & Dressings

Pickled Cucumber Salad

Salads

Dressed Green Salad V

Serves 4 Preparation 15 mins
Per portion 117 kcals, 12g fat (1.5g saturated)

1 cos or romaine lettuce
1 garlic clove, peeled (optional)
French dressing made with 4 tbsp oil
(page 62)

Wash lettuce well and shake dry.
Halve garlic clove, if using. Rub cut sides against base and sides of salad bowl.
Tear lettuce into bite-size pieces and put into bowl. Just before serving, pour over dressing. Toss lettuce in dressing until evenly coated.

Variations

Mixed Salad V

Follow recipe and method for Dressed Green Salad. Add torn-up watercress and/or frisée.

Summer Salad V

Follow recipe and method for Dressed Green Salad. Add chunks of cucumber, tomatoes, radishes, strips of red or green pepper and spring onions.

Tomato & Onion Salad V

Serves 4 Preparation 15 mins plus chilling
Per portion 128 kcals, 12g fat (1.6g saturated)

450g (1lb) tomatoes, sliced
French dressing made with 4 tbsp oil
(page 62)
½ onion, peeled and finely chopped
2 tbsp chopped parsley

Arrange tomatoes in a large shallow serving dish.
Pour over dressing and sprinkle with onion and parsley. Serve chilled.

Cucumber Salad V

Serves 4 Preparation 15 mins
Per portion 94 kcals, 7g fat (1.8g saturated)

½ cos or romaine lettuce
1 small cucumber, diced
150g (5oz) natural yogurt
2 tbsp mayonnaise
1 tbsp lemon juice
Salt and freshly ground black pepper

Wash lettuce and shake dry. Tear leaves into bite-size pieces and put into a serving dish. Add cucumber and mix well.
Combine yogurt with mayonnaise and lemon juice. Season to taste.
Pour over lettuce and cucumber and toss well.

Pickled Cucumber Salad V

Serves 4 Preparation 25 mins
Per portion 76 kcals, 6g fat (0.8g saturated)

400g (14oz) cucumber, sliced very thinly
Sea salt
1 mild red chilli, deseeded and finely chopped
4 tbsp chopped mint
2 tbsp olive oil
2 tbsp white wine vinegar
4 tsp clear honey

Place cucumber in a sieve and sprinkle with salt. Leave for 10 minutes.
Rinse cucumber slices, drain well and place in a serving bowl.
Mix together all remaining ingredients to make the dressing.
Pour over cucumber. Leave to stand for 10 minutes, then serve.

Green Bean Salad V

Serves 4 Preparation 15 mins plus standing Cooking 10 mins Per portion 204 kcals, 20g fat (6.1g saturated)

450g (1lb) green beans
4 tbsp olive oil
¼ tsp mustard powder
Salt and freshly ground black pepper
1 garlic clove, peeled and crushed
2 tbsp white wine vinegar
2 tbsp chopped parsley
2 tbsp chopped chives
4 tbsp double cream

Trim beans and cut into 2.5cm (1in) lengths. Cook in boiling water until tender.
Beat oil with mustard, seasoning to taste and garlic.
Gradually beat in vinegar and continue beating until dressing is thick.
Stir in 1 tbsp each parsley and chives.
Drain beans. While still hot, stir in dressing. Cool then refrigerate for 2 hours. Just before serving stir in cream and sprinkle with remaining herbs.

Mozzarella and Tomato Salad V

Serves 4   Preparation 10 mins   Cooking 5 mins
Per portion 458 kcals, 43g fat (11.8g saturated)

6 tbsp olive oil
1 garlic clove, peeled and crushed
1 tsp caster sugar
225g (8oz) cherry tomatoes
2 ripe avocados, halved, stoned and peeled
250g (9oz) Mozzarella cheese, drained and thinly sliced
2 tbsp balsamic vinegar
2 tbsp chopped parsley
Salt and freshly ground black pepper

Gently heat oil in a non-aluminium frying pan. Add garlic, sugar and tomatoes and cook gently until tomatoes burst.
Slice avocados and arrange on serving plates with Mozzarella.
Stir vinegar and herbs into tomatoes and season to taste. Heat for 1-2 minutes.
Spoon tomato mixture over avocados. Serve immediately.

Mixed Bean Salad V

Serves 4   Preparation 20 mins
Per portion 434 kcals, 19g fat (10.2g saturated)

400g can red kidney beans, rinsed and drained
410g can cannellini beans, rinsed and drained
400g can chickpeas, rinsed and drained
50g (2oz) radishes, sliced
110g (4oz) cooked peas
175g (6oz) Red Leicester cheese, cubed
150g (5oz) natural yogurt
1 tsp chopped chervil (optional)
2 tsp horseradish sauce
2 tbsp milk

Mix together beans, chickpeas, vegetables and cheese.
Mix all remaining ingredients together.
Serve salad with dressing drizzled over.

Curried Rice & Bean Salad V

Serves 6   Preparation 35 mins   Cooking 30 mins
Per portion 308 kcals, 14g fat (2.6g saturated)

175g (6oz) long grain brown rice
1 tbsp curry paste
4 tbsp mayonnaise
2 tbsp chopped coriander or parsley
400g can red kidney beans, rinsed and drained
110g (4oz) mushrooms, wiped and sliced
½ green pepper, deseeded and chopped
½ orange pepper, deseeded and chopped
50g (2oz) currants
50g (2oz) roasted peanuts

Cook rice in boiling water for 25–30 minutes, until tender.
Rinse in cold water and drain well.
Blend curry paste and mayonnaise.
Add dressing to rice with remaining ingredients and mix well.

Fruity Bean Salad V

Serves 4   Preparation 45 mins plus chilling
Per portion 248 kcals, 5g fat (1.4g saturated)

400g can chickpeas, rinsed and drained
220g can red kidney beans, rinsed and drained
110g (4oz) bean sprouts
110g (4oz) radishes, sliced
2 carrots, peeled and chopped
1 green pepper, deseeded and chopped
2 oranges, peeled, segmented and chopped
110g (4oz) seedless green grapes, halved
1 eating apple, cored, chopped and dipped in lemon juice
275g (10oz) natural yogurt
¼ tsp ground ginger
2 tbsp chopped mint
½ tsp sugar

Mix together chickpeas, beans, vegetables and fruit. Chill.
Mix a spoonful of yogurt with ground ginger then stir into remaining yogurt with mint and sugar. Chill.
Serve salad with sauce drizzled over.

Pulses

Pulses are edible seeds grown from a pod. They include beans, lentils and peas. Pulses are a low-fat source of protein, fibre, vitamins and minerals.
If using dried pulses, cook first to soften them. Kidney beans contain toxins that need to be removed by cooking. Soak for 12 hours, then drain and rinse. Cover with fresh water and bring to the boil. Boil for at least 45 minutes until tender.

Fiesta Salad

Fiesta Salad

Serves 4   Preparation 25 mins   Cooking 30 mins
Per portion 200 kcals, 7g fat (1g saturated)

110g (4oz) long grain brown rice
175g (6oz) frozen broad beans
½ red pepper, deseeded and diced
½ orange pepper, deseeded and diced
110g (4oz) seedless red grapes, halved
3 tbsp French Dressing (page 62)
4 tbsp chopped parsley

Cook rice in boiling water for 30 minutes.
Add broad beans 5 minutes before end of cooking time.
Drain rice and beans and rinse in cold water.
Leave until cold.
Add peppers, grapes, dressing and chopped parsley and mix well.

V Coleslaw

Serves 4   Preparation 25 mins
Per portion 137 kcals, 8g fat (4.8g saturated)

2 eating apples, cored and grated
1 tbsp lemon juice
½ white cabbage, finely shredded
1 carrot, peeled and grated
1 small onion, peeled and chopped
2 tbsp chopped parsley
150ml (¼ pint) soured cream
2 tbsp milk
½ tsp Worcestershire sauce

Sprinkle apples with lemon juice. Mix with vegetables and parsley.
Mix soured cream with milk and Worcestershire sauce. Pour over cabbage mixture and mix well.

Potato Salad   V

Serves 4   Preparation 10 mins
Per portion 446 kcals, 40g fat (10.9g saturated)

450g (1lb) cold cooked potatoes, cubed
2 spring onions, trimmed and finely sliced
150g (5oz) mayonnaise
5 tbsp double cream
Snipped chives or paprika to garnish

Mix potatoes with onions.
Add mayonnaise and double cream and stir gently until potato cubes are thickly coated with dressing.
Pile into a serving dish and sprinkle with chives or paprika.

Apple & Walnut Salad   V

Serves 4   Preparation 25 mins
Per portion 542 kcals, 52g fat (11.6g saturated)

½ cos or romaine lettuce
3 large eating apples, cored and chopped
Juice of 1 lemon
6 celery sticks, sliced
75g (3oz) walnut pieces, coarsely chopped
150g (¼ pint) mayonnaise
5 tbsp double cream or soured cream
1 tbsp white wine vinegar

Wash lettuce leaves and shake dry. Tear into bite-size pieces and use to cover base of serving dish.
Dip two of the apples in lemon juice. Add to celery, together with nuts and mix well.
Combine mayonnaise with cream and vinegar. Pour over apple mixture and toss until ingredients are thickly coated. Arrange over lettuce.
Cut remaining apple into thin slices. Dip into lemon juice to prevent browning then arrange on top of salad.

Shallot & Rocket Salad   V

Serves 4   Preparation 5 mins   Cooking 20 mins
Per portion 165 kcals, 13g fat (2.7g saturated)

20 shallots, peeled
4 tbsp olive oil
2 tbsp balsamic vinegar
Salt and freshly ground black pepper
50g (2oz) wild rocket
2 cooked beetroot, thinly sliced
Parmesan shavings

Place shallots in a roasting tin and drizzle with 2 tbsp oil. Roast at 200°C/400°F/Mark 6 for 20 minutes.
Drizzle shallots with remaining oil and vinegar and stir to coat. Season.
Divide rocket between four plates. Scatter over beetroot and shallots and drizzle with dressing.
Serve with Parmesan shavings.

Fruity Greek Salad   V

Serves 4   Preparation 20 mins plus chilling
Per portion 224 kcals, 16g fat (8g saturated)

1 green pepper, deseeded and cut into chunks
2 peaches, stoned and sliced
¼ cucumber, cut into chunks
1 small red onion, peeled and thinly sliced
1 cos or romaine lettuce, torn into pieces
75g (3oz) pitted black olives
200g pack Feta cheese, cubed
6 tbsp Greek natural yogurt
3 tbsp lemon juice
1 tsp mint sauce
2 tbsp chopped mint
Salt and freshly ground black pepper

In a bowl mix together pepper, peaches, cucumber, onion, lettuce, olives and Feta. Cover and chill for at least an hour.
Mix together remaining ingredients and chill until required.
Serve salad drizzled with yogurt dressing.

Fruity Stilton Salad   V

Serves 4   Preparation 10 mins
Per portion 279 kcals, 21g fat (7.8g saturated)

6 tbsp raspberry vinegar
4 tbsp olive oil
1 tsp Dijon mustard
1 tsp caster sugar
250g (9oz) raspberries
150g bag salad leaves
1 mango, peeled, stoned and cubed
110g (4oz) Blue Stilton cheese, cubed

Whisk vinegar, oil, mustard, sugar together.
Mash half of raspberries into dressing.
Divide salad, mango, cheese and remaining raspberries between four plates.
Drizzle with raspberry dressing.

Caesar-Style Salad

Bulghur Wheat Salad

Serves 4 Preparation 30 mins plus soaking
Per portion 280 kcals, 9g fat (1.3g saturated)

225g (8oz) bulghur wheat
4 spring onions, trimmed and sliced
½ red pepper, deseeded and diced
¼ cucumber, diced
25g (1oz) chopped parsley
2 tbsp chopped mint
2 tbsp chopped coriander
1 garlic clove, peeled and crushed
3 tbsp olive oil
3 tbsp lemon juice

Place bulghur wheat in a bowl and cover with water. Leave to soak for 30 minutes.

Line a sieve with a piece of kitchen paper and drain bulghur wheat through it. Press out as much water as possible.

Place bulghur wheat in a bowl. Add all remaining ingredients and mix well.

V Caesar-Style Salad

Serves 4 Preparation 20 mins
Per portion 494 kcals, 41g fat (9.7g saturated)

1 large cos or romaine lettuce, torn into pieces
1 bunch watercress
125ml (4fl oz) extra-virgin olive oil
1 clove garlic, peeled and crushed
Juice of ½ lemon
1 egg, placed in boiling water for 1 minute
16 anchovy fillets, drained
75g (3oz) croûtons
75g (3oz) Parmesan cheese, grated
Freshly ground black pepper

Place lettuce and watercress in a bowl.

Mix together oil, garlic and lemon juice. Pour over salad leaves.

Crack egg over salad and toss gently until egg is blended with dressing.

Mix in anchovies, croûtons and Parmesan and season well with pepper.

Prawn & Pineapple Salad

Herring Salad

Serves 4   Preparation 30 mins plus chilling
Per portion 205 kcals, 15g fat (6.5g saturated)

½ **cos or romaine lettuce, shredded**
3 rollmop herrings
150ml (¼ pint) soured cream
2 tbsp milk
½ **tsp paprika**
½ **tsp grated lemon rind**
2 eggs, hard-boiled, shelled and chopped
1 small gherkin, sliced

Place lettuce in the base of a serving dish.
Drain rollmops well, unroll and cut into
strips. Place in a bowl and add soured cream,
milk, paprika, lemon rind and chopped eggs.
Mix well then pile onto lettuce.

Garnish with slices of gherkin and serve
chilled.

Prawn & Pineapple Salad

Serves 4   Preparation 15 mins
Per portion 244 kcals, 18g fat (5.3g saturated)

1 cos or romaine lettuce
227g can pineapple slices, drained and
chopped
175g (6oz) cooked peeled prawns
Soured Cream Dressing (page 63)
2 tbsp single cream
Black pepper to garnish (optional)

Wash lettuce and shake leaves dry. Tear into
bite-size pieces and place on 4 individual
plates.
Mix pineapple with prawns. Pile equal
amounts on top of lettuce.
Mix soured cream dressing with cream. Pour
over salad.
Garnish with black pepper if using.

Tuna & Bacon Salad

Serves 4   Preparation 25 mins   Cooking 5 mins
Per portion 577 kcals, 51g fat (10.8g saturated)

225g (8oz) bacon, chopped
½ cos or romaine lettuce, shredded
2 spring onions, trimmed and chopped
185g can tuna, drained and flaked
2 eggs, hard-boiled, shelled and chopped
Cucumber Mayonnaise made with 4 tbsp
soured cream (page 62)

Fry bacon in its own fat until crisp. Drain on
kitchen paper.
Place lettuce in a large bowl. Add bacon,
onions, tuna and eggs. Toss well and transfer
to a serving dish.
Pour a little dressing over salad. Serve
remainder separately.

Chicken & Sweetcorn Salad

Serves 4   Preparation 20 mins
Per portion 280 kcals, 14g fat (2.9g saturated)

1 head of chicory
340g can sweetcorn, drained
½ red pepper, deseeded and chopped
225g (8oz) cooked chicken meat, cubed
4 tbsp Garlic Mayonnaise (page 62)
2 tbsp natural yogurt

Separate chicory leaves and place in a
serving dish.
Mix together vegetables and chicken.
Add mayonnaise and yogurt. Stir to mix.
Pile mixture into centre of chicory leaves.

Turkey & Chestnut Salad

Serves 3   Preparation 20 mins
Per portion 323 kcals, 8g fat (1.6g saturated)

250g (9oz) cooked, peeled chestnuts
225g (8oz) cooked turkey, sliced
1 satsuma, peeled and segmented
1 apple, cored and sliced
25g (1oz) lambs lettuce
25g (1oz) rocket
2 celery sticks, sliced
1 clove garlic, peeled and crushed
1 tsp wholegrain mustard
1 tbsp red wine vinegar
4 tbsp olive oil
1 tsp caster sugar

Place chestnuts, turkey, satsuma, apple,
lambs lettuce, rocket and celery in a large
bowl.
In a separate bowl whisk together garlic,
mustard, red wine vinegar, olive oil and
sugar.
Pour dressing over salad and leave to stand
for 10 minutes before serving.

Sandringham Salad

Serves 4   Preparation 25 mins
Per portion 372 kcals, 21g fat (4.2g saturated)

175g (6oz) red cabbage, shredded
1 green pepper, deseeded and sliced
175g (6oz) beansprouts
350g (12oz) cooked duck meat, shredded
2 large oranges, peeled and segmented
3 tbsp raisins
French Dressing made with 4 tbsp oil
(page 62)
1 tbsp soy sauce

Place cabbage, pepper, beansprouts, duck,
orange segments and raisins in a serving
bowl.
Whisk together French dressing and soy
sauce.
Pour dressing over salad and mix well to
coat.

Swedish Sausage Salad

Serves 4   Preparation 25 mins
Per portion 554 kcals, 42g fat (11.8g saturated)

½ round lettuce
1 eating apple, cored and diced
1 tbsp lemon juice
350g (12oz) cooked sausages, sliced
225g (8oz) cooked potatoes, diced
1 green pepper, deseeded and sliced
110g (4oz) canned red kidney beans
Swedish Mayonnaise made with 65g (2½oz)
apple purée (page 62)

Wash lettuce, shake leaves dry and use to
cover base of a serving dish.
Sprinkle apple with lemon juice.
Place apple, sausages, potato, pepper, beans
and Swedish mayonnaise in a large bowl and
mix well.
Spoon sausage mixture onto lettuce and
serve.

Salad Dressings

All quantities of dressings are sufficient for 4-6 servings.

Mayonnaise   V

Makes about 300ml (½ pint)
Preparation 20 mins

2 egg yolks
½ tsp each of mustard powder, salt and sugar
Freshly ground black pepper
300ml (½ pint) olive oil
2 tbsp white wine vinegar or lemon juice
1 tbsp hot water

All ingredients for mayonnaise should be at room temperature.
Place yolks, mustard, salt, sugar and pepper in a bowl. Beat until smooth.
Beating more quickly, add 150ml (¼ pint) oil, slowly, a drop at a time and continue beating until mayonnaise is very thick.
Stir in 1 tbsp vinegar or lemon juice. Beat in remaining oil gradually, about 2 tsp at a time.
When all the oil has been added, stir in remaining vinegar or lemon juice and 1 tbsp hot water (this helps prevent separation).
Adjust seasoning to taste. Transfer to a covered container. Will keep in a refrigerator for up to 2 weeks.

Variations

Thousand Island Dressing   V

Follow recipe and method for Mayonnaise. Stir 4 tbsp double cream, 4 tsp tomato ketchup, ½ tsp chilli sauce, 2 tbsp finely chopped stuffed olives, 2 tsp finely chopped onion, 1 tbsp finely chopped green pepper, 1 hard-boiled egg, shelled and finely chopped and 3 tbsp chopped parsley into the mayonnaise after adding the hot water.

Garlic Mayonnaise   V

Follow recipe and method for Mayonnaise. Stir 1 crushed garlic clove into mayonnaise after adding hot water. Chill before using.

Curry Mayonnaise   V

Follow recipe and method for Mayonnaise. Stir 2 tsp curry powder, 1 tsp finely chopped onion, a pinch of cayenne pepper and 1 tbsp sweet pickle into the mayonnaise after adding the hot water.

Swedish Mayonnaise   V

Follow recipe and method for Mayonnaise. Stir 150g (5oz) apple sauce, 1 tbsp horseradish sauce and 5 tbsp soured cream into mayonnaise after adding hot water.

Tartare Sauce   V

Follow recipe and method for Mayonnaise. Stir 1 tbsp each finely chopped capers and parsley and 2 tbsp finely chopped gherkins to mayonnaise after adding the hot water.

Cucumber Mayonnaise   V

Preparation 15 mins

½ recipe Mayonnaise
4 tbsp soured cream
½ small cucumber, finely diced
1 tsp lemon juice
1 tbsp chopped chives

Place all ingredients in a bowl and mix well.

French Dressing   V

Preparation 10 mins

½ tsp salt
½ tsp sugar
½ tsp mustard powder
4 tbsp extra-virgin olive oil
2 tbsp white wine vinegar or lemon juice

Put salt, sugar and mustard into a basin.
Gradually add oil and beat until smooth.
Gradually beat in vinegar or lemon juice.

Variations

Balsamic Dressing   V

Follow recipe and method for French Dressing. Omit salt, sugar and mustard and use balsamic vinegar in place of white wine vinegar.

Blue Stilton Dressing   V

Follow recipe and method for French Dressing. Gradually beat dressing into 25–50g (1–2oz) finely mashed Blue Stilton cheese.

Creamed Onion Dressing   V

Follow recipe and method for French Dressing. Gradually beat dressing into 75g (3oz) cream cheese. Add 1 tsp finely grated onion and 1 tsp chopped parsley.

Soured Cream Dressing   V

Preparation 5 mins plus 15 mins standing

150ml (¼ pint) soured cream
1 tbsp milk
1 tbsp lemon juice or white wine vinegar
1 tsp sugar
Salt and freshly ground black pepper

Beat soured cream together with milk and lemon juice or vinegar.
Stir in sugar. Season to taste.
If a thinner dressing is preferred, add a little extra milk. Leave to stand for 15 minutes before using to allow the flavours to develop.
Alternatively any one of the following can be added to the dressing before standing for 15 minutes.

3 tbsp chopped parsley
1 tsp wholegrain mustard
1 tbsp horseradish sauce
2 tbsp tomato ketchup
2 tsp paprika blended with 2 tsp milk

Creamy Stilton Dressing   V

Preparation 10 mins plus 15 mins standing

50g (2oz) Blue Stilton cheese
150ml (¼ pint) soured cream
2 tbsp milk
Salt and freshly ground black pepper

Mash Stilton finely in a bowl.
Gradually blend in cream and milk. Season. Stand for 15 mins before using.
Add more milk for a thinner dressing.

Mustard Dressing   V

Preparation 5 mins   Cooking 10 mins

1 tbsp plain flour
Pinch of cayenne pepper
4 tsp caster sugar
1 tsp mustard powder
½ tsp salt
150ml (¼ pint) milk
2 egg yolks, beaten
4 tbsp white wine vinegar

Mix dry ingredients with a little cold milk until smooth.
Bring remaining milk up to boil then stir into the blended ingredients.
Return to pan and bring to the boil, stirring.

Cool slightly, stir in egg yolks and return pan to heat. Cook gently until mixture thickens, but do not allow to boil.
When cool, stir in vinegar.

Yogurt Dressing   V

Preparation 5 mins plus 15 mins standing

150g (¼ pint) natural yogurt
2 tbsp single cream
1 tbsp lemon juice
1 tsp caster sugar
Salt and freshly ground black pepper

Pour yogurt into a bowl. Beat in cream, lemon juice and sugar.
Season to taste and leave to stand for 15 minutes before using to allow flavours to develop.

Variations

Piquant Yogurt Dressing

Follow recipe and method for Yogurt Dressing. Add 1 tsp Worcestershire sauce, ¼ tsp cayenne pepper, 1 tsp paprika and ½ crushed garlic clove, before standing.

Curry Yogurt Dressing   V

Follow recipe and method for Yogurt Dressing. Add 2 tsp curry powder and 1 tbsp sweet pickle before standing.

Tomato Yogurt Dressing   V

Follow recipe and method for Yogurt Dressing. Add 1 tbsp each tomato ketchup, horseradish sauce and 3 finely chopped spring onions before standing.

Mixed Cheese Dressing

Preparation 10 mins

50g (2oz) Blue Stilton cheese
110g (4oz) cream cheese
25g (1oz) Cheddar, finely grated
½ garlic clove, peeled and crushed (optional)
150ml (¼ pint) milk
Salt and finely ground pepper

Mash Blue Stilton and cream cheese together.
Add Cheddar and garlic if using.
Gradually beat in milk. Season to taste.

Crunchy Wraps

Open Sandwiches or Wraps

Use any bread of your choice, or a flour tortilla, and one of the following toppings.

Ideas for Toppings

Bean salad and grated carrot with cherry tomatoes.

Sliced Double Gloucester cheese with grated carrot and onion chutney.

Sliced Brie and grapes.

Cottage cheese with a selection of fresh fruit.

Sliced egg and tomato with mayonnaise and chopped chives.

Cooked salmon with sliced cucumber and lemon.

Smoked mackerel with cucumber and tomato.

Tuna and mayonnaise with dill and sliced pickled cucumber.

Prawns and mayonnaise with paprika and lemon slices.

Cooked sliced chicken with mayonnaise, chopped tomato and asparagus tips.

Cooked sliced duck with cucmber sticks and hoisin sauce.

Sliced Blue Stilton cheese with cooked ham and watercress.

Cooked sliced pork loin and mayonnaise with sliced apple and orange.

Salami and cottage cheese with chopped parsley.

Sliced cooked sausage and coleslaw with parsley.

Cheese & Celery Sandwich   V

Serves 6   Preparation 10 mins
Per portion 271 kcals, 11g fat (6.6g saturated)

12 large slices of brown bread
175g (6oz) Cheshire cheese, thinly sliced
1 celery stick, chopped
40g (1½oz) light soft cheese

Sandwich bread together, in pairs, with cheese followed by celery well mixed with soft cheese.

Cut each sandwich into 2 or 4 pieces.

Variation

Cheese & Apple Sandwich   V

Follow recipe and method for Cheese & Celery Sandwich. Add 1 grated apple and use 3 tbsp mayonnaise instead of the soft cheese.

Cheese & Carrot Sandwich   V

Serves 6   Preparation 10 mins
Per portion 293 kcals, 13g fat (7.8g saturated)

12 large slices of brown bread
175g (6oz) Double Gloucester cheese, sliced
6 tbsp grated carrot
4 tbsp soured cream or natural yogurt

Sandwich bread slices together, with cheese, then carrot mixed with cream or yogurt.

Cheese & Peanut Sandwich   V

Serves 4   Preparation 20 mins
Per portion 398 kcals, 23g fat (10.8g saturated)

25g (1oz) butter
110g (4oz) Cheddar cheese, grated
50g (2oz) roasted peanuts, chopped
1 stick of celery, chopped
8 slices of wholemeal bread

Cream together butter and cheese, then stir in peanuts and celery.

Sandwich between slices of bread.

Nutty Sweetcorn Sandwich   V

Serves 1   Preparation 5 mins
Per portion 433 kcals, 23g fat (4.5g saturated)

2 slices of wholemeal bread
50g (2oz) peanut butter
25g (1oz) canned sweetcorn, drained
Alfalfa sprouts or bean sprouts

Spread 1 slice of bread with peanut butter.

Cover with remaining ingredients and bread.

Crunchy Wraps   V

Serves 2   Preparation 20 mins
Per portion 424 kcals, 22g fat (9.7g saturated)

2 tbsp natural yogurt
1 tbsp mayonnaise
2 tortilla wraps
1 pear, cored and chopped
1 tbsp lemon juice
75g (3oz) Red Leicester cheese, grated
1 carrot, peeled and grated
¼ cucumber, chopped
50g (2oz) white cabbage, shredded

Mix yogurt with mayonnaise and spread onto each wrap.

Toss pear in lemon juice and scatter on wraps with remaining ingredients. Roll up.

Stilton & Radish Sandwich · V

Serves 2 Preparation 20 mins
Per portion 382 kcals, 22g fat (13.2g saturated)

4 slices granary bread
Butter
50g (2oz) Blue Stilton cheese, crumbled
6 radishes, trimmed and sliced
2 spring onions, trimmed and sliced

Spread bread with butter.
Place cheese, radishes and spring onions on 2 slices of the buttered bread.
Top with remaining bread and cut in half.

Berry Brie Sandwich · V

Serves 2 Preparation 15 mins
Per portion 277 kcals, 9g fat (4.5g saturated)

1 small baguette
2 tbsp cranberry jelly
50g (2oz) Brie, sliced
Lettuce

Split baguette and spread with jelly.
Arrange Brie in baguette and cover with lettuce. Cut in half.

Malted Cheese Sandwich · V

Serves 2 Preparation 10 mins
Per portion 404 kcals, 9g fat (2.7g saturated)

8 slices of malt loaf
50g (2oz) light soft cheese
Fresh fruit to garnish

Make malt loaf and soft cheese into sandwiches with fruit.

Cheese & Bean Pittas · V

Serves 4 Preparation 20 mins
Per portion 379 kcals, 11g fat (6.2g saturated)

415g can mixed bean salad
½ red pepper, deseeded and diced
110g (4oz) Cheddar cheese, cubed
4 pitta breads
Frisée or lettuce, shredded

Drain beans, reserving 4 tbsp of liquid.
Stir in pepper, cheese and reserved liquid.
Halve pitta breads and open to form pockets.
Place a little frisée or lettuce in each one, then fill with bean mixture.

Smoked Mackerel Sandwich

Serves 4 Preparation 15 mins
Per portion 355 kcals, 16g fat (4.3g saturated)

175g (6oz) smoked mackerel fillets, flaked
110g (4oz) cottage cheese
75g (3oz) canned sweetcorn, drained
1 tbsp chopped parsley
8 slices of brown bread

Mix mackerel, cottage cheese, sweetcorn and parsley together.
Divide filling between 4 slices of bread.
Cover with remaining slices of bread.

Orange & Mackerel Sandwich

Serves 2 Preparation 20 mins
Per portion 440 kcals, 22g fat (5.6g saturated)

½ orange, peeled and segmented
3 tbsp natural yogurt
75g (3oz) seedless green grapes, halved
2 poppy seed rolls
110g (4oz) smoked mackerel fillets, flaked

Chop orange segments and stir into yogurt with grapes.
Split rolls in half lengthways.
Fill rolls with mackerel and yogurt mixture.

Mango Chicken Sandwich

Serves 2 Preparation 20 mins
Per portion 320 kcals, 7g fat (2.1g saturated)

110g (4oz) cooked chicken, chopped
3 tbsp natural yogurt
1 tsp curry powder
2 tbsp mango chutney
4 slices of granary bread
Lettuce

Mix together chicken, natural yogurt, curry powder and mango chutney.
Divide filling between 2 slices of bread.
Top with lettuce and remaining 2 slices of bread.

Variation

Cranberry Chicken Sandwich

Follow recipe and method for Mango Chicken Sandwich. Omit curry powder and replace mango chutney with cranberry sauce. Replace lettuce with sliced grapes.

Salami & Cheese Sandwich

Serves 2   Preparation 10 mins
Per portion 235 kcals, 11g fat (5g saturated)

2 wholemeal rolls
25g (1oz) salami
25g (1oz) Cheddar cheese, sliced
1 tomato, sliced

Split rolls and fill with salami, cheese and tomato.

BLT Sandwich

Serves 2   Preparation 10 mins
Per portion 329 kcals, 15g fat (4.2g saturated)

4 slices of granary bread
1 tbsp mayonnaise
Lettuce
2 tomatoes, sliced
4 rashers streaky bacon, well grilled

Spread 2 slices bread with mayonnaise.
Top with lettuce, tomato and bacon. Add bread.

Stilton & Ham Sandwich

Serves 4   Preparation 10 mins
Per portion 642 kcals, 36g fat (21.7g saturated)

12 large slices of bread
Butter
175g (6oz) Blue Stilton cheese, sliced
6 thin slices lean cooked ham
Lettuce, shredded

Spread bread with butter.
Sandwich slices together, in pairs, with Stilton, ham and lettuce. Cut each in half.

Cheesy Avocado Toasts   V

Serves 2   Preparation 15 mins   Cooking 10 mins
Per portion 302 kcals, 19g fat (7.8g saturated)

2 slices of wholemeal bread
½ ripe avocado, peeled, stoned and chopped
Lemon juice
110g (4oz) cottage cheese
50g (2oz) Cheddar cheese, grated

Toast bread on one side only.
Dip avocado in lemon juice and mix with cottage cheese and half the Cheddar.
Spoon on to untoasted side of bread and cover with remaining cheese. Grill.

Fruity Cheese Toast   V

Serves 1   Preparation 5 mins   Cooking 5 mins
Per portion 311 kcals, 10g fat (5.7g saturated)

1 slice of soft grain bread
1 tbsp mango chutney
1 small banana
25g (1oz) Double Gloucester cheese, grated

Toast bread on one side only.
Spread untoasted side with chutney.
Peel and slice banana, then arrange on top of chutney. Cover with cheese and grill. Serve hot.

Welsh Rarebit

Serves 4   Preparation 5 mins   Cooking 10 mins
Per portion 239 kcals, 15g fat (8.9g saturated)

4 large slices of bread
25g (1oz) butter, softened
1 tsp mustard
¼ tsp Worcestershire sauce
110g (4oz) Lancashire or Cheddar cheese, grated
2 tbsp milk

Toast bread on one side only.
Cream butter well. Stir in mustard, salt, Worcestershire sauce, cheese and milk.
Spread equal amounts thickly over untoasted sides of bread.
Brown under a hot grill.

Variation

Buck Rarebit

Follow recipe and method for Welsh Rarebit. Serve each slice with a poached egg on top.

Croque Monsieur

Serves 2   Preparation 5 mins   Cooking 5 mins
Per portion 418 kcals, 22g fat (12.6g saturated)

4 large slices of bread
25g (1oz) butter, softened
4 slices smoked ham
50g (2oz) Gruyére cheese, grated

Butter bread on both sides
Sandwich bread together with ham and grated cheese.
Places sandwiches under a hot grill and cook until browned on both sides.

Cheese & Apple Toastie V

Serves 4   Preparation 10 mins   Cooking 10 mins
Per portion 399 kcals, 22g fat (13g saturated)

8 large slices of bread
Butter
110g (4oz) Lancashire cheese, crumbled
2 eating apples, peeled, cored and sliced

Spread bread with butter.
Sandwich together in pairs with filling.
Toast each sandwich lightly on both sides.
Press down firmly and cut each into 2
triangles. Serve immediately.

Variations

Cheese & Pickle Toastie V

Follow recipe and method for Cheese &
Apple Toastie. Omit Lancashire cheese and
apples. Fill with 110g (4oz) sliced Cheddar
and pickle of your choice.

Bacon & Mushroom Toastie

Follow recipe and method for Cheese &
Apple Toastie. Omit Lancashire cheese and
apples. Fill with 225g (8oz) grilled bacon
rashers and 110g (4oz) sliced and fried or
grilled mushrooms.

Beef & Tomato Toastie

Follow recipe and method for Cheese &
Apple Toastie. Omit Lancashire cheese and
apples. Fill with 110g (4oz) cold, sliced roast
beef, mustard and 4 sliced tomatoes.

Hawaiian Club Sandwich V

Serves 1   Preparation 15 mins   Cooking 5 mins
Per portion 529 kcals, 28g fat (16.3g saturated)

3 large slices of toast
Butter
4 small crisp lettuce leaves
1 canned pineapple slice, well drained
25g (1oz) Cheshire cheese, sliced
Mild mustard

Spread first slice of toast with butter.
Cover with lettuce leaves and pineapple
slice.
Top with second slice of toast. Cover with
cheese. Spread cheese with a little mustard.
Butter third slice of toast. Put on top of
cheese, buttered side down.

Variation

Sausage Club Sandwich

Follow recipe and method for Hawaiian Club
Sandwich. For first layer, use lettuce topped
with slices of cold cooked sausages. For
second layer, use sliced Wensleydale cheese
covered with sweet pickle or onion chutney.

Prawn Toasties

Serves 2   Preparation 10 mins   Cooking 7 mins
Per portion 289 kcals, 11g fat (6.5g saturated)

2 large slices of bread
110g (4oz) peeled prawns
110g (4oz) cottage cheese
50g (2oz) Cheshire cheese, grated

Toast bread on one side only.
Mix together prawns, cottage cheese and
half of the Cheshire cheese.
Spoon on to untoasted sides of bread.
Sprinkle with remaining cheese.
Grill until heated through and serve.

Bacon & Banana Toasts

Serves 4   Preparation 10 mins
Per portion 432 kcals, 10g fat (3.1g saturated)

2 ciabatta loaves, halved
3 bananas, peeled and mashed
12 rashers bacon, grilled
Maple syrup

Lightly toast ciabatta on both sides. Cut each
in half.
Spread cut side with mashed bananas and
top with bacon rashers.
Drizzle with a small amount of maple syrup
and serve hot.

Sausage & Apple Grills

Serves 2   Preparation 20 mins   Cooking 10 mins
Per portion 337 kcals, 18g fat (8.6g saturated)

2 large slices of bread
1 eating apple, cored and sliced
2 sausages, cooked and sliced
Apple or onion chutney
50g (2oz) Lancashire cheese, grated

Toast bread on both sides
Top with apple and sausage.
Spread a little chutney over sausage and
sprinkle with cheese. Grill until hot.

Ham & Cheese Toastie

Serves 4   Preparation 15 mins   Cooking 2 mins
Per portion 432 kcals, 23g fat (13.2g saturated)

8 slices of wholemeal bread
50g (2oz) butter, softened
4 tbsp mango chutney
4 slices lean cooked ham
110g (4oz) Double Gloucester cheese, grated

Butter one side of each slice of bread.
Spread other side with chutney.
Put ham and cheese on top of chutney.
Top with remaining slices of bread, butter side up.
Press together and place in a non-stick frying pan. Cook for about 2 minutes until crisp and browned. Serve hot.

Peperami Muffins

Serves 2   Preparation 20 mins   Cooking 10 mins
Per portion 348 kcals, 15g fat (7.5g saturated)

2 English muffins
4 tbsp tomato chutney
40g (1½oz) mushrooms, wiped and sliced
25g (1oz) Red Leicester cheese, grated
25g (1oz) Wensleydale cheese, grated
25g (1oz) stick of snack salami, sliced

Split muffins and toast one side of each.
Spread chutney over untoasted side of each one. Arrange mushrooms on top.
Mix together cheeses and salami, divide between muffins. Grill until hot.

Variation

Chorizo Muffins

Follow recipe and method for Peperami Muffins. Replace mushrooms with 6 halved cherry tomatoes, use Caerphilly in place of both cheeses and chorizo instead of salami.

Nutty Stilton Crumpets   V

Makes 8   Preparation 15 mins   Cooking 10 mins
Per portion 225 kcals, 12g fat (5.5g saturated)

175g (6oz) Blue Stilton cheese, crumbled
1 tbsp port
1 tbsp natural yogurt
25g (1oz) chopped mixed nuts
8 crumpets
8 walnut halves

Combine cheese, port and yogurt. Stir in nuts.
Toast one side of each crumpet.
Spread cheese mixture onto untoasted side of crumpets.
Grill until cheese is bubbling.
Top with walnuts. Serve hot.

Pizza-Style Crumpets

Serves 3   Preparation 10 mins   Cooking 10 mins
Per portion 408 kcals, 18g fat (9g saturated)

400g can chopped tomatoes, drained
1 tsp dried mixed herbs
2 tbsp chopped basil
½ tsp caster sugar
1 garlic clove, peeled and crushed
Salt and freshly ground black pepper
6 crumpets
200g (7oz) Mozzarella cheese, drained and thinly sliced
6 anchovy fillets, drained
12 pitted black olives, drained

Mix together tomatoes, herbs, sugar and garlic. Season to taste.
Toast crumpets on each side.
Spoon tomato mixture on top of each and top with cheese.
Grill until hot.
Garnish with anchovies and olives and serve immediately.

Ham & Pineapple Crumpets

Serves 4   Preparation 10 mins   Cooking 15 mins
Per portion 288 kcals, 13g fat (7g saturated)

4 crumpets
110g (4oz) Cheddar cheese, grated
½ tsp mustard powder
2 tbsp milk
4 slices thick cut ham
4 pineapple slices
Watercress

Toast crumpets.
Mix cheese, mustard and milk together.
Spread on top of each toasted crumpet and grill until golden brown.
Place ham on top of toasted cheese and crown with slices of pineapple.
Heat through under grill. Top with sprigs of watercress.

Vegetable Curry

Vegetable Casserole ❄ V

Serves 4 Preparation 35 mins Cooking 40 mins
Per portion 298 kcals, 9g fat (4.4g saturated)

2 onions, peeled and sliced
2 garlic cloves, peeled and crushed
225g (8oz) carrots, peeled and sliced
4 celery sticks, sliced
1 large potato, peeled and cubed
2 tbsp paprika
25g (1oz) butter
400g can red kidney beans, drained
300ml (½ pint) vegetable stock
450ml (¾ pint) milk
2 tbsp tomato purée
2 tbsp cornflour

Fry onions, garlic, carrots, celery, potato and paprika in butter for 5 minutes, until soft but not browned.
Add beans, stock, milk and tomato purée.
Bring to the boil and simmer for 20–30 minutes or until tender.
Blend cornflour with a little water and add to casserole, then stir until thickened.
Serve immediately.

Parsnip Roast ❄ V

Serves 6 Preparation 40 mins Cooking 35 mins
Per portion 294 kcals, 21g fat (9.2g saturated)

680g (1½lb) parsnips, sliced
25g (1oz) butter
4 tbsp double cream
75g (3oz) Cheddar cheese, grated
Salt and freshly ground black pepper
75g (3oz) roasted peanuts, chopped
25g (1oz) wholemeal breadcrumbs

Cook parsnips in boiling water until tender. Drain well.
Mash parsnips and stir in butter, cream and 50g (2oz) grated cheese. Season to taste.
Spoon half the mixture into a greased 1.1 litre (2 pint) ovenproof dish.
Cover with half the peanuts then remaining parsnip mixture.
Mix remaining peanuts and grated cheese with breadcrumbs and sprinkle over top.
Bake at 220°C (425°F) Mark 7 for 15 minutes or until top is golden.
Serve immediately.

Vegetable Curry ❄ V

Serves 4 Preparation 5 mins Cooking 25 mins
Per portion 268 kcals, 10g fat (5g saturated)

1 tbsp olive oil
1 onion, peeled and chopped
1 tbsp curry powder
1 tsp paprika
2 tsp tomato purée
2 tsp lemon juice
1 tbsp redcurrant jelly
300ml (½ pint) milk
50g (2oz) raisins
400g (14oz) carrots, peeled and sliced
400g (14oz) caulifower, broken into florets
400g (14oz) potatoes, peeled and cubed
Salt and freshly ground black pepper

Heat oil in a large saucepan and fry onion until soft.
Add curry powder and paprika and cook for 2–3 minutes.
Add tomato purée, lemon juice, redcurrant jelly, milk and raisins.
Bring to the boil, then simmer uncovered for 10 minutes.
Meanwhile cook vegetables in a pan of boiling water for 5–10 minutes (or steam for 10 minutes), until tender.
Drain vegetables and stir into curry. Simmer for 2–3 minutes.
Season to taste and serve immediately.

Peanut & Cheese Loaf ❄ V

Serves 6 Preparation 30 mins Cooking 40 mins
Per portion 216 kcals, 14g fat (5.5g saturated)

75g (3oz) peanuts, chopped
75g (3oz) mushrooms, wiped and chopped
110g (4oz) wholemeal breadcrumbs
1 onion, peeled and chopped
1 carrot, peeled and grated
½ tsp dried mixed herbs
110g (4oz) Cheddar cheese, grated
1 egg, beaten
Salt and freshly ground black pepper

In a large bowl mix together all ingredients.
Spoon into a greased 900g (2lb) loaf tin.
Cook at 190°C (375°F) Mark 5 for 40 minutes.
Turn out on to a serving dish.
Serve hot or cold.

Carrot & Cheese Bake ❄ V

Serves 4   Preparation 20 mins   Cooking 30 mins
Per portion 414 kcals, 28g fat (15.5g saturated)

50g (2oz) butter, melted
75g (3oz) porridge oats
150g (5oz) Cheddar cheese, grated
400g (14oz) carrots, peeled and grated
25g (1oz) plain wholemeal flour
3 tbsp milk
¼ tsp dried thyme
1 tbsp sesame seeds
1 tbsp poppy seeds

Mix together all ingredients, except seeds.
Spoon into a greased ovenproof dish and press in. Sprinkle seeds over top.
Bake at 190°C (375°F) Mark 5 for 30 minutes.

Cheshire Aubergine Layer ❄ V

Serves 4   Preparation 30 mins plus standing   Cooking 55 mins   Per portion 450 kcals, 35g fat (21.3g saturated)

700g (1½lb) aubergines, sliced
Salt and freshly ground black pepper
90g (3½oz) butter
1 onion, peeled and chopped
1 garlic clove, peeled and crushed
400g can chopped tomatoes
25g (1oz) plain flour
300ml (½ pint) milk
2 tbsp natural yogurt
175g (6oz) Cheshire cheese, grated

Sprinkle aubergines with salt and leave to drain in a colander for 30 minutes. Drain, rinse and pat dry.
Heat 15g (½oz) butter in a pan and fry onion until soft. Add garlic and tomatoes and simmer for 5 minutes.
Heat 25g (1oz) butter, flour and milk in a saucepan, whisking, until sauce thickens, boils and is smooth. Cook for 1 minute.
Stir in yogurt and 110g (4oz) cheese.
Melt remaining butter in a frying pan and fry aubergines on both sides until golden.
Arrange a third of aubergines in an ovenproof dish.
Cover with half the tomato mixture, then top with half the cheese sauce. Repeat layers, finishing with aubergines. Sprinkle with remaining cheese.
Bake at 180°C (350°F) Mark 4 for 40 minutes.

Root Vegetable Gratin ❄ V

Serves 4   Preparation 20 mins   Cooking 1½ hours
Per portion 200 kcals, 8g fat (4.5g saturated)

500g (1lb 2oz) potatoes, peeled and thinly sliced
500g (1lb 2oz) celeriac, peeled and thinly sliced
Salt and freshly ground black pepper
1 tbsp dried mixed herbs
300ml (½ pint) milk
125ml (4fl oz) single cream
25g (1oz) butter

Place a layer of potatoes into a greased 1.25 litre (2 pint) shallow ovenproof dish.
Season and sprinkle with some of the herbs.
Repeat with celeriac, seasoning and sprinkling with more herbs.
Repeat the layers, ending with a layer of potato slices.
Mix together milk and cream and pour over potato. Dot with butter.
Place on a baking tray and bake at 200°C (400°F) Mark 6 for 1¼–1½ hours, until cooked and golden brown.

Cashew & Vegetable Stir Fry V

Serves 4   Preparation 45 mins   Cooking 6 mins
Per portion 396 kcals, 32g fat (13g saturated)

25g (1oz) butter
2 garlic cloves, peeled and crushed
225g (8oz) carrots, peeled and thinly sliced
2 peppers, deseeded and chopped
4 celery sticks, sliced
175g (6oz) mushrooms, wiped and sliced
8 spring onions, trimmed and sliced
110g (4oz) cashew nuts, toasted
2 tbsp chopped fresh or 2 tsp dried marjoram
75ml (3fl oz) double cream
110g (4oz) fromage frais

Melt butter in a large frying pan or wok and fry garlic and carrots for 3 minutes.
Add remaining vegetables and cook for 1–2 minutes, stirring continuously.
Stir in nuts and transfer to a warm serving dish.
Add herbs and cream to pan and heat until hot.
Remove from heat and stir in fromage frais.
Serve sauce with vegetables.

Chilli Bean Moussaka

Leek & Carrot Medley ❄ V

Serves 4 Preparation 35 mins Cooking 25 mins
Per portion 458 kcals, 26g fat (11.8g saturated)

900g (2lb) leeks, washed and thickly sliced
680g (1½ lb) carrots, peeled and thickly sliced
450ml (¾ pint) vegetable stock
450ml (¾ pint) milk
50g (2oz) cashew nuts, toasted
40g (1½oz) plain flour
40g (1½oz) butter
75g (3oz) Cheddar cheese, grated
¼ tsp dried sage
Salt and freshly ground black pepper
50g (2oz) wholemeal breadcrumbs

Place vegetables in a saucepan with stock.
Bring to the boil, cover and simmer for 15 minutes.
Drain and reserve liquid. Make up to 900ml (1½ pints) with milk.
Place vegetables and cashew nuts in a flameproof dish.
Keep warm.
Place flour, butter and liquid in a saucepan and heat, whisking continuously, until sauce thickens, boils and is smooth.
Cook for a minute.
Remove pan from heat, add cheese and sage and stir until melted. Season to taste.
Pour sauce over vegetables.
Sprinkle breadcrumbs over and grill until golden brown.

Chilli Bean Moussaka   V

Serves 4 Preparation 25 mins plus standing Cooking 25 mins Per portion 268 kcals, 10g fat (4.1g saturated)

2 aubergines, sliced
Salt
1 onion, peeled and sliced
1 garlic clove, peeled and crushed
1 tbsp vegetable oil
400g can chopped tomatoes
1 tsp dried thyme
½ tsp ground cinnamon
420g can kidney beans in chilli sauce
1 tbsp cornflour
150g (5oz) natural yogurt
150ml (¼ pint) milk
1 egg, beaten
½ tsp ground nutmeg
50g (2oz) Red Leicester cheese, grated

Sprinkle aubergines with salt and leave to drain in a colander for 30 minutes. Rinse and drain well.
Fry onion and garlic in oil for 5 minutes.
Add tomatoes, thyme, cinnamon, beans and aubergines. Simmer for 15 minutes, stirring occasionally, until aubergines are soft.
Blend cornflour with some yogurt, then with remaining yogurt, milk, egg and nutmeg.
Transfer aubergine mixture into a flameproof dish, spoon yogurt mixture over, and top with cheese.
Grill until cheese has melted.

73

Spinnach & Cheese Roulade

Spinach & Cheese Roulade ❄ V

Serves 4–6   Preparation 30 mins   Cooking 30 mins
Per portion 474 kcals, 42g fat (20.1g saturated)

25g (1oz) butter, melted

275g (10oz) spinach, fresh or frozen, rinsed

3 eggs, separated

275g (10oz) full fat soft cheese

Salt and freshly ground black pepper

2 tbsp natural yogurt

4 spring onions, trimmed and sliced

50g (2oz) walnuts, roughly chopped

75g (3oz) Double Gloucester cheese, grated

½ tsp cayenne pepper

Line a 30 x 23cm (12 x 9in) Swiss roll tin with greaseproof paper. Brush with butter.

Cook spinach in a pan for 4–5 minutes until tender. Drain well. Press out as much liquid as possible.

Beat in egg yolks and 75g (3oz) soft cheese. Season to taste.

Whisk egg whites until softly stiff and fold into mixture.

Turn into prepared tin, smooth over and bake at 190°C (375°F) Mark 5 for 15 minutes until firm to the touch.

Turn out onto greaseproof paper. Cool slightly, then peel off baking paper. Trim off outside edges and roll up with greaseproof paper.

Mix all remaining ingredients together.

Unroll roulade when cool and remove paper. Spread with filling and roll up. Serve chilled

Parsnip & Tomato Bake ❋ V

Serves 4 Preparation 50 mins Cooking 50 mins
Per portion 555 kcals, 28g fat (15.6g saturated)

2 large parsnips, peeled and sliced
2 large leeks, washed and sliced
110g (4oz) pasta, cooked
1 tsp dried mixed herbs
1 garlic clove, peeled and crushed
25g (1oz) plain flour
40g (½oz) butter
300ml (½ pint) milk
Salt and freshly ground black pepper
1 tsp mustard
175g (6oz) Cheddar cheese, grated
50g (2oz) breadcrumbs
6 tomatoes, sliced

Place parsnips and leeks in a pan of boiling water, cover and simmer for 10 minutes or until just tender.
Drain well and mix with cooked pasta, herbs and garlic.
Place flour, 25g (1oz) butter and milk in a saucepan and heat, whisking continuously, until sauce thickens, boils and is smooth. Cook for a minute then remove from heat.
Season to taste. Stir in mustard and 150g (5oz) cheese.
Melt remaining butter in a pan and fry breadcrumbs until golden brown. Set aside.
Place half the vegetables and pasta mixture in base of an ovenproof dish, cover with a layer of tomatoes, then half the sauce.
Repeat layers. Top with breadcrumbs and remaining cheese.
Bake at 190°C (375°F) Mark 5 for 30 minutes.

Courgette & Tomato Bake ❋ V

Serves 4 Preparation 35 mins Cooking 45 mins
Per portion 459 kcals, 32g fat (7.5g saturated)

4 large courgettes
25g (1oz) butter
1 onion, peeled and chopped
50g (2oz) walnut pieces, chopped
50g (2oz) hazelnuts, chopped
75g (3oz) wholemeal breadcrumbs
1 tbsp chopped parsley
400g can chopped tomatoes with herbs
295g can condensed cream of tomato soup
50g (2oz) Wensleydale cheese, grated

Cook whole courgettes in boiling water for 5 minutes.
Rinse under cold water, drain and cool.
Halve lengthways, scoop out flesh, chop and reserve.
Place courgette cases in a greased ovenproof dish.
Melt butter in a saucepan, add onion and fry for 3 minutes.
Add chopped courgette flesh and cook for 2 minutes.
Remove from heat, stir in nuts, breadcrumbs, parsley and half the tomatoes. Spoon into courgette cases.
Place any remaining stuffing in dish.
Mix remaining tomatoes with tomato soup and half the cheese.
Pour over courgettes and top with remaining cheese.
Cover and bake at 200°C (400°F) Mark 6 for 35 minutes.

Pepper & Brie Bake V

Serves 4 Preparation 20 mins plus standing Cooking 30 mins Per portion 541 kcals, 35g fat (18.6g saturated)

25g (1oz) butter, softened
75g (3oz) hard Italian cheese (Parmesan substitute suitable for vegetarians), grated
75g (3oz) plain flour
4 eggs
600ml (1 pint) milk
Salt and freshly ground black pepper
290g jar marinated peppers, drained and sliced
200g (7oz) Brie, cubed
Handful of torn basil

Generously brush a baking dish with melted butter.
Scatter over half the Italian cheese, tipping out any excess.
Chill dish.
Place flour, eggs, milk and seasoning in a food processor and whizz until smooth. Leave batter to rest for 30 minutes.
Place pepper slices in baking dish and pour over batter.
Scatter over cubes of Brie, basil and remaining Italian cheese.
Bake at 190°C (375°F) Mark 5 for 20–30 minutes, until puffed and golden.

Vegetable & Nut Cobbler ❄ V

Serves 4 Preparation 40 mins Cooking 50 mins plus chilling   Per portion 851 kcals, 54g fat (28g saturated)

150g (5oz) butter

175g (6oz) cauliflower florets

6 baby onions, peeled

175g (6oz) carrots, peeled and sliced

1 parsnip, peeled and sliced

175g (6oz) green beans, sliced

240g (8½oz) wholemeal self raising flour

400g can butter beans, drained

1 vegetable stock cube

600ml (1 pint) milk

110g (4oz) Red Leicester cheese, grated

Freshly ground black pepper

2 tsp baking powder

50g (2oz) walnuts, chopped

Melt 25g (1oz) butter in a saucepan. Add raw vegetables. Cover and cook gently for 15–20 minutes, stirring occasionally, until soft.

Stir in 15g (½oz) flour. Add butter beans, stock cube, 450ml (¾ pint) milk, half the cheese and seasoning.

Bring up to the boil, stirring, until the sauce is smooth.

Transfer to an ovenproof casserole.

Sift remaining flour and baking powder. Rub in remaining butter until mixture resembles fine breadcrumbs and add nuts. Stir in most of the remaining milk and mix to a soft dough. Chill for 10 minutes.

Roll out to slightly smaller than size of casserole on a floured work surface. Cut into 6 wedges.

Place scones on top of casserole. Brush with milk and sprinkle with remaining cheese.

Cook at 180°C (350°F) Mark 4 for 25 minutes or until scones are cooked.

Gloucester Pie   V

Serves 4 Preparation 25 mins plus standing Cooking 30 mins Per portion 437 kcals, 25g fat (14.3g saturated)

8 slices of bread, crusts removed

Butter

110g (4oz) Double Gloucester cheese, thinly sliced

225g (8oz) tomatoes, sliced

150ml (¼ pint) milk

1 egg

1 tsp mustard

Salt and freshly ground black pepper

Butter bread slices and sandwich together with cheese and tomatoes.

Cut each sandwich into 4 triangles. Arrange in a greased shallow ovenproof dish.

Beat milk with egg and mustard and season to taste. Pour over sandwiches.

Leave to stand for 30 minutes or until bread has absorbed liquid.

Bake at 190°C (375°F) Mark 5 for 25–30 minutes or until top is crisp and golden.

Chilli Quorn Cottage Pie   ❄ V

Serves 4 Preparation 15 mins Cooking 55 mins
Per portion 384 kcals, 6g fat (1g saturated)

900g (2lb) potatoes, peeled and cubed
1 egg, beaten
4 tbsp fromage frais
4 tbsp chopped parsley
Salt and freshly ground black pepper
1 large onion, peeled and chopped
300ml (½ pint) vegetable stock
350g (12oz) Quorn mince
400g can chopped tomatoes with garlic
½-1 tsp hot chilli powder
½-1 tsp ground cumin
400g can kidney beans, drained and rinsed

Place potatoes in a saucepan of water and bring to the boil. Simmer for 10 minutes, until tender.
Drain and mash with half of egg and fromage frais.
Stir in parsley and season to taste.
Place onion and half of stock in a saucepan. Bring to the boil. Cover and simmer for 5 minutes.
Stir in remaining stock, Quorn, tomatoes, chilli powder, cumin and kidney beans. Bring to the boil and simmer for 5 minutes.
Transfer Quorn mixture to an ovenproof dish and top with mashed potatoes.
Stand on a baking sheet and brush with remaining egg.
Bake at 200°C (400°F) Mark 6 for 30–35 minutes, until golden.

Lancashire Mushroom Rolls   V

Serves 4 Preparation 30 mins Cooking 25 mins
Per portion 359 kcals, 19g fat (10.9g saturated)

1 onion, peeled and finely chopped
2 garlic cloves, peeled and crushed
40g (1½oz) butter
110g (4oz) mushrooms, wiped and chopped
75g (3oz) wholemeal breadcrumbs
1 tsp dried basil
110g (4oz) Lancashire cheese, crumbled
8 sheets of filo pastry

Cook onion and garlic in a non-stick saucepan with 15g (½oz) butter for 1 minute.
Add mushrooms and cook for a further 2 minutes.

Remove from heat, then stir in breadcrumbs, basil and cheese.
Brush half of each sheet of pastry with melted remaining butter and fold in half lengthways.
Divide filling between pastry. Fold over sides of pastry and roll up.
Place on a greased baking sheet and brush with melted butter.
Bake at 190°C (375°F) Mark 5 for 20 minutes, until golden brown.

Cheese & Onion Pasties   ❄ V

Serves 4 Preparation 35 mins Cooking 25 mins
Per portion 704 kcals, 52g fat (32g saturated)

Flaky Pastry made with 225g (8oz) flour (page 228)
175g (6oz) Wensleydale cheese, finely grated
1 tbsp finely grated onion
Beaten egg to bind
Salt and freshly ground black pepper
Milk for brushing

Roll out pastry into 40 x 20cm (16 x 8in) rectangle.
Cut into eight 10cm (4in) squares.
Mix cheese with onion.
Bind fairly stiffly with egg. Season to taste.
Put equal amounts of cheese mixture onto the centres of pastry squares.
Moisten edges of pastry with water. Fold squares in half to form triangles. Press edges well together to seal.
Make 2 or 3 snips across top of each pasty with scissors.
Transfer to a damp baking sheet.
Brush with milk.
Bake at 220°C (425°F) Mark 7 for 10 minutes.
Reduce to 200°C (400°F) Mark 6 and bake for a further 10–15 minutes or until well puffed and golden brown.
Serve hot.

Variation

Cheese & Apple Pasties   ❄ V

Follow recipe and method for Cheese & Onion Pasties. Replace Wensleydale cheese with Cheshire cheese. Omit onion and use 1 large dessert apple, peeled, cored and cut into small cubes. Add 4 tbsp chopped parsley, if wished.

Fish & Shellfish

Deep Fried Fish

Fish

Grilled Whole Plaice

Serves 4   Preparation 5 mins   Cooking 25 mins
Per portion 127 kcals, 4g fat (1.6g saturated)

4 x 175g (6oz) whole plaice, cleaned
50g (2oz) butter, melted
Salt and freshly ground black pepper
Lemon wedges and parsley to garnish

Line grill pan or rack with aluminium foil.
Arrange 2 plaice on top, brush with melted
butter and season to taste.
Grill for 5–6 minutes.
Turn plaice over, brush with more butter
and season to taste. Grill for a further
5–6 minutes. Transfer to a warm platter and
keep hot.
Cook remaining plaice in the same way.
Garnish with lemon and parsley.

Portuguese Plaice

Serves 4   Preparation 25 mins   Cooking 30 mins
Per portion 229 kcals, 7g fat (1.3g saturated)

120g can sardines in oil, drained
40g (1½oz) breadcrumbs
2 tbsp chopped parsley
Grated rind of 1 lemon
1 tsp finely grated onion
Salt and freshly ground black pepper
Beaten egg to bind
8 x 75g (3oz) plaice fillets, skinned

Mash sardines well in a large bowl and
combine with breadcrumbs, parsley, lemon
rind, onion and seasoning. Bind loosely with
beaten egg.
Spread sardine mixture over skinned side of
plaice fillets and roll up.
Arrange plaice in a greased shallow
ovenproof dish.
Cover and cook at 180°C (350°F) Mark 4 for
30 minutes.

Deep Fried Fish

Serves 4   Preparation 5 mins   Cooking 20 mins
Per portion 511 kcals, 30g fat (5.5g saturated)

Vegetable oil for frying
8 fillets of fish (about 750g/1½lb)
Coating Batter (page 172)
Lemon wedges to garnish

Half-fill a deep saucepan with oil.
Heat until a faint haze rises from it (or until
bread cube sinks to bottom of pan, rises
to top immediately and turns golden in 50
seconds).
Coat 2 pieces of fish with batter. Lift into pan
with fork or kitchen tongs.
Fry for 4–5 minutes until crisp and golden.
Remove from pan. Drain on kitchen paper.
Repeat with remaining fish.
Garnish with lemon.

Thai Fish Curry

Serves 4   Preparation 15 mins   Cooking 15 mins
Per portion 334 kcals, 20g fat (14.5g saturated)

2 red chillis, halved and deseeded
1 lemon grass stalk, trimmed and sliced
1 shallot, peeled and quartered
2 garlic cloves, peeled and halved
2.5cm (1in) piece root ginger, peeled
and sliced
Small handful of coriander, plus extra
chopped coriander
Grated rind of 1 lime
1 tbsp fish sauce
400ml can coconut milk
1 tsp caster sugar
1 tbsp sunflower oil
500g (1lb 2oz) monkfish fillet, skinned
and cubed
250g (9oz) haddock fillet, cubed

Put chillis, lemon grass, shallot, garlic,
ginger, coriander, lime rind (reserving some
to garnish), fish sauce, 6 tablespoons of the
coconut milk and sugar in a blender and
whizz to make a thick paste.
Heat oil in a wok and tip in the paste and fry
for 2 minutes.
Add the remaining coconut milk, bring to a
simmer and cook gently for
5 minutes.
Carefully add monkfish and haddock cubes
and coat in curry paste. Cook for 8–10
minutes or until the fish is cooked through.
Stir every now and then very gently so the
fish doesn't break up.
Serve in small bowls with microwavable
fragrant Thai jasmine rice (cooked as on the
packet's instructions), garnished with the
extra chopped coriander and grated lime
rind.

Cheese-Baked Haddock ❄

Serves 4   Preparation 10 mins   Cooking 40 mins
Per portion 282 kcals, 10g fat (5.9g saturated)

680g (1½lb) haddock fillets
Salt and freshly ground black pepper
1 onion, peeled and finely chopped
1 garlic clove, peeled and crushed
400g can tomatoes
25g (1oz) butter
¼ tsp dried thyme
2 tsp chopped parsley
25g (1oz) fresh breadcrumbs
50g (2oz) Lancashire cheese, crumbled

Skin fish and cut into 4 portions.
Arrange in a shallow ovenproof dish and season to taste.
Put onion and garlic into a saucepan with tomatoes, butter, thyme and parsley. Simmer slowly for 10 minutes.
Cover fish with tomato mixture and sprinkle with breadcrumbs and cheese.
Bake in the oven at 180°C (350°F) Mark 4 for 30 minutes.

Savoury Haddock Casserole ❄

Serves 4   Preparation 30 mins   Cooking 45 mins
Per portion 239 kcals, 7g fat (3.5g saturated)

680g (1½lb) haddock fillets
2 tbsp plain flour
Salt and freshly ground black pepper
25g (1oz) butter
Juice of 1 small lemon
110g (4oz) mushrooms, wiped and chopped
1 onion, peeled and chopped
225g (8oz) tomatoes, chopped
1 small green pepper, deseeded and chopped
1 tsp dried mixed herbs
2 tsp soft brown sugar

Skin fish and cut into 4 portions.
Coat with seasoned flour. Fry quickly in butter in a non-stick pan until golden.
Transfer to a 900ml (1½ pint) greased ovenproof dish and sprinkle with lemon juice.
Mix together vegetables and herbs and spread over fish. Scatter with brown sugar.
Cover and bake at 190°C (375°F) Mark 5 for 30–40 minutes.

Baked Haddock with Cream

Serves 4   Preparation 10 mins   Cooking 30 mins
Per portion 315 kcals, 21g fat (11.5g saturated)

550g (1¼lb) haddock fillets
Salt and freshly ground black pepper
2 tbsp lemon juice
1 tsp mustard
1 small onion, grated
1 tsp Worcestershire sauce
2 tsp cornflour
150ml (¼ pint) double cream
Chopped parsley and paprika to garnish

Season haddock to taste.
Arrange fillets in a greased shallow ovenproof dish.
Combine lemon juice with mustard, onion, Worcestershire sauce and cornflour.
Stir in cream and pour over fish.
Bake uncovered at 190°C (375°F) Mark 5 for 25–30 minutes or until fish is tender.
Sprinkle with parsley and paprika.

Crusted Sea Bass

Serves 2   Preparation 5 mins   Cooking 15 mins
Per portion 261 kcals, 14g fat (7.1g saturated)

Finely grated rind and 2 tsp juice of 1 lemon
2 x 110g (4oz) sea bass fillets
25g (1oz) ciabatta bread, torn into crumbs
2 spring onions, trimmed and finely sliced
2 tbsp chopped parsley
Salt and freshly ground black pepper
25g (1oz) butter, melted

Brush lemon juice over the flesh of the fish fillets and place the fillets, skin side down, on a baking tray.
Tip breadcrumbs into a bowl and stir in the lemon rind, spring onions, parsley and seasoning, and then stir in the butter.
Press the crumb mixture on top of the fish fillets.
Bake at 200°C (400°F) Mark 6 for 12–15 minutes, or until the crust is light golden in colour.
Remove from oven and serve immediately while the fillets are piping hot.

Kedgeree

Kedgeree

Serves 4   Preparation 20 mins   Cooking 15 mins
Per portion 411 kcals, 16g fat (7.1g saturated)

1 onion, peeled and chopped
25g (1oz) butter
150g (5oz) long-grain rice
½ tsp turmeric
600ml (1 pint) fish stock
1 bay leaf
Salt and freshly ground black pepper
450g (1lb) smoked haddock fillets
75g (3oz) frozen peas
75ml (3fl oz) single cream or milk
3 eggs, hard-boiled, shelled and chopped
2 tbsp chopped parsley (optional)

Fry onion in butter until softened.

Stir in rice and turmeric and cook for 1 minute.

Pour in stock; add bay leaf and seasoning.

Place fish on top, cutting to fit if necessary, and bring stock up to the boil. Cover and simmer for 10 minutes or until fish flakes easily.

Remove fish and continue to cook rice for a further 5–10 minutes, until tender.

Skin and flake the fish, removing any bones. Return to pan with peas and warm through.

Stir in cream and serve topped with boiled eggs and parsley if using.

81

Fish & Soured Cream Bake

Serves 4   Preparation 15 mins   Cooking 35 mins
Per portion 513 kcals, 42g fat (12.8g saturated)

25g (1oz) plain flour
Salt and freshly ground black pepper
450g (1lb) white fish fillets or steaks
150ml (¼ pint) soured cream
150g (5oz) mayonnaise
2 spring onions, trimmed and finely chopped
1 tsp dried dill
1 tsp lemon juice
50g (2oz) Cheddar cheese, grated

Season flour and coat fish. Place in a greased ovenproof dish.

Mix together soured cream, mayonnaise, onions, dill and lemon juice. Spoon over fish. Sprinkle with cheese.

Cook at 180°C (350°F) Mark 4 for 30–35 minutes until fish flakes with a fork.

Cod & Potato Bake

Serves 4   Preparation 40 mins   Cooking 50 mins
Per portion 440 kcals, 18g fat (10.3g saturated)

450g (1lb) cod fillet, skinned
300ml (½ pint) milk
1 bay leaf
25g (1oz) plain flour
25g (1oz) butter
110g (4oz) Cheddar cheese, grated
Salt and freshly ground black pepper
680g (1½lb) new potatoes, cooked and sliced
50g can anchovy fillets, drained

Place fish in a saucepan with milk and bay leaf. Bring to the boil and simmer for 15 minutes or until fish flakes easily.

Drain, reserving liquid. Flake fish. Discard bay leaf. Make fish liquid up to 300ml (½ pint) with extra milk.

Place fish liquid, flour and butter in a pan. Heat, whisking continuously, until sauce thickens, boils and is smooth.

Stir in fish and half the cheese. Season.

Arrange half the potatoes in a greased ovenproof dish. Pour over sauce and cover with remaining potatoes. Sprinkle with remaining cheese. Arrange anchovies over cheese.

Bake at 200°C (400°F) Mark 6 for 30 minutes.

Danish-Style Cod

Serves 4   Preparation 15 mins   Cooking 30 mins
Per portion 263 kcals, 13g fat (6.1g saturated)

110g (4oz) streaky bacon, chopped
110g (4oz) chestnut mushrooms, wiped and halved
110g (4oz) frozen peas
4 x 150g (5oz) cod cutlets or fillets
Salt and freshly ground black pepper
25g (1oz) butter

Arrange bacon, mushrooms and peas in a greased shallow ovenproof dish.

Season cod and place on top of bacon and vegetables. Put a piece of butter on each cutlet.

Cover and bake at 180°C (350°F) Mark 4 for 20 minutes. Remove lid and bake for a further 10 minutes.

Cod with Orange & Walnuts

Serves 4   Preparation 15 mins   Cooking 35 mins
Per portion 277 kcals, 11g fat (4g saturated)

25g (1oz) butter
75g (3oz) fresh wholemeal breadcrumbs
1 garlic clove, crushed
25g (1oz) finely chopped walnuts
Finely grated rind and juice of 1 orange
4 x 175g (6oz) cod cutlets
Salt and freshly ground black pepper
Watercress to garnish

Melt butter in a pan. Stir in breadcrumbs, garlic, walnuts and orange rind.

Cook over a low heat, stirring frequently, until breadcrumbs absorb butter.

Season fish and place in a greased shallow ovenproof dish.

Pour orange juice over fish and cover with breadcrumb mixture.

Bake, uncovered, at 180°C (350°F) Mark 4 for 20–30 minutes, or until fish is tender.

Garnish with watercress.

White fish

Cod has dense white flesh, but due to over-fishing is not so readily available, so haddock is a good alternative. It has a slightly sweeter taste than cod and is often available smoked, which has a distinctive salty flavour.

Mixed Fish Pie

Family Fish Pie

Serves 4–6   Preparation 40 mins   Cooking 20 mins
Per portion 545 kcals, 22g fat (12g saturated)

50g (2oz) butter

50g (2oz) flour

600ml (1 pint) milk plus extra for **mashing**

600g (1lb 6oz) smoked haddock, skinned and cubed

110g (4oz) frozen peas

2 tbsp chopped parsley

350g (12oz) potatoes, peeled, diced and freshly cooked

225g (8oz) swede, peeled diced **and freshly** cooked

50g (2oz) Red Leicester cheese, grated

Poach fish in milk for 10 minutes.
Reserve the milk; skin and flake the fish.
Place butter, flour and reserved milk in a saucepan.

Heat, whisking continuously until sauce thickens, boils and is smooth. Cook for a minute.

Add fish, peas and parsley.

Cook for 2 minutes.

Pour into a large flameproof dish.

Mash warm potato and swede with a little extra milk. Spoon on to fish mixture.

Sprinkle cheese over and place under a hot grill for a few minutes until cheese has melted.

Variation

Mixed Fish Pie

Follow recipe and method for Family Fish Pie. Use 300g (10oz) each white fish fillet and smoked fish fillet and 200g (7oz) cooked, peeled prawns. Replace swede with more potato.

Smoked Fish Florentine

Smoked Fish Florentine

Serves 4   Preparation 10 mins   Cooking 25 mins
Per portion 299 kcals, 15g fat (8.6g saturated)

450g (1lb) smoked cod or haddock fillets,
each cut in half
450ml (¾ pint) milk
225g (8oz) frozen chopped spinach
25g (1oz) butter
25g (1oz) plain flour
75g (3oz) Double Gloucester cheese,
grated
Freshly ground black pepper

Place fish in a large frying pan and pour over
sufficient milk to cover.

Bring to the boil and simmer gently for
10–12 minutes or until fish is tender.

Cook spinach as directed on packet.

Drain well and spread over the base of a
700ml (1½ pint) flameproof dish. Place in a
low oven to keep warm.

Drain fish and reserve milk. Remove and
discard skin and bones. Flake the fish and
keep warm.

Make up reserved milk to 300ml (½ pint) and
place in a saucepan with butter and flour.
Heat, whisking continuously, until sauce
thickens, boils and is smooth. Cook for a
minute.

Remove from heat, add 50g (2oz) cheese
and stir until melted.

Season to taste. Add fish to sauce and pour
over spinach.

Sprinkle with remaining cheese and grill
until it melts and browns.

Normandy Whiting

Serves 4 Preparation 10 mins Cooking 30 mins
Per portion 177 kcals, 6g fat (3.4g saturated)

550g (1¼lb) whiting fillets
1 small onion, peeled and finely chopped
1 tbsp French mustard
4 tbsp white wine or cider
Juice of ½ lemon
25g (1oz) butter
1 tbsp chopped parsley

Arrange fish in a greased ovenproof dish. Sprinkle onion over fish.
Heat mustard, wine or cider, lemon juice, butter and parsley in a small saucepan until butter melts. Pour over fish.
Cover and cook at 180°C (350°F) Mark 4 for 15 minutes.
Uncover and continue to cook for a further 10 minutes.

Trout with Almonds

Serves 4 Preparation 5 mins Cooking 15 mins
Per portion 497 kcals, 32g fat (12.4g saturated)

75g (3oz) butter
2 tsp oil
50g (2oz) blanched and halved almonds
4 trout, cleaned
4 tbsp flour
Salt
Cayenne pepper
Lemon wedges and parsley to garnish

Melt butter and oil in a large non-stick frying pan.
Add almonds and fry gently until golden brown. Remove and drain.
Wash trout thoroughly and wipe dry with kitchen paper.
Season flour with salt and cayenne pepper and coat fish well.
Fry trout in remaining butter in pan, until cooked through and golden (about 4–5 minutes each side).
Remove trout to serving dish and then keep warm.
Pour hot butter and almonds over the cooked fish.
Garnish with lemon and parsley and serve immediately.

Trout with Watercress Sauce

Serves 4 Preparation 15 mins Cooking 20 mins
Per portion 207 kcals, 12g fat (5.7g saturated)

4 x 110g (4oz) trout fillets
1 garlic clove, peeled and crushed
1 tbsp lemon juice
Salt and freshly ground black pepper
1 bunch of watercress, finely chopped
½ tsp French mustard
150ml (¼ pint) soured cream

Lay a large piece of aluminium foil on a baking sheet. Arrange trout on foil.
Spread garlic and 2 tsp lemon juice over fish. Season to taste. Fold foil over and seal.
Bake at 180°C (350°F) Mark 4 for 20 minutes.
Stir watercress, mustard and remaining lemon juice into soured cream. Season and chill.
Remove fish from oven. Transfer fish to a serving plate and serve sauce separately.

Salmon with Avocado Sauce

Serves 4 Preparation 5 mins Cooking 30 mins
Per portion 551 kcals, 44g fat (15.4g saturated)

1 ripe avocado
1 tbsp lemon juice
450ml (¾ pint) fish stock
150ml (¼ pint) white wine
4 x 150g (5oz) salmon steaks or fillets
1 tsp cornflour
150ml (¼ pint) double cream
½ tsp dried dill
Freshly ground black pepper
Fresh dill to garnish

Peel avocado and mash with lemon juice.
Place stock and wine in a large frying pan. Bring to the boil and add salmon.
Cover and simmer for 5 minutes. Remove from heat and keep warm.
Pour 300ml (½ pint) of cooking liquid into a pan and boil rapidly until reduced to 150ml (¼ pint).
Blend cornflour with cream, dill and pepper. Stir in reduced stock. Pour sauce back into pan and heat gently until thickened.
Remove from heat and stir in avocado.
Remove and discard skin from fish.
Garnish with fresh dill and serve with avocado sauce.

Salmon Fish Cakes

Salmon Fish Cakes

Serves 4   Preparation 10 mins   Cooking 35 mins
Per portion 326 kcals, 22g fat (10.9g saturated)

450g (1lb) potatoes, peeled and cut into chunks
75g (3oz) butter
213g can red salmon, drained
1 tbsp chopped parsley
1 tsp grated lemon rind
Freshly ground black pepper
1 tbsp vegetable oil
Lemon wedges to garnish

Cook potatoes in boiling water in a saucepan until tender.

Drain and mash with 25g (1oz) butter, salmon, parsley and lemon rind.

Season to taste with pepper. Leave mixture to cool.

Turn out on to floured board. Divide into 8 equal-sized pieces and shape into cakes.

Fry in a non-stick frying pan in remaining butter and oil until crisp and golden, allowing about 3–4 minutes each side.

Drain on kitchen paper. Garnish with lemon.

Tuna with Hot Tomato Butter

Serves 4 Preparation 5 mins plus marinating Cooking
2–3 mins Per portion 525 kcals, 36g fat (13.4g saturated)

4 tbsp olive oil

Grated rind of 1 lemon

Salt

2 tsp mixed ground peppercorns

4 x 200g (7oz) fresh tuna steaks

75g (3oz) butter

1 tbsp tomato paste

¼ tsp chilli powder

3 tbsp chopped coriander

Lemon wedges to garnish

Mix together 2 tbsp olive oil with lemon rind,
a pinch of salt and peppercorns in a shallow
container.

Add tuna steaks, cover and leave to marinate
for 1 hour.

Blend butter with tomato paste, chilli
powder and coriander.

Heat remaining oil in a frying pan.

Cook tuna steaks for 1 minute on each side,
until just opaque in centre.

Top with tomato butter and serve with
lemon wedges.

Soused Herrings

Serves 4 Preparation 25 mins Cooking 45 mins plus
chilling Per portion 313 kcals, 20g fat (3.4g saturated)

4 large herrings, cleaned and filleted

1 large onion, peeled and thinly sliced

1 tbsp pickling spice

2 small bay leaves, halved

150ml (¼ pint) malt vinegar

1 tsp caster sugar

½ tsp salt

Wash and dry herrings. Roll up from head
to tail, with skin outside.

Arrange herring rolls in a 900ml (1½ pint)
ovenproof dish.

Scatter onion over herrings and sprinkle
with pickling spice and bay leaves.

Combine 5 tbsp water with malt vinegar,
caster sugar and salt. Pour vinegar mixture
over fish.

Cover and bake at 170°C (325°F) Mark 3 for
45 minutes or until tender.

Leave herrings to cool in dish and chill
thoroughly before serving.

Fried Herrings in Oatmeal

Serves 4 Preparation 5 mins Cooking 10 mins
Per portion 505 kcals, 34g fat (10.3g saturated)

4 large herrings, cleaned and filleted

110g (4oz) porridge oats or oatmeal

½ tsp salt

Black pepper

50g (2oz) butter

2 tsp vegetable oil

Lemon wedges to garnish

Wash and dry herrings.

Season oats with salt and pepper. Coat the
fish with the seasoned oats.

Fry in hot butter and oil, allowing 4–5
minutes each side.

Drain on kitchen paper.

Transfer to a serving dish and garnish.

Jugged Kippers

Serves 4 Preparation 5 mins Cooking 6–8 mins
Per portion 395 kcals, 33g fat (9.1g saturated)

4 kippers

40g (1½oz) butter

Put kippers into a tall jug and cover with
boiling water. Leave for 6–8 minutes and
drain.

Serve immediately and top each with pieces
of butter.

If kippers are very large it may be necessary
to trim away the head.

Marinated Mackerel

Serves 4 Preparation 25 mins plus marinating Cooking
30 mins Per portion 424 kcals, 29g fat (5.9g saturated)

4 x 250g (9oz) mackerel, cleaned and filleted

1 tbsp honey

½ tsp chilli powder

½ tsp grated fresh ginger

2 tbsp white wine vinegar

150ml (¼ pint) fish stock

2 carrots, peeled and cut into matchsticks

2 celery sticks, finely sliced

4 spring onions, trimmed and sliced

Place fish in a large ovenproof dish.

Mix together honey, chilli powder, ginger,
vinegar and stock. Pour over fish.

Scatter vegetables over fish, cover and chill
for 1 hour.

Bake at 190°C (375°F) Mark 5 for 30 minutes.

Shellfish

Scallops

If they have not already been opened and cleaned by the fishmonger, put them into a hot oven and leave for a few minutes until the shells open. Remove the dark frill (beard) from round the scallop, then carefully wash the white portion and bright orange roe.

Fried Scallops

Serves 4   Preparation 5 mins   Cooking 8 mins
Per portion 163 kcals, 8g fat (3.7g saturated)

8 scallops
Salt and freshly ground black pepper
1 tbsp lemon juice
3 tbsp plain flour
25g (1oz) butter
2 tsp vegetable oil
Lemon wedges to garnish

Cut washed scallops in half. Pat dry with kitchen paper.
Season to taste and sprinkle with lemon juice. Toss in flour.
Fry in hot butter and oil until golden, allowing about 4 minutes each side.
Serve immediately garnished with lemon wedges.

Variation

Fried Scallops with Bacon

Follow recipe and method for Fried Scallops. Cook 200g (7oz) smoked bacon lardons in frying pan for 5–6 minutes before adding scallops.

Coquille St Jacques

Serves 4   Preparation 30 mins   Cooking 40 mins
Per portion 390 kcals, 21g fat (12.6g saturated)

4 scallops
4 tbsp white wine
110g (4oz) mushrooms, wiped and sliced
Mornay sauce made with 300ml (½ pint) milk (page 180)
25g (1oz) Cheddar cheese, grated
25g (1oz) breadcrumbs
225g (8oz) potatoes, peeled, boiled and mashed
15g (½oz) butter

Remove scallops from their shells. Discard darker intestine. Wash thoroughly.
Place scallops with their orange roes in a saucepan with wine and mushrooms and poach for 10 minutes.
Make mornay sauce (page 180).
Drain scallops; add wine and mushrooms to sauce.
Place scallops and roes back in their shells or in individual flameproof dishes. Pour sauce over and around.
Mix together cheese and breadcrumbs and sprinkle over sauce.
Cream potatoes with butter and spoon around the edge of each shell or dish.
Brown under a hot grill and serve immediately.

Mussels

Mussels should be purchased tightly closed or close when tapped. Discard any open ones before cooking. Cut away beards with scissors, then put into a colander and wash under cold running water. Shake colander continuously to prevent mussel shells from opening. Scrub with stiff brush and wash again to ensure no grit is left with the shells.

Moules Mariniére

Serves 4   Preparation 30 mins   Cooking 20 mins
Per portion 170 kcals, 8g fat (3.6g saturated)

25g (1oz) butter
6 shallots or small onions, peeled and chopped
1 garlic clove, peeled and crushed
150ml (¼ pint) dry white wine
1 bay leaf
1.8 kg (4lb) mussels, scrubbed and beards removed
3 tbsp chopped parsley

Melt butter in a large saucepan. Add shallots or onions and garlic. Fry gently until pale gold.
Add wine and bay leaf and simmer gently for 7 minutes.
Add mussels and cook over a brisk heat, shaking pan frequently, until shells open (about 6–8 minutes).
Discard any mussels that do not open.
Pour into warm serving dishes, sprinkle with parsley and serve immediately.

Prawn Stir-Fry

Prawn Stuffed Courgettes

Serves 4   Preparation 40 mins   Cooking 40 mins
Per portion 540 kcals, 27g fat (15.6g saturated)

4 courgettes, halved lengthways
50g (2oz) butter
1 onion, peeled and chopped
250g (9oz) cooked long grain brown rice,
(about 75g (3oz) raw)
3 tomatoes, chopped
198g can sweetcorn, drained
1 tsp mustard
1 tbsp chopped parsley
110g (4oz) Cheddar cheese, grated
4 tbsp single cream
110g (4oz) cooked peeled prawns
25g (1oz) plain flour
300ml (½ pint) milk
Salt and freshly ground black pepper
50g (2oz) wholemeal breadcrumbs

Cook courgettes in boiling water in a
saucepan for 10 minutes.
Drain and cool. Scoop out flesh and reserve.
Place cases in a greased ovenproof dish.
Melt 25g (1oz) butter in a saucepan and cook
onion until soft.
Chop reserved courgette flesh and mix with
onion, rice, tomatoes, sweetcorn, mustard,
parsley, 50g (2oz) cheese, cream and prawns.
Spoon into courgette cases, adding any
leftover filling to dish.

Place remaining butter with flour and milk in
a saucepan.
Heat, stirring, until sauce thickens, boils and
is smooth. Cook for a minute.
Season to taste and pour over courgettes.
Mix breadcrumbs and remaining cheese and
sprinkle over sauce.
Bake at 200°C (400°F) Mark 6 for 15–20
minutes, until golden brown.

Prawn Stir-Fry

Serves 2   Preparation 5 mins   Cooking 5 mins
Per portion 289 kcals, 12g fat (6.8g saturated)

25g (1oz) butter
1 garlic clove, peeled and crushed
Pinch of ground ginger
170g (6oz) baby sweetcorn, halved
300g (10oz) pack fresh stir-fry
vegetables
200g (7oz) cooked peeled prawns
2 tbsp soy sauce
2 tbsp dry sherry

Melt butter in a large frying pan or wok.
Add garlic, ginger and sweetcorn and cook
for 2 minutes.
Add vegetables and prawns and stir-fry for
2–3 minutes, until prawns are hot. Sprinkle
on soy sauce and sherry.
Serve immediately.

Poultry & Game

Roast Chicken

Chicken

Roast Chicken ❄

Serves 4–6   Preparation 15 mins
Cooking 1 hr 40 mins
Per portion 470 kcals, 27g fat (8.9g saturated)

1.8kg (4lb) oven-ready chicken
Small bunch of herbs
25g (1oz) butter
Salt and freshly ground black pepper
Streaky bacon rashers (optional)
Accompany with
Gravy (page 181)
Bread Sauce (page 183)
Small cooked sausages
Boiled or Roast Potatoes (page 155)
Assorted vegetables

If chicken is frozen, thaw completely.
Remove giblet pack, if necessary.
Wash bird. Dry thoroughly with kitchen
paper. Stand in a roasting tin.
Sprinkle a few herbs onto chicken breast and
dot with butter. Season. Place bacon rashers
onto breast if using. Put herbs into cavity.
Cover with foil and roast at 190°C (375°F)
Mark 5 allowing 20 minutes per 450g (1lb)
plus 20 minutes. 30 minutes before the end
of cooking remove foil and lift bacon onto
the base of the tin.
Test the deepest part of each thigh with a
skewer to check that juices run clear and bird
is cooked through. Transfer to a board or
carving dish.
Leave to rest for 5 minutes before carving.
Serve with accompaniments.

Variations

Roast Stuffed Chicken ❄

Follow recipe and method for Roast Chicken.
Stuff neck end (not body cavity) with suitable
stuffing (page 188). Fold neck skin under
bird. Allow an extra 5 minutes per 450g (1lb)
roasting time.

French-Style Roast Chicken ❄

Follow recipe and method for Roast Chicken.
Mix 40g (1½oz) softened butter with 1 tsp
dried rosemary and 1 tsp French mustard.
Place half of butter in body cavity and smear
remainder over chicken skin before roasting.

Chicken with Almonds

Serves 3–4   Preparation 30 mins   Cooking 30 mins
Per portion 452 kcals, 26g fat (10.2g saturated)

1 small onion, peeled and chopped
50g (2oz) mushrooms, wiped and sliced
25g (1oz) butter
2 tsp cornflour
300ml (½ pint) milk
350g (12oz) cooked chicken meat, chopped
¼ tsp ground ginger
¼ tsp ground nutmeg
150g (5oz) natural yogurt
1 egg yolk
Salt and freshly ground black pepper
25g (1oz) flaked almonds, toasted

Fry onion and mushrooms in butter, in a
saucepan, until pale gold. Add cornflour, cook
for 1 minute then gradually blend in milk.
Cook stirring until sauce boils. Add chicken,
ginger and nutmeg. Simmer for 5–7 minutes.
Beat together yogurt and egg yolk, then add
to chicken. Cook very slowly, without boiling,
until thickened.
Season to taste and pour into a serving dish.
Scatter with almonds.

Leftover Chicken Bake ❄

Serves 3   Preparation 15 mins   Cooking 1¼ hrs
Per portion 655 kcals, 25g fat (9.8g saturated)

500g (1lb 2oz) potatoes, peeled
1 tbsp sunflower oil
1 onion, peeled and thinly sliced into rings
1–2 bacon rashers, cut into thin strips
225g (8oz) cooked chicken, chopped
1 tsp mixed dried herbs
150ml (¼ pint) single cream or milk
150ml (¼ pint) chicken stock
25g (1oz) butter, melted

Cut potatoes into 5m (¼in) thick slices. Place
in a saucepan, cover with water, add a little
salt and bring up to boil. Drain in a colander.
Heat oil in a frying pan, add onion and bacon
and cook gently until onion is softened.
Mix chicken and herbs into onion and bacon,
and transfer to a shallow baking dish.
Pour cream or milk and stock over chicken,
and cover top with overlapping potato slices.
Brush with butter and bake at 200°C (400°F)
Gas 6 for 45 minutes–1 hour.

Chicken Cacciatore ❄

Serves 4   Preparation 40 mins   Cooking 1¼ hrs
Per portion 490 kcals, 30g fat (7.9g saturated)

4 x 275g (10oz) chicken portions
4 tbsp plain flour
Salt and freshly ground black pepper
2 tbsp olive oil
1 large onion, peeled and chopped
1 garlic clove, peeled and crushed
450g (1lb) tomatoes, skinned and chopped
1 tsp sugar
150ml (¼ pint) chicken stock
110g (4oz) mushrooms, sliced

Toss chicken in seasoned flour.
Heat oil in large pan and fry chicken until crisp and golden on both sides. Remove to a plate.
Fry onion and garlic in remaining oil until pale gold.
Add tomatoes, sugar and stock. Replace chicken, bring to the boil slowly, cover, lower heat and simmer for 45 minutes.
Add mushrooms and simmer for 15 minutes.

Chicken Maryland

Serves 4   Preparation 30 mins   Cooking 40 mins
Per portion 655 kcals, 25g fat (9.8g saturated)

4 x 225g (8oz) chicken joints, skinned
Milk
175g (6oz) plain flour
Salt and freshly ground black pepper
2 eggs
50g (2oz) breadcrumbs
50g (2oz) butter
2 tbsp olive oil
Pinch of nutmeg
¼ tsp mustard powder
150ml (¼ pint) milk
340g can sweetcorn, drained

Dip chicken joints in milk. Toss in 50g (2oz) seasoned flour.
Break 1 egg in a bowl and beat. Dip in chicken, then coat with breadcrumbs. Shake off surplus crumbs.
Place butter and 1 tbsp oil in a roasting tin. Heat at 190°C (375°F) Mark 5 for 10 minutes. Add chicken and baste with hot fat.
Return to oven for 30 minutes or until chicken is tender.

Meanwhile, make corn fritters. Mix together remaining flour, nutmeg and mustard.
Break in remaining egg and milk. Beat to form a smooth batter. Stir in sweetcorn.
Heat remaining oil in a non-stick frying pan.
Drop spoonfuls of fritter mixture into pan, turn over when underside is golden.
Cook for a further 3–4 minutes until cooked through.
Remove from pan and keep warm. Repeat with remaining mixture.
Serve chicken with corn fritters.

Fricassée of Chicken ❄

Serves 4   Preparation 30 mins   Cooking 1¼ hrs
Per portion 402 kcals, 17g fat (7.5g saturated)

1.6kg (3½lb) chicken joints, skinned and cut into 8 portions
300ml (½ pint) chicken stock
300ml (½ pint) milk
110g (4oz) streaky bacon, chopped
4 cloves
1 large onion, peeled
¼ tsp ground nutmeg
50g (2oz) mushrooms, wiped and sliced
¼ tsp dried mixed herbs
Salt and freshly ground black pepper
25g (1oz) butter
25g (1oz) plain flour
4 rashers streaky bacon, halved, rolled and grilled to garnish
4 lemon wedges to garnish
1 tbsp chopped parsley to garnish

Put chicken into a saucepan with stock, milk and bacon.
Press cloves into onion and add to chicken with nutmeg, mushrooms, herbs and seasoning.
Bring to the boil and remove any scum.
Lower heat, cover and simmer gently for 1–1½ hours or until chicken is tender.
Transfer chicken to plate, keep hot.
Strain chicken liquid and reserve.
Melt butter in a clean saucepan, add flour and cook for 1 minute. Gradually blend in chicken liquid.
Cook stirring until sauce boils and thickens. Cook for 1 minute.
Pour sauce over chicken and garnish with bacon, lemon and parsley.

Coq au Vin

Chicken & Parsley Casserole ❋

Serves 4   Preparation 40 mins   Cooking 1¾ hrs
Per portion 526 kcals, 25g fat (12.2g saturated)

4 x 275g (10oz) chicken portions, skinned
50g (2oz) butter
110g (4oz) streaky bacon, chopped
2 large onions, peeled and chopped
50g (2oz) plain flour
600ml (1 pint) milk
1 bay leaf
1 tsp dried mixed herbs
1 chicken stock cube
Salt and freshly ground black pepper
110g (4oz) mushrooms, wiped and sliced
2 tbsp chopped parsley to garnish

Fry chicken in 25g (1oz) butter until golden. Transfer to a large casserole.

Add bacon and onions to same pan and fry gently until pale gold. Sprinkle over chicken.

Melt remaining butter, stir in flour and cook for 1 minute. Gradually blend in milk.

Add bay leaf, herbs and crumbled stock cube. Cook, stirring, until sauce boils and thickens. Cook for 1 minute.

Season to taste and pour over chicken. Cover and cook at 170°C (325°F) Mark 3 for 1 hour.

Add mushrooms, cover and cook for a further 30 minutes.

Serve garnished with chopped parsley.

Coq au Vin ❋

Serves 4   Preparation 40 mins   Cooking 1½ hrs
Per portion 394 kcals, 16g fat (4.5g saturated)

4 x 275g (10oz) chicken portions, skinned
4 tbsp plain flour
Salt and freshly ground black pepper
2 tbsp olive oil
1 large onion, peeled and chopped
1 garlic clove, peeled and crushed
110g (4oz) smoked streaky bacon, chopped
8 small onions or shallots, peeled
2 or 3 sprigs of thyme
1 bay leaf
300ml (½ pint) dry red wine
110g (4oz) mushrooms, wiped and sliced

Toss chicken joints in seasoned flour.

Heat oil in a large saucepan and fry chicken until crisp and golden on both sides. Remove to a plate.

Add chopped onion, garlic and bacon to remaining oil in pan.

Fry gently until pale gold. Return chicken to pan.

Add small onions, thyme, bay leaf, wine and 4 tbsp water. Bring to the boil then lower heat, cover and simmer for 1 hour or until chicken is cooked through. Top up with more water if needed.

Add mushrooms and simmer for 10 minutes.

Chicken Pie ❄

Serves 4–6   Preparation 40 mins   Cooking 1¾ hrs
Per portion 868 kcals, 46g fat (26.5g saturated)

4 x 275g (10oz) chicken portions, skinned
2 carrots, peeled and halved
3 onions, peeled
2 celery sticks, sliced
Salt and freshly ground black pepper
40g (1½oz) butter
110g (4oz) mushrooms, wiped and sliced
40g (1½oz) plain flour
300ml (½ pint) milk
4 tbsp double cream
Shortcrust Pastry made with 225g (8oz) flour
(page 225)
Beaten egg to glaze

Place chicken, carrots, 2 onions (cut into
quarters), celery and 1.1 litres (2 pints) water
in a large saucepan and season to taste.
Bring to the boil, remove any scum then
cover and simmer for 1 hour.
Remove chicken, discard bones and cut
meat into bite-size pieces.
Strain chicken liquid, reserving carrots and
150ml (¼ pint) of liquid.
Chop carrots and remaining onion.
Melt butter in a saucepan and fry onion and
mushrooms until soft.
Add flour and cook for 1 minute. Gradually
stir in milk and reserved chicken liquid.
Cook stirring until sauce comes to the boil
and thickens. Cook for a minute.
Remove from heat and stir in reserved
chicken, carrots and cream. Season to taste.
Spoon into a 1.1 litre (2 pint) pie dish.
Roll out pastry on a floured work surface
until 5cm (2in) larger than pie dish.
Cut a 2.5cm (1in) wide strip off pastry and
place on dampened rim of dish. Brush strip
with water. Cover with pastry lid and press
lightly to seal edges.
Trim off excess pastry, knock edges back to
seal and crimp. Brush with egg to glaze.
Stand on a baking sheet and bake at 220°C
(425°F) Mark 7 for 25–30 minutes or until
pastry is cooked.
Use remaining chicken liquid to make soup.
Alternatively use 450g (1lb) cooked chicken,
2 sliced and cooked carrots and 150ml (¼
pint) of ready-made chicken stock. Omit
steps 1–3.

Variations

Chicken & Leek Pie ❄

Follow recipe and method for Chicken Pie.
Use 2 sliced leeks in place of mushrooms.

Chicken & Ham pie ❄

Follow recipe and method for Chicken Pie.
Add 110g (4oz) cooked, diced ham at step 9.

Thai Chicken Curry with Noodles ❄

Serves 4   Preparation 10 mins   Cooking 25 mins
Per portion 547 kcals, 26g fat (16.6g saturated)

1 tbsp vegetable oil
3 tsp Thai curry paste
8 skinless, boneless chicken thighs, each cut
into 4 or 6 pieces
400ml can coconut milk
1 aubergine, cut into 2.5cm (1in) chunks
10 baby sweetcorn, halved lengthways
110g (4oz) tenderstem broccoli, cut into 5cm
(2in) lengths
300g pack straight-to-wok noodles
Grated rind and juice of 1 lime
2 tbsp Thai fish sauce
2 tbsp chopped coriander
1 red chilli, deseeded and finely sliced, to
serve (optional)
Lime wedges to serve (optional)

Heat oil in a saucepan. Stir in curry paste and
cook for 30 seconds.
Add chicken and fry until sealed.
Stir in coconut milk, aubergine and baby
sweetcorn. Bring to the boil. Simmer for 10
minutes.
Add broccoli and cook for 2 minutes.
Stir in noodles. Simmer, uncovered, for 3–5
minutes. Add lime rind and juice, fish sauce
and coriander.
Garnish with chilli and lime and serve.

> **Thai Curry Paste**
> The three most popular Thai curry
> pastes are red, green and yellow, red
> being the hottest and yellow the most
> fragrant. Whatever the colour, the main
> ingredients are lemongrass, chillies,
> garlic, glangal, cumin and fish sauce.

Chicken Kiev

Chicken Kiev

Serves 2   Preparation 10 mins   Cooking 25 mins
Per portion 454 kcals, 17g fat (8.9g saturated)

2 chicken breasts, skinned
25g (1oz) butter, softened
1 garlic clove, peeled and crushed
1 tbsp chopped parsley
Salt and freshly ground black pepper
1 tbsp plain flour
1 tbsp grated Parmesan cheese
1 egg, beaten
50g (2oz) cornflakes

Cut a small slit horizontally into chicken.
Mix together butter, garlic, parsley and
seasoning. Push mixture into chicken pockets
Mix together flour and Parmesan.
Dust chicken in flour, then beaten egg and
then cornflakes
Place on a baking tray and bake at 180°C
(350°F) Mark 4 for 20–25 minutes, until
cooked and golden.

Pippin Chicken

Serves 4   Preparation 15 mins   Cooking 25 mins
Per portion 236 kcals, 6g fat (3.1g saturated)

15g (½oz) butter
1 onion, peeled and chopped
4 x 110g (4oz) chicken breasts, skinned
15g (½oz) cornflour
300ml (½ pint) milk
1 chicken stock cube
1 tsp dried mixed herbs
125ml (4fl oz) apple juice
110g (4oz) seedless black grapes

Melt butter in a large frying pan and fry
onion and chicken for 3 minutes.
Blend cornflour with milk and add to chicken
with crumbled stock cube and herbs.
Bring to the boil, stirring, then add apple
juice. Cover and simmer for 20 minutes,
stirring occasionally and turning chicken
over half way.
Add grapes just before serving.

Chicken in Orange Cream

Serves 4   Preparation 10 mins   Cooking 1 hr
Per portion 313 kcals, 14g fat (8.4g saturated)

25g (1oz) butter
4 x 110g (4oz) chicken breasts, skinned
1 onion, peeled and chopped
2 tbsp plain flour
300ml (½ pint) orange juice
150ml (¼ pint) soured cream
1 tbsp marmalade
½ tsp dried marjoram

Melt butter in a non-stick frying pan and brown chicken on both sides. Transfer to ovenproof casserole.
Fry onion in remaining butter until soft.
Stir in flour and cook for 1 minute.
Blend in orange juice. Bring to the boil, stirring, until thickened. Stir in remaining ingredients and pour over chicken.
Cover and cook at 180°C (350°F) Mark 4 for 45 minutes, or until chicken is tender.

Variation

Turkey in Citrus Cream

Follow recipe and method for Chicken in Orange Cream. Omit chicken and use 4 turkey breast steaks. Also use three fruits marmalade in place of orange marmalade.

Chicken & Broccoli Bake

Serves 4   Preparation 15 mins   Cooking 55 mins
Per portion 458 kcals, 27g fat (8.3g saturated)

225g (8oz) broccoli florets
4 x 175g (6oz) chicken breasts, skinned
295g can condensed cream of chicken soup
50g (2oz) mayonnaise
4 tbsp double cream
½ tsp curry powder
25g (1oz) Cheddar cheese, grated

Cook broccoli in boiling water until almost tender. Drain well.
Place drained broccoli and chicken in a shallow ovenproof dish.
Mix together soup, mayonnaise, cream and curry powder. Spoon over chicken and broccoli, coating them well. Sprinkle with cheese.
Bake at 190°C (375°F) Mark 5 for 45–50 minutes or until chicken is tender.

Italian Chicken

Serves 4   Preparation 45 mins   Cooking 35 mins
Per portion 281 kcals, 8g fat (4g saturated)

15g (½oz) butter
1 onion, peeled and sliced
1 green pepper, deseeded and sliced
275g (10oz) courgettes, sliced
400ml (14fl oz) passata
1 tsp Italian herb seasoning
350g (12oz) chicken breasts, cubed
1 tbsp cornflour
110g (4oz) wholemeal bread, lightly toasted and cubed
4 tbsp grated Parmesan cheese

Melt butter in a saucepan and cook onion and pepper for 3 minutes. Add courgettes, passata, herbs and chicken.
Bring to the boil, cover and simmer for 10–15 minutes until chicken is cooked.
Blend cornflour with a little cold water and stir into chicken. Cook until thickened.
Spoon into a flameproof dish, scatter bread and cheese over top and grill to melt cheese.

Cheesy Chicken & Mushrooms

Serves 4   Preparation 10 mins   Cooking 30 mins
Per portion 482 kcals, 27g fat (11.6g saturated)

110g (4oz) goat's cheese
4 chicken breasts, skin-on
1 tbsp olive oil
4 rashers smoked streaky bacon
250g (8oz) chestnut mushrooms, sliced
25g (1oz) butter
1 tbsp plain flour
250ml (9fl oz) white wine
½ chicken stock cube, crumbled
Salt and freshly ground black pepper

Divide goat's cheese into 4 and push a portion under skin of each chicken breast.
Heat oil in a frying pan and cook chicken, skin-side down, for 4–5 minutes until golden.
Turn the chicken over and cook for 3–4 minutes. Remove from pan. Add bacon and cook for 2–3 minutes, then remove.
Cook mushrooms in butter for 2–3 minutes.
Stir in flour, then stir in wine and 100ml (3½ fl oz) water. Add stock cube, chicken and bacon.
Cook for 10–15 minutes, until chicken is cooked. Season to taste and serve.

Parsley Pesto Chicken

Tarragon Chicken ❄

Serves 4–6 Preparation 40 mins Cooking 25 mins
Per portion 465 kcals, 31g fat (17.7g saturated)

450g (1lb) chicken breasts, cut into strips
25g (1oz) plain flour
25g (1oz) butter
1 onion, peeled and chopped
1 small green pepper, deseeded and sliced
Grated rind of 1 lemon
1 garlic clove, peeled and crushed
150ml (¼ pint) dry white wine
1 tbsp finely chopped fresh tarragon
150ml (¼ pint) double cream
2 tsp wholegrain mustard
50g (2oz) Cheddar cheese, grated

Coat chicken in flour.
Melt butter in a non-stick frying pan. Add onion and cook for 2 mins or until soft.
Add chicken, pepper, lemon rind, garlic, wine and tarragon.
Cook for 10–15 minutes.
Stir in cream, mustard and cheese. Heat through.

Parsley Pesto Chicken

Serves 4 Preparation 20 mins Cooking 10 mins
Per portion 415 kcals, 29g fat (8.1g saturated)

15g (½oz) walnuts, roughly chopped
1 clove garlic, peeled and chopped
½ tsp salt
50g (2oz) flat-leaved parsley, thick stalks removed
3 tbsp grated Parmesan cheese
6 tbsp olive oil
4 chicken breasts, skinned, cut into thin strips
4 tbsp crème fraîche

Dry-fry walnuts in a non-stick frying pan until lightly toasted.
Put walnuts, garlic, salt and parsley into a food processor and pulse to a rough texture.
Add Parmesan and 5 tbsp oil. Whizz to blend, but still leave slightly chunky.
Heat remaining oil in a wok or frying pan and add chicken strips. Cook for 4–5 minutes until browned.
Add crème fraîche and 3 tbsp of parsley pesto and simmer for 5 minutes.
Mix in 2 tbsp extra pesto and serve.

Lemon Chicken

Serves 4   Preparation 10 mins   Cooking 55 mins
Per portion 504 kcals, 26g fat (8.9g saturated)

4 potatoes, peeled and cut into wedges
3 tbsp olive oil
4 garlic cloves, unpeeled
2 lemons, 1 sliced and 1 cut into wedges
4 chicken breasts, skin-on
Salt and freshly ground black pepper
Grated nutmeg
4 slices Parma ham
150ml (¼ pint) chicken stock
4 tbsp crème fraîche

Cook potatoes in boiling water for 5 minutes.
Drain well and place on a baking sheet with
2 tbsp oil and garlic.
Squeeze juice from lemon wedges onto
potatoes and add wedges to tray.
Roast for 50 minutes at 190°C (375°F) Mark 5,
turning twice.
Meanwhile, place chicken in a roasting tin
and season with salt, pepper and nutmeg.
Top each chicken breast with ham and
lemon slices. Drizzle with remaining oil.
Bake chicken above potato wedges for 20
minutes.
Pour stock over chicken and cook for 20
minutes. Keep chicken and potatoes warm.
Pour roasting tin juices into a saucepan,
then bring to the boil and reduce to 90ml
(3fl oz).
Whisk crème fraîche into sauce and serve
with chicken and potato wedges.

Chicken Tikka

Serves 4   Preparation 25 mins plus marinating Cooking
20 mins   Per portion 189 kcals, 4g fat (1.8g saturated)

275g (10oz) natural yogurt
Juice and rind of 1 lemon
4 spring onions, trimmed and finely
chopped
2 garlic cloves, peeled and crushed
1 tbsp vinegar
1 tsp chilli powder
1 tsp ground coriander
1 tsp turmeric
1 tsp salt
1 tbsp grated fresh ginger
450g (1lb) chicken breasts, cubed
Lemon wedges to serve

Mix together all ingredients except chicken
in a bowl. Stir in chicken and mix well.
Cover and leave to marinate in refrigerator
overnight or for at least 2 hours. Stir
occasionally.
Thread on to skewers.
Cook under a preheated medium grill or
over a barbecue for 15–20 minutes. Turn
regularly and baste with marinade.
Serve with lemon.

Tandoori Chicken

Serves 4   Preparation 10 mins plus marinating Cooking
40 mins   Per portion 193 kcals, 4g fat (1.7g saturated)

3 garlic cloves, peeled and crushed
275g (10oz) natural yogurt
2 tsp garam masala
1 tsp paprika
1 tsp ground ginger
½ tsp chilli powder
½ tsp mustard powder
½ tsp turmeric
4 x 110g (4oz) chicken breasts, skinned
Coriander to garnish

Mix garlic, yogurt and spices together in a
large bowl.
Cut a few slashes into flesh of chicken and
cover with yogurt mixture.
Cover and refrigerate overnight or for at least
2 hours.
Place on a wire roasting rack and bake at
200°C (400°F) Mark 6 for 40 minutes until
brown and tender.
Serve garnished with coriander.

Stir-Fried Chicken

Serves 4   Preparation 20 mins   Cooking 10 mins
Per portion 171 kcals, 7g fat (1.2g saturated)

1 tbsp groundnut oil
1 tbsp sunflower oil
½ tsp five spice powder
350g (12oz) chicken breast, cut into strips
355g pack stir-fry vegetables
2 tsp soy sauce

Heat oils in a large frying pan, then add
spice and chicken. Cook for 6 minutes until
browned and cooked.
Add vegetables and soy sauce and stir-fry for
2 minutes.

Turkey

Roast Turkey ✵

Preparation 20 mins   Cooking according to chart (below)

1 oven-ready turkey
Stuffing (page 188)
1 onion, peeled
1 eating apple, halved
50–110g (2–4oz) butter, softened
Streaky bacon rashers (optional)
Accompany with
Gravy (page 181)
Bread Sauce (page 183)
Cranberry Sauce (page 181)
Small cooked sausages
Grilled bacon rolls
Boiled and Roast Potatoes (page 155)
Brussels sprouts

If turkey is frozen, place in its bag on a large plate in a cool place until completely thawed; see chart for thawing times. Check that there are no icy crystals in turkey cavity and legs are flexible. Remove giblet pack, if necessary. Wash fresh or thawed bird. Dry with kitchen paper. Cook straight away or refrigerate.
Stuff neck end (not body cavity) and fold neck skin under bird just before roasting.
Place onion and apple into body cavity.
Place in a roasting tin and smear butter over skin. Place bacon rashers over breast if using.
Roast at 190°C (375°F) Mark 5 according to recommended times in chart (below).
Remove bacon rashers or foil for last 30 minutes of cooking time to allow skin to brown and crisp. Test the deepest part of each thigh with a skewer to check that juices run clear and bird is cooked through.
Leave to stand for 30 minutes before carving. Serve with accompaniments.

Turkey Roasting Times

Small turkey (under 6kg/13lb), stuffed
Cook at 200°C (400°F) Mark 6 for 12 mins per 450g (1lb), plus 20 mins, plus resting time of 30 mins.
Large turkey (over 6kg/13lb), stuffed
Cook at 180°C (350°F) Mark 4 for 16 mins per 450g (1lb), plus resting time of 30 mins.

Creamy Turkey ✵

Serves 4   Preparation 15 mins   Cooking 20 mins
Per portion 433kcals, 28g fat (14.7g saturated)

1 onion, peeled and sliced
15g (½oz) butter
350g (12oz) cooked turkey meat, cut into strips
1 red pepper, deseeded and sliced
150ml (¼ pint) dry white wine
Salt and freshly ground black pepper
150ml (¼ pint) double cream
110g (4oz) canned sweetcorn

Fry onion in butter until soft.
Stir in turkey. Add pepper, wine and seasoning. Bring to the boil and simmer for 10 minutes.
Stir in cream and sweetcorn and then reheat and serve.

Turkey in Paprika

Serves 4   Preparation 20 mins   Cooking 30 mins
Per portion 295 kcals, 13g fat (5.7g saturated)

1 large onion, peeled and chopped
1 large green pepper, deseeded and chopped
25g (1oz) butter
2 tsp olive oil
1 tbsp plain flour
1½ tbsp paprika
1 tbsp tomato purée
1 tsp caster sugar
300ml (½ pint) chicken or turkey stock
Salt and freshly ground black pepper
¼ tsp caraway seeds (optional)
350g (12oz) cooked turkey meat, cut into bite-sized pieces
150g (5oz) natural yogurt

Fry onion and pepper in butter and oil until pale gold and soft.
Remove from heat and stir in flour, paprika, tomato purée and sugar.
Gradually blend in stock, seasoning and caraway seeds if using. Cook, stirring, until sauce boils and thickens.
Cover saucepan and simmer gently for 15 minutes.
Add turkey to sauce with yogurt. Heat through for a further 5 minutes without boiling.

Turkey & Broccoli Bake ❋

Serves 4 Preparation 20 mins Cooking 30 mins
Per portion 402 kcals, 26g fat (11.4g saturated)

175g (6oz) broccoli florets
25g (1oz) plain flour
25g (1oz) butter
300ml (½ pint) milk
Salt and freshly ground black pepper
110g (4oz) Cheddar cheese, grated
50g (2oz) flaked almonds, toasted
1 garlic clove, peeled and crushed
225g (8oz) cooked turkey meat, chopped

Cook broccoli florets in boiling water for 2–3 minutes. Drain well.
Place flour, butter and milk in a saucepan. Heat, whisking continuously until the sauce thickens, boils and is smooth.
Cook for a minute. Season and remove pan from heat. Add 75g (3oz) cheese, 40g (1½oz) almonds, garlic, turkey and broccoli.
Place in an ovenproof dish.
Mix remaining cheese and almonds and sprinkle over turkey. Bake at 190°C (375°F) Mark 5 for 15–20 minutes.

Turkey á la King

Serves 4 Preparation 20 mins Cooking 30 mins
Per portion 337 kcals, 19g fat (9.8g saturated)

1 green pepper, deseeded and diced
25g (1oz) butter
2 tsp olive oil
110g (4oz) mushrooms, wiped and sliced
25g (1oz) plain flour
150ml (¼ pint) stock
150ml (¼ pint) milk
350g (12oz) cooked turkey meat, cut into bite-sized pieces
150ml (¼ pint) single cream
1 tbsp dry sherry or lemon juice
Salt and freshly ground black pepper

Fry pepper gently in butter and oil for 5 minutes. Add mushrooms and fry gently for 5 minutes. Transfer to a plate.
Stir flour into remaining butter and oil in pan and cook, stirring, for 2 minutes.
Gradually blend in stock and milk. Cook, stirring, until sauce thickens and boils.
Lower heat and add pepper, mushrooms and turkey. Heat for 10 minutes. Add cream and sherry or lemon juice and season to taste.

Turkey Pilaf ❋

Serves 4 Preparation 25 mins Cooking 30 mins
Per portion 468 kcals, 15g fat (4.8g saturated)

1 large onion, peeled and chopped
25g (1oz) butter
2 tsp olive oil
225g (8oz) long-grain rice
600ml (1 pint) chicken or turkey stock
225g (8oz) cooked turkey meat, cut into bite-sized pieces
50g (2oz) raisins
½ tsp grated orange rind
110g (4oz) tomatoes, skinned and chopped
25g (1oz) almonds, toasted and chopped
1 tbsp chopped parsley

Fry onion in butter and oil until pale gold.
Add rice and fry for 1 minute, stirring.
Pour in stock. Bring to the boil, cover, lower heat and simmer for 15 minutes.
Add remaining ingredients. Continue simmering for 7–10 minutes or until the rice has absorbed all the liquid and is tender.

Turkey, apple & sage meatballs

Serves 4 Preparation 10 mins plus chilling Cooking 40 mins Per portion 353 kcals, 10g fat (1.2g saturated)

450g (1lb) turkey mince
8 tbsp sage and onion stuffing mix
4 tbsp apple sauce
Freshly ground black pepper
2 tbsp vegetable oil
1 large onion, peeled and thinly sliced
600ml (1 pint) chicken stock
1 tbsp plain flour

Put mince in a bowl, add stuffing and apple and stir. Season with pepper and combine.
Divide into 12 and form into balls. Place on a plate, cover and chill for 30 minutes.
Heat half oil in a frying pan and fry onion for 10 minutes until softened. Drain, set aside.
Heat remaining oil and fry meatballs, turning frequently, for about 5 minutes until sealed.
Pour in stock to just cover bottom of pan. Bring to the boil, cover, reduce heat and simmer for about 20 minutes until meatballs cooked through. Drain, reserving any stock.
In same pan, reheat onion and add flour. Blend stock into flour and bring to the boil, stirring, until thickened. Simmer for 2 minutes. Pour gravy over meatballs.

Spicy Turkey Stew

Turkey with Ham & Cheese

Serves 4 Preparation 15 mins Cooking 25 mins
Per portion 261 kcals, 13g fat (7.8g saturated)

4 x 110g (4oz) turkey breast steaks
25g (1oz) garlic butter, melted
2 slices cooked ham, halved
40g (1½oz) Cheddar cheese, grated
40g (1½oz) Double Gloucester cheese, grated
1 tbsp chopped parsley
1 tbsp milk

Dip turkey steaks in melted butter and coat thoroughly. Place on a non-stick baking sheet.
Bake at 200°C (400°F) Mark 6 for 20 minutes.
Place a piece of ham on top of each piece of turkey.
Mix together cheeses, parsley and milk and spoon on top of ham.
Continue cooking for 5 minutes until cheese has melted.

Spicy Turkey Stew

Serves 4 Preparation 35 mins Cooking 50 mins
Per portion 280 kcals, 13g fat (6.7g saturated)

225g (8oz) onions, peeled and chopped
1 garlic clove, peeled and crushed
50g (2oz) bacon, chopped
40g (1½oz) butter
450g (1lb) boneless turkey fillet, cubed
1 tbsp garam masala
1 large green pepper, deseeded and chopped
227g can chopped tomatoes
150ml (¼ pint) chicken or turkey stock

Fry onion, garlic and bacon in butter until lightly browned.
Add turkey and cook until golden.
Stir in garam masala and mix well. Add pepper, tomatoes and stock. Bring to the boil, cover and simmer for 40 minutes or until turkey is tender. Uncover for last 10 minutes of cooking time.

Spiced Turkey Kebabs

Turkey Marengo ❄ ## Spiced Turkey Kebabs

Serves 4   Preparation 30 mins   Cooking 50 mins
Per portion 344 kcals, 10g fat (4.2g saturated)

Serves 4   Preparation 30 mins plus marinating Cooking
20 mins   Per portion 282 kcals, 14g fat (4.5g saturated)

700g (1½lb) boneless turkey fillet, cubed
3 tbsp plain flour
Salt and freshly ground black pepper
25g (1oz) butter
1 tbsp olive oil
1 large onion, peeled and chopped
1 garlic clove, peeled and crushed
150ml (¼ pint) chicken or turkey stock
150ml (¼ pint) dry white wine
400g can chopped tomatoes
225g (8oz) mushrooms, peeled and halved
2 tbsp chopped parsley

Coat turkey in seasoned flour.
Heat butter and oil in a pan, add turkey and
cook until golden. Remove to a plate.
Add onion and garlic, then cook until soft.
Return turkey to pan and stir in stock, wine,
tomatoes and mushrooms.
Bring to the boil, cover and simmer for 40
minutes or until turkey is tender. Stir.
Uncover and boil rapidly to reduce sauce
slightly. Sprinkle with parsley and serve.

450g (1lb) turkey meat, cubed
4 tbsp peanut butter
1 tbsp soy sauce
1 tsp ground cumin
1 tsp chilli powder
150ml (¼ pint) milk
175g (6oz) fromage frais
Wedges of lime to serve

Thread turkey on to skewers.
Blend peanut butter with soy sauce, cumin,
chilli and milk.
Pour over kebabs and leave to marinate for
2 hours.
Grill kebabs under high heat, basting with
marinade.
Place remaining marinade in a pan, bring to
the boil and cook, stirring, for 2 minutes or
until thickened.
Remove from heat and stir in fromage frais.
Reheat without boiling.
Serve with sauce and lime.

Duck, Goose & Guinea Fowl

Roast Duck
Preparation 10 mins Cooking 30 mins per 450g (1lb)
Allow at least 450g (1lb) raw weight per person

1 oven-ready duckling
Salt
Accompany with
Gravy (page 181)
Apple Sauce (page 182)
Mashed or Roast Potatoes (page 155)
Peas or petit pois

Wash inside of bird out under running water. Dry thoroughly with kitchen paper.

Remove and discard any loose fat from inside cavity.

Weigh and calculate cooking time, allowing 30 minutes per 450g (1lb).

Stand on a rack in a roasting tin, if possible, so bird does not stand in fat.

Prick skin all over with a fork. Sprinkle well with salt.

Roast at 180°C (350°F) Mark 4 for calculated cooking time. Do not baste or cover.

Carefully drain off excess fat if it starts to reach level of rack.

Transfer to a board or serving dish. Leave for 5 minutes before carving.

Serve with accompaniments.

Duck & Orange Sauce
Serves 4 Preparation 20 mins Cooking 2¾ hrs
Per portion 888 kcals, 75g fat (20.3g saturated)

2.3kg (5lb) oven-ready duckling
Salt
1 tbsp plain flour
Grated rind and juice of 2 oranges
2 tbsp red wine
2 tbsp redcurrant jelly
50ml (2fl oz) dry sherry
Sliced oranges and watercress to garnish

Cook duck according to recipe for Roast Duck.

Cut duck into 4 joints and keep hot.

Pour off all but 1 tbsp fat from roasting tin.

Stir in plain flour and cook for 2 minutes on hob.

Add orange rind and juice, wine, redcurrant jelly and sherry.

Cook gently, stirring, until jelly dissolves and sauce comes to the boil and thickens.

Pour a little sauce over duck. Garnish with orange and watercress.

Serve remaining sauce separately.

Chinese Duck with Noodles
Serves 4 Preparation 10 mins Cooking 25 mins
Per portion 779 kcals, 58g fat (17.1g saturated)

2 tsp Chinese five-spice powder
4 duck breasts
25g (1oz) butter
1 tbsp sesame oil
6 spring onions, trimmed and sliced
1 garlic clove, peeled and crushed
2.5cm (1in) piece root ginger, peeled and grated
1 red chilli, deseeded and sliced
150g (5oz) straight-to-wok noodles
110g (4oz) sugar snap peas, shredded
1 tbsp honey
1 tbsp soy sauce
1 tbsp plum sauce
2 tbsp chopped coriander
1 tbsp sesame seeds

Rub five-spice powder into skin of duck.

Cook duck in a hot frying pan, skin-side down, for 5 minutes.

Remove from pan and place duck on a baking sheet. Bake for 12–15 minutes at 200°C (400°F) Mark 6.

Meanwhile, heat butter and oil in the pan and cook onions, garlic, ginger and chilli for 1–2 minutes.

Add noodles and sugar snap peas and cook for 1–2 minutes, until hot.

Stir in honey, soy sauce and plum sauce.

Slice duck and stir into noodles with coriander. Serve sprinkled with sesame seeds.

Five-Spice Powder
Chinese cuisine places great weight on the five flavours – sweet, sour, bitter, pungent and salty – and five-spice powder contains them all. The ingredients are peppercorns, star anise, cloves, cinnamon and fennel seeds, all of which are ground. Use the powder sparingly as it is pungent.

Roast Guinea Fowl

Roast Goose ❄

Preparation 10 mins   Cooking 20 mins per 450g (1lb)
plus 20 mins
Allow at least 450g (1lb) raw weight per person

1 oven-ready goose
Salt
Accompany with
Gravy (page 181)
Apple Sauce (page 182)
Boiled or Roast potatoes (page 155)
Peas or petit pois

Wash inside of bird out under running water.
Dry thoroughly with kitchen paper. Remove
and discard any loose fat from inside cavity.
Weigh and calculate cooking time.
Stand on a rack in a roasting tin, if possible,
so bird does not stand in fat.
Prick skin with a fork. Sprinkle well with salt.
Roast at 200°C (400°F) Mark 6 for cooking
time. Do not baste or cover. Carefully drain
off excess fat if it starts to reach level of rack.
Transfer to a board. Leave for 20 minutes
before carving. Serve with accompaniments.

Roast Guinea Fowl ❄

Serves 4   Preparation 10 mins   Cooking 1–1½ hrs
Per portion 368 kcals, 17g fat (6.5g saturated)

1 oven-ready guinea fowl
1 lemon, cut into wedges
25g (1oz) butter
150ml (¼ pint) chicken stock
Accompany with
Thin Gravy (page 181)
Roast Potatoes (page 155)
Steamed vegetables

Place guinea fowl in a roasting tin.
Stuff lemon wedges and butter inside bird's
cavity and then pour stock all over and
around bird.
Roast at 200°C (400°F) Mark 6 for 1¼ hours.
Test the deepest part of each thigh with a
skewer to check that juices run clear and bird
is cooked through.
Transfer to a warm serving platter.
Accompany with gravy, roast potatoes and
vegetables.

Game

Fresh game is only available during the hunting season, which is different for each bird/animal. However, farmed varieties are usually available year-round. It is generally hung to improve the flavour and to tenderise the flesh.

Roast Quail

Serves 2 Preparation 10 mins Cooking 20–25 mins
Per portion 542 kcals, 39g fat (12.6g saturated)

4 oven-ready quail
4 slices pancetta
15g (½oz) butter, melted
Accompany with
Thin Gravy (page 181)
Game Chips (page 155)
Green Salad (page 55)

Stand quail in roasting tin. Cover breast with pancetta and melted butter.
Roast at 220°C (425°F) Mark 7 for 20–25 minutes.
Transfer to a warm serving platter. Accompany with gravy, game chips and salad.

Roast Pheasant

Serves 2–3 Preparation 10 mins Cooking 1–1½ hrs
Per portion 378 kcals, 26g fat (10.9g saturated)

1 oven-ready pheasant
4 rashers streaky bacon
15g (½oz) butter, melted
Accompany with
50g (2oz) fresh breadcrumbs fried in 25g (1oz) butter
Bread Sauce (page 183)
Thin Gravy (page 181)
Game Chips (page 155)
Green Salad (page 55)

Stand pheasant in roasting tin. Cover breast with bacon rashers and melted butter.
Roast at 200°C (400°F) Mark 6 for 1–1½ hours, depending on size and until cooked through, basting frequently.
Transfer to a warm serving platter. Accompany with a small dish of fried breadcrumbs (for sprinkling over each portion), bread sauce, gravy, game chips and salad.

Variation

Roast Grouse

Follow recipe and method for Roast Pheasant. Use 2 plucked, drawn and trussed grouse instead of pheasant. Put 25g (1oz) butter inside each bird and roast for 30–35 minutes or until tender.

Raised Game Pie

Serves 6–8 Preparation 1¼ hrs plus cooling Cooking 2½ hrs Per portion 507 kcals, 24g fat (9.8g saturated)

Hot Water Crust Pastry made with 350g (12oz) flour (page 230)
225g (8oz) pork sausagemeat
450g (1lb) raw game (pheasant, partridge, pigeon or a mixture)
350g (12oz) rump steak, diced
110g (4oz) lean bacon, chopped
2 pickled walnuts, chopped
1 small onion, peeled and grated
½ tsp dried mixed herbs
300ml (½ pint) vegetable stock
1 egg, beaten
2 tsp powdered gelatine

Roll out two-thirds of pastry on a floured work surface. Use to line a raised pie mould or 18cm (7in) loose-bottomed cake tin.
Cover base with sausagemeat.
Cut game into neat pieces. Discard bones, skin and gristle.
Put game, steak, bacon, walnuts and onion into a bowl. Add herbs and mix well. Put into pie mould or cake tin. Pour in half stock.
Roll out remaining pastry into a lid. Moisten edges with water and cover pie.
Press edges of pastry together. Trim any surplus. Brush top with egg and decorate with pastry leaves. Brush with more egg.
Make a hole in top to allow steam to escape. Stand on a baking sheet.
Bake at 200°C (400°F) Mark 6 for 30 minutes.
Reduce to 180°C (350°F) Mark 4 for a further 1¾–2 hours. Cover top with greaseproof paper during last 30 minutes to prevent pastry from browning too much.
Remove pie from oven. Heat remaining stock. Sprinkle in gelatine and stir to dissolve.
Pour into pie through hole in top and leave to cool for 12 hours.
Remove cake tin or mould before serving.

Roast Rabbit ❄

Serves 4   Preparation 10 mins   Cooking 15 mins per 450g (1lb) plus 15 mins

1 oven-ready rabbit
4 rashers streaky bacon
40g (1½oz) butter, melted
Accompany with
Gravy (page 181)
Cranberry Sauce (page 181)
Steamed vegetables

Weigh rabbit and calculate cooking time allowing 15 minutes per 450g (1lb) roasting time plus 15 minutes.
Stand in roasting tin. Top with bacon and coat with melted butter.
Roast in oven at 220°C (425°F) Mark 7 for 15 minutes.
Reduce to 180°C (350°F) Mark 4. Continue to roast for required amount of time, basting frequently with butter.
Accompany with gravy, cranberry sauce and vegetables.

Rabbit Casserole ❄

Serves 4   Preparation 25 mins   Cooking 2 hrs
Per portion 316 kcals, 15g fat (7.8g saturated)

25g (1oz) butter
450g (1lb) boneless rabbit, cubed
1 bacon rasher, chopped
2 carrots, peeled and sliced
600ml (1 pint) milk
 Salt and freshly ground black pepper
¼ tsp ground nutmeg
15g (½oz) cornflour
1 tbsp chopped parsley

Melt butter in a flameproof casserole. Add rabbit and then bacon and cook until browned.
Add carrots, milk, seasoning and nutmeg. Bring to the boil.
Cover and bake at 180°C (350°F) Mark 4 for 1½–2 hours, or until rabbit is tender.
Blend cornflour with a little cold water and stir into casserole.
On the hob, cook, stirring, until sauce thickens, boils and is smooth. Cook for 3 minutes.
Sprinkle with parsley.

Rabbit Pie ❄

Serves 4   Preparation 40 mins   Cooking 1½ hrs
Per portion 868 kcals, 45g fat (23.6g saturated)

6 rabbit joints, about 1.1kg (2½lb) in total
15g (½oz) butter
4 rashers bacon, chopped
2 potatoes, peeled and sliced
2 leeks, washed and sliced
2 carrots, peeled and sliced
1 tbsp chopped parsley
¼ tsp dried mixed herbs
Salt and freshly ground black pepper
Vegetable stock
Shortcrust pastry made with 225g (8oz) flour (page 225)
Beaten egg to glaze

Wash rabbit joints. Put in a pan with butter to brown. Add chopped bacon.
Layer rabbit, bacon and vegetables alternately in pie dish. Sprinkle each layer with parsley, mixed herbs and seasoning.
Half-fill dish with stock. Roll out pastry on a floured work surface and use to cover dish.
Make a hole in centre to allow steam to escape. Decorate with pastry leaves and glaze with beaten egg.
Bake at 220°C (425°F) Mark 7 for 15–20 minutes, until pastry is set.
Reduce heat to 170°C (325°F) Mark 3 and cook for about 1¼ hours. Cover with aluminium foil if pastry becomes too brown.

Game Seasons

Wild game can only be shot during certain times of the year. However, lots of wild game is now available frozen all year round.

The table below shows the shooting seasons, when fresh game should be available.

Game	Season
Grouse	August–November
Hare	August–February
Partridge	September–January
Pheasant	October–January
Pigeon	All Year
Quail	All Year
Rabbit	All Year
Venison	July–April (varies by species)

Collops of Venison

Jugged Hare ❄

Serves 4   Preparation 25 mins   Cooking 3½ hrs
Per portion 827 kcals, 43g fat (21.2g saturated)

75g (3oz) butter
1 hare, jointed
2 onions, peeled and sliced
2 carrots, peeled and sliced
1 celery stick, sliced
1 bouquet garni
Salt and freshly ground black pepper
25g (1oz) plain flour
125ml (4fl oz) port
1 tbsp redcurrant jelly
110g (4oz) fresh breadcrumbs
50g (2oz) shredded suet
1 tsp dried mixed herbs
½ tsp grated lemon rind
Milk to bind

Melt 25g (1oz) butter in a large flameproof casserole. Add hare and fry until brown. Remove to a plate.
Add vegetables to pan and fry gently for 6–7 minutes.
Replace hare, add 900ml (1½ pints) water, bouquet garni and seasoning.
Cover and bake at 180°C (350°F) Mark 4 for 2–3 hours, or until hare is tender. Transfer joints of hare to a serving dish and keep hot.
Strain liquor from casserole. Pour into a

clean pan. Add flour (mixed to a paste with 2 tbsp water), port and redcurrant jelly.
Cook, stirring, until sauce boils and thickens. Simmer for 2 minutes. Remove from heat.
Make forcemeat balls. Mix breadcrumbs with suet, herbs and lemon rind and bind with milk.
Shape into 12 small balls. Fry in remaining butter until crisp and golden. Pour sauce over hare. Serve with forcemeat balls.

Collops of Venison

Serves 4   Preparation 10 mins   Cooking 20 mins
Per portion 452 kcals, 28g fat (15.1g saturated)

25g (1oz) butter
4 x 175g (6oz) venison or sirloin steaks
2 eating apples, peeled, cored and sliced
2 tbsp whisky
1 tsp honey
150ml (¼ pint) double cream
5 juniper berries, crushed

Melt butter in a frying pan and cook steaks for 3–5 minutes each side, until cooked to your liking. Remove when cooked and keep warm.
Fry apple slices until heated through.
Mix together whisky, honey, cream and berries. Add to pan and heat until warm.
Pour sauce over steaks.

Roast Pork

Pork

Roast Pork ❄

Preparation 10 mins   Cooking 30 mins per 450g (1lb) plus 30 mins

Choose shoulder, loin, leg or belly
When buying allow (raw per person) about
110–175g (4–6oz) meat without bone
175–350g (6–12oz) meat with bone
2 tbsp olive oil
Salt
Accompany with
Gravy (page 181)
Apple Sauce (page 182)
Mashed or boiled potatoes
Steamed vegetables

Rub pork with oil and salt and stand in a roasting tin.
Calculate cooking time (see above).
Cook at 220°C (425°F) Mark 7 for 30 minutes to make crackling crisp, then 180°C (350°F) Mark 4 for the remaining cooking time.
A meat thermometer should show 85°C.
Remove from oven, stand joint on a board to carve. Remove string or skewers.
Carve and serve with accompaniments.

Cotswold Chops

Serves 4   Preparation 25 mins   Cooking 50 mins
Per portion 554 kcals, 45g fat (21.2g saturated)

50g (2oz) Double Gloucester cheese, grated
75g (3oz) reduced fat soft cheese
25g (1oz) breadcrumbs
1 tsp horseradish sauce
2 tsp chopped parsley
4 x 150g (5oz) pork chops
25g (1oz) butter
3 tbsp sherry
3 tbsp double cream

Mix together cheeses, breadcrumbs, horseradish and parsley.
Cut a pocket in flesh of each chop and fill with cheese mixture.
Melt butter in a roasting tin, add chops and fry to brown on both sides.
Cover and bake at 190°C (375°F) Mark 5 for 30 minutes, uncover and cook for a further 10 minutes. Remove from oven, take out chops and keep warm.

Add sherry to tin, scrape up any sediment and heat on hob. Boil until syrupy.
Remove from heat and stir in cream. Spoon over chops to serve.

Pork Chops with Cheese & Beer

Serves 4   Preparation 10 mins   Cooking 25 mins
Per portion 478 kcals, 36g fat (17.2g saturated)

4 x 175g (6oz) pork chops
175g (6oz) Lancashire cheese, grated
2 tsp mustard
4 tbsp beer

Stand chops in grill pan. Grill for 8–10 minutes, depending on thickness.
Turn over and grill for 8–10 minutes again.
Mix cheese with mustard and beer. Spread equal amounts over chops. Grill until brown.

Somerset Pork Chops ❄

Serves 4   Preparation 15 mins   Cooking 50 mins
Per portion 343 kcals, 20g fat (8.9g saturated)

4 x 150g (5oz) pork chops, trimmed of fat
25g (1oz) butter
1 onion, peeled and thinly sliced
25g (1oz) plain flour
150ml (¼ pint) cider
1 garlic clove, peeled and crushed
Salt and freshly ground black pepper
Pinch of dried sage
2 tbsp single cream (optional)

Fry chops in butter with onion. When chops are brown, remove from pan. Continue cooking onion until soft.
Add flour and cook gently until brown.
Stir in cider, 75ml (3fl oz) water, garlic, seasoning and sage.
Place pork chops and onion in a shallow ovenproof dish. Pour sauce over.
Cover and bake at 190°C (375°F) Mark 5 for 30–40 minutes.
Pour cream, if using, over chops and serve.

Variation

Hawaiian Pork Chops ❄

Follow recipe and method for Somerset Pork Chops. Omit cider, garlic and sage. Use 90ml (3fl oz) pineapple juice, 60ml (2fl oz) water, 2 tsp soy sauce and 4 slices of canned pineapple, chopped.

Braised Pork Chops

Braised Pork Chops ❋

Serves 4   Preparation 40 mins   Cooking 1½ hrs
Per portion 473 kcals, 23g fat (9.9g saturated)

4 x 175g (6oz) pork chops, trimmed
of fat
2 tbsp plain flour
Salt and freshly ground black pepper
25g (1oz) butter
1 large onion, peeled and chopped
4 potatoes, peeled and sliced
2 large celery sticks, chopped
225g (8oz) tomatoes, chopped
2 tsp caster sugar
1 tsp Worcestershire sauce

Toss chops in seasoned flour.
Fry chops in butter until crisp and golden on
both sides. Transfer to a plate and keep warm
until ready to put in oven.
Add onion to remaining butter in frying pan.
Fry until golden.
Cover the base of a fairly shallow ovenproof
dish with potatoes.
Add celery, tomatoes, sugar and
Worcestershire sauce to onion in frying pan.
Mix well. Pour over potatoes and arrange
chops on top.
Cover and bake at 180°C (350°F) Mark 4 for
1–1¼ hours.

Pork in Cream Sauce ❋

Serves 4   Preparation 30 mins   Cooking 30 mins
Per portion 307 kcals, 15g fat (8.6g saturated)

4 x 110g (4oz) pork escalopes
75g (3oz) butter
1 celery stick, sliced
50g (2oz) leeks, washed and sliced
½ eating apple, peeled, cored and chopped
Freshly ground black pepper
25g (1oz) Cheddar cheese, grated
1 onion, peeled and chopped
15g (½oz) plain flour
300ml (½ pint) milk
110g (4oz) mushrooms, wiped and sliced
2 tbsp double cream

Place escalopes between 2 sheets of
greaseproof paper. Beat until thin.
Melt 25g (1oz) butter in a large frying pan
and fry celery, leek and apple. Season.
Remove from pan and cool. Mix in cheese.
Place some stuffing on to each escalope,
then roll up. Secure with cocktail sticks.
Melt remaining butter in pan. Add pork and
brown. Remove from pan.
Add onion and cook until soft. Stir in flour for
2 minutes. Stir in milk and bring to boil. Add
pork, cover and simmer for 10 minutes.
Add mushrooms and simmer for 5 minutes.
Stir in cream and serve.

Peppered Pork

Serves 4 Preparation 30 mins Cooking 20 mins
Per portion 356 kcals, 20g fat (10.6g saturated)

450g (1lb) pork fillet, cut into strips
Freshly ground black pepper
25g (1oz) butter
225g (8oz) carrots, peeled and cut into strips
1 large onion, peeled and chopped
110g (4oz) mushrooms, wiped and sliced
3 tbsp Irish whiskey
150ml (¼ pint) soured cream
Chopped parsley to garnish

Liberally sprinkle pork with pepper.
Melt butter in a large frying pan, add pork and carrots and stir-fry for 5 minutes.
Add onion and mushrooms and cook until soft.
Stir in whiskey and soured cream and heat through; do not boil.
Serve pork strips garnished with chopped parsley.

Blackberry & Apple Pork

Serves 4 Preparation 10 mins Cooking 20 mins
Per portion 229 kcals, 6g fat (1.6g saturated)

1 tbsp vegetable oil
450g (1lb) pork fillet, thinly sliced
150ml (¼ pint) unsweetened apple juice
150ml (¼ pint) chicken stock
1 tbsp clear honey
1 tbsp chopped sage
Salt and freshly ground black pepper
2 Granny Smith apples, cored and sliced
150g (5oz) blackberries
2 tsp cornflour

Cook pork in oil for about 3 minutes on each side until browned. Transfer to a plate and set aside.
Pour apple juice and stock into pan and add honey, sage and seasoning. Bring to boil, stirring, and reduce to a simmer.
Return pork to pan and add apples. Cover and cook for 5 minutes. Add blackberries, cover and cook gently for 5 minutes.
Blend cornflour with 4 tsp cold water and stir into mixture. Raise heat slightly and cook for a minute, stirring constantly, until lightly thickened.

Baked Pork Creole

Serves 4 Preparation 40 mins Cooking 1½ hrs
Per portion 280 kcals, 13g fat (5.9g saturated)

450g (1lb) pork fillet, thinly sliced
4 tbsp plain flour
Salt and freshly ground black pepper
25g (1oz) butter
1 large onion, peeled and chopped
225g (8oz) tomatoes, chopped
1 large celery stick, chopped
1 small green pepper, deseeded and chopped
4 tbsp tomato juice

Coat pork in seasoned flour.
Fry in butter until golden. Transfer meat to a casserole dish.
Add onion to remaining butter in pan and fry gently until pale gold.
Add to casserole with tomatoes, celery and green pepper. Season to taste and add tomato juice.
Cover and bake at 180°C (350°F) Mark 4 for 1 hour.
Uncover and cook for a further 15 minutes.

Variation

Chilli Pork Creole

Follow recipe and method for Baked Pork Creole. Add 2 tsp chilli powder at step 3.

Normandy Pork & Rice

Serves 6 Preparation 25 mins Cooking 40 mins
Per portion 286 kcals, 8g fat (3.5g saturated)

25g (1oz) butter
350g (12oz) pork fillet, cut into strips
1 small onion, peeled and chopped
1 eating apple, peeled, cored and sliced
300ml (½ pint) cider
600ml (1 pint) chicken stock
225g (8oz) long grain rice
4 tbsp double cream (optional)

Melt butter in a frying pan and cook pork until brown and almost cooked through.
Add onion and cook until soft.
Add apple, cider, stock and rice. Bring to the boil, cover and simmer for about 30 minutes or until rice is cooked, stirring occasionally and adding more liquid if needed.
Stir cream into rice, if using.

Peking Pork Stir-Fry ❄

Serves 4   Preparation 35 mins   Cooking 15 mins
Per portion 249 kcals, 11g fat (5g saturated)

2 tbsp sunflower oil
275g (10oz) pork fillet, cut into strips
225g (8oz) carrots, peeled and cut into thin strips
175g (6oz) baby corn, cut in half lengthways
225g (8oz) courgettes, cut into thin strips
1 red, green or yellow pepper, deseeded and cut into strips
4 spring onions, trimmed and sliced
110g (4oz) hoisin sauce

Heat sunflower oil in a large frying pan or wok, add pork and stir-fry over a high heat for 5 minutes.
Add carrots and baby corn and continue stir-frying for 3 minutes.
Add remaining vegetables and stir-fry for 3–4 minutes.
Stir in hoisin sauce and heat through.

Chinese-Style Pork ❄

Serves 4   Preparation 35 mins plus marinating   Cooking 20 mins   Per portion 262 kcals, 13g fat (6g saturated)

1 tbsp soy sauce
1 tsp brown sugar
1 tbsp dry white wine
1 tbsp plain flour
450g (1lb) pork fillet, trimmed and cut into thin slices
25g (1oz) butter
1 onion, peeled and chopped
110g (4oz) mushrooms, wiped and sliced
2 large tomatoes, chopped
50g (2oz) frozen peas

Mix soy sauce, sugar and wine with flour. Add pork and mix well. Leave to marinate for 30 minutes.
Melt 15g (½oz) butter in a non-stick frying pan until hot.
Add onion and fry until soft but not brown. Remove from pan.
Melt remaining butter in pan, add pork and cook for 5 minutes, stirring.
Add fried onion and then mushrooms, tomatoes and peas.
Cook for 5–10 minutes, or until pork is cooked. Stir frequently.

Oriental Pork ❄

Serves 4   Preparation 20 mins plus marinating   Cooking 35 mins   Per portion 274 kcals, 13g fat (5.9g saturated)

2 tbsp soy sauce
1 tbsp Worcestershire sauce
4 tbsp tomato ketchup
1 tbsp honey
1 tsp mustard
450g (1lb) pork fillet, sliced
25g (1oz) butter
1 onion, peeled and chopped
150ml (¼ pint) chicken or pork stock
1 red or green pepper, deseeded and sliced
75g (3oz) mushrooms, wiped and sliced

Mix sauces, ketchup, honey and mustard. Add pork and marinate for 30 minutes.
Melt butter and fry onion and meat (reserve marinade) until coloured.
Add stock and marinade, then cover and simmer for 20 minutes, until pork is cooked.
Add vegetables and cook for 3 minutes or until sauce has reduced.

Pork & Pineapple Curry ❄

Serves 4   Preparation 25 mins   Cooking 1¾ hrs
Per portion 379 kcals, 15g fat (7.5g saturated)

2 large onions, peeled and chopped
1 garlic clove, peeled and crushed
40g (1½oz) butter
550g (1¼lb) lean pork, diced
1 tbsp plain flour
1–2 tbsp curry powder (to taste)
227g can pineapple slices, drained and chopped
1 tbsp tomato purée
50g (2oz) raisins
1 tbsp lemon juice
1 bay leaf
1 tsp ground ginger
300ml (½ pint) chicken or pork stock
150ml (¼ pint) milk

Fry onions and garlic in butter until golden.
Add pork and fry briskly for 5 minutes, stirring.
Stir in flour and curry powder.
Add remaining ingredients and bring to the boil.
Lower heat, cover and simmer gently for 1–1½ hours or until pork is tender. Stir frequently.

Pork & Cheese Burgers

Pork & Vegetable Crumble ❄

Serves 4   Preparation 30 mins   Cooking 50 mins
Per portion 530 kcals, 26g fat (13.9g saturated)

65g (2½oz) butter
450g (1lb) lean pork, trimmed and cubed
150g (5oz) wholemeal flour
450ml (¾ pint) milk
Salt and freshly ground black pepper
2 tsp chopped sage
2 leeks, washed and sliced
110g (4oz) mushrooms, wiped and sliced
½ red pepper, deseeded and diced
1 tsp mustard powder
1 tsp paprika
50g (2oz) Red Leicester cheese, grated
25g (1oz) porridge oats

Melt 15g (½oz) butter in a non-stick frying pan and fry pork until browned.
Add 25g (1oz) flour and cook for a minute. Gradually stir in milk and cook stirring until sauce thickens, boils and is smooth.
Season, add sage and vegetables, bring to the boil and simmer for 10 minutes.
Pour pork mixture into an ovenproof dish.
Rub remaining butter into remaining flour until mixture resembles breadcrumbs.

Stir in remaining ingredients and sprinkle over pork mixture. Bake at 200°C (400°F) Mark 6 for 30 minutes.

Variation

Garlic Pork Crumble ❄

Follow recipe and method for Pork & Vegetable Crumble. Omit butter, sage, mustard and paprika. Use 65g (2½oz) garlic butter and add 1 tsp dried mixed herbs to sauce.

Pork & Cheese Burgers ❄

Serves 4   Preparation 15 mins   Cooking 20 mins
Per portion 293 kcals, 16g fat (7.9g saturated)

450g (1lb) minced lean pork
1 tbsp Taco seasoning
110g (4oz) Lancashire cheese, grated
1 egg

Place meat in a bowl and break up with a fork.
Add Taco seasoning, most of cheese and egg. Mix until combined.
Using dampened hands form into 8 burgers.
Grill until well browned and cooked.
Sprinkle with remaining cheese and grill until melted.

Pork Pie

Serves 4–6   Preparation 1¼ hrs   Cooking 2 hrs
Per portion 816 kcals, 45g fat (25.4g saturated)

Hot Water Crust Pastry made with 350g (12oz) flour (page 230)
500g (1lb 2oz) lean diced pork
110g (4oz) bacon, chopped
1 tsp dried sage
Pinch of ground nutmeg
Freshly ground black pepper
Beaten egg for brushing
1½ tsp powdered gelatine

Roll out two-thirds of pastry. Keep remaining pastry covered.

Place inside a 15cm (6in) round cake tin and draw pastry up sides to cover base and sides completely.

Mix pork with bacon, sage, nutmeg and pepper.

Pack into pastry case. Moisten edges of pastry with water.

Roll out remaining pastry into a lid. Cover pie, pressing pastry edges together to seal. Make a hole in top to allow steam to escape.

Brush with beaten egg. Decorate with pastry leaves, cut from trimmings. Then brush with more egg.

Bake at 200°C (400°F) Mark 6 for 15 minutes.

Reduce temperature to 180°C (350°F) Mark 4 and bake for a further 1¾ hours.

Heat 90ml (3fl oz) water. Add gelatine and stir briskly until dissolved.

Pour into hot pie through the hole on top, using a small funnel.

Leave until completely cold before removing from tin and cutting.

Baked Glazed Gammon

Serves 12–14 Preparation 30 mins Cooking 3 hrs
Per portion 195 kcals, 12g fat (4.9g saturated)

1.6–1.8 kg (3½–4lb) gammon joint
Cloves
75g (3oz) soft brown sugar
2 tsp mustard powder
50g (2oz) butter, melted
2 tbsp cider or apple juice
1 tsp Worcestershire sauce

Put gammon into a saucepan, cover with cold water and bring to the boil. Drain.
Cover with fresh water. Bring slowly to the boil and remove any scum. Cover and simmer gently for 1¾–2 hours.
Drain and cool slightly. Strip off the skin, if necessary. Score fat into a diamond pattern with a sharp knife.
Press a clove into each alternate diamond. Put gammon into a roasting tin.
Mix together sugar, mustard, butter, cider or apple juice and Worcestershire sauce. Coat fat with mixture.
Cook at 190°C (375°F) Mark 5 for 30 minutes or until fat is golden brown, basting three to four times. Serve hot or cold.

Gammon Steaks with Apples

Serves 4 Preparation 30 mins Cooking 50 mins
Per portion 422 kcals, 26g fat (10.3g saturated)

2 tbsp soft brown sugar
1 tsp mustard powder
Freshly ground pepper
4 x 150g (5oz) gammon steaks, trimmed of fat
12 shallots, peeled and halved
150ml (¼ pint) apple juice or cider
2 cooking apples, peeled, cored and sliced
3 cloves
15g (½oz) butter

Combine 1 tbsp sugar with mustard and pepper.
Rub on to both sides of gammon steaks.
Transfer to a greased ovenproof dish. Surround with shallots. Pour in apple juice or cider and cover tightly.
Bake at 200°C (400°F) Mark 6 for 30 minutes.
Turn gammon steaks over. Cover with apples, remaining sugar and cloves.
Dot with butter and cook at 180°C (350°F) Mark 4 for 20 minutes.

Gammon with Pineapple

Serves 4 Preparation 5 mins Cooking 20 mins
Per portion 183 kcals, 9g fat (3.4g saturated)

4 x 110g (4oz) gammon steaks
227g can pineapple rings in juice, drained

Snip fat with scissors at 2.5cm (1in) intervals to prevent gammon from curling as it cooks.
Stand in grill pan and grill for 5–7 minutes (or until fat becomes transparent).
Turn over and grill for a further 5–7 minutes, or until cooked.
Remove gammon and keep warm.
Place pineapple rings under grill and cook until heated through. Serve gammon with hot pineapple rings.

Fruity Gammon Casserole

Serves 4 Preparation 30 mins Cooking 1½ hrs
Per portion 733 kcals, 35.7g fat (14g saturated)

680g (1½lb) unsmoked gammon joint
50g (2oz) butter
12 button onions or shallots, peeled
350g (12oz) baby potatoes, scrubbed
350g (12oz) baby carrots, scrubbed
2 tbsp flour
350ml (12fl oz) chicken stock
300ml (½ pint) strong cider
1 sprig parsley, rosemary, thyme and bay leaf
225g (8oz) broad beans, fresh or frozen
12 large pitted prunes
4 Cox's apples, cored
4 tbsp single cream
Chopped flat-leaved parsley

Cut rind and excess fat from gammon. Cut meat from bone and then into 2.5cm (1in) cubes.
Heat butter in a flameproof casserole, add gammon and cook until browned. Add onions, potatoes and carrots.
Cook at 180°C (350°F) Mark 4 for 2–3 minutes and stir in flour.
Stir in stock and cider and bring to boil.
Add herbs, cover with greaseproof paper and then with lid or foil and cook for about 1¼ hours.
After 1 hour, add beans, prunes and apples. Return to oven until vegetables are cooked.
Remove from oven, stir in cream, sprinkle with parsley – and serve.

Sausage with Beans ❄

Serves 4   Preparation 15 mins   Cooking 30 mins
Per portion 401 kcals, 16g fat (6.6g saturated)

15g (½oz) butter
1 onion, peeled and sliced
4 carrots, peeled and sliced
1 tsp chilli powder
450g (1lb) reduced fat sausages, sliced
25g (1oz) wholemeal flour
300ml (½ pint) milk
1 tbsp Worcestershire sauce
1 tbsp tomato purée
200g can baked beans
110g (4oz) frozen peas

Melt butter in a non-stick frying pan and fry onion, carrots and chilli for 5 minutes.
Add sausages, cover and cook for 15 minutes. Stir in flour and cook for 1 minute.
Slowly add milk, whisking continuously, until sauce thickens, boils and is smooth.
Cook for a minute. Stir in remaining ingredients and cook for 5 minutes.

Sausage & Leek Bake ❄

Serves 6   Preparation 30 mins   Cooking 45 mins
Per portion 469 kcals, 26g fat (11.4g saturated)

680g (1½lb) potatoes, peeled and sliced
25g (1oz) butter
450g (1lb) pork and herb sausages, sliced
1 onion, peeled and sliced
4 leeks, washed and sliced
40g (1½oz) plain flour
450ml (¾ pint) milk
110g (4oz) Cheddar cheese, grated
25g (1oz) fresh breadcrumbs

Cook potatoes in boiling water for 5–10 minutes. Drain.
Melt butter in a large frying pan, add sausages and cook for 5 minutes. Add onion and leeks. Cook for 5 minutes. Add flour, cook for 1 minute, then gradually add milk.
Slowly add milk, whisking continuously, until sauce thickens, boils and is smooth.
Remove from heat, add 75g (3oz) cheese and stir until melted.
Transfer to ovenproof dish, arrange potato slices on top, sprinkle over breadcrumbs and remaining cheese. Bake at 200°C (400°F) Mark 6 for 30 minutes until browned.

Sausages with Devilled Sauce

Serves 4   Preparation 10 mins   Cooking 20 mins
Per portion 344 kcals, 24g fat (8.7g saturated)

450g (1lb) pork sausages
15g (½oz) butter
1 onion, peeled and chopped
1 tbsp plain flour
2 tbsp sweet pickle
2 tsp Worcestershire sauce
2 tbsp tomato ketchup
1 tsp mustard
1 tbsp vinegar

Grill sausages until cooked.
Meanwhile, melt butter in a non-stick saucepan and fry onion until golden.
Stir in flour and cook for a minute, continuously stirring.
Gradually stir in 150ml (¼ pint) water. Add remaining ingredients and bring to the boil, stirring. Cook for a minute.
Serve sauce with cooked sausages.

Sausages with Apples & Squash

Serves 4   Preparation 10 mins   Cooking 30 mins
Per portion 512 kcals, 34g fat (10g saturated)

1 small butternut squash or pumpkin, halved, deseeded, peeled and cut into wedges
1 red onion, peeled and thickly sliced
2 Granny Smith apples, cored, peeled and thickly sliced
2 tbsp lemon juice
2 tbsp maple syrup
1 tsp ground cinnamon
2 tbsp vegetable oil
Salt and freshly ground black pepper
8 thick pork sausages
2 tbsp chopped parsley

Arrange squash or pumpkin, onion and apple slices evenly in a roasting tin lined with baking parchment.
In a small bowl, mix lemon juice, maple syrup, cinnamon and oil.
Drizzle over vegetables, mixing to coat. Season well.
Arrange sausages on top and bake at 200°C (400°F) Mark 6 for about 30 minutes, turning occasionally, until cooked through.
Serve sprinkled with parsley.

Lamb

Roast Lamb ❋

Preparation 5 mins   Cooking times
25 mins per 450g (1lb) plus 25 mins (medium)
30 mins per 450g (1lb) plus 30 mins (well done)

Choose leg, shoulder, loin, best end of neck or stuffed boned breast
When buying allow (raw per person) about
110–175g (4–6oz) meat without bone
175–350g (6–12oz) meat with bone
Accompany with
Gravy (page 181)
Mint sauce (page 182)
Boiled or Roast Potatoes (page 155)
Steamed vegetables

Tie or skewer joint into a neat shape if necessary and stand in a roasting tin.
Calculate cooking time (above). Cook at 180°C (350°F) Mark 4 for calculated cooking time. A meat thermometer may be used to assess the final temperature, which should be 75°C for medium and 82°C for well done.
Remove from oven and stand joint on a board to carve. Remove string or skewers.
Carve and serve with accompaniments.

Crown Roast of Lamb

Serves 6   Preparation 1 hr
Cooking 30 mins per 450g (1lb) plus 30 mins
Per portion 604 kcals, 44g fat (22.9g saturated)

1 crown roast of lamb
Suitable stuffing (see stuffings on page 188)
Fresh rosemary to garnish
Accompany with
Gravy (page 181)
Mint Sauce (page 182)
Boiled or Roast Potatoes (page 155)
Steamed vegetables

Ask your butcher to prepare a crown from 2 best end necks of lamb, each with 6 or 7 cutlets.
Alternatively, to make a crown yourself, buy 2 best end necks, already chined. Trim away meat from upper parts of bones, leaving 2.5cm (1in) of bone bare. With skin side inside, curve both necks round to form a crown. Hold together by stitching ends together with fine string and a trussing needle.

Place in a roasting tin and place stuffing in centre of crown. Weigh with stuffing to calculate roasting time, allowing 30 minutes per 450g (1lb), plus 30 minutes. Cover tops of bones with pieces of foil to prevent over browning.
Roast at 180°C (350°F) Mark 4 for calculated cooking time. Remove from oven. Transfer to a board or serving dish.
Garnish with rosemary and serve with accompaniments.

Braised Shoulder of Lamb ❋

Serves 4–6   Preparation 25 mins   Cooking 2¼ hrs
Per portion 853 kcals, 53g fat (26.6g saturated)

50g (2oz) butter
225g (8oz) onions, peeled and chopped
1 garlic clove, peeled and crushed
110g (4oz) lean bacon, chopped
225g (8oz) carrots, peeled and sliced
110g (4oz) turnips, peeled and diced
2 large celery sticks, chopped
150ml (¼ pint) red wine
1 tsp dried rosemary
Salt and freshly ground black pepper
1.4 kg (3lb) shoulder of lamb, boned and rolled

Heat butter in a large saucepan. Add onions, garlic, bacon, carrots, turnips and celery.
Cover saucepan. Fry gently for 10 minutes, shaking pan frequently.
Add wine, 150ml (¼ pint) water, rosemary and season to taste.
Bring to the boil. Stand lamb on top.
Cover and simmer very gently for 2 hours or until meat is tender.
Transfer lamb to a warm serving dish and surround with vegetables from saucepan.

Lamb

Lamb is sweet-flavoured meat from sheep less than a year old. British lamb has the finest flavour, but New Zealand lamb can be cheaper. Smaller cuts generally taste the best – so it may be worth buying two small joints rather than one large one to cater for more people. Lamb is popular in European and Middle Eastern cooking, especially in rich stews, kebabs and rice and curry dishes. Go for the leanest cuts with firm, creamy-white fat.

Spiced Lamb Shanks

Spiced Lamb Shanks ❄

Serves 4   Preparation 25 mins   Cooking 2¼ hrs
Per portion 921 kcals, 52g fat (24.9g saturated)

1 tbsp olive oil
25g (1oz) butter
4 lamb shanks
450g (1lb) small onions or shallots, peeled
2 tbsp plain flour
2 tsp mixed spice
Grated rind and juice of 2 oranges
300ml (½ pint) lamb stock
150g (5oz) ready-to-eat prunes

Heat oil and butter in a flameproof casserole and brown lamb shanks all over. Set aside.
Cook onions in casserole for 2–3 minutes.
Stir in flour, spice, orange rind and juice and stock. Bring to the boil, stirring.
Place lamb in casserole with prunes and transfer to the oven.
Bake at 180°C (350°F) Mark 4 for 2 hours. Turn lamb after 1 hour.

Lamb and Barley Casserole ❄

Serves 4   Preparation 20 mins   Cooking 55 mins
Per portion 630 kcals, 34g fat (17.3g saturated)

15g (½oz) butter
2 onions, peeled and sliced
4 lamb chops
15g (½oz) wholemeal flour
175g (6oz) pearl barley
225g (8oz) mushrooms, wiped and halved
4 sticks celery, sliced
300ml (½ pint) lamb stock
600ml (1 pint) milk

In a large saucepan melt butter and fry onions until soft.
Add lamb and cook until brown on both sides.
Add flour and cook for 1 minute.
Stir in barley, mushrooms, celery and stock.
Simmer gently without a lid for 45 minutes or until lamb and barley are tender.
Add milk, bring to the boil and serve.

Lancashire Hot Pot

Serves 4   Preparation 30 mins   Cooking 1¾ hrs
Per portion 728 kcals, 54g fat (28.1g saturated)

680g (1½lb) best end neck of lamb
2 lamb's kidneys
450g (1lb) potatoes, peeled and thinly sliced
225g (8oz) onions, peeled and thinly sliced
Salt and freshly ground black pepper
150ml (¼ pint) lamb or chicken stock
25g (1oz) butter, melted

Cut lamb into cutlets, removing any surplus fat.
Remove and discard skin and core from kidneys. Cut into slices.
Cover base of a 1.7 litre (3 pint) casserole with some of the potato slices.
Stand lamb on top, then cover with kidneys and onions. Season to taste.
Arrange overlapping rings of remaining potatoes on top.
Pour in stock. Brush with butter.
Cover dish with lid or foil.
Bake at 180°C (350°F) Mark 4 for 1¼ hours.
Uncover dish and continue to cook for a further 30 minutes or until potatoes are tender and golden brown.

Variation

Traditional Lancashire Hot Pot

Follow recipe and method for Lancashire Hot Pot, adding 8 shelled oysters along with the lamb.

Mediterranean Casserole

Serves 4   Preparation 30 mins   Cooking 1½ hrs
Per portion 336 kcals, 21g fat (10.8g saturated)

1 aubergine, halved and sliced
Salt and freshly ground black pepper
25g (1oz) butter
450g (1lb) lamb neck fillet, cubed
1 onion, peeled and sliced
1 garlic clove, peeled and crushed
110g (4oz) mushrooms, wiped and sliced
15g (½oz) plain flour
150ml (¼ pint) lamb stock
400g can chopped tomatoes
½ tsp dried rosemary
225g (8oz) courgettes, sliced

Sprinkle aubergine with salt and leave to stand for 30 minutes.
Rinse and drain well.
Melt butter in a frying pan and brown lamb. Remove to an ovenproof dish.
Add onion, garlic and mushrooms to pan and cook for 3 minutes.
Add flour and cook, continuously stirring, for 1 minute.
Stir in stock, tomatoes and aubergine.
Bring to the boil, stirring, and cook for a minute. Pour into ovenproof dish with rosemary and courgettes.
Cover and cook at 190°C (375°F) Mark 5 for 1¼ hours or until lamb is tender.

Lamb Stew

Serves 4   Preparation 20 mins   Cooking 2 hrs
Per portion 438 kcals, 30g fat (15.8g saturated)

1.1kg (2½lb) middle neck of lamb
2 tbsp plain flour
Salt and freshly ground black pepper
25g (1oz) butter
1 large onion, peeled and chopped
2 tbsp pearl barley
450ml (¾ pint) lamb stock

Divide lamb into neat pieces. Cut away surplus fat. Toss in seasoned flour.
Fry briskly in hot butter until crisp and brown. Transfer to plate.
Add onion to remaining butter in frying pan. Fry slowly until pale gold.
Replace lamb. Add barley and stock and season to taste.
Bring slowly to the boil. Lower heat and cover pan. Simmer gently for 1½–2 hours or until meat is tender.

Grilled Lamb Cutlets or Chops

Serves 4   Cooking 10–20 mins
Per portion 412 kcals, 33g fat (17g saturated)

8 best end neck cutlets or 4 loin chops

Stand chops in grill pan. Cook under pre-heated grill for 1 minute.
Turn over. Grill for a further minute. Continue to grill for a total of 7–9 minutes for cutlets, or 10–18 minutes for loin chops. Turn frequently.
Transfer to 4 individual plates or a warm serving dish and serve.

Fruity Lamb Stew

Fruity Lamb Stew ❊

Serves 4   Preparation 15 mins   Cooking 1½ hrs
Per portion 331 kcals, 14g fat (6.7g saturated)

680g (1½lb) boneless leg of lamb, trimmed
and cubed
1 onion, peeled and chopped
1 tbsp vegetable oil
½ tsp ground ginger
½ tsp ground coriander
½ tsp ground cinnamon
900ml (1½ pints) lamb stock
50g (2oz) ready-to-eat prunes, halved
50g (2oz) ready-to-eat dried apricots, halved

Fry lamb and onion in oil until browned.
Place ingredients except fruit in a saucepan.
Bring to the boil, cover and simmer for
1¼ hours or until the meat is tender.
Add fruit and bring back to the boil.
Simmer for 15 minutes.

Variation

Fruity Pork Stew

Follow recipe and method for Fruity Lamb
Stew. Use 680g (1½lb) cubed boneless pork.

Eastern Lamb

Serves 4   Preparation 25 mins   Cooking 1 hr
Per portion 461 kcals, 18g fat (10g saturated)

50g (2oz) butter
350g (12oz) lamb neck fillet, cut into strips
1 small onion, peeled and chopped
400g can chopped tomatoes
175g (6oz) long grain rice
50g (2oz) raisins
2 tsp brown sugar
4 tbsp vinegar
1 tsp turmeric
1 tsp ground ginger
2 garlic cloves, peeled and crushed
300ml (½ pint) lamb stock
Salt and freshly ground black pepper

Melt butter in a flameproof casserole and fry
lamb until browned. Remove meat to a plate.
Add onion to casserole and fry for 3 minutes.
Return lamb to casserole with tomatoes,
rice, raisins, sugar, vinegar, spices, garlic and
stock. Stir to mix.
Cover and cook at 190°C (375°F) Mark 5 for
50 minutes or until rice and meat are tender.
Remove from oven and season to taste.

Lamb Korma

Serves 4   Preparation 25 mins   Cooking 35 mins
Per portion 378 kcals, 23g fat (9.6g saturated)

25g (1oz) butter
1 onion, peeled and chopped
2 garlic cloves, peeled and crushed
5cm (2in) piece root ginger, peeled and grated
2 tsp ground coriander
2 tsp ground cumin
1 tsp ground turmeric
½ tsp ground cinnamon
275g (10oz) natural yogurt
450g (1lb) lamb (leg or shoulder), trimmed and cubed
50g (2oz) cashew nuts
2 tbsp chopped coriander

Melt butter in a large saucepan and fry onion and garlic until soft.

Add ginger and spices and cook for a few minutes.

Gradually stir in yogurt, then add lamb, nuts and half the coriander.

Cook on low heat for 30 minutes, until meat is tender.

Garnish with remaining chopped coriander and serve.

Variation

Chicken Korma

Follow recipe and method for Lamb Korma. Omit lamb and use 450g (1lb) boneless chicken breast fillet, cubed.

Lamb Kebabs

Serves 4   Preparation 30 mins plus 3 hrs marinating
Cooking 26 mins
Per portion 372 kcals, 23g fat (11g saturated)

450g (1lb) boneless leg of lamb, cubed
Yogurt Marinade made with 300g (10oz) yogurt (page 189)
4 shallots or small onions, peeled
8 rashers streaky bacon
8 cherry tomatoes
8 button mushrooms
Fresh coriander to garnish

Add lamb to yogurt marinade and refrigerate for 3 hours.

Cook shallots or onions in boiling water for 10 minutes. Drain and halve.

Cut bacon rashers in half. Roll up each one like a Swiss roll.

Thread lamb on to 4 skewers alternately with halved shallots or onions, bacon rolls, tomatoes and mushrooms.

Stand in grill pan. Cook under preheated hot grill for 16 minutes, turning frequently.

Serve garnished with coriander.

Kofta Curry

Serves 4   Preparation 20 mins   Cooking 40 mins
Per portion 460 kcals, 30g fat (12.2g saturated)

450g (1lb) minced lamb
1 onion, peeled and finely chopped
1cm (¾in) piece root ginger, peeled and grated
2 garlic cloves, peeled and crushed
1 fresh green chilli, deseeded and finely chopped
2 tbsp chopped coriander
1 egg, beaten
15g (½oz) butter
2 tsp ground coriander
1 tsp ground cumin
½ tsp ground turmeric
½ tsp ground cinnamon
450ml (¾ pint) milk
1 tbsp tomato purée
50g (2oz) blanched almonds
150g (5oz) natural yogurt

Mix together meat, half the onion, ginger, garlic, chilli, fresh coriander and egg.

Shape into 16 small balls with dampened hands.

In a non-stick frying pan, fry meatballs in butter, in batches, until evenly browned. Lift out and drain off excess fat from pan.

Place remaining onion in pan and fry lightly.

Add spices and cook for 1 minute, stirring.

Add milk and tomato purée and bring to the boil.

Return meatballs to pan, cover and simmer gently for 30 minutes.

Add almonds and stir in yogurt gradually. Do not boil.

Lamb & Apricot Coucous

Lamb & Apricot Couscous

Serves 4   Preparation 10 mins   Cooking 1 hr 40 mins
Per portion 335 kcals, 11g fat (3.9g saturated)

1 tbsp olive oil
350g (12oz) lean lamb, diced
1 tsp ground cinnamon
1 tsp ground turmeric
1 onion, peeled and sliced
1 leek, washed and sliced
2 red peppers, deseeded and chopped
150g (5oz) ready-to-eat dried apricots
Grated zest and juice of 1 lemon
450ml (¾ pint) lamb stock
110g (4oz) couscous
Salt and freshly ground black pepper
2 tbsp chopped parsley

Heat oil in a flameproof casserole and brown lamb.

Add cinnamon and turmeric to casserole and cook for 1 minute, continuously stirring, to relase flavour.

Add onion, leek, peppers, apricots, lemon zest and juice to the casserole and mix thoroughly with meat.

Pour in stock. Bring to the boil, then simmer, covered, for 1¼–1½ hours, until lamb is tender.

Stir in couscous and cook, covered, for a further 3–5 minutes until couscous has fluffed up.

Season and serve sprinkled with chopped parsley.

Shepherd's Pie ❄

Serves 4 Preparation 15 mins Cooking 1¾ hrs
Per portion 437 kcals, 21g fat (10.8g saturated)

450g (1lb) minced lamb

1 onion, peeled and chopped

2 tbsp plain flour

300ml (½ pint) lamb or beef stock

1 tbsp tomato purée

½ tsp dried mixed herbs

Salt and freshly ground black pepper

680g (1½lb) potatoes, peeled and chopped

25g (1oz) butter

3 tbsp milk

Dry fry lamb in a non-stick frying pan until browned. Add onion and cook for 5 minutes, stirring occasionally.

Add flour and cook, stirring, for 1 minute. Gradually blend in stock, tomato purée and herbs and season to taste.

Cook, stirring, until mixture thickens and boils. Cover and simmer for 25 minutes.

Turn mince into a 1.25 litre (2 pint) ovenproof dish.

Meanwhile, cook potatoes in boiling water for 20 minutes until tender.

Drain well, then mash with butter and milk.

Cover mince mixture with potato. Bake at 190°C (375°F) Mark 5 for 1¼ hours.

Moussaka ❄

Serves 4 Preparation 15 mins plus standing Cooking 1¼ hrs Per portion 464 kcals, 32g fat (14.3g saturated)

2 aubergines

Salt and freshly ground black pepper

2 tbsp olive oil

2 large onions, peeled and sliced

450g (1lb) minced lamb or beef

1 tbsp tomato purée

1 egg, beaten

200g (7oz) Greek-style natural yogurt

50g (2oz) Cheddar cheese, grated

Cut aubergines into 5mm (¼in) thick slices. Sprinkle with salt and leave for 30 minutes.

Rinse and drain. Fry in oil until golden on both sides. Remove from pan and set aside.

Fry onions in remaining oil until pale gold.

Add meat and cook until browned. Add 150ml (¼ pint) water and tomato purée.

Season to taste.

Line base of an oblong or square ovenproof dish with half the aubergine slices.

Cover with meat mixture and onions. Arrange remaining aubergine slices on top.

Beat egg into most of cheese and yogurt. Pour over aubergine slices. Sprinkle with remaining cheese.

Bake at 180°C (350°F) Mark 4 for 45 minutes–1 hour.

Variation

Lamb & Potato Bake ❄

Follow recipe and method for Moussaka. Omit aubergines and steps 1 and 2. Use 680g (1½lb) potatoes, cooked and sliced in place of aubergines.

Cheshire Lamb Crumble ❄

Serves 4 Preparation 20 mins Cooking 1¼ hrs
Per portion 464 kcals, 30g fat (16.6g saturated)

450g (1lb) minced lamb

1 onion, peeled and chopped

75g (3oz) wholemeal flour

1 tbsp tomato purée

300ml (½ pint) beef stock

Salt and freshly ground black pepper

50g (2oz) butter

50g (2oz) Cheshire cheese, grated

25g (1oz) oats

½ tsp dried mixed herbs

Dry fry meat and onion in a non-stick frying pan for 10 minutes.

Mix in 15g (½oz) flour, tomato purée, stock and seasoning.

Turn into a shallow ovenproof dish.

In a bowl, rub butter into remaining flour, then stir in cheese, oats, herbs and seasoning.

Spoon crumble over meat.

Bake at 190°C (375°F) Mark 5 for 45 minutes–1 hour.

Variation

Beef crumble

Follow recipe and method for Cheshire Lamb Crumble but replace minced lamb with minced beef and Cheshire cheese with Cheddar cheese.

Lamb & Mint Pasty

Lamb Burgers ❄

Serves 4   Preparation 15 mins   Cooking 15 mins
Per portion 328 kcals, 23g fat (11.2g saturated)

1 onion, peeled and chopped
1 garlic clove, peeled and crushed
15g (½oz) butter
450g (1lb) minced lamb
1 tbsp chopped parsley
½ tsp dried mint
1 egg, beaten
4 streaky bacon rashers

Fry onion and garlic in butter until soft.
Place lamb, onion, garlic and herbs in a bowl.
Add egg and mix well.
Cut bacon rashers in half, giving 8 long thin strips.
Divide lamb mixture into 8 equal pieces.
Shape into burgers using dampened hands.
Wrap a piece of bacon carefully around sides of each burger. Secure bacon with wooden cocktail sticks.
Cook under a hot grill until brown and cooked through. Turn twice.

Lamb & Mint Pasty ❄

Serves 4   Preparation 20 mins   Cooking 40 mins
Per portion 602 kcals, 41g fat (19.3g saturated)

350g (12oz) minced lamb
1 onion, peeled and finely chopped
1 tbsp mint jelly
75g (3oz) cooked peas
375g (13oz) puff pastry
Beaten egg to seal and glaze

Dry fry lamb until browned, then add onion and cook for 5 minutes.
Remove from heat and stir in mint jelly and peas.
Roll out pastry on a floured work surface to a 30cm (12in) square. Cut in half. Place one half on a baking sheet.
Spoon lamb mixture into centre of pastry on baking sheet. Brush edges with egg.
Fold remaining pastry in half lengthways and cut slits to within 2.5cm (1in) of edge, spaced 1cm (½in) apart. Unfold.
Place cut pastry over filling and seal edges. Brush with beaten egg.
Bake at 200°C (400°F) Mark 6 for 30 minutes.

Beef

Roast Beef ❄

Preparation 5 mins   Cooking times
20 mins per 450g (1lb) plus 20 mins rare
25 mins per 450g (1lb) plus 25 mins medium
30 mins per 450g (1lb) plus 30 mins well done

Choose sirloin, fore rib, topside, silverside, thick flank or brisket
When buying allow (raw per person) about
110–175g (4–6oz) meat without bone
175–350g (6–12oz) meat with bone
Accompany with
Gravy (page 181)
Yorkshire Pudding (page 172)
Horseradish Sauce or mustard
Boiled or Roast Potatoes (page 155)
Vegetables

Tie or skewer joint into a neat shape, if necessary, and stand in a roasting tin.
Calculate cooking time (above).
Cook at 180°C (350°F) Mark 4 for calculated cooking time.
A meat thermometer may be used to assess the final temperature, which should be 60°C for rare, 70°C for medium, 80°C for well done.
Remove from oven, then stand joint on a board to carve. Remove string or skewers.
Carve and serve with accompaniments.

Pot Roasted Beef ❄

Serves 4   Preparation 30 mins   Cooking 2¼ hrs
Per portion 569 kcals, 35g fat (13.6g saturated)

2 tbsp olive oil
900g (2lb) topside or thick flank of beef
1 onion, peeled and chopped
2 large carrots, peeled and sliced
2 large celery sticks, chopped
1 large tomato, chopped
300ml (½ pint) beef stock
150ml (¼ pint) red wine
Salt and freshly ground black pepper
12 small onions or shallots, peeled

Heat oil in a large saucepan. Brown beef briskly on all sides. Lift out.
Add onion, carrots and celery to remaining oil and fry until golden.
Replace meat. Add tomato, stock, wine and seasoning.

Bring to the boil, lower heat, cover and simmer gently for 1 hour, turning meat at least twice.
Add onions or shallots, cover and continue to simmer for 45 minutes–1 hour or until meat is tender.

Beef Wellington

Serves 8   Preparation 30 mins   Cooking 1 hr 10 mins plus resting Per portion 531 kcals, 34g fat (13g saturated)

1.4kg (3lb) fillet of beef
Freshly ground black pepper
1 tbsp vegetable oil
25g (1oz) butter
225g (8oz) mushrooms, wiped and sliced
110g (4oz) smooth liver pâté
375g pack ready-to-roll puff pastry
1 egg, beaten

Season fillet with pepper. In a large frying pan, fry for 5 minutes on each side in oil and 15g (½oz) butter.
Wrap in cling film and place in a loaf tin so meat 'sets' in a good shape. Cool, then chill.
Meanwhile, add remaining butter to frying pan and fry mushrooms until softened.
Allow mushrooms to cool, then mix thoroughly into pâté.
On a floured surface, unroll pastry. If necessary, roll out a little larger.
Spread pâté mixture in a strip down centre of pastry. Place beef on top, near short end.
Fold pastry edges over beef, sticking edges together with egg and encasing meat. Trim away edges where pastry is double thickness.
Turn over and tuck joins underneath. Brush all over with egg. Re-roll trimmings and create pastry leaves to decorate the top. Brush with egg.
Place on a baking tray and bake at 220°C (425°F) Mark 7 for 50–60 minutes. Cover with foil after 25 minutes.
Allow to rest for 10 minutes before serving.

Beef Wellington

The origin of the name of this dish is disputed. Some say it was named after the 1st Duke of Wellington, who loved this combination of food, but it could simply have been named by a patriotic chef during the Napoleonic Wars.

Beef Stew ❄

Serves 4   Preparation 30 mins   Cooking 2½ hrs
Per portion 354 kcals, 15g fat (7.8g saturated)

680g (1½lb) lean stewing beef, trimmed and cubed

2 tbsp plain flour

Salt and freshly ground black pepper

40g (1½oz) butter

2 onions, peeled and chopped

3 carrots, peeled and sliced

½ small swede, peeled and diced (optional)

450ml (¾ pint) beef stock

Toss meat in seasoned flour. In a large saucepan, fry meat in butter until browned, turning constantly. Remove to a plate.

Add vegetables to saucepan and fry for 7 minutes until golden.

Add meat and stock. Bring to the boil, cover and simmer gently for 2 hours or until meat is tender, stirring occasionally.

Variation

Beef & Tomato Stew ❄

Follow recipe and method for Beef Stew. Use 227g can chopped tomatoes and 200ml (7fl oz) tomato juice in place of stock.

Beef & Beer Casserole ❄

Serves 4   Preparation 30 mins   Cooking 2¾ hrs
Per portion 486 kcals, 17g fat (7.9g saturated)

680g (1½lb) lean stewing beef, trimmed and cubed

40g (1½oz) butter

3 onions, peeled and sliced

1 garlic clove, peeled and crushed

2 tbsp flour

300ml (½ pint) brown ale

1 tsp wine vinegar

150ml (¼ pint) beef stock

Salt and freshly ground black pepper

8 slices of French bread

4 tbsp wholegrain mustard

Fry beef in butter until brown. Transfer beef to an ovenproof casserole.

Add onions and garlic to frying pan and fry in remaining butter until lightly browned.

Add flour and cook, stirring, until it turns light brown.

Gradually stir in liquids. Season to taste.

Bring to the boil and pour over meat. Cover and cook at 170°C (325°F) Mark 3 for 2 hours.
Spread one side of bread with mustard. Push, mustard side down, into casserole.
Return to oven and cook, uncovered, for 30 minutes.

Coconut Beef Curry

Serves 6   Preparation 10 mins plus marinating   Cooking 2 hrs   Per portion 286 kcals, 12g fat (7.4g saturated)

150g (5oz) natural yogurt

1 garlic clove, peeled and crushed

1 tbsp curry powder

900g (2lb) lean stewing beef, cubed

50g (2oz) desiccated coconut

150ml (¼ pint) milk

300ml (½ pint) beef stock

400g can chopped tomatoes

150g (5oz) ready-to-eat dried tropical fruit, chopped (optional)

Combine yogurt, garlic and curry powder.
Stir in beef and leave to marinate for 1 hour.
Meanwhile, soak coconut in milk.
Place beef and marinade in a saucepan with coconut, milk, stock, tomatoes and dried fruit, if using.
Bring to the boil, cover and simmer for 2 hours or until meat is tender. Stir occasionally.

Beef Stroganoff

Serves 4   Preparation 25 mins   Cooking 15 mins
Per portion 411 kcals, 25g fat (14.1g saturated)

700g (1½lb) rump or fillet steak

1 onion, peeled and sliced

50g (2oz) butter

175g (6oz) button mushrooms, wiped and sliced

3 tbsp white wine

150ml (¼ pint) soured cream

Salt and freshly ground black pepper

1 tbsp chopped parsley to garnish

Cut steak into 1.5 x 5cm (¼ x 2in) strips.
Fry onion in 25g (1oz) butter for 5 minutes.
Add remaining butter and steak strips. Fry for a further 5 minutes, stirring.
Add mushrooms and fry for 3 minutes, stirring.
Stir in wine and cream and reheat gently without boiling. Season to taste.
Garnish with parsley and serve.

Grilled Steak au Poivre

Grilled Steak

Serves 4   Preparation 5 mins   Cooking 15 mins
Per portion 320 kcals, 17g fat (7.9g saturated)

4 x 175g (6oz) fillet, rump or sirloin steaks, trimmed of excess fat
Flavoured butter (page 191) to garnish
4 whole grilled tomatoes, watercress and fried mushrooms to garnish

Stand steak on grill rack. Grill for 1 minute, turn over. Grill for 1 minute.

Turn over. Grill for a further 2–3 minutes each side for rare; 4–5 minutes each side for medium; up to 6–7 minutes each side for well done.

Remove from grill. Top each with a piece of flavoured butter. Garnish with tomatoes, watercress and mushrooms.

Variation

Grilled Steak au Poivre

Follow recipe and method for Grilled Steak. An hour before grilling, press 2 tbsp crushed black peppercorns (use rolling pin for crushing) well into steaks with palm of hand. Chill until ready to cook.

Fried Steak & Onions

Serves 4   Preparation 10 mins   Cooking 15 mins
Per portion 342 kcals, 17g fat (9.4g saturated)

350g (12oz) onions, peeled and sliced
50g (2oz) butter
4 x 175g (6oz) rump steaks, trimmed of fat

Fry onions gently in butter until golden. Transfer to a plate and keep warm.

Add steaks to frying pan. Fry briskly for 1 minute on each side.

Lower heat. Continue to fry for a further 3–4 minutes for rare; 4–5 minutes for medium; about 7–8 minutes for well done.

Turn steaks about every minute to ensure even cooking.

Transfer to 4 individual warm plates and serve with fried onions.

Beef Fajitas

Serves 4   Preparation 5 mins   Cooking 10 mins
Per portion 695 kcals, 36g fat (16.2g saturated)

8 flour tortillas

2 tbsp vegetable oil

450g (1lb) rump steak, trimmed of fat and cut into strips

1 green pepper, deseeded and sliced

1 yellow pepper, deseeded and sliced

1 onion, peeled and cut into 8 wedges

2 red chillis, deseeded and sliced

150ml (¼ pint) soured cream

150g (5oz) Cheddar cheese, grated

Wrap tortillas in foil and warm in oven at 220°C (425°F) Mark 7.

Heat oil in a large frying pan and fry beef for 4 minutes. Transfer to a plate and keep warm.

Add vegetables to oil and fry for 5 minutes.

Top each tortilla with beef, vegetables, soured cream and cheese. Roll up and serve.

Steak & Kidney Pie ❄

Serves 4   Preparation 35 mins   Cooking 2½ hrs
Per portion 908 kcals, 50g fat (28.2g saturated)

450g (1lb) lean stewing beef, trimmed and cubed

175g (6oz) lamb's kidneys, chopped

2 tbsp plain flour

Salt and freshly ground black pepper

25g (1oz) butter

1 tbsp olive oil

1 large onion, peeled and chopped

300ml (½ pint) beef stock

Shortcrust Pastry made with 350g (12oz) flour (page 225)

Milk for brushing

Toss steak and kidneys in seasoned flour.

Fry steak and kidneys in hot butter and oil until well browned. Remove to a plate.

Add onion to remaining butter in frying pan and fry gently until pale gold.

Replace meat, add stock and bring to boil.

Lower heat, cover and simmer gently for 1¾–2 hours, stirring occasionally, or until meat is tender. Leave until completely cold.

Roll out half of pastry on a floured surface. Use to cover a lightly greased 23cm (9in) ovenproof pie plate. Trim away surplus pastry.

Roll out remaining pastry to make a lid.

Pile cold meat with sufficient gravy in centre. Moisten edges of pastry with water.

Cover with lid, pressing edges together to seal, then trim away surplus pastry. Flake by cutting with back of a knife. Flute and stand pie on a baking sheet.

Brush with milk and bake at 220°C (425°F) Mark 7 for 25–30 minutes or until golden.

Variation

Steak & Mushroom Pie ❄

Prepare meat filling as for Steak & Kidney Pie, omitting kidneys and adding 110g (4oz) sliced mushrooms with onions. Transfer to a 600ml (1 pint) pie dish. Cover with Puff Pastry (page 229) and bake at 230°C (450°F) Mark 8 for 20–30 minutes or until pastry is puffed and golden.

Steak & Kidney Pudding ❄

Serves 4   Preparation 35 mins   Cooking 4 hrs
Per portion 916 kcals, 30g fat (13.2g saturated)

Suet Crust Pastry made with 225g (8oz) flour (page 230)

450g (1lb) stewing steak, trimmed and cubed

175g (6oz) lamb's kidney, chopped

1 tbsp plain flour

Salt and freshly ground black pepper

1 large onion, peeled and chopped

Roll out two-thirds of pastry. Use to line a greased 900ml (1½ pint) pudding basin.

Toss steak and kidneys in seasoned flour. Layer in basin with onion. Add 3 tbsp water.

Moisten edges of pastry with water. Cover with lid, rolled from remaining pastry. Press pastry edges well together to seal.

Cover with double thickness of buttered greaseproof paper or single thickness of greased foil. Pleat once for pudding to rise.

Secure with string. Use extra string to make a handle for ease of removal.

Place in a steamer over a pan of hot water. Or place a metal trivet in a large saucepan and add boiling water to come halfway up the sides of basin. Add pudding and cover.

Steam steadily for 3½–4 hours. Replenish boiling water as necessary.

Remove from steamer, then serve.

Alternatively, cook filling as for Steak & Kidney Pie prior to making pastry. Then assemble and steam for 2 hours.

Country Beef Bake

Chilli con Carne

Serves 4   Preparation 25 mins   Cooking 1¼ hrs
Per portion 339 kcals, 14g fat (5.7g saturated)

2 streaky bacon rashers, chopped
1 large onion, peeled and chopped
1 garlic clove, peeled and crushed
450g (1lb) lean minced beef
400g can chopped tomatoes
2 tbsp tomato purée
1 green pepper, deseeded and chopped
1–2 tsp chilli powder
150ml (¼ pint) beef stock
400g can red kidney beans, drained

[handwritten: 1 level tsp. cut seeds]

Cook bacon in a non-stick frying pan for 5 minutes, stirring.
Add onion and garlic and cook until soft.
Add beef and cook, stirring, until browned.
Stir in tomatoes, tomato purée, pepper, chilli powder to taste and stock. Bring to the boil, cover and simmer for 45 minutes, stirring occasionally.
Stir in beans and cook for 10 minutes.

Variations

Chilli Cobbler

Follow recipe and method for Chilli con Carne. To make the cobbler topping, rub 25g (1oz) butter into 110g (4oz) wholemeal self-raising flour. Stir in 65ml (2½fl oz) milk to form a soft dough. Roll out on a floured work surface to 1cm (½in) thick and cut into 5cm (2in) rounds. Place hot chilli into an ovenproof dish and overlap scones around the edge of the dish. Brush with a little milk and bake at 200°C (400°F) Mark 6 for 10 minutes or until scones are golden and cooked.

Chilli Tacos

Follow recipe and method for Chilli con Carne. Serve in 12 warmed taco shells topped with soured cream.

Country Beef Bake

Serves 4   Preparation 20 mins   Cooking 55 mins
Per portion 458 kcals, 22g fat (11.6g saturated)

450g (1lb) lean minced beef
1 onion, peeled and sliced
110g (4oz) mushrooms, wiped and sliced
198g can sweetcorn with peppers
225ml (8fl oz) beef stock
1 tsp dried mixed herbs
40g (1½oz) Cheddar cheese, grated
40g (1½oz) Double Gloucester cheese, grated
450g (1lb) Mashed Potato (page 155)

Dry fry mince in a non-stick frying pan until browned. Add the onion and mushrooms and cook for 5 minutes, stirring occasionally.
Add sweetcorn, stock and herbs.
Bring to the boil, cover and simmer for 15 minutes. Top up with stock if neccessary.
Transfer to an ovenproof dish.
Mix together cheeses and stir half into potato. Spoon on top of meat.
Sprinkle remaining cheese over potato.
Bake at 190°C (375°F) Mark 5 for 30 minutes.

Meatball Casserole ❄

Serves 4 Preparation 30 mins Cooking 1 hr
Per portion 384 kcals, 19g fat (9g saturated)

450g (1lb) lean minced beef
1 onion, peeled and chopped
1 tbsp dried mixed herbs
1 egg, beaten
25g (1oz) butter
2 potatoes, peeled and diced
1 green pepper, deseeded and sliced
1 carrot, peeled and thinly sliced
1 tbsp cornflour
300ml (½ pint) stock
290g can oxtail soup

Mix together meat, half the onion, all the herbs and egg.

Using dampened hands, shape into 16 small balls.

Gently fry batches of meatballs in butter in a pan until browned on the surface.

Remove browned meatballs to an ovenproof casserole.

Add remaining onion and vegetables to butter in frying pan and fry for 5 minutes until softened.

Blend cornflour with a little stock, then add to pan with remaining stock and soup. Bring to the boil, stirring and cook for a minute. Pour into casserole.

Cover and cook at 190°C (375°F) Mark 5 for 40 minutes.

Beef Burgers ❄

Serves 4 Preparation 20 mins Cooking 10 mins
Per portion 225 kcals, 13g fat (5.2g saturated)

450g (1lb) lean minced beef
1 small onion, peeled and finely chopped
½ tsp mustard
1 tsp Worcestershire sauce
Salt and freshly ground black pepper
1 egg, beaten

Put all ingredients in a bowl and mix together well.

Using dampened hands, divide into 8 equal pieces and shape into 1cm (½in) thick burgers.

Grill or dry fry in a non-stick frying pan for 8–10 minutes or until cooked through. Turn once.

Cheese Burgers ❄

Serves 4 Preparation 20 mins plus chilling Cooking 20 mins Per portion 347 kcals, 22g fat (11.2g saturated)

450g (1lb) lean minced beef
1 onion, peeled and chopped
1 tsp dried mixed herbs
110g (4oz) Cheddar cheese, grated
1 tbsp tomato purée
1 egg, beaten

Put all ingredients in a bowl and mix well.

Using dampened hands, shape mixture into 4 burgers. Chill for 30 minutes.

Grill or dry fry in a non-stick frying pan for 8–10 minutes on each side until golden brown and cooked through. Turn once.

Harvest Bake

Serves 4 Preparation 35 mins Cooking 1 hr
Per portion 474 kcals, 20g fat (9.2g saturated)

450g (1lb) lean minced beef
25g (1oz) plain flour
300ml (½ pint) beef stock
1 tbsp dried mixed herbs
2 tbsp tomato purée
110g (4oz) leeks, washed and sliced
175g (6oz) cauliflower florets
110g (4oz) carrots, peeled and diced
450g (1lb) potatoes, cooked and sliced
1 egg, beaten
275g (10oz) natural yogurt
50g (2oz) Cheddar cheese, grated

Dry fry mince in a non-stick frying pan until browned. Stir in flour. Gradually stir in stock. Heat, whisking continuously, until sauce thickens, boils and is smooth.

Add 2 tsp herbs, tomato purée, leeks, cauliflower and carrots.

Bring to the boil, cover and simmer for 15 minutes. Stir occasionally.

Transfer to an ovenproof dish. Cover with sliced potatoes.

Whisk together egg, yogurt and remaining herbs. Pour over potatoes and top with cheese.

Bake at 190°C (375°F) Mark 5 for 40 minutes until potatoes are golden.

Offal

Fried Liver

Serves 4   Preparation 10 mins plus soaking Cooking
10 mins   Per portion 263 kcals, 15g fat (7.2g
saturated)

450g (1lb) lamb's, calf's or pig's liver,
sliced
Milk
4 tbsp plain flour
Salt and freshly ground black pepper
40g (1½oz) butter

Put liver into a shallow dish. Cover with milk.
Soak for 30 minutes.
Drain. Pat dry with kitchen paper. Toss in
seasoned flour.
Heat butter in a frying pan. Add liver, a few
pieces at a time.
Fry until liver is crisp and golden, allowing
2–3 minutes each side.
Drain on kitchen paper.

Braised Liver   ❄

Serves 4   Preparation 45 mins   Cooking 40 mins
Per portion 351 kcals, 18g fat (8.5g saturated)

450g (1lb) lamb's liver, sliced
4 tbsp flour
Salt and freshly ground black pepper
50g (2oz) butter
1 onion, peeled and chopped
2 carrots, peeled and grated
1 large potato, peeled and grated
2 celery sticks, chopped
2 tbsp chopped parsley
1 lemon, sliced

Toss liver in seasoned flour.
Melt butter in a saucepan. Fry liver until crisp
and well sealed, turning all the time. Remove
to a plate.
Add onion to remaining butter. Fry slowly
until pale gold.
Stir in any left-over flour, together with
carrots, potato, celery, parsley and 300ml
(½ pint) water.
Season to taste.
Mix well. Bring to the boil. Replace liver, and
top with lemon slices.
Lower heat. Cover and simmer for 30
minutes or until liver is tender.

Grilled Liver

Serves 4   Preparation 5 mins plus soaking Cooking
4 mins   Per portion 182 kcals, 10g fat (3.9g saturated)

450g (1lb) lamb's, calf's or pig's liver,
sliced
Milk
15g (½oz) butter, melted

Put liver into a shallow dish. Cover with milk.
Soak for 30 minutes.
Drain and pat dry with kitchen paper.
Stand on grill rack. Brush all over with melted
butter.
Cook under a hot grill for 1–2 minutes.
Turn over. Brush with more butter. Grill for a
further 1–2 minutes.
Serve immediately.

Liver & Bacon

Serves 4   Preparation 5 mins   Cooking 25 mins
Per portion 335 kcals, 20g fat (7.2g saturated)

1 tbsp sunflower oil
4 smoked back bacon rashers
450g (1lb) lamb's liver, thinly sliced
2 tbsp plain flour
25g (1oz) butter
2 onions, peeled and sliced
1 tsp caster sugar
1 tsp balsamic vinegar
300ml (½ pint) lamb stock
1 tbsp wholegrain mustard
Salt and freshly ground black pepper

Heat oil in a frying pan and cook bacon for
2–3 minutes on each side. Remove to a plate
and keep warm.
Put flour on plate and coat liver (reserving
remaining flour).
Fry liver in oil for 30 seconds–1 minute on
each side. Remove to a plate and keep warm.
Melt butter in frying pan, add onions and
sugar and cook for 8–10 minutes until
softened.
Stir in vinegar and remaining flour, then
gradually stir in stock (allowing to boil
between each addition of stock).
Simmer for 2 minutes.
Stir in mustard and seasoning to taste.
Return bacon and liver to frying pan and
heat through.

Spicy Peanut Liver

Serves 4   Preparation 25 mins   Cooking 15 mins
Per portion 434 kcals, 26g fat (10.9g saturated)

50g (2oz) plain flour
Salt and freshly ground black pepper
½ tsp turmeric
1 tsp chilli powder
450g (1lb) lamb's liver, cut into strips
50g (2oz) butter
1 onion, peeled and sliced
1 garlic clove, peeled and crushed
1 tbsp soy sauce
50g (2oz) dry roasted peanuts
450ml (¾ pint) milk

Mix flour, seasoning and spices in a plastic bag, add liver and shake to coat with flour.
Melt butter in a frying pan, add liver and fry for 3 minutes or until browned.
Add onion and garlic and fry for 3 minutes.
Stir in any remaining flour, soy sauce and peanuts. Cook, stirring for 2 minutes.
Slowly add milk, stirring continuously, until sauce thickens, boils and is smooth.
Cover and simmer for 5 minutes.

Liver Special

Serves 4   Preparation 30 mins   Cooking 15 mins
Per portion 417 kcals, 20g fat (9.6g saturated)

50g (2oz) plain flour
½ tsp curry powder
450g (1lb) lamb's liver, cut into strips
50g (2oz) butter
1 onion, peeled and sliced
1 green pepper, deseeded and diced
400ml (14fl oz) milk
198g can sweetcorn, drained
1 eating apple, peeled, cored and sliced

Mix flour and curry powder in a large plastic bag, add liver and shake to coat with flour.
Melt butter in a frying pan, add liver and fry for 3 minutes.
Add onion and pepper. Cook, stirring, for 3 minutes.
Slowly add milk, stirring continuously, until sauce thickens, boils and is smooth.
Cook for 1 minute.
Add sweetcorn and apple and allow to heat through.

Kidney Turbigo

Serves 4   Preparation 20 mins   Cooking 30 mins
Per portion 396 kcals, 23g fat (9g saturated)

12 pickling onions or shallots, peeled
450g (1lb) lamb's kidneys, halved
25g (1oz) butter
225g (8oz) chipolata sausages
110g (4oz) button mushrooms, wiped and halved
1 tbsp plain flour
2 tsp tomato purée
2 tbsp sherry
300ml (½ pint) stock
1 bay leaf
Salt and freshly ground black pepper
2 slices of bread
1 tbsp chopped parsley

Boil onions or shallots for 5 minutes. Drain.
Remove and discard skin and cores from kidneys.
Melt butter in a large non-stick frying pan and cook kidneys and sausages until browned. Remove and keep warm.
Add mushrooms and cook for 3 minutes, continuously stirring.
Stir in flour, tomato purée, sherry and stock. Bring to the boil, stirring.
Add kidneys and sausages to pan with bay leaf and seasoning.
Cover and simmer for 15 minutes.
Cut crusts off bread and cut into triangles. Toast or fry until brown.
Serve with toasts and parsley.

Devilled Kidneys

Serves 2   Preparation 20 mins   Cooking 10 mins
Per portion 527 kcals, 41g fat (23.6g saturated)

350g (12oz) lamb's kidneys
25g (1oz) butter
110g (4oz) mushrooms, wiped and sliced
1 tbsp Worcestershire sauce
2 tbsp tomato ketchup
1 tsp English mustard
125ml (4fl oz) whipping cream
Chopped parsley to garnish

Remove and discard cores from kidneys and cut into bite-size pieces.
Melt butter in a saucepan, add kidneys and cook for 2 minutes, stirring.

Add mushrooms and continue cooking for 3 minutes, continuously stirring.
Add sauce, ketchup, mustard and cream. Mix well and heat without boiling.
Serve sprinkled with chopped parsley.

Kidneys with Black Bean Sauce

Serves 4   Preparation 20 mins   Cooking 15 mins
Per portion 220 kcals, 11g fat (5.3g saturated)

450g (1lb) lamb's kidneys
25g (1oz) butter
175g (6oz) green beans, cut into 2.5cm (1in) pieces
3 tomatoes, quartered
120g pack black bean stir-fry sauce
75g (3oz) fromage frais

Remove and discard cores and skin from kidneys. Cut a criss-cross design three-quarters of way through each kidney half.
Fry in butter until browned.
Add beans to kidneys. Cook, stirring, for 4 minutes.
Add tomatoes and black bean sauce and heat until piping hot.
Remove from heat and stir in fromage frais.

Haggis, Neeps & Tatties

Serves 4   Preparation 20 mins   Cooking 1½ hrs
Per portion 750 kcals, 48g fat (28.8g saturated)

680g (1½lb) haggis
1 turnip or swede, peeled and chopped
Salt and freshly ground black pepper
450g (1lb) potatoes, peeled and chopped
50g (2oz) butter
3 tbsp warm milk
Snipped chives for garnishing

Cook haggis according to manufacturer's instructions.
Cook turnip or swede in lightly salted, simmering water for about 15 minutes until tender. Drain and return to saucepan.
Cook potatoes for about 15 minutes until tender. Drain well and return to saucepan.
Mash turnip or swede and potatoes and add half butter to each. Season to taste. Stir milk into potato. Cover and keep warm.
Remove skin from haggis and scoop on to serving plates with mashed 'neeps' and 'tatties'.
Sprinkle with snipped chives.

Meals for One or Two

Fish Kebabs

Serves One

Butter Bean Bake   V

Serves 1   Preparation 15 mins   Cooking 40 mins
Per portion 613 kcals, 34g fat (1.8g saturated)

15g (½oz) butter
1 small onion, peeled and chopped
½ green pepper, deseeded and diced
400g can chopped tomatoes with herbs
225g (8oz) canned butter beans, rinsed
2 tsp tomato purée
1 egg
110g (4oz) cottage cheese
25g (1oz) Double Gloucester cheese, grated

Melt butter in a small non-stick frying pan.
Fry onion and pepper for 3 minutes.
Add tomatoes, bring to the boil and simmer
for 5 minutes.
Stir in butter beans and tomato purée.
Spoon into a 600ml (1 pint) ovenproof dish.
Beat egg into cottage cheese and stir in
half the grated cheese. Spoon over tomato
mixture and top with remaining cheese.
Bake at 180°C (350°F) Mark 4 for 30 minutes.

Mushroom Risotto   V

Serves 1   Preparation 10 mins   Cooking 25 mins
Per portion 543 kcals, 30g fat (1.5g saturated)

15g (½oz) butter
1 small onion, peeled and sliced
2–3 button mushrooms, wiped and sliced
50g (2oz) risotto rice
295g can condensed mushroom soup
1 tbsp chopped parsley
Salt and freshly ground black pepper
Grated Cheddar cheese

Melt butter and cook onion for 5 minutes,
until softened but not browned.
Add mushrooms and cook for 3–4 minutes.
Tip rice into frying pan and cook for 1
minute, stirring continuously.
Pour in soup and 150ml (¼ pint) boiling
water. Bring to the boil.
Reduce heat and simmer for 15 minutes,
stirring occasionally. If it appears too dry, add
a little boiling water.
Stir in the parsley and seasoning. Serve
sprinkled with cheese.

Spicy Pasta

Serves 1   Preparation 15 mins   Cooking 12 mins
Per portion 606 kcals, 25g fat (9.8g saturated)

75g (3oz) pasta shapes
110g (4oz) fromage frais
1 tbsp sweet chilli sauce
25g (1oz) salami or garlic sausage, cut into
strips
½ yellow or red pepper, deseeded and
diced
2 spring onions, trimmed and sliced
25 (1oz) pitted black olives, halved
Parsley to garnish

Cook pasta in boiling water for 10–12
minutes.
Combine fromage frais with chilli sauce in
bowl.
Drain pasta and stir into sauce with salami or
sausage, pepper, onions and olives.
Serve garnished with parsley.

Fish Kebabs

Serves 1   Preparation 25 mins   Cooking 10 mins
Per portion 268 kcals, 4g fat (1.5g saturated)

110g (4oz) white fish fillet, cubed
4 unpeeled prawns
1 pepper, deseeded and cut into chunks
1 small courgette, cut into chunks
1 tsp lemon juice
Cayenne pepper
65g (2½oz) natural yogurt
½ tsp grated lemon rind
½ tsp chopped dill

Thread fish, prawns, pepper and courgette
on to 2 skewers, brush with lemon juice and
sprinkle with cayenne pepper.
Place under grill and cook for 10 minutes or
until fish is cooked, turning occasionally.
Blend together yogurt, lemon rind and
chopped dill.
Serve kebabs with yogurt dip.

Variation

Mixed Fish Kebabs

Follow recipe for Fish Kebabs. Omit prawns
and pepper. Use 75g (3oz) white fish fillet
and 75g (3oz) smoked fish fillet, cubed.
Thread on to 2 skewers with courgette, 4
cherry tomatoes and 4 button mushrooms.

Tuna Pasta

Serves 1   Preparation 20 mins   Cooking 15 mins
Per portion 624 kcals, 19g fat (1.7g saturated)

50g (2oz) pasta shapes
2 tsp cornflour
175ml (6fl oz) milk
Pinch of nutmeg
Salt and freshly ground black pepper
40g (1½oz) Double Gloucester cheese, grated
25g (1oz) mushrooms, wiped and sliced
¼ green pepper, deseeded and sliced
¼ red pepper, deseeded and sliced
50g (2oz) canned sweetcorn, drained
120g can tuna, drained and flaked

Cook pasta in boiling water for 10–12 minutes. Drain well.
Meanwhile, blend cornflour with a little milk. Stir in remaining milk.
Heat, whisking continuously until sauce boils, thickens and is smooth. Cook for a minute. Add nutmeg and season to taste.
Add cheese, vegetables, tuna and pasta. Mix well and heat through.

Pan-fried chicken with figs

Serves 1   Preparation 20 mins   Cooking 15 mins
Per portion 532 kcals, 23g fat (1.5g saturated)

1 chicken breast, skinned
Salt and freshly ground black pepper
25g (1oz) butter
Juice of ½ lemon
125ml (4fl oz) white wine
4 ready-to-eat dried figs
1 tbsp honey
½ tsp Dijon mustard

Make two long cuts in rounded side of chicken breast. Season well.
Melt butter in a frying pan, cook chicken breast, scored-side down, for 3–4 minutes until lightly browned.
Turn chicken and cook the other side until it's no longer pink in the centre. Keep warm.
Skim off any excess fat from pan juices, then add lemon juice, wine and figs. Bring to the boil, stirring.
Remove figs. Add honey and mustard to frying pan and boil gently, stirring continuously, until the sauce is slightly reduced and thickened.
Serve chicken and figs with sauce.

One-Pan Pasta for One

Serves 1   Preparation 5 mins   Cooking 25 mins
Per portion 552 kcals, 18g fat (3.1g saturated)

1 tbsp sunflower oil
1 chicken breast, skinned and chopped
1 small courgette, chopped
1 small red pepper, deseeded and sliced
1 garlic clove, peeled and crushed, optional
227g can chopped tomatoes
50g (2oz) pasta shapes
1 tbsp pesto sauce
Salt and freshly ground black pepper

Heat oil and cook chicken for 1–2 minutes, turning occasionally.
Add courgette, pepper, and garlic, if using. Cook for 5–7 minutes, until vegetables have softened, stirring regularly.
Add tomatoes and 150ml (¼ pint) boiling water and bring to the boil.
Add pasta and cook for 15 minutes or until the pasta is tender. Stir occasionally to prevent sticking.
Stir in pesto sauce and season to taste.

Pork Simla

Serves 1   Preparation 10 mins   Cooking 30 mins
Per portion 598 kcals, 33g fat (1.1g saturated)

110g (4oz) pork fillet, diced
15g (½oz) plain flour
15g (½oz) butter
1 small onion, peeled and chopped
½ tsp curry powder
½ tsp cayenne pepper
150ml (¼ pint) milk
1 tbsp mango chutney
15g (½oz) sultanas
50ml (2fl oz) soured cream

Coat pork in flour.
Melt butter in a saucepan, then fry onion and pork until browned.
Stir in curry powder, cayenne pepper and milk.
Bring to the boil and simmer until pork is tender.
Add chutney and sultanas and simmer for 5 minutes.
Remove pork from heat. Add cream and reheat but do not let boil.

Corned Beef Hash

Corned Beef Hash ❄

Serves 1   Preparation 15 mins   Cooking 20 mins
Per portion 634 kcals, 36g fat (1.7g saturated)

225g (8oz) potatoes, peeled and halved
15g (½oz) butter
1 tbsp olive oil
1 small onion, peeled and chopped
¼ green pepper, deseeded and chopped
¼ yellow pepper, deseeded and chopped
110g (4oz) corned beef, cubed
Freshly ground pepper

Boil potatoes for 10 minutes until just tender but firm. Drain, cool slightly and cube.

Heat butter and 2 tsp oil in a non-stick frying pan. Add potatoes and fry until golden. Remove to a plate.

Add remaining oil, onion and peppers. Cook for 3 minutes, stirring. Add beef and potatoes.Cook until heated through. Season.

Quick Kidneys ❄

Serves 1   Preparation 10 mins   Cooking 20 mins
Per portion 360 kcals, 18g fat (9.4g saturated)

150g (5oz) lamb's kidneys, halved
15g (½oz) butter
227g can chopped tomatoes
50ml (2fl oz) lamb or chicken stock
50g (2oz) mushrooms, wiped and sliced
50g (2oz) frozen sweetcorn
50g (2oz) frozen peas

Remove and discard skin and core from kidneys and cut into bite-size pieces.

Melt butter in a non-stick frying pan, add kidneys and cook until lightly brown.

Add tomatoes, stock and mushrooms. Bring to the boil and simmer for 10 minutes.

Add frozen vegetables, bring back to the boil and cook for a further 5 minutes. Stir occasionally.

Serves Two

Spicy Beanburgers   V

Serves 2 Preparation 5 mins Cooking 15 mins
Per portion 396 kcals, 22g fat (3.2g saturated)

3 tbsp olive oil
1 small red onion, finely chopped
1 garlic clove, peeled and crushed
Pinch of chilli flakes
400g can butter beans, rinsed
2 tbsp chopped coriander
50g (2oz) breadcrumbs
1 tbsp ground cumin
1 egg yolk
Salt and freshly ground black pepper

Heat 1 tbsp oil in a frying pan and cook onion, garlic and chilli for 2–3 minutes, until softened but not browned.
Mash butter beans. Stir in onion mixture and remaining ingredients (except oil).
Shape mixture into two burgers and chill until required.
Fry burgers in remaining oil for 3–4 minutes on each side until golden.

Leicester Cheese Pudding   V

Serves 2 Preparation 20 mins plus 30 mins standing
Cooking 30 mins
Per portion 667 kcals, 43g fat (2.5g saturated)

4 slices wholemeal bread, crusts removed
15g (½oz) butter, softened
25g (1oz) crunchy peanut butter
110g (4oz) Red Leicester cheese, grated
1 tbsp chopped parsley
2 eggs
300ml (½ pint) milk
½ tsp mustard
Salt and freshly ground black pepper

Make sandwiches using bread, butter, peanut butter and 50g (2oz) cheese.
Cut into triangles and arrange in a shallow, greased 600ml (1 pint) ovenproof dish.
Mix parsley and remaining cheese together and sprinkle over sandwiches.
Whisk together eggs, milk, mustard and seasoning. Pour over sandwiches and leave to stand for 30 minutes.
Bake at 180°C (350°F) Mark 4 for 30 minutes until set and golden.

Spinach & Pine Nut Pasta   V

Serves 2 Preparation 10 mins Cooking 20 mins
Per portion 880 kcals, 40g fat (19.4g saturated)

225g (8oz) pasta shapes
Salt and freshly ground black pepper
15g (½oz) butter
300g (11oz) baby spinach, washed
110g (4oz) blue cheese
4 tbsp single cream
45g (1½oz) seedless raisins
Pinch of ground nutmeg
25g (1oz) pine nuts, toasted

Cook pasta according to packet. Drain, return to saucepan and add butter.
Put spinach in clean saucepan, cover and cook for 4–5 minutes until wilted. Drain, then chop finely.
Crumble cheese into a saucepan with cream and raisins. Heat until sauce is creamy. Add spinach, pepper and nutmeg and stir.
Toss pasta in the sauce and serve with pine nuts over scattered over the top.

Gingered Fish

Serves 2 Preparation 20 mins Cooking 15 mins
Per portion 324 kcals, 15g fat (8.6g saturated)

15g (½oz) butter
1 onion, peeled and sliced
1cm (½in) piece root ginger, peeled and chopped
1 garlic clove, peeled and crushed
1 small red pepper, deseeded and chopped
175g (6oz) cauliflower florets
225g (8oz) boned monkfish, cubed
¼ tsp turmeric
150ml (¼ pint) milk
110g (4oz) reduced fat soft cheese
Chopped chives to garnish

Melt butter in a non-stick saucepan and add onion, ginger and garlic. Cook until soft.
Add pepper, cauliflower, fish and turmeric. Cook stirring for 2 minutes.
Add milk, bring to the boil, cover and simmer for 5 minutes.
Mix soft cheese with a little of the hot milk and stir into vegetables and fish. Heat gently without boiling.
Serve sprinkled with chopped chives.

Herby Chicken Couscous

Tuna Baked Aubergine ❄

Serves 2 Preparation 25 mins plus 30 mins standing
Cooking 45 mins
Per portion 390 kcals, 21g fat (1.2g saturated)

1 aubergine
Salt
15g (½oz) butter
1 onion, peeled and finely chopped
1 garlic clove, peeled and crushed
110g (4oz) canned tuna, drained and flaked
110g (4oz) cooked brown rice
Pinch of ground bay leaves
½ tsp lemon juice
2 tbsp chicken stock
½ tsp tomato purée
75g (3oz) Double Gloucester cheese, grated

Halve aubergine lengthways. Sprinkle cut
surfaces with salt and stand for 30 minutes.
Rinse and dry with kitchen paper. Scoop out
flesh, leaving shell intact. Chop flesh.
Melt butter in saucepan, add onion, garlic
and aubergine. Cook for 4 minutes, stirring.
Stir in tuna, rice, bay leaves, lemon juice,
stock, tomato purée and half the cheese.
Fill aubergine shells with stuffing. Place in
an ovenproof dish and top with remaining
cheese. Add 3 tbsp water to dish.
Bake at 190°C (375°F) Mark 5 for 40 minutes.
Cover with foil after 20 minutes.

Herby Chicken Couscous

Serves 2 Preparation 5 mins Cooking 15 mins
Per portion 809 kcals, 37g fat (5g saturated)

200g (7oz) couscous
300ml (½ pint) hot chicken stock
50g (2oz) pine nuts
2 chicken breasts, skinned and thinly
sliced
3 tbsp olive oil
2 tbsp chopped mint
75g (3oz) raisins
Salt and freshly ground black pepper
2 tbsp lemon juice

Put couscous in a large bowl, add stock and
leave for 5 minutes.
Heat a frying pan, add pine nuts and toast for
about 2 minutes.
Tip pine nuts over couscous.
Add 1 tbsp of olive oil to frying pan and
cook chicken for 6–8 minutes, until cooked
through.
Meanwhile, add chopped mint and raisins
to couscous and season. Toss ingredients
together.
Mix remaining olive oil in a small bowl with
lemon juice.
Spoon couscous on to serving plates, pile
chicken on top and drizzle with lemon
dressing.

Bacon & Cheese Potatoes

Savoury Crumble

Serves 2   Preparation 15 mins   Cooking 35 mins
Per portion 599 kcals, 28g fat (1.7g saturated)

50g (2oz) wholemeal flour
50g (2oz) butter
½ tsp mustard powder
Pinch of cayenne pepper
½ tsp paprika
15g (½oz) oats
225g (8oz) chicken breasts, diced
25g (1oz) plain flour
150ml (¼ pint) milk
150g (5oz) natural yogurt
175g (6oz) broccoli florets, blanched
15g (1oz) ready-to-eat dried apricots, chopped

Place wholemeal flour in a bowl and rub in 25g (1oz) butter until mixture resembles fine breadcrumbs.
Stir in mustard, cayenne pepper, paprika and oats.
Place chicken and remaining butter in a saucepan. Fry gently for 10 minutes.
Stir in plain flour and cook for a minute.
Gradually add milk and yogurt. Heat, stirring continuously, until sauce boils, thickens and is smooth.

Add broccoli and apricots. Cook for 2 minutes.
Pour sauce mixture into a 600ml (1 pint) ovenproof dish and top with crumble.
Bake at 190°C (375°F) Mark 5 for 20 minutes.

Variation

Pork & Broccoli Crumble

Follow recipe and method for Savoury Crumble. Omit chicken and dried apricots. Use 225g (8oz) diced pork fillet.

Bacon & Cheese Potatoes

Serves 2   Preparation 10 mins   Cooking 1 hr 5 mins
Per portion 402 kcals, 15g fat (8.6g saturated)

2 x 225g (8oz) potatoes, scrubbed
2 bacon rashers
175g (6oz) cottage cheese
½ tsp chopped parsley
50g (2oz) Cheddar cheese, grated

Prick potato skins and bake at 200°C (400°F) Mark 6 for 1 hour or until soft when pinched.
Crisply grill bacon.
Chop bacon and mix with cottage cheese and parsley.
Cut open potatoes and spoon in filling. Top with grated cheese.

Variation

Spicy Sweet Potatoes

Follow recipe and method for Bacon & Cheese Potatoes. Use sweet potatoes in place of the potatoes. For the filling, mix cottage cheese with 1 tsp sweet chilli sauce (or to taste) and chopped coriander. Top with grated cheese.

Smoky Cauliflower Supper ❄

Serves 2   Preparation 25 mins   Cooking 25 mins
Per portion 578 kcals, 36g fat (1.9g saturated)

1 cauliflower, cut into florets
4 rashers streaky bacon, cut in half
25g (1oz) butter
1 small onion, peeled and chopped
25g (1oz) plain flour
300ml (½ pint) milk
Salt and freshly ground black pepper
75g (3oz) smoked Cheddar cheese, grated
½ tsp French mustard
1 rye crispbread, crushed

Steam cauliflower for 10 minutes or until tender.
When cooked, drain and place in a shallow flameproof dish.
Stretch bacon and roll up. Grill until crisp.
Melt butter in a saucepan. Add onion and fry until soft.
Stir in plain flour and milk and heat, whisking continuously, until sauce thickens, boils and is smooth.
Cook for a minute. Add seasoning.
Remove from heat, add 50g (2oz) cheese and mustard. Stir until melted. Pour over cauliflower.
Combine crispbread and remaining Cheddar cheese. Sprinkle over cauliflower and grill until golden.
Garnish cauliflower with bacon rolls and serve.

Redcurrant Lamb Chops

Serves 2   Preparation 5 mins   Cooking 25 mins
Per portion 457 kcals, 30g fat (1.3g saturated)

4 lamb loin chops
2 tbsp redcurrant jelly
1 tsp orange juice
Pinch of ground ginger

Grill chops for 5–10 minutes on each side, depending on thickness.
Place remaining ingredients in a small saucepan, heat until jelly has melted. Stir to mix well.
Brush over chops and grill for a further minute. Turn chops over and repeat.

Steak in Red Wine Sauce

Serves 2   Preparation 5 mins   Cooking 15 mins
Per portion 408 kcals, 26g fat (1g saturated)

25g (1oz) butter
2 x 175g (6oz) sirloin steaks, trimmed of excess fat
50g (2oz) mushrooms, wiped and sliced
1 tsp wholegrain mustard
75ml (3fl oz) red wine
50ml (2fl oz) beef stock

Melt butter in a frying pan and when foaming add steaks.
Fry briskly for 1 minute each side.
Lower heat. Continue to fry for a further 3–4 minutes for rare, 4–5 minutes for medium or 7–8 minutes for well-done steak.
Turn steaks about every minute to ensure even cooking.
Transfer steaks to a plate and keep warm.
Add mushrooms and cook for 2 minutes.
Blend mustard with wine and stock. Add to pan and boil for 2 minutes to reduce liquid.
Serve steaks with sauce.

Steaks with Stilton Sauce

Serves 2   Preparation 10 mins   Cooking 15 mins
Per portion 758 kcals, 63g fat (34.5g saturated)

2 x 175g (6oz) sirloin steaks, trimmed of excess fat
15g (½oz) butter
1 small onion, peeled and finely chopped
2 tbsp sherry
125ml (4fl oz) double cream
50g (2oz) Stilton cheese, crumbled
1 tbsp chopped chives

Grill steaks to your liking (see recipe above).
Melt butter in a saucepan and cook onion until soft.
Add sherry and boil to reduce slightly.
Add cream and boil for 1 minute.
Stir in Stilton and chives.
Serve steaks with sauce.

Pilau Rice

Rice

Boiled Rice

Method One
Serves 4   Cooking 20 mins
Per portion 203 kcals, 1g fat (0g saturated)

225g (8oz) long grain rice

Rinse rice thoroughly under running cold water. Place in a large saucepan with 600ml (1 pint) water.

Bring to the boil, then stir to loosen grains.

Cover with a well fitting lid. Reduce heat and simmer for 15–20 minutes or until rice is tender and water has been absorbed, but the rice isn't sticking to the bottom of the saucepan.

Stir with a fork to separate grains.

This volume method of cooking rice depends on having twice the amount of liquid to rice. This can be used for any quantity of rice.

Cook brown rice in 750ml (1¼ pints) water for 25–30 minutes.

Variations

Onion Rice

Follow the recipe and method for Boiled Rice. After cooking add 1 chopped onion, fried in butter.

Lemon & Butter Rice

Add a thick slice of lemon to the rice before cooking. Follow recipe and method for Boiled Rice. Remove lemon and stir in 40g (1½oz) butter before serving.

Boiled Rice

Method Two
Serves 4   Cooking 20 mins
Per portion 203 kcals, 1g fat (0.4g saturated)

225g (8oz) long grain rice, rinsed

Place rice in a large saucepan of boiling water.

Bring back to the boil and stir to loosen grains.

Cover saucepan, lower heat and simmer for 15–20 minutes or until rice is tender.

Drain and rinse with a kettle of boiling water through a colander or sieve.

Cook brown rice for 25–30 minutes.

Pilau Rice   ❄ V
Serves 4–6   Preparation 5 mins plus 30 mins soaking
Cooking 25 mins
Per portion 257 kcals, 3g fat (0.4g saturated)

275g (10oz) basmati rice
1 tbsp olive oil
½ tsp cumin seeds
4 green cardamoms
4 cloves
2.5cm (1in) stick of cinnamon
1 bay leaf

Place rice in a sieve and wash under cold running water.

Leave to soak in cold water for 30 minutes. Drain well.

Heat oil in a saucepan, add spices and fry for 1 minute.

Stir in rice. Add sufficient cold water to come to 2.5cm (1in) above top of rice.

Bring to the boil, cover, reduce heat and simmer for 20 minutes or until rice is tender and water absorbed.

Gently stir with a fork to separate grains and serve.

Alternatively, add 1 tsp turmeric to rice before cooking for yellow pilau rice.

Nutty Rice Salad   V
Serves 4–6   Preparation 5 mins   Cooking 30 mins
Per portion 454 kcals, 20g fat (3.5g saturated)

225g (8oz) long grain brown rice
175g (6oz) frozen peas
175g (6oz) frozen sweetcorn
French Dressing made with 4 tbsp oil (page 62)
50g (2oz) roasted peanuts

Place rice in a large saucepan of boiling water.

Bring back to the boil and stir to loosen grains.

Cover saucepan, lower heat and simmer for 25–30 minutes or until rice is tender.

Add peas and sweetcorn for last 5 minutes of cooking time.

Drain and rinse under cold water until rice is tepid.

Stir dressing and peanuts into rice.

Spoon into a serving bowl and chill until ready to serve.

Thai Prawn & Rice Salad

Serves 4   Preparation 20 mins   Cooking 15 mins
Per portion 565 kcals, 33g fat (20.7g saturated)

150g (5oz) long grain rice
250ml carton coconut cream
1–2 tsp Thai green curry paste
350g (12oz) large frozen peeled prawns, thawed
¼ cucumber, diced
½ red onion, peeled and thinly sliced
4 tbsp chopped parsley
75g (3oz) cashew nuts, toasted

Cook rice in boiling water for 15–20 minutes until tender.
Rinse and drain rice.
In a large bowl, mix together coconut cream and curry paste.
Add rice, prawns, cucumber, onion and 3 tbsp parsley. Mix well.
Serve scattered with remaining parsley and cashew nuts.

Stuffed Peppers   V

Serves 4   Preparation 15 mins   Cooking 25 mins
Per portion 346 kcals, 22g fat (13.2g saturated)

4 red or green peppers
225g (8oz) freshly cooked rice (about 110g/4oz raw)
75g (3oz) cooked sliced mushrooms
50g (2oz) cooked peas
110g (4oz) Lancashire cheese, grated
½ tsp English mustard
150ml (¼ pint) single cream
Salt and freshly ground black pepper
25g (1oz) butter

Cut tops off peppers. Remove inside seeds and fibres.
Put peppers into a large saucepan of boiling water and simmer for 2 minutes.
Carefully lift out peppers. Stand upside down to drain on absorbent kitchen paper. Set aside.
Mix together rice, mushrooms, peas, cheese, mustard and cream. Season to taste.
Stand peppers in a shallow ovenproof dish. Fill with cheese and rice mixture.
Put a knob of butter on top of each pepper. Cover with foil.
Bake at 180°C (350° F) Mark 4 for 20 minutes.

Squash & Bean Risotto   V

Serves 4   Preparation 10 mins   Cooking 40 mins
Per portion 570 kcals, 24g fat (11.6g saturated)

1 butternut squash (about 900g/2lb), peeled, deseeded and chopped
2 tbsp olive oil
50g (2oz) butter
1 onion, peeled and chopped
1 garlic clove, peeled and crushed
250g (9oz) arborio or risotto rice
150ml (¼ pint) dry cider
750ml (1¼ pints) vegetable stock
150g (5oz) frozen broad beans
Salt and freshly ground black pepper
75g (3oz) Stilton cheese, crumbled
8 sage leaves, shredded

Roast squash with 1 tbsp oil at 200°C (400°F) Mark 6 for 40 minutes.
Heat remaining oil with butter in a large saucepan and cook onion for 5 minutes.
Add garlic and rice and cook for 2 minutes.
Pour in cider and cook until almost absorbed. Add 200ml (7fl oz) stock. Cook over a low heat, adding stock a little at a time.
With last addition of stock, add beans.
When rice is cooked, mash squash and add to risotto with juices from roasting tin. Season and serve scattered with crumbled cheese and shredded sage.

Nutty Bean Pilaff   V

Serves 4–6   Preparation 5 mins   Cooking 40 mins
Per portion 506 kcals, 23g fat (6.9g saturated)

225g (8oz) brown basmati rice
25g (1oz) butter
1 onion, peeled and chopped
3 celery sticks, sliced
110g (4oz) chestnut mushrooms, wiped and sliced
400g can red kidney beans, rinsed
2 tbsp pesto sauce
110g (4oz) cashew nuts, toasted

Cook rice in boiling water for about 25 minutes or until tender. Drain.
Meanwhile, melt butter in a saucepan. Add onion, celery and mushrooms and cook, stirring, for 5 minutes.
Add mushroom mixture, beans, pesto and nuts to rice. Heat through and stir to mix.

Koulibiac

Koulibiac

Serves 4   Preparation 35 mins   Cooking 1 hr
Per portion 812 kcals, 53g fat (23.6g saturated)

110g (4oz) long grain rice
418g can red salmon, drained
25g (1oz) butter
1 small onion, peeled and chopped
50g (2oz) mushrooms, wiped and sliced
2 eggs, hard-boiled, shelled and chopped
2 tbsp chopped parsley
4 tbsp double cream
2 tbsp sherry
Salt and freshly ground black pepper
375g (13oz) puff pastry
Beaten egg to glaze

Cook rice in boiling water for 8–10 minutes, or until tender. Drain well.
Remove and discard skin and bones from salmon. Flake the flesh.
Melt butter in a saucepan and fry onion and mushrooms for 3 minutes.
Add to rice with salmon, eggs, parsley, cream and sherry. Season to taste.
Roll out pastry on a floured work surface to a 30cm (12in) square.
Spoon filling down centre of pastry. Brush edges of pastry with beaten egg.
Bring together edges of pastry and seal at ends and down the centre. Invert on to a baking sheet and brush with beaten egg.

Score pastry with a knife in a diamond pattern.
Bake at 200°C (400° F) Mark 6 for 40 minutes or until golden brown.

Risotto Milanese

Serves 4   Preparation 10 mins   Cooking 30 mins
Per portion 404 kcals, 11g fat (6.1g saturated)

Few saffron strands
25g (1oz) butter
1 small onion, peeled and finely chopped
350g (12oz) arborio or risotto rice
900ml (1½ pints) hot chicken stock
Salt and freshly ground black pepper
50g (2oz) mature Cheddar, grated

Place saffron in a cup with 3 tbsp hot water and leave to stand.
Melt butter in a large saucepan. Add onion and fry for 5 minutes.
Add rice and stir to coat with butter.
Add 125ml (4fl oz) hot stock to rice, cook gently, stirring frequently, until absorbed.
Add a little more stock; when it is absorbed, add a little more. Stir frequently.
Continue until all the stock has been added. This should take about 25 minutes until rice is thick, creamy and tender.
Add saffron in its water and season to taste.
Stir in most of the cheese. Serve with remaining cheese.

145

Paella

Serves 4–6 Preparation 25 mins Cooking 35 mins
Per portion 620 kcals, 16g fat (6g saturated)

25g (1oz) butter
1 tbsp olive oil
8 chicken thighs, skinned
1 onion, peeled and chopped
2 garlic cloves, peeled and crushed
225g (8oz) long grain rice
1 tsp saffron strands
600ml (1 pint) chicken stock
1 bay leaf
225g (8oz) frozen peas
1 red pepper, deseeded and diced
2 tomatoes, quartered
110g (4oz) cooked peeled prawns
110g (4oz) cooked shelled mussels
Lemon wedges to garnish

Heat butter and oil in a large frying pan. Add chicken and fry until lightly browned. Remove and keep warm.
Add onion and garlic to pan and fry until golden.
Add rice and cook for a minute, stirring.
Return chicken to pan with saffron, stock and bay leaf. Bring to the boil, cover and simmer slowly for 15 minutes.
Stir occasionally and add more stock if necessary.
Uncover and stir in vegetables. Recover and cook for 5 minutes, or until peas are cooked through.
Add cooked prawns and mussels and heat through.
Serve garnished with lemon wedges.

Special Fried Rice

Serves 6 Preparation 15 mins Cooking 20 mins
Per portion 201 kcals, 9g fat (4.4g saturated)

40g (1½oz) butter
6 spring onions, trimmed and sliced
1 garlic clove, peeled and crushed
50g (2oz) mushrooms, wiped and sliced
2 eggs, beaten
350g (12oz) cooked long grain rice
75g (3oz) cooked ham, diced
110g (4oz) frozen peas
110g (4oz) frozen sweetcorn
Soy sauce to serve

Melt butter in a wok or frying pan. Add onions, garlic and mushrooms. Cook stirring for 5 minutes. Remove to a plate.
Add eggs to wok or pan and cook until lightly scrambled.
Return onion mixture to wok or pan, then add rice, ham and remaining vegetables.
Cook, stirring, for 5–10 minutes or until rice is heated and peas and sweetcorn are cooked through.
Serve accompanied with soy sauce.

Stuffed Minced Beef Peppers ❄

Serves 4 Preparation 15 mins Cooking 30 mins
Per portion 280 kcals, 12g fat (5.6g saturated)

4 red or green peppers
225g (8oz) lean minced beef
1 onion, peeled and finely chopped
75g (3oz) mushrooms, wiped and sliced
225g (8oz) freshly cooked rice (about 110g/4oz raw)
2 tomatoes, chopped
2 tsp Worcestershire sauce
Salt and freshly ground black pepper
25g (1oz) butter

Cut tops off peppers. Remove inside seeds and fibres.
Put peppers into a large saucepan of boiling water and simmer for 2 minutes.
Carefully lift out peppers. Stand upside down to drain on absorbent kitchen paper. Set aside.
Dry fry beef in a non-stick frying pan until browned. Add onion and mushrooms and cook for 3 minutes.
Stir in rice, tomatoes and Worcestershire sauce. Season to taste.
Stand peppers in a shallow ovenproof dish. Stuff with meat and rice mixture.
Pour 65ml (2½fl oz) water into dish. Put a knob of butter on top of each pepper.
Bake at 180°C (350° F) Mark 4 for 20 minutes.

Rice

There are more than 100,000 varieties of rice. The most commonly used type is white or brown long-grain (Patna) rice. Basmati rice is often served with curry. There are also medium-grain and short-grain rices that have a softer texture.

Pasta

Salmon Pasta Bake ❄

Serves 4   Preparation 20 mins   Cooking 25 mins
Per portion 350 kcals, 15g fat (7.5g saturated)

110g (4oz) pasta shapes
15g (½oz) butter
1 onion, peeled and chopped
25g (1oz) wholemeal flour
300ml (½ pint) milk
75g (3oz) Cheddar cheese, grated
213g can pink salmon, drained and flaked
1 tbsp chopped parsley
Freshly ground black pepper
1 tomato, sliced
25g (1oz) wholemeal breadcrumbs

Cook pasta in boiling water for 10–12 minutes until tender.
Meanwhile, melt butter in a saucepan and cook onion until soft.
Stir in flour, then gradually stir in milk and cook, stirring, until sauce thickens, boils and is smooth. Cook for a minute.
Remove from heat, then stir in half the cheese, flaked salmon, drained pasta, parsley and pepper. Spoon into a flameproof dish.
Arrange tomato on top.
Mix breadcrumbs and remaining cheese and sprinkle over tomato.
Either grill until toasted or bake at 200°C (400° F) Mark 6 for 15 minutes.

Macaroni Cheese ❄ V

Serves 4   Preparation 10 mins   Cooking 15 mins
Per portion 540 kcals, 26g fat (15.4g saturated)

225g (8oz) macaroni
40g (1½oz) butter
40g (1½oz) plain flour
½ tsp mustard powder
600ml (1 pint) milk
175g (6oz) Lancashire or Cheddar cheese, grated
Salt and freshly ground black pepper

Cook macaroni in boiling water for 7–10 minutes until tender.
Meanwhile, melt butter in a saucepan, add flour and mustard and cook slowly for 2 minutes. Stir often and do not allow mixture to brown.

Gradually blend in milk. Cook, stirring, until sauce thickens, boils and is smooth. Simmer for 2 minutes and remove from heat.
Stir in 110g (4oz) cheese. Season to taste.
Drain macaroni, then add to sauce and mix.
Transfer to a 1.1litre (2 pint) greased flameproof dish.
Sprinkle remaining cheese on top and brown under a hot grill.
If prepared in advance, reheat at 200°C (400° F) Mark 6 for 25 minutes.

Variation

Macaroni Cheese with Bacon ❄

Follow recipe and method for Macaroni Cheese. Add 110g (4oz) chopped and lightly fried bacon to sauce with macaroni.

Pasticcio ❄

Serves 4   Preparation 30 mins   Cooking 50 mins
Per portion 652 kcals, 27g fat (14.6g saturated)

225g (8oz) macaroni
225g (8oz) lean minced beef
50g (2oz) bacon, chopped
1 onion, peeled and chopped
1 carrot, peeled and chopped
1 celery stick, sliced
1 garlic clove, peeled and crushed
2 tbsp tomato purée
225ml (8fl oz) beef stock
225g (8oz) frozen peas
50g (2oz) plain flour
50g (2oz) butter
600ml (1 pint) milk
50g (2oz) Double Gloucester cheese, grated

Cook macaroni in boiling water for 7–10 minutes until tender.
Brown beef in a non-stick frying pan.
Add bacon, onion, carrot, celery, garlic, tomato purée and stock. Bring to the boil, cover and simmer gently for 40 minutes.
Mix meat, drained macaroni and peas. Place in an ovenproof dish.
Place flour, butter and milk in a saucepan. Heat, stirring, until sauce thickens, boils and is smooth. Cook for a minute.
Remove from heat, add half the cheese and stir until melted. Season to taste.
Pour over beef and sprinkle with remaining Double Gloucester cheese.

Beef & Noodle Bake

Beef & Noodle Bake

Serves 4–6 Preparation 20 mins Cooking 1 hr 5 mins
Per portion 651 kcals, 35g fat (17.6g saturated)

450g (1lb) lean minced beef
1 onion, peeled and chopped
1 green pepper, deseeded and chopped
2 garlic cloves, peeled and chopped
300g canned chopped tomatoes
1 vegetable stock cube
175g (6oz) egg noodles
275g (10oz) soured cream
225g (8oz) cottage cheese
50g (2oz) Double Gloucester cheese, grated
1 egg, beaten
Salt and freshly ground black pepper

Brown mince in a non-stick frying pan.
Add vegetables, garlic, tomatoes and stock
cube, bring to the boil, cover and simmer for
15 minutes, stirring occasionally.
Spoon into an ovenproof dish.
Meanwhile, cook noodles as on packet's
instructions and drain.
Mix soured cream and cottage cheese with

noodles. Spoon over meat.
Mix cheese with egg and seasoning and
spoon over the top.
Cook at 180°C (350° F) Mark 4 for 45 minutes.

Spaghetti Neapolitan   V

Serves 4 Preparation 2 mins Cooking 12 mins
Per portion 475 kcals, 14g fat (6.6g saturated)

350g (12oz) spaghetti
Freshly made tomato sauce made with 400g
(14oz) tomatoes (page 182)
110g (4oz) Cheddar cheese, grated

Cook spaghetti in boiling water for 10–12
minutes or until tender.
Drain well. Transfer equal amounts to
plates. Pour sauce over. Sprinkle with cheese.

Variation

Spaghetti Marinara

Follow recipe and method for Spaghetti
Neapolitan. Add 175g (6oz) cooked, peeled
prawns and 110g (4oz) cooked, shelled
mussels and heat through before serving.

Spaghetti Bolognese

Serves 4   Preparation 20 mins   Cooking 1 hr
Per portion 593 kcals, 19g fat (6.5g saturated)

1 tbsp olive oil
50g (2oz) streaky bacon, chopped
1 onion, peeled and finely chopped
2 celery sticks, finely chopped
1 carrot, peeled and finely chopped
110g (4oz) mushrooms, wiped and sliced
1 garlic clove, peeled and crushed
450g (1lb) lean minced beef
350ml (12fl oz) beef stock
2 tbsp tomato purée
1 bay leaf
½ tsp dried oregano
350g (12oz) spaghetti

Heat oil in a saucepan and cook bacon until it starts to brown.
Add vegetables and garlic and cook, stirring, until golden.
Add beef and cook until brown.
Add stock, tomato purée and herbs and bring to the boil. Cover and cook for 45–50 minutes on a low heat. Stir occasionally.
Meanwhile, cook spaghetti in boiling water for 10–12 minutes or until tender, stirring often to prevent sticking. Drain.
Serve pasta with Bolognese sauce.

Tagliatelle with Ham

Serves 4   Preparation 15 mins   Cooking 10 mins
Per portion 549 kcals, 27g fat (14.7g saturated)

275g (10oz) tagliatelle
15g (½oz) butter
1 onion, peeled and chopped
175g (6oz) frozen peas
175g (6oz) frozen sweetcorn
150ml (¼ pint) vegetable stock
1 tbsp cornflour
300ml (½ pint) single cream
175g (6oz) cooked smoked ham, cut into strips
Freshly ground black pepper
50g (2oz) Caerphilly cheese, grated

Cook tagliatelle in boiling water for 8–10 minutes or until tender.
Meanwhile, melt butter in a saucepan and cook onion until soft. Add peas, sweetcorn and stock and cook for 2 minutes.

Blend cornflour with a little cold water. Stir into vegetables with cream and ham. Cook gently until thickened. Season to taste.
Drain tagliatelle and stir into sauce. Serve sprinkled with cheese.

Variation

Tagliatelle with Tuna

Follow recipe and method for Tagliatelle with Ham. Omit smoked ham and Caerphilly cheese. Use a 185g can of tuna, drained and flaked, and 50g (2oz) grated Double Gloucester cheese.

Broccoli & Bacon Tagliatelle

Serves 4   Preparation 20 mins   Cooking 20 mins
Per portion 528 kcals, 19g fat (9.9g saturated)

275g (10oz) tagliatelle
175g (6oz) broccoli florets
25g (1oz) butter
75g (3oz) mushrooms, wiped and sliced
110g (4oz) smoked bacon, chopped
2 garlic cloves, peeled and crushed
1 tbsp chopped basil
40g (1½oz) plain flour
600ml (1 pint) milk
50g (2oz) Red Cheshire cheese, grated
Salt and freshly ground black pepper

Cook tagliatelle in boiling water for 5 minutes.
Add broccoli, return to the boil and cook for a further 5 minutes or until tender.
Melt butter in a saucepan, add mushrooms, bacon, garlic and basil. Cook for 5 minutes.
Add flour and milk and heat, stirring continuously, until sauce thickens, boils and is smooth. Cook for 1 minute.
Remove from heat. Add most of the cheese and stir until melted. Season to taste.
Stir drained tagliatelle into sauce. Serve sprinkled with remaining cheese.

Pasta

Pasta is available dried, fresh and stuffed, and can be made at home with a machine. It comes in many shapes, which are designed to trap the sauce they are served with. Two basic groups are long pastas such as spaghetti, and short varieties such as penne.

Vegetable Cannelloni

Vegetable Cannelloni ❋ V

Serves 4   Preparation 35 mins   Cooking 45 mins
Per portion 560 kcals, 22g fat (12.7g saturated)

15g (½oz) butter
1 small onion, peeled and finely chopped
110g (4oz) aubergines, diced
110g (4oz) courgettes, diced
2 tomatoes, chopped
1 garlic clove, peeled and crushed
125ml (4fl oz) tomato juice
40g (1½oz) plain flour
40g (1½oz) butter
450ml (¾ pint) milk
Salt and freshly ground black pepper
75g (3oz) Cheddar cheese, grated
4 tbsp natural yogurt
12 no pre-cook cannelloni tubes

Melt butter in a saucepan, then add vegetables, tomatoes, garlic and tomato juice. Cook for 10 minutes.

Place flour, butter and milk in a saucepan. Heat, stirring continuously, until sauce thickens, boils and is smooth. Cook for a minute. Season to taste.

Add 50g (2oz) cheese and yogurt to sauce, stir until melted.

Spoon vegetable mixture into cannelloni tubes. Place in an ovenproof dish and pour over sauce. Sprinkle with remaining cheese.

Bake at 180°C (350° F) Mark 4 for 30 minutes.

Vegetable Lasagne ❋ V

Serves 4   Preparation 45 mins   Cooking 50 mins
Per portion 542kcals, 30g fat (17.7g saturated)

350g (12oz) carrots, peeled and thinly sliced
350g (12oz) courgettes, thinly sliced
110g (4oz) mushrooms, wiped and sliced
1 onion, peeled and thinly sliced
1 green pepper, deseeded and thinly sliced
110g (4oz) celery, thinly sliced
1 vegetable stock cube
4 tbsp plain flour
50g (2oz) butter
600ml (1 pint) milk
Salt and freshly ground black pepper
110g (4oz) no pre-cook lasagne
175g (6oz) Cheddar cheese, grated

Place vegetables in a saucepan with stock cube and 200ml (7fl oz) water. Bring to the boil, cover and simmer for 10–15 minutes.

Place flour, butter and milk in a saucepan and heat, whisking continuously, until sauce thickens, boils and is smooth. Cook for a minute and season to taste.

Place half the vegetable mixture in base of a 25 x 20cm (10 x 8in) ovenproof dish.

Cover with half of the lasagne, some sauce and cheese. Repeat layers.

Top with remaining sauce and cheese.

Bake at 190°C (375° F) Mark 5 for 35 minutes.

Lentil Lasagne V

Serves 4 Preparation 25 mins Cooking 1 hr
Per portion 534 kcals, 21g fat (10.7g saturated)

15g (½oz) butter
1 onion, peeled and chopped
1 green pepper, deseeded and chopped
175g (6oz) split red lentils
400g can chopped tomatoes
300ml (½ pint) vegetable stock
300ml (½ pint) milk
2 tsp tomato purée
1 tsp dried mixed herbs
Freshly ground black pepper
110g (4oz) no pre-cook lasagne
2 eggs
225g (8oz) natural yogurt
110g (4oz) Cheddar cheese, grated

Melt butter in a saucepan, add onion and cook until soft.
Add pepper, lentils, tomatoes, stock, 150ml (¼ pint) milk, tomato purée, herbs and pepper. (It may look curdled to begin with, but just keep on stirring.)
Bring to the boil, cover and simmer for 15–20 minutes until lentils are tender.
Place half the lentil mixture in a 25 x 20cm (10 x 8in) ovenproof dish.
Cover with half the lasagne; repeat layers.
Whisk together eggs, remaining milk and yogurt. Stir in half the cheese and pour over lasagne.
Sprinkle remaining cheese over lasagne and bake at 200°C (400° F) Mark 6 for 35 minutes or until golden brown.

Broccoli & Stilton Lasagne V

Serves 4–6 Preparation 15 mins Cooking 1 hr
Per portion 591 kcals, 33g fat (19g saturated)

750g (1lb 10oz) broccoli florets
2 red peppers, deseeded and sliced
2 courgettes, sliced
50g (2oz) butter
50g (2oz) plain flour
600ml (1 pint) milk
175g (6oz) Stilton cheese, crumbled
Salt and freshly ground black pepper
6–8 sheets no pre-cook lasagne
Grated nutmeg
2 tbsp grated Cheddar cheese

Cook broccoli in boiling water for 2 minutes.
Add peppers and courgettes to saucepan and cook for a further 2 minutes.
Drain and cool vegetables under cold running water.
Place butter, flour and milk in a saucepan and heat, stirring constantly, until the sauce boils and is smooth.
Melt Stilton in sauce and season.
Spoon half of vegetables into a lasagne dish and top with a third of sauce. Cover with lasagne sheets.
Spoon remaining vegetables on top, then half of remaining sauce. Top with lasagne.
Pour remaining sauce on top, then sprinkle with nutmeg and cheese.
Bake for 40–50 minutes at 200°C (400°F) Mark 6, until bubbling and golden (cover with foil if browning too quickly).

Tuna & Sweetcorn Lasagne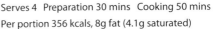

Serves 4 Preparation 30 mins Cooking 50 mins
Per portion 356 kcals, 8g fat (4.1g saturated)

400g can chopped tomatoes with herbs
1 onion, peeled and chopped
50g (2oz) mushrooms, wiped and sliced
1 green pepper, deseeded and sliced
1 garlic clove, peeled and crushed
2 x 185g cans tuna in brine, drained and flaked
110g (4oz) canned sweetcorn, drained
110g (4oz) ready-to-cook lasagne
2 tbsp cornflour
½ tsp mustard powder
450ml (¾ pint) milk
50g (2oz) mature Cheddar cheese, grated

Place vegetables and garlic in a saucepan, bring to the boil and cook for 3 minutes.
Stir in tuna and sweetcorn.
Layer in a 25 x 20cm (10 x 8in) ovenproof dish with lasagne.
Blend together cornflour, mustard and a little milk.
Heat remaining milk to boiling point, pour on to cornflour and stir well.
Return to heat and cook, stirring, until sauce thickens, boils and is smooth.
Stir in half the cheese and pour over lasagne.
Sprinkle remaining cheese over lasagne.
Bake at 200°C (400° F) Mark 6 for 35–40 minutes.

Seafood Lasagne

Seafood Lasagne

Serves 6   Preparation 20 mins   Cooking 50 mins
Per portion 368 kcals, 18g fat (10.3g saturated)

400g (14oz) smoked haddock
600ml (1 pint) milk
50g (2oz) butter
50g (2oz) plain flour
200g (7oz) cooked peeled prawns
75g (3oz) peas
Grated rind of ½ lemon
125g (5oz) fresh lasagne
1 egg, beaten
150g (5oz) natural yogurt
110g (4oz) Cheddar cheese, grated

Poach fish in milk for 10 minutes.

Reserve the milk; skin and flake the fish.

Place butter, flour and reserved milk in a saucepan. Heat, whisking, until sauce thickens and is smooth. Cook for a minute.

Add fish, prawns, peas and lemon rind.

Place half the mixture in a 25 x 20cm (10 x 8in) ovenproof dish.

Cover with half the lasagne and repeat.

Whisk together egg and yogurt, stir in half the cheese and pour over lasagne.

Sprinkle over remaining cheese and bake at 200°C (400° F) Mark 6 for 35 minutes.

Lasagne

Serves 4   Preparation 10 mins   Cooking 40 mins
Per portion 583 kcals, 31g fat (14.8g saturated)

25g (1oz) plain flour
25g (1oz) butter
450ml (¾ pint) milk
Pinch of ground nutmeg
½ tsp mustard
75g (3oz) Cheddar cheese, grated
Salt and freshly ground black pepper
75ml (3fl oz) beef stock
Bolognese sauce made with 450g (1lb) beef (page 149)
125g (4½oz) fresh lasagne

Place flour, butter and milk in a saucepan and heat, whisking, until sauce thickens, boils and is smooth. Cook for a minute.

Remove from heat. Add nutmeg, mustard and half the cheese and stir until melted. Season to taste.

Add stock to Bolognese sauce and place half the mixture in a 25 x 20cm (10 x 8in) ovenproof dish. Cover with half the lasagne sheets, repeat layers.

Pour cheese sauce over lasagne and sprinkle remaining cheese on top.

Bake at 200°C (400° F) Mark 4 for 35 minutes until golden and pasta is tender.

Pizza

Pizza Neapolitan ❋ V

Serves 2 Preparation 30 mins Cooking 35 mins
Per portion 465 kcals, 22g fat (9.8g saturated)

1 tbsp olive oil
1 small onion, peeled and finely chopped
1 garlic clove, peeled and crushed
227g can chopped tomatoes
2 tsp tomato purée
2 tsp dried mixed herbs
25g (1oz) button mushrooms, wiped and sliced
145g packet pizza base or bread mix
½ green pepper, deseeded and sliced
50g (2oz) Mozzarella cheese, grated
50g (2oz) Cheddar cheese, grated

Heat olive oil in a saucepan and fry onion and garlic until soft.

Add tomatoes, tomato purée and herbs. Bring to the boil and simmer for 5–10 minutes.

Add mushrooms and continue cooking for 5–10 minutes or until most of the liquid has evaporated.

Make up pizza base mix as directed on packet. (To obtain hand hot water to make up dough, mix ⅓ boiling water with ⅔ cold water.)

Lightly grease a pizza tin or baking sheet.

Roll out dough on a floured work surface to approximately 20cm (8in) and place in tin.

Spoon tomato mixture on to dough, then arrange pepper on top.

Sprinkle with cheeses and bake at 240°C (475°F) Mark 9 for 8–10 minutes.

For a thicker base, allow dough to stand for 15 minutes before adding the tomato topping.

Variations

Fruity Pizza V

Follow recipe and method for Pizza Neapolitan, adding 25g (1oz) sultanas, 25g (1oz) capers and 25g (1oz) pine nuts to tomato sauce and topping with 50g (2oz) black olives and 2 slices of canned pineapple, chopped.

Ratatouille Pizza V

Follow recipe and method for Pizza Neapolitan, and use 390g can ratatouille instead of tomato sauce and omit steps 1–3. Top with 75g (3oz) sliced mushrooms and cheese.

Seafood Pizza

Follow recipe and method for Pizza Neapolitan, adding 50g (2oz) cooked peeled prawns to sauce and topping with 50g can drained anchovy fillets.

Pepperoni Pizza ❋

Follow recipe and method for Pizza Neapolitan, add an extra 50g (2oz) mushrooms to sauce and top with 50g (2oz) sliced pepperoni.

Beef & Tomato Pizza ❋

Follow recipe and method for Pizza Neapolitan, adding 225g (8oz) minced beef with onion and garlic. Also add 2 tbsp Worcestershire sauce to sauce, and cook for 20 minutes.

Hot & Spicy Pizza ❋

Serves 4 Preparation 25 mins Cooking 12–15 mins
Per portion 508 kcals, 22g fat (13.1g saturated)

225g (8oz) self-raising flour
50g (2oz) butter
125ml (4fl oz) milk
400g can chopped tomatoes, drained
198g can sweetcorn, drained
120g can tuna in brine, drained and flaked
2 green chillis, deseeded and sliced
110g (4oz) Double Gloucester cheese, grated
50g can anchovies, drained

Place flour in a bowl, then rub in butter with your fingertips until mixture resembles breadcrumbs.

Add milk and mix to a dough.

Roll out to 28 x 18cm (11 x 7in).

Place on a greased baking sheet and spread with tomatoes.

Generously arrange remaining ingredients on top of the base.

Bake at 220°C (425°F) Mark 7 for 12–15 minutes until golden brown.

Vegetables

Roast Potatoes

Minted New Potatoes ❄ V

Serves 4 Preparation 5 mins Cooking 15–20 mins
Per portion 147 kcals, 4g fat (2g saturated)

680g (1½lb) unpeeled new potatoes, scrubbed
15g (½oz) butter
3 mint leaves

Cook potatoes for 15–20 minutes in boiling water until tender. Drain.
Stand saucepan of potatoes over a low heat. Add butter and mint.
Cover and leave over a low heat for 2 minutes, shaking pan frequently.
Remove mint and serve.

Roast Potatoes

Serves 4 Preparation 20 mins Cooking 55 mins
Per portion 194 kcals, 8g fat (2.5g saturated)

680g (1½lb) potatoes, peeled
2 tbsp goose fat

Cut potatoes into quarters or leave whole if new.
Cook in boiling water for 5–7 minutes. Drain. Shake in saucepan to roughen surface.
Heat goose fat in a roasting tin.
Add potatoes and turn in tin until well coated.
Roast at 200°C (400°F) Mark 6 for 45 minutes or until crisp and golden, basting at least twice during that time.

Mashed Potatoes ❄ V

Serves 4 Preparation 20 mins Cooking 20 mins
Per portion 177 kcals, 6g fat (3.3g saturated)

680g (1½ lb) potatoes, peeled and quartered
15g (½oz) butter
3 tbsp single cream or milk
Salt and freshly ground black pepper

Cook potatoes for 15–20 minutes in boiling water until tender. Drain.
Mash finely with a potato masher.
Add butter, cream or milk and stir until well mixed. Season to taste.

Variation

Mashed Potatoes with Swede V

Follow recipe and method for Mashed Potatoes. Cook 175g (6oz) chopped swede with potatoes and mash together.

Chipped Potatoes V

Serves 4 Preparation 5 mins plus standing Cooking 20 mins Per portion 226 kcals, 1g fat (1.5g saturated)

680g (1½lb) potatoes, peeled and cut into thick sticks
Sunflower oil

Leave prepared potatoes in a bowl of cold water for 30 minutes to remove excess starch.
Drain and dry well.
Heat oil in a saucepan or deep-fryer. Test to see if one chip will rise to surface immediately.
Cook for 7–10 minutes, in batches, until golden. Drain on kitchen paper and serve.

Variation

Game Chips V

Follow recipe and method for Chipped Potatoes but cut potatoes into thin slices instead of sticks.

Sauté Potatoes V

Serves 4 Preparation 15 mins Cooking 20 mins
Per portion 269 kcals, 16g fat (7.3g saturated)

680g (1½lb) potatoes, peeled and halved
50g (2oz) butter
2 tbsp olive oil

Cook potatoes in boiling water for 5–7 minutes. Drain and cool.
Cut into 5mm (¼in) thick slices.
Heat butter and oil in a large frying pan. Add potato slices. Fry until golden brown on both sides, turning occasionally.

Variation

Potatoes Lyonnaise V

Follow recipe and method for Sauté Potatoes. When potatoes are golden brown, add 225g (8oz) fried, sliced onions. Mix well and serve.

Jacket Potatoes V

Serves 4 Preparation 5 mins Cooking 1 hr
Per portion 131 kcals, 0.4g fat (0g saturated)

4 large potatoes, about 175g (6oz) each

Prick potatoes all over with a fork.
Stand on a baking sheet. Bake at 200°C (400°F) Mark 6 for 1 hour or until tender.
Alternatively, cook in the microwave for 5–8 minutes and then bake for 30 minutes.

Potato Wedges V

Serves 4 Preparation 2 mins Cooking 40 mins
Per portion 180 kcals, 9g fat (0.8g saturated)

4 large potatoes, scrubbed
2 tbsp olive oil
Salt and freshly ground black pepper

Microwave the potatoes for 5–7 minutes, until just cooked.
Cut potatoes into wedges and toss in oil. Season to taste.
Place in a roasting tin and bake at 200°C (400°F) Gas 6 for 30 minutes, turning once.

Potatoes Anna V

Serves 4 Preparation 40 mins Cooking 2 hrs
Per portion 201 kcals, 9g fat (5.2g saturated)

680g (1½lb) potatoes, peeled and very thinly sliced
40g (1½oz) butter, melted
Salt and freshly ground black pepper

Dry potatoes on kitchen paper.
Brush a 1.1 litre (2 pint) ovenproof dish with butter. Fill with layers of potato slices arranged in overlapping circles.
Brush each layer with butter and season.
Brush top layer with butter.
Cover with greased foil. Bake at 190°C (375°F) Mark 5 for 1¼–1½ hours.
Turn out on to a warm ovenproof plate (potatoes should stay moulded).
Return to oven for a further 20–30 minutes, or until outside is golden brown

Casseroled Potatoes V

Serves 4 Preparation 30 mins Cooking 1 hr
Per portion 208 kcals, 7g fat (4g saturated)

680g (1½lb) potatoes, peeled and thinly sliced
Salt and freshly ground black pepper
25g (1oz) butter
300ml (½ pint) milk

Dry potatoes on kitchen paper.
Fill a 1.1 litre (2 pint) greased ovenproof dish with layers of potato slices, seasoning between each.
Melt 15g (½oz) butter and mix with milk. Pour into dish. Cover top with remaining butter, cut into thick flakes.
Cook at 190°C (375°F) Mark 5 for 1 hour, or until potatoes are tender.

Duchesse Potatoes ❄ V

Serves 4 Preparation 35 mins Cooking 35 mins
Per portion 171 kcals, 9g fat (4.2g saturated)

450g (1lb) potatoes, peeled and halved
25g (1oz) butter
2 egg yolks
2 tsp hot milk
A little egg white

Cook potatoes for 15–20 minutes in boiling water until tender. Drain.
Mash then rub through a fine sieve and return to saucepan.
Stand over a low heat.
Add butter, egg yolks and milk. Beat until smooth.
Transfer to a piping bag fitted with a large star-shaped nozzle.
Pipe fairly small mounds or whirls on to a greased baking sheet.
Leave potato until cold, then brush with egg white.
Bake at 220°C (425° F) Mark 7 for 15 minutes or until golden.

Root Vegetable Bake V

Serves 4–6 Preparation 30 mins Cooking 1¼ hrs
Per portion 230 kcals, 9g fat (4g saturated)

225g (8oz) potatoes, peeled
225g (8oz) carrots, peeled
225g (8oz) parsnips, peeled
15g (½oz) butter
½ onion, peeled and sliced
2 eggs, beaten
450ml (¾ pint) milk
Salt and freshly ground black pepper
Paprika

Cut potatoes, carrots and parsnips into wedges
Grease an ovenproof dish with a little of the butter.
Mix together all vegetable wedges with onion and place in dish.
Whisk together eggs and milk, season and pour over vegetables.
Dot with remaining butter and dust with paprika.
Bake at 190°C (375° F) Mark 5 for 1¼ hours until vegetables are tender and egg mixture has set.

Dauphinois Potatoes

Dauphinois Potatoes ❄ V

Serves 4   Preparation 25 mins   Cooking 35 mins
Per portion 398 kcals, 27g fat (15.3g saturated)

680g (1½ lb) potatoes, peeled and thinly sliced
Salt and freshly ground black pepper
1 garlic clove, peeled and crushed
Ground nutmeg
50g (2oz) mature Cheddar cheese, grated
150ml ((¼ pint) double cream
7g (¼oz) butter

Par-boil the potatoes in boiling water for 4
minutes until just tender.
Arrange layer of potato slices in a greased
1.1 litre (2 pint) ovenproof dish. Season
lightly, add a little garlic, nutmeg and cheese.
Repeat, then pour cream over potatoes.
Dot with butter and bake at 190°C (375°F)
Mark 5 for 30 minutes until golden.

Right Potato for the Right Job

To ensure you get the best results when
cooking potatoes, choose a suitable
variety.
Here are some of the most popular ones:

Boiling	Baking	Roasting	Chipping	Mashing
Desiree	Desiree	Desiree	Celine	Epicure
King Edward	Estima	Romano	Desiree	Desiree
Jersey Royal	King Edward	King Edward	Majestic	King Edward
Maris Piper		Maris Piper	Maris Piper	Majestic
Romano				Maris Piper

Seasoned Roast Vegetables

Seasoned Roast Vegetables V

Serves 4   Preparation 15 mins plus standing   Cooking 45 mins   Per portion 490 kcals, 29g fat (5.6g saturated)

2 baking potatoes, scrubbed and cut into wedges

3 sweet potatoes, peeled and cut into wedges

3 red onions, peeled and quartered

125ml (4fl oz) groundnut oil

1 tsp sea salt

1 tsp mixed peppercorns

2 tsp dried mixed herbs

8 garlic cloves, skin on

Place all ingredients in a bowl and mix well. Leave to stand for 30 minutes.

Tip into a large roasting tin and bake at 220°C (425°F) Gas 7 for 40–45 minutes, until softened and golden.

Remove garlic cloves and serve.

Honey Roast Parsnips V

Serves 4   Preparation 5 mins   Cooking 35 mins
Per portion 308 kcals, 18g fat (7.3g saturated)

2 tbsp olive oil

50g (2oz) butter

900g (2lb) parsnips, peeled and quartered lengthways

2 tbsp clear honey

Black pepper

Heat oil and butter in a roasting tin on the hob. When hot, add parsnips and fry until golden.

Bake at 220°C (425° F) Mark 7 for 20 minutes.

Toss in honey and bake for another 5 minutes, until tender. Season with pepper.

Creamed Swede V

Serves 4   Preparation 20 mins   Cooking 20 mins
Per portion 72 kcals, 5g fat (2.8g saturated)

450g (1lb) swede, peeled and diced

15g (½oz) butter

2 tbsp single cream or milk

Large pinch of ground nutmeg

Salt and freshly ground black pepper

Cook swede in boiling water for about 20 minutes, or until tender.

Drain and mash finely.

Stand saucepan over low heat. Add butter, cream or milk and nutmeg.

Beat until smooth and creamy. Season to taste.

Variation

Creamed Turnips V

Follow recipe and method for Creamed Swede. Use 450g (1lb) young turnips instead of swede.

Vichy Carrots V

Serves 4 Preparation 15 mins Cooking 20 mins
Per portion 91 kcals, 6g fat (3.3g saturated)

450g (1lb) carrots, peeled and thinly
sliced
25g (1oz) butter
1 tsp sugar
1 tsp lemon juice
1 tbsp chopped parsley to garnish

Put carrots into a saucepan with water to
cover.
Add half the butter and all of the sugar and
lemon juice and cover.
Simmer gently for 15–20 minutes, or until
tender and liquid has evaporated.
Stir in remaining butter and sprinkle with
parsley to serve.

Carrots in Parsley Sauce V

Serves 4 Preparation 10 mins Cooking 15 mins
Per portion 137 kcals, 7g fat (4g saturated)

450g (1lb) baby carrots, scrubbed
300ml (½ pint) Parsley Sauce (page 179)

Cook whole carrots in boiling water until just
tender. Drain.
Transfer to a serving dish and coat with hot
sauce.

Poached Asparagus V

Serves 4 Preparation 5 mins Cooking 15 mins
Per portion 261 kcals, 25g fat (14.8g saturated)

24 asparagus spears
Hollandaise Sauce (page 180) or Clarified
Butter (page 183)

Trim off 2.5cm (1in) from base of asparagus.
Put into a large, fairly shallow saucepan or
frying pan and half-fill with water.
Bring slowly to the boil, then lower heat.
Cover and simmer for 12–15 minutes, or until
tender.
Drain and serve with sauce.

Variations

Grilled Asparagus V

Trim the asparagus as for Poached
Asparagus, but cook under a medium–hot
grill for 5–8 minutes, turning a few times to
avoid burning.

Braised Celery V

Serves 4 Preparation 10 mins Cooking 25 mins
Per portion 40 kcals, 4g fat (2g saturated)

1 head of celery
Juice of ½ lemon
150ml (¼ pint) vegetable stock
15g (½oz) butter

Cut celery sticks into 7.5cm (3in) lengths.
Wash thoroughly.
Put in a saucepan with lemon juice, stock
and butter.
Cover and simmer for 20 minutes, or until
tender.
Lift out celery and place in a serving dish.
Keep hot.
Briskly boil any liquid left in saucepan, until
reduced to about 75ml (3fl oz).
Pour over celery.

Buttered Corn on the Cob V

Serves 4 Preparation 10 mins Cooking 5 mins
Per portion 141 kcals, 7g fat (3.3g saturated)

4 corn on the cob
25g (1oz) butter
Salt and freshly ground black pepper

Remove husks and silk from corn. Put into a
saucepan, half full of gently boiling water.
Boil for 4–5 minutes only, turning corn husks
over once if water is insufficiently deep to
cover them.
Drain and serve with butter and seasoning.

Parched Corn & Chilli Butter V

Serves 6 Preparation 8 mins Cooking 7 mins
Per portion 226 kcals, 14g fat (6.6g saturated)

75g (3oz) butter, softened
½ tsp hot chilli powder
1 tsp paprika
1 tbsp chopped coriander
Salt and freshly ground black pepper
4 sweetcorn cobs

Place butter in a bowl and thoroughly mix
in chilli powder, paprika, coriander and
seasoning. Cover and chill.
Remove leaves and husk from corn and boil
in a saucepan of water for 2 minutes. Drain
and set aside.
Cook under hot grill for 4–5 minutes, turning,
until charred. Serve with flavoured butter.

French-Style Peas V

Serves 4   Preparation 5 mins   Cooking 10 mins
Per portion 129 kcals, 6g fat (3.7g saturated)

450g (1lb) frozen peas
6 large lettuce leaves, shredded
25g (1oz) butter
3 spring onions, trimmed and finely sliced
½ tsp caster sugar
75ml (3fl oz) vegetable stock

Put all ingredients into a saucepan.
Slowly bring to the boil, cover and simmer gently for 5–10 minutes, or until peas are tender. Add a little extra water if necessary.

Swiss Peas with Rice V

Serves 4   Preparation 5 mins   Cooking 15 mins
Per portion 164 kcals, 6g fat (3.6g saturated)

350g (12oz) frozen peas
1 small onion, peeled and chopped
1 garlic clove, peeled and crushed
25g (1oz) butter
175g (6oz) freshly cooked rice (about 75g/3oz raw)
2 tbsp chopped parsley

Cook peas in boiling water for 3–5 minutes or until tender. Fry onion and garlic in butter until pale gold.
Drain peas and stir into onions with rice and parsley.
Heat through, gently, for about 5 minutes. Stir frequently.

Pease Pudding V

Serves 4–6   Preparation Soaking overnight   Cooking 2¾ hrs   Per portion 416 kcals, 7.5g fat (3.4g saturated)

450g (1lb) split peas, soaked overnight
15g (½oz) butter
1 egg yolk
Salt and freshly ground black pepper

Drain split peas and place in a saucepan. Cover with boiling water and bring slowly to the boil. Boil rapidly for 10 minutes.
Cover saucepan and simmer gently for 1¾–2 hours, stirring occasionally. Add extra boiling water if peas become dry.
Process in a blender or push through a sieve.
Add butter and egg yolk. Mix and season.
Place in a greased ovenproof dish, then bake at 180°C (350°F) Mark 4 for 30 minutes.

Green Beans with Bacon & Soy

Serves 4   Preparation 25 mins   Cooking 15 mins
Per portion 95 kcals, 5g fat (1.1g saturated)

450g (1lb) runner beans
4 rashers lean bacon, chopped
1 small onion, peeled and chopped
1 small garlic clove, peeled and crushed
1 tbsp olive oil
2 tbsp soy sauce

Top and tail beans and remove stringy sides. Slice diagonally into thin strips.
Cook in boiling water for 10–15 minutes, or until tender.
Fry bacon, onion and garlic in oil until pale gold.
Drain beans and return to saucepan.
Stir in bacon mixture and soy sauce.
Heat through gently, stirring frequently.

Creamed Broad Beans V

Serves 4   Preparation 15 mins   Cooking 20 mins
Per portion 300 kcals, 26g fat (14.6g saturated)

450g (1lb) shelled broad beans
50g (2oz) mushrooms, wiped and sliced
25g (1oz) butter
150ml (¼ pint) double cream

Cook beans in boiling water for 15–20 minutes, or until tender.
Meanwhile, fry mushrooms in butter and keep warm.
Drain beans and return to saucepan.
Add mushrooms and pan juices with cream. Mix well. Reheat gently.
Alternatively, use 300ml (½ pint) Basic White Coating Sauce (page 179) instead of cream.

Buttery Steamed Cabbage V

Serves 4   Preparation 15 mins   Cooking 12 mins
Per portion 72 kcals, 3g fat (2g saturated)

680g (1½lb) white cabbage
15g (½oz) butter

Shred cabbage finely, discarding hard stalks.
Steam for 10 minutes, over a saucepan of boiling water.
Tip into colander and drain well.
Return to saucepan and add butter
Cover. Stand over a low heat for a further 2 minutes, shaking saucepan frequently.

Sweet-Sour White Cabbage   V

Serves 4   Preparation 10 mins   Cooking 15 mins
Per portion 100 kcals, 6g fat (3.3g saturated)

680g (1½lb) white cabbage, shredded
25g (1oz) butter
2 tbsp water
2 tbsp white wine vinegar
Pinch of mixed spice
2 tsp soft brown sugar
Salt and freshly ground black pepper

Put cabbage in a saucepan with all remaining ingredients.
Cover and cook over a low heat for 7–10 minutes, or until cabbage is just tender but still slightly crisp. Shake saucepan frequently while cabbage is cooking.
Uncover and cook fairly briskly until no liquid remains (about 5 minutes).

Savoury Cabbage

Serves 4   Preparation 15 mins   Cooking 10 mins
Per portion 112 kcals, 6g fat (2.9g saturated)

680g (1½lb) white cabbage
15g (½oz) butter
2 streaky bacon rashers, chopped
1 onion, peeled and finely chopped
Pinch of ground nutmeg

Shred cabbage finely, discarding hard stalks.
Heat butter in a large saucepan.
Add cabbage, bacon, then onion and nutmeg. Cover and cook gently for 7–10 minutes, shaking saucepan frequently, or until cabbage is tender.

Sweet-Sour Red Cabbage   V

Serves 4–6   Preparation 20 mins   Cooking 25 mins
Per portion 185 kcals, 6g fat (3.3g saturated)

25g (1oz) butter
900g (2lb) red cabbage, shredded
2 tbsp soft brown sugar
1 tsp caraway seeds
3 cloves
450g (1lb) cooking apples, peeled, cored and chopped
1 tbsp cornflour
4 tbsp vinegar
Salt and freshly ground black pepper

Melt butter in a large saucepan. Add cabbage and fry briskly for 5 minutes, shaking saucepan frequently.
Stir in sugar, caraway seeds, cloves and apples.
Mix cornflour to a paste with vinegar. Add 300ml (½ pint) water and pour over cabbage.
Cook, stirring, until mixture comes to the boil and thickens. Season to taste.
Reduce heat. Cover saucepan and simmer very slowly for 20 minutes. Stir occasionally.

Colcannon   V

Serves 4   Preparation 30 mins   Cooking 20 mins
Per portion 190 kcals, 6.8g fat (3.7g saturated)

450g (1lb) savoy cabbage, shredded
450g (1lb) potatoes, peeled and cut into chunks
2 leeks, washed and finely chopped
150ml (¼ pint) milk
25g (1oz) butter
Pinch of ground mace
Salt and freshly ground black pepper

Boil cabbage in water for 5 minutes until cooked, drain well and keep warm.
Meanwhile, place potatoes and leeks in a saucepan with milk. Bring to the boil, cover and simmer for 15–20 minutes until cooked.
Mash potatoes with leeks, butter and mace, then season. Add cabbage to potatoes and mix well.

Brussels Sprouts & Chestnuts   V

Serves 4   Preparation 25 mins   Cooking 20 mins
Per portion 192 kcals, 7g fat (2.4g saturated)

275g (10oz) chestnuts
450g (1lb) Brussels sprouts
15g (½oz) butter

Slit shells of chestnuts with a sharp knife.
Place in a saucepan of cold water and bring to the boil. Cook for 5 minutes. Drain and leave to cool.
Peel, removing shell and brown skin.
Remove outer leaves from sprouts and cut a cross in the stem end of each sprout.
Cook sprouts in boiling water for 10 minutes.
Drain sprouts and return to saucepan. Add chestnuts and butter and stand over a low heat for 2 minutes, shaking saucepan frequently.
Alternatively, use ready-to-eat vacuum-packed or frozen chestnuts.

Broccoli Hollandaise

Broccoli Hollandaise V

Serves 4   Preparation 10 mins   Cooking 12 mins
Per portion 285 kcals, 26g fat (14.8g saturated)

680g (1½lb) broccoli
Hollandaise Sauce (page 180)

Remove large leaves and cut away tough parts of stalks from broccoli.
Cook in boiling water for 10–12 minutes or until stalks are tender.
Drain thoroughly and transfer to a serving dish.
Coat with hollandaise sauce.

Cauliflower Cheese V

Serves 4   Preparation 10 mins   Cooking 15 mins
Per portion 241 kcals, 15g fat (8.1g saturated)

1 cauliflower, cut into florets
300ml (½ pint) Cheese Sauce (page 179)
25g (1oz) Cheddar cheese, grated

Steam cauliflower over a saucepan of boiling water for 10 minutes until tender.
Drain and transfer to a flameproof dish.
Coat with hot sauce. Sprinkle with cheese.
Brown under a hot grill.

Variations

Crumbed Cauliflower Cheese V

Follow recipe and method for Cauliflower Cheese, but mix 25g (1oz) breadcrumbs into Cheddar cheese before sprinkling.

Cauliflower Cheese & Bacon

Follow recipe and method for Cauliflower Cheese, but grill 4 bacon rashers while cauliflower is cooking. Chop and add to dish with cauliflower.

Leeks with White or Hollandaise Sauce V

Serves 4   Preparation 10 mins   Cooking 15 mins
Per portion 135 kcals, 7g fat (4g saturated)

4 leeks, washed and sliced
Basic White Coating Sauce (page 179) or Hollandaise Sauce (page 180)

Put leeks into a saucepan containing 5cm (2in) boiling water.
Cover and simmer for 10 minutes or until tender. Drain leeks and transfer to a serving dish. Coat with hot sauce.

Fried Onions   V

Serves 4   Preparation 10 mins   Cooking 10 mins
Per portion 115 kcals, 8g fat (5.3g saturated)

40g (1½oz) butter
3 onions, peeled and thinly sliced

Heat butter in a frying pan.
Add onion slices and fry until golden brown, stirring frequently to prevent burning.

Glazed Sweet Onions   V

Serves 4   Preparation 10 mins   Cooking 20 mins
Per portion 162 kcals, 11g fat (6.6g saturated)

12 small onions, peeled
50g (2oz) butter
Pinch of salt
1 tbsp soft brown sugar

Cook onions in boiling water for 15 minutes, or until tender.
Drain, then dry on absorbent kitchen paper.
Melt butter in a frying pan, add salt and sugar. Heat for 1 minute.
Add onions. Toss in butter mixture until well coated.
Cook over a very low heat until glazed and golden.

Bacon-Stuffed Onions

Serves 4   Preparation 30 mins   Cooking 1¼ hrs
Per portion 204 kcals, 9g fat (3.8g saturated)

4 large onions, peeled
50g (2oz) breadcrumbs
110g (4oz) bacon, chopped
Single cream
Freshly ground black pepper

Cook onions in boiling water for 30 minutes. Drain and reserve 5 tbsp onion water.
Cut the top off each onion. Carefully remove centres, leaving 1cm (½in) thick onion shells.
Chop onion centres finely. Mix with breadcrumbs and bacon.
Add sufficient cream to bind mixture together. Season to taste.
Spoon mixture carefully back into onion shells.
Stand filled onions in a shallow ovenproof dish. Pour in onion water.
Bake at 190°C (375° F) Mark 5 for about 45 minutes until tender.

Stuffed Red Onions   V

Serves 4   Preparation 35 mins   Cooking 40 mins
Per portion 172 kcals, 10.8g fat (6.6g saturated)

50g (2oz) bulgur wheat
425ml (¾ pint) hot vegetable stock
4 red onions, peeled
25g (1oz) butter
275g (10oz) tomatoes, chopped
2 tbsp chopped coriander
2 tbsp chopped mint
3 tbsp chopped parsley
Salt and freshly ground black pepper

Soak bulgur wheat in stock for 30 minutes.
Cook onions in boiling water for 5 minutes. Drain. Slice top off each onion and remove centres leaving 1cm (½in) thick onion shells.
Chop half of centres and soften in butter.
Drain bulgur wheat, reserving stock.
Mix wheat with chopped onion, tomatoes, herbs and seasoning. Fill onions with stuffing and place in an ovenproof dish.
Replace tops and add 8 tbsp stock. Cover with foil. Bake at 190°C (375°F) Mark 5 for 35–40 minutes.

Battered Onion Rings   V

Serves 4   Preparation 15 mins   Cooking 10 mins
Per portion 316 kcals, 26g fat (3.1g saturated)

4 onions, peeled and thinly sliced
Milk
Self-raising flour
Salt and freshly ground black pepper
Oil for deep-frying

Separate onions into rings.
Dip in milk, then toss in seasoned flour.
Fry in hot oil until crisp and golden.
Drain on kitchen paper.

Onions in Cheese Sauce   V

Serves 4   Preparation 5 mins   Cooking 15 mins
Per portion 201 kcals, 11g fat (6.8g saturated)

8 small onions, peeled
300ml (½ pint) Cheese Sauce (page 179)
1 tbsp toasted breadcrumbs to garnish

Cook onions in boiling water for 15 minutes, or until tender. Drain. Transfer to a dish.
Coat with hot sauce and sprinkle with breadcrumbs.

163

Ratatouille ❄ V

Serves 4   Preparation 25 mins   Cooking 1 hr
Per portion 122 kcals, 7g fat (0.9g saturated)

1 large onion, peeled and thinly sliced
1 garlic clove, peeled and crushed
2 tbsp olive oil
2 aubergines, sliced
225g (8oz) courgettes, sliced
1 green pepper, deseeded and chopped
400g can tomatoes
Salt and freshly ground black pepper
2 tbsp chopped parsley

Fry onion and garlic gently in oil for 3–4 minutes.
Add remaining vegetables to frying pan with tomatoes, seasoning and parsley.
Cover pan. Simmer gently for 1 hour.

Fried Aubergine V

Serves 4   Preparation 35 mins   Cooking 7 mins
Per portion 129 kcals, 11g fat (5.6g saturated)

1 aubergine
Salt
Milk
Flour
40g (1½oz) butter
1 tbsp olive oil

Cut aubergine into 5mm (¼in) thick slices.
Sprinkle with salt and leave for 30 minutes.
Rinse and drain. Dry on kitchen paper.
Dip in milk then coat in flour.
Fry gently in hot butter and oil for 5–7 minutes until crisp, golden and tender.
Drain on kitchen paper.

Stuffed Aubergines ❄ V

Serves 4   Preparation 40 mins   Cooking 30 mins
Per portion 282 kcals, 17g fat (8.9g saturated)

2 aubergines
1 large onion, peeled and finely chopped
4 streaky bacon rashers, chopped
1 small green pepper, deseeded and chopped
450g (1lb) tomatoes, chopped
25g (1oz) butter
110g (4oz) mushrooms, wiped and sliced
50g (2oz) breadcrumbs
Salt and freshly ground black pepper
75g (3oz) Lancashire cheese, grated

Halve aubergines lengthways. Scoop out flesh, leaving 5mm (¼in) thick shells.
Chop flesh. Put into saucepan with onion, bacon, green pepper, tomatoes and butter.
Simmer gently until aubergine is tender.
Remove from heat. Stir in mushrooms and breadcrumbs. Season to taste.
Spoon mixture into aubergine shells. Sprinkle with cheese.
Bake at 200°C (400° F) Mark 6 for 20 minutes.

Artichokes & Aubergines V

Serves 4   Preparation 10 mins   Cooking 15 mins
Per portion 336 kcals, 33g fat (4.2g saturated)

280g jar artichoke antipasto in oil, drained and 2 tbsp reserved for cooking
Small aubergine, trimmed, halved and cut roughly into 2.5cm (1in) cubes
2 large spring onions, trimmed and cut diagonally into 7.5cm (3in) pieces
1–2 tsp medium curry powder
8–10 cherry tomatoes
2 tbsp chopped coriander

Heat artichoke oil in a frying pan. Add aubergine and stir-fry for 6–8 minutes until softened and lightly browned.
Add artichokes and spring onions and cook for 2–3 minutes until onions are softened.
Stir in curry powder and tomatoes and cook for 3–4 minutes, or until tomatoes are hot.
Mix in coriander and serve.

Italian Tomato Bake V

Serves 4   Preparation 20 mins   Cooking 25 mins
Per portion 254 kcals, 19g fat (11.5g saturated)

15g (½oz) basil, chopped
65g (2½oz) Parmesan cheese, grated
40g (1½oz) breadcrumbs
680g (1½lb) tomatoes, sliced
Salt and freshly ground black pepper
65g (2½oz) butter, melted

Mix a quarter of basil with cheese and breadcrumbs.
Place tomatoes in a greased 1½ litre (2½ pint) ovenproof dish. Season each layer and sprinkle with basil and melted butter.
Cover with cheese mixture and sprinkle with any remaining butter.
Bake at 220°C (425°F) Gas 7 for 20–25 minutes, until topping is golden and crisp.

Tasty Courgette Bake

Serves 4   Preparation 30 mins   Cooking 1 hr
Per portion 310 kcals, 21.1g fat (10g saturated)

680g (1½lb) courgettes, sliced
75g (3oz) smoked streaky bacon, chopped
1 onion, peeled and sliced
3 eggs
300ml (½ pint) milk
½ tsp dried marjoram
110g (4oz) Cheddar cheese, grated

Blanch courgettes in boiling water for 2 minutes, drain well and cool.
Place bacon and onion in a non-stick frying pan and cook, stirring, for 5 minutes.
Lightly grease a large ovenproof dish. Place courgettes, bacon and onion in dish.
Beat together eggs, milk and marjoram.
Stir in 75g (3oz) cheese and pour over courgettes.
Sprinkle with remaining cheese.
Bake at 180°C (350° F) Mark 4 for 55 minutes or until set.

Marrow Provençal   ❄ V

Serves 4   Preparation 50 mins   Cooking 45 mins
Per portion 200 kcals, 14g fat (8.8g saturated)

1 marrow, peeled
25g (1oz) butter
1 onion, peeled and grated
1 garlic clove, peeled and crushed
1 green pepper, deseeded and chopped
225g (8oz) tomatoes, chopped
110g (4oz) Lancashire cheese or Cheddar cheese, grated

Cut marrow into 2.5cm (1in) rings and remove seeds from centres. Cut rings into 2.5cm (1in) cubes.
Melt butter in a large saucepan and fry marrow for 6–7 minutes or until golden. Transfer to a plate.
Place onion, garlic and green pepper in remaining butter in saucepan.
Fry until softened.
Add tomatoes and marrow and mix well.
Place half mixture in an ovenproof dish.
Cover with 50g (2oz) cheese, then the remaining marrow mixture. Sprinkle with remaining cheese.
Bake at 190°C (375° F) Mark 5 for 30 minutes.

Spinach with Cream Sauce   V

Serves 4   Preparation 10 mins   Cooking 15 mins
Per portion 166 kcals, 14g fat (8g saturated)

680g (1½lb) spinach
25g (1oz) butter
2 tsp flour
150ml (¼ pint) single cream
Salt and freshly ground black pepper

Cut away any tough stems from spinach. Wash leaves thoroughly under cold running water to remove grit.
Tear into small pieces. Put into a saucepan with 2 tbsp water.
Cover and cook for 5–10 minutes, or until tender.
Drain well, pressing water out with the back of a spoon.
Melt butter in a saucepan. Stir in flour. Cook for 2 minutes without browning.
Gradually blend in cream. Cook, stirring, until sauce comes to the boil, thickens and is smooth.
Add spinach and season to taste.
Heat through gently.

Fried Mushrooms   V

Serves 2   Preparation 5 mins   Cooking 5 mins
Per portion 108 kcals, 11g fat (6.6g saturated)

25g (1oz) butter
225g (8oz) mushrooms, wiped and halved

Melt butter in a saucepan. Add mushrooms and stir until well coated with butter.
Fry briskly, uncovered, for 5 minutes. Shake saucepan often.

Grilled Mushrooms   V

Serves 2–4   Preparation 5 mins   Cooking 5 mins
Per portion 93 kcals, 9g fat (5.6g saturated)

225g (8oz) large open mushrooms, stalks removed
25g (1oz) butter
Salt and freshly ground black pepper

Stand mushrooms, brown sides down in a grill pan. Place a little butter on each mushroom.
Grill for 2–2½ minutes, depending on size.
Turn over. Put a knob of remaining butter on each. Season and grill for a further 2–2½ minutes.

Eggs & Egg Dishes

Boiled Eggs

Eggs

Fried Egg   V

Serves 1   Cooking 3 mins
Per portion 108 kcals, 9g fat (2g saturated)

Vegetable oil for frying
1 egg

Heat a little oil in a frying pan over a medium heat.
Break egg into frying pan. Baste with hot oil, tipping pan if necessary to pool fat.
Cook until white is firm and yolk is cooked to your liking. Remove from pan with a fish slice.

Poached Egg   V

Serves 1   Preparation 2 mins   Cooking 5 mins
Per portion 88 kcals, 7g fat (1.8g saturated)

1 tbsp white wine vinegar
1 egg

Half fill a saucepan with water. Add vinegar to water and bring to the boil.
Crack egg into a cup and slide into water.
Cook gently for 3–5 minutes until lightly set then lift out with a slotted spoon.

Eggs Benedict   ❄

Serves 4   Preparation 10 mins   Cooking 10 mins
Per portion 404 kcals, 32g fat (17g saturated)

4 small slices of bread
4 eggs
4 thin slices of lean ham
Freshly made Hollandaise Sauce (page 180)

Toast bread on both sides.
Poach eggs (see above).
Top each slice of toast with a slice of ham. Place drained poached eggs on top.
Spoon over sauce and serve.

Boiled Eggs   V

Method One
Serves 1–2   Cooking 5½–7 mins
Per portion 88 kcals, 7g fat (1.8g saturated)

2 eggs

Place eggs in a saucepan of enough boiling water to cover them completely.
Bring back to the boil and simmer gently for 5½–7 minutes depending on how set you like your eggs.

Boiled Eggs   V

Method Two
Serves 1–2   Cooking 5–6 mins
Per portion 88 kcals, 7g fat (1.8g saturated)

2 eggs

Place eggs in a saucepan and cover with cold water. Bring to the boil and simmer gently for 3–5 minutes.
Time from when water comes to the boil.

Hard-Boiled Eggs   V

Serves 1–2   Cooking 12 mins
Per portion 88 kcals, 7g fat (1.8g saturated)

2 eggs

Place eggs in a saucepan of enough boiling water to cover them completely.
Bring back to the boil and simmer gently for 10–12 minutes.
Drain and place under running cold water to prevent them from cooking further.
Leave to cool, then crack shells and peel.
Rinse and dry on kitchen paper.

Scrambled Eggs   V

Serves 1   Preparation 1 min   Cooking 1½ mins
Per portion 240 kcals, 19g fat (7.4g saturated)

2 eggs
1 tbsp milk
Salt and freshly ground black pepper
7g (¼oz) butter

Break eggs into a bowl, add milk and seasoning and beat with a fork until mixed.
Melt butter in a small saucepan.
Pour in eggs and stir over a gentle heat moving eggs from bottom and sides of saucepan.
Remove from heat when lightly set as eggs continue cooking slightly.

Variations

Scrambled Eggs & Tomatoes   V

Follow recipe for Scrambled Eggs, adding a finely chopped tomato to saucepan once eggs start to cook.

Scrambled Eggs & Salmon   V

Follow recipe for Scrambled Eggs, adding a slice of chopped smoked salmon to saucepan once eggs start to cook.

Creamed Corn & Ham Scramble

Piperade   V

Serves 4 Preparation 35 mins Cooking 35 mins
Per portion 303 kcals, 22g fat (7.8g saturated)

350g (12oz) onions, peeled and chopped
1 tbsp olive oil
3 green peppers, deseeded and cut into strips
450g (1lb) tomatoes, chopped
¼ tsp dried marjoram or basil
Salt and freshly ground black pepper
6 eggs
4 tbsp double cream

Fry onion gently in oil until soft but not brown. Add peppers to pan.
Cook slowly with onion until soft.
Add tomatoes to frying pan with herbs and seasoning. Cover and simmer for 20 minutes or until most of liquid has evaporated.
Beat eggs lightly with cream. Pour over vegetable mixture.
Cook, stirring, until eggs are scrambled.

Egg & Mushroom Savoury   V

Serves 4 Preparation 5 mins Cooking 15 mins
Per portion 277 kcals, 22g fat (9.8g saturated)

25g (1oz) butter
225g (8oz) mushrooms, wiped and halved
6 eggs
2 tbsp milk
2 tbsp chopped parsley
2 large tomatoes, sliced
75g (3oz) Lancashire cheese, grated

Melt butter in a saucepan, add mushrooms and cook for 3–5 minutes until soft.
Transfer mushrooms to a 600ml (1 pint) greased flameproof dish.
Beat eggs with milk and parsley.
Pour eggs into saucepan and scramble lightly until set.
Spoon over mushrooms, top with slices of tomato and sprinkle with cheese.
Brown under a hot grill.

Creamed Corn & Ham Scramble

Serves 4 Preparation 7 mins Cooking 5 mins
Per portion 407 kcals, 24g fat (10.6g saturated)

6 eggs
4 tbsp single cream
15g (½oz) butter
198g can sweetcorn
110g (4oz) lean ham, finely chopped
Large pinch of ground nutmeg
Salt and freshly ground black pepper
4 slices hot buttered toast
Fresh parsley to garnish

Beat eggs and cream well together. Pour into frying pan.
Add butter, drained sweetcorn, ham, ground nutmeg and seasoning.
Scramble eggs over a low heat until they are creamy.
Pile equal amounts on to buttered toast.
Garnish with parsley.

Omelettes

Plain or French Omelette   V

Serves 1   Preparation 2 mins   Cooking 3–5 mins
Per portion 293 kcals, 26g fat (11.4g saturated)

2 eggs
Salt and freshly ground black pepper
15g (½oz) butter
Parsley to garnish

Beat eggs and 2 tsp water lightly together. Season to taste.
Put butter into omelette pan or non-stick frying pan. Heat until sizzling but not brown.
Swirl round to coat base and sides of pan. Pour in beaten eggs.
After about 5 seconds, move edges of setting omelette to centre of pan with a fork.
At same time tilt pan quickly in all directions so that uncooked egg flows to edges.
Continue until mixture is lightly set and top is slightly soft. Remove from heat.
Fold in half in pan and slide out on to a warm plate. Garnish with parsley and serve.

Variations

Cooked Breakfast Omelette

Fry in a little butter 1 tbsp each chopped bacon, mushrooms and onion. Add to beaten eggs just before making plain omelette.

Herb Omelette   V

Add 1 tbsp finely chopped fresh herbs to egg mixture before cooking. Parsley, chives or chervil can be used.

Omelette Fillings

Add before folding the omelette.

Cheddar Cheese   V

40g (1½oz) grated Cheddar cheese.

Stilton & Onion   V

40g (1½oz) crumbled Stilton cheese mixed with 2 sliced spring onions.

Mushroom   V

50g (2oz) sliced mushrooms fried in butter.

Prawn

50g (2oz) cooked peeled prawns.

Ham

50g (2oz) lean chopped ham.

Spanish Omelette   V

Serves 2   Preparation 25 mins   Cooking 15 mins
Per portion 435 kcals, 28g fat (10.8g saturated)

25g (1oz) butter
2 tsp olive oil
1 large onion, peeled and thinly sliced
1 large peeled boiled potato, diced
110g (4oz) tomatoes, chopped
50g (2oz) red or green peppers, deseeded and chopped
4 eggs
Salt and freshly ground black pepper

Put butter and oil into a 23cm (9in) non-stick frying pan. When hot and sizzling, add onion and potato.
Fry gently until pale gold, turning often.
Add tomatoes and pepper. Fry for a further 2–3 minutes.
Beat eggs lightly with 2 tsp water. Season to taste then pour into frying pan over vegetables.
Cook gently until base is firm.
Cook under a preheated hot grill for 1–2 minutes, until just set. Slide unfolded omelette on to a plate. Cut into 2 portions.

Sweet Soufflé Omelette   V

Serves 4   Preparation 10 mins   Cooking 10 mins
Per portion 108 kcals, 6g fat (2.9g saturated)

2 eggs, separated
15g (½oz) sugar
¼ tsp vanilla extract
15g (½oz) butter
2 tbsp jam, warmed
Icing sugar to serve

Beat egg yolks with sugar and vanilla until very thick and pale in colour.
Beat egg whites to a stiff snow.
Gently fold into egg yolk mixture.
Melt butter in omelette pan or non-stick frying pan. Swirl round to coat sides and base.
When hot and sizzling, pour in egg mixture.
Cook without moving for 2–2½ minutes or until base is set and underside is golden.
Stand below a preheated hot grill for 2–3 minutes or until top is puffed and golden.
Run a spatula around edges to loosen it. Score a line down centre, spread with jam, fold in half, dust with icing sugar and serve immediately.

Batters

Pancakes V

Makes 8   Preparation 5 mins   Cooking 20 mins
Per portion 94 kcals, 4g fat (1.9g saturated)

110g (4oz) flour
Pinch of salt
1 egg
300ml (½ pint) milk
Melted butter or vegetable oil for frying

Sift flour and salt into a bowl. Break in egg.
Gradually add half the milk, beating to form a smooth batter.
Pour in remaining milk and beat until quite smooth.
Lightly brush base of a 20cm (8in) non-stick frying pan with melted butter or oil. Stand over a medium heat.
When frying pan and fat are hot, pour in 3 tbsp of batter, tilting pan to cover base.
Cook until pancake moves freely, turn and cook until golden.
Repeat with remaining batter.

Variations

Lemon or Orange Pancakes ※ V

Follow recipe and method for Pancakes. Sprinkle with sugar and lemon or orange juice. Roll up and serve with lemon or orange wedges.

Seafood Pancakes

Serves 4   Preparation 15 mins   Cooking 15 mins
Per portion 479 kcals, 22g fat (9.7g saturated)

25g (1oz) plain flour
450ml (¾ pint) milk
25g (1oz) butter
350g (12oz) white fish fillet, cut into 2.5cm (1in) cubes
75g (3oz) frozen peas
110g (4oz) peeled cooked prawns or chopped seafood sticks
2 tsp wholegrain mustard
50g (2oz) cheese with garlic and herbs, grated
8 freshly cooked pancakes (see above)

Place flour, milk and butter in a saucepan and heat, whisking continuously, until sauce thickens, boils and is smooth.
Add fish and peas and cook for 5 minutes.

Add prawns or seafood sticks and heat through.
Remove from heat, add mustard and cheese and stir until melted.
Divide filling between pancakes and roll up or fold into triangles.

Chicken Pancakes

Serves 4   Preparation 15 mins   Cooking 10 mins
Per portion 506 kcals, 24g fat (9.4g saturated)

15g (½oz) plain flour
15g (½oz) butter
300ml (½ pint) milk
Pinch of dried basil
350g (12oz) cooked chicken meat, diced
225g (8oz) cooked broccoli, in small florets
225g (8oz) cooked carrots, diced
8 freshly cooked pancakes (see left)
50g (2oz) Cheddar cheese, grated

Place flour, butter and milk in a saucepan and heat, whisking, until sauce thickens, boils and is smooth. Cook for a minute.
Stir in basil, chicken and vegetables and cook until heated through.
Divide between pancakes and roll up.
Place in a baking dish in one layer. Sprinkle with cheese and grill until melted.

Chilli Pancakes V

Serves 4   Preparation 20 mins   Cooking 25 mins
Per portion 453 kcals, 14g fat (4.8g saturated)

1 onion, peeled and chopped
1 garlic clove, peeled and crushed
400g can red kidney beans, rinsed
415g can baked beans
400g can chopped tomatoes
2 tsp chilli powder
225g (8oz) frozen green beans
1 yellow pepper, deseeded and chopped
8 freshly cooked pancakes (see left)
50g (2oz) Red Leicester cheese, grated

Place onion, garlic, kidney and baked beans, tomatoes and chilli in a saucepan and simmer for 15 minutes.
Add green beans and pepper, cook for a further 5 minutes or until mixture is thick.
Divide filling between pancakes and fold into triangles.
Place in a baking dish in one layer. Sprinkle with cheese and grill until melted.

Crêpes Suzette

Crêpes Suzette   V

Serves 4 Preparation 5 mins Cooking 10 mins
Per portion 378 kcals, 19g fat (8.3g saturated)

---

8 cooked pancakes (see left)
50g (2oz) butter
25g (1oz) caster sugar
½ tsp grated lemon rind
½ tsp grated orange rind
4 tbsp Cointreau, Curaçao or Grand
Marnier
2 tbsp brandy

Fold pancakes into fan shapes.
Melt butter in a frying pan. Add sugar, lemon
and orange rind and liqueur.
Bring to the boil. Add pancakes.
Heat through, turning twice.
Warm brandy or liqueur and pour into frying
pan. Set alcohol alight and allow it to flame.
Serve pancakes as soon as flames have
subsided.

Mock Crêpes Suzette   V

Serves 4 Preparation 5 mins Cooking 10 mins
Per portion 360 kcals, 19g fat (8.3g saturated)

---

8 cooked pancakes (see left)
50g (2oz) butter
50g (2oz) caster sugar
Finely grated rind and juice of 1 large orange
3 tbsp sweet sherry or white wine

Fold pancakes into fan shapes.
Melt butter in a frying pan. Add sugar,
orange rind and juice and sherry or wine.
Bring to the boil. Add pancakes.
Heat through, turning twice.

American Pancakes   ❄ V

Makes 8 Preparation 5 mins Cooking 16 mins
Per portion 188 kcals, 7g fat (3.9g saturated)

225g (8oz) plain flour
4 tsp baking powder
2 tsp caster sugar
1 tsp salt
2 eggs
350ml (12fl oz) milk
25g (1oz) butter, melted
Butter for frying
Maple syrup and whipped cream to serve

Sift flour, baking powder, sugar and salt into
a bowl.
Whisk eggs, milk and melted butter
together. Stir into dry ingredients and mix
until evenly blended.
Heat a little butter in a non-stick frying
pan then pour in sufficient batter to give a
12.5cm (5in) pancake, 5mm (¼in) thick.
Cook until top of pancake looks bubbly, then
turn and cook until golden.
Repeat, making 8 pancakes.
Serve with maple syrup and cream.

Yorkshire Pudding   V

Serves 6–8   Preparation 5 mins   Cooking 555 mins
Per portion 150 kcals, 8g fat (4.3g saturated)

110g (4oz) plain flour
Pinch of salt
1 egg
300ml (½ pint) milk
40g (1½oz) butter

Sift flour and salt into a bowl. Break in egg.
Gradually add half the milk, beating to form a smooth batter.
Pour in remaining milk and beat until smooth.
Preheat oven to 220°C (425°F) Mark 7. Put butter into a 25 x 30cm (10 x 12in) baking tin. Heat for 10 minutes or until a faint haze just appears.
Pour in batter.
Bake just above centre of oven for 40–45 minutes.

Variation

Small Yorkshire Puddings   V

Follow recipe and method for Yorkshire Pudding. Place butter in a 12-section bun tin and heat as step 4. Pour in batter and cook for 15–20 minutes.

Toad in the Hole

Serves 4–6   Preparation 5 mins   Cooking 55 mins
Per portion 545 kcals, 37g fat (13.8g saturated)

25g (1oz) butter
450g (1lb) sausages
110g (4oz) plain flour
Pinch of salt
1 egg
300ml (½ pint) milk

Place butter and sausages in a 25 x 30cm (10 x 12in) roasting tin.
Cook at 220°C (425°F) Mark 7 for 10 minutes.
Meanwhile, sift flour and salt into a bowl. Break in egg.
Gradually add half the milk, beating to form a smooth batter.
Pour in remaining milk and beat until smooth.
Pour batter into roasting tin and bake for 40–45 minutes, until batter is well risen and golden.

Variations

Toad in the Hole with a Twist

Follow recipe and method for Toad in the Hole but put 2 red onions, peeled and cut into thin wedges, and 2 sweet potatoes, peeled and cut into chunks into roasting tin and layer sausages over top.

Rosemary Batter Pudding

Follow recipe and method for Toad in the Hole and add 1 tbsp finely chopped rosemary to batter.

Meatball Batter Pudding

Follow recipe and method for Toad in the Hole but omit sausages. After pouring batter into roasting tin add 450g (1lb) lean minced beef, seasoned and shaped into 12 meatballs.

Apple Batter Pudding   V

Follow recipe and method for Toad in the Hole but omit sausages. Add 450g (1lb) peeled, cored and thickly sliced apples to butter and 50g (2oz) sugar, and 1 tsp cinnamon to batter.

Coating Batter   V

Preparation 5 mins

110g (4oz) plain or self-raising flour
¼ tsp salt
1 egg
1 tbsp melted butter
150ml (¼ pint) milk

For coating fish, meat and vegetables.
Sift flour and salt into a bowl.
Beat to a smooth batter with unbeaten egg, butter and milk.
Use as required.

Tempura Batter   V

Serves 4   Preparation 5 mins   Cooking 1–2 mins

1 egg, beaten
110g (4oz) plain flour

For coating vegetables.
Stir egg and flour together with 150ml (¼ pint) iced water.
Use to coat chosen vegetables and deep fry for about 1 minute, until crispy.

Cheese Soufflé

Soufflés

Cheese Soufflé

Serves 4   Preparation 15 mins   Cooking 1 hr
Per portion 356 kcals, 26g fat (14.7g saturated)

50g (2oz) butter
50g (2oz) plain flour
300ml (½ pint) milk, warmed
110g (4oz) Cheddar Cheese, grated
1 tsp mustard
Salt and freshly ground black pepper
¼ tsp Worcestershire sauce
3 egg yolks
4 egg whites

Melt butter in a saucepan and add flour. Cook for 2 minutes without browning, stirring all the time.

Gradually whisk in warm milk (using a whisk rather than a spoon). Continue whisking gently until sauce thickens, boils and is smooth.

Simmer sauce for about 2 minutes. It should eventually be quite thick and leave sides of pan clean.

Remove from heat and cool slightly. Beat in cheese, mustard, seasoning, Worcestershire sauce and egg yolks.

Beat egg whites to a stiff snow. Gently fold into sauce mixture with a large metal spoon.

Transfer to a greased 1.5 litre (2½ pint) soufflé dish (or similar straight-sided, heatproof dish.)

Bake at 190°C (375°F) Mark 5 for 50 minutes. The soufflé should be well-risen and golden.

Remove from oven and serve immediately.

It is vital not to open the oven door while the soufflé is baking or it will collapse.

Variations

Ham Soufflé

Follow recipe and method for Cheese Soufflé but omit cheese. Before beating in egg yolks, add 110g (4oz) finely chopped ham.

Smoked Mackerel Soufflé

Follow recipe and method for Cheese Soufflé. Add half the cheese. Before beating in egg yolks, add 110g (4oz) finely flaked, smoked mackerel.

Mushroom Soufflé   V

Follow recipe and method for Cheese Soufflé but omit cheese and Worcestershire sauce. Before beating in egg yolks, add 110g (4oz) finely chopped, fried mushrooms.

Bacon Soufflé

Follow recipe and method for Cheese Soufflé but omit cheese. Before beating in egg yolks, add 110g (4oz) finely chopped, grilled bacon.

Hot Chocolate Soufflé   V

Serves 4   Preparation 15 mins   Cooking 45 mins
Per portion 260 kcals, 13g fat (5.8g saturated)

50g (2oz) plain chocolate chips
4 tbsp plain flour
150ml (¼ pint) milk
50g (2oz) caster sugar
15g (½oz) butter
3 egg yolks
4 egg whites
Icing sugar to serve

Place chocolate chips in a bowl with 2 tbsp water and melt over a saucepan of barely simmering water.

Blend flour with a little cold milk to make a smooth paste.

Heat remaining milk with sugar.

Mix hot milk with melted chocolate then pour on to flour paste, stirring to mix.

Return to saucepan and bring to the boil, stirring continuously.

Cook for 2 minutes, stirring occasionally.

Remove from heat, stir in butter and cool slightly.

Stir in egg yolks.

Whisk egg whites to a stiff snow and gently fold in to chocolate mixture.

Transfer to a well greased 1.25 litre (2 pint) soufflé dish.

Bake at 200°C (400°F) Mark 6 for 35 minutes until well risen with a high crown.

Dust with icing sugar and serve immediately in case soufflé collapses.

Variations

Hazelnut or Walnut Soufflé   V

Follow recipe and method for Chocolate Soufflé but omit chocolate. Add 75g (3oz) finely chopped hazelnuts or walnuts before beating in egg yolks.

Coffee Soufflé   V

Follow recipe and method for Chocolate Soufflé but omit chocolate. Add 1 tbsp instant coffee granules to hot milk.

Banana Soufflé   V

Follow recipe and method for Chocolate Soufflé but omit chocolate. Add 2 small bananas mashed with 2 tsp lemon juice before beating in egg yolks.

Cold Soufflé

To prepare a soufflé dish for a cold soufflé, first cut a strip of greaseproof paper long enough to go around the outside of the soufflé dish. It should be deep enough to stand about 5cm (2in) above the top of the dish. Secure paper with string around outside of dish. It should fit closely around the rim to prevent mixture escaping down sides of dish. Brush inside of greaseproof paper with a little oil and stand prepared dish on a small tray.

Lemon Soufflé

Serves 4   Preparation 30 mins   Cooking 2 mins
Per portion 700 kcals, 59g fat (28.6g saturated)

1 tbsp (about 15g packet) powdered gelatine
4 eggs, separated
110g (4oz) caster sugar
Grated rind and juice of 2 lemons
300ml (½ pint) double cream, softly whipped
40g (1½oz) almonds
Whipped cream to decorate

Prepare dish as for cold soufflé.

Sprinkle gelatine over 3 tbsp water in a basin. Stand for 10 minutes.

Dissolve gelatine over a pan of boiling water. Leave to cool.

Whisk egg yolks and sugar together in a bowl over a pan of hot water until very thick and pale.

Remove bowl from hot water and continue whisking until mixture is cool.

Gently whisk in dissolved gelatine, lemon rind and juice.

Leave until just beginning to thicken and set.

Beat egg whites to a stiff snow.

Gently fold cream into lemon mixture. Fold in beaten egg whites.

Pour into prepared soufflé dish. Chill until firm and set.

Toast almonds under grill for 2–3 minutes, then chop.

Just before serving, ease greaseproof paper away from mixture with a knife dipped into hot water.

Gently press chopped nuts against sides of soufflé.

Decorate top with whipped cream.

Meringues (with fresh cream)

Meringues

Meringues ❄ V

Makes 16   Preparation 20 mins   Cooking 2½ hrs
Per meringue 35 kcals, 0g fat (0g saturated)

2 egg whites
Pinch of cream of tartar (optional)
110g (4oz) caster sugar
25g (1oz) granulated sugar

Brush a large baking sheet with oil. Cover with a double thickness of greaseproof or non-stick baking paper. Do not brush paper with more oil.

Put egg whites into a clean dry bowl. Add cream of tartar, if using. Beat until stiff and peaky.

Add half the caster sugar.

Continue beating until meringue is shiny and stands in firm peaks.

Add remaining caster sugar. Beat until meringue is very stiff and silky-looking and texture is fairly close. Gently fold in granulated sugar.

Pipe or spoon 16 rounds or ovals on to prepared sheet.

Bake at 110°C (225°F) Mark ¼ for 2½ hours or until crisp and firm.

Transfer to a wire cooling rack and leave until cold.

Variations

Coffee Meringues ❄ V

Follow recipe and method for Meringues. Add 2 tsp instant coffee powder with granulated sugar. Sandwich together with whipped cream or Butter Cream (page 269).

Brown Sugar Meringues ❄ V

Follow recipe and method for Meringues. Use 110g (4oz) light soft brown sugar in place of caster sugar. Sandwich together with whipped cream.

Walnut Chocolate Fingers ❄ V

Follow recipe and method for Meringues. Add 50g (2oz) very finely chopped walnuts with granulated sugar. Pipe 20 x 7.5cm (3in) lengths of mixture on to a prepared baking sheet. When cold, dip ends in melted chocolate. Sandwich together with whipped cream.

175

Meringue Topping ❄ V
Preparation 15 mins

2 egg whites
75g (3oz) caster sugar
1 tbsp granulated sugar (optional)

Put egg whites into a clean, dry bowl. Beat until stiff and peaky.

Gently fold in caster sugar with a large metal spoon.

Pile meringue over pie or pudding, etc., and sprinkle with granulated sugar, if using.

Baking

Quick cooking is essential if meringue is used as decoration on frozen or chilled desserts. Flash bake dish for 1–3 minutes towards top of a hot oven 230°C (450°F) Mark 8 until meringue just starts turning gold.

If meringue is on a pudding or pie that is made to be served cold later, dry out the meringue thoroughly, otherwise it will sag on standing and become wet and syrupy. Put dish into centre of a very slow oven 110°C (225°F) Mark ¼ and bake for 1½–2 hours, or until meringue is firm, crisp and golden.

For a hot pudding topped with meringue, bake in centre of a slow oven 150°C (300°F) Mark 2 for 20–30 minutes, or until pale gold.

Pear & Hazelnut Meringue V
Serves 6–8 Preparation 50 mins Cooking 45 mins
Per meringue 451 kcals, 30g fat (12g saturated)

4 egg whites
275g (10oz) caster sugar
Few drops of vanilla extract
1 tsp white wine vinegar
110g (4oz) ground hazelnuts, toasted
450g (1lb) pears, peeled, cored and chopped
300ml (½ pint) double cream, whipped
Whole hazelnuts to decorate

Whisk egg whites until stiff, then whisk in 250g (9oz) of sugar a spoonful at a time.

Continue whisking until meringue is very stiff and holds its shape.

Fold in vanilla extract, vinegar and nuts.

Divide between two lined and greased 20cm (8in) sandwich tins and spread evenly.

Bake at 180°C (350°F) Mark 4 for 45 minutes.

Place pears, remaining sugar and 50ml (2fl oz) water in a saucepan. Cover and cook for 10–15 minutes until tender.

Strain off any liquid and leave until cold. Fold into three quarters of the cream.

Sandwich meringue rounds together with pear and cream filling.

Decorate with remaining cream and nuts.

Lemon Meringues V
Serves 4 Preparation 30 mins Cooking 40 mins
Per meringue 258 kcals, 10g fat (4.9g saturated)

25g (1oz) cornflour
300ml (½ pint) milk
110g (4oz) caster sugar
25g (1oz) butter, diced
Grated rind and juice of 1 lemon
2 eggs, separated

Blend cornflour with milk.

Pour into a small saucepan and heat, stirring, until sauce thickens, boils and is smooth.

Add 50g (2oz) sugar, butter and lemon rind. Stir in lemon juice.

Cool slightly. Stir in egg yolks.

Turn mixture into 4 ramekin dishes.

Whisk egg whites stiffly. Fold in all but a dessertspoonful of remaining sugar.

Pile meringue over lemon filling in each dish. Sprinkle with remaining sugar.

Bake at 150°C (300°F) Mark 2 for 20–30 minutes until golden brown.

Berry Meringue V
Serves 6 Preparation 20 mins Cooking 25 mins
Per meringue 150 kcals, 0g fat (0g saturated)

150g (5oz) strawberries, hulled and sliced
450g (1lb) mixed fresh berries
175g (6oz) caster sugar
25g (1oz) plain flour
2 egg whites

Put strawberries and berries in a bowl. Add 50g (2oz) sugar and all flour and mix gently.

Spread in a baking dish measuring about 25cm (9½in) wide x 3.5cm (1½in) deep.

Whisk egg whites to stiff peaks. Gradually whisk in remaining sugar to stiff peaks.

Spoon into large piping bag fitted with a large star nozzle and pipe in overlapping swirls on top of fruit and all around the edge. Pipe a large swirl in centre.

Place on a baking tray and cook at 190°C (375°F) Mark 5 for 20–25 minutes, or until meringue is lightly browned.

Strawberry Pavlova

Almond & Apricot Meringue   V

Serves 6–8   Preparation 45 mins   Cooking 1¼ hrs
Per meringue 467 kcals, 36g fat (17.6g saturated)

---

4 egg whites
225g (8oz) caster sugar
Pinch of cream of tartar
75g (3oz) ground almonds
110g (4oz) canned apricots, drained
450ml (¾ pint) double cream
Grated chocolate to decorate

Line two baking sheets with greased
greaseproof or non-stick baking paper.
Draw a 20cm (8in) circle on the under side of
each piece of paper.
Whisk egg whites until stiff; add 1 tbsp caster
sugar and cream of tartar. Whisk for 1 minute.
Fold in remaining sugar and almonds.
Spread mixture over marked circles.
Bake at 140°C (275°F) Mark 1 for 1¼ hours or
until bottoms of meringues are firm.
Remove paper and leave to cool.
Purée apricots in a blender until smooth.
Whip cream until softly stiff. Fold apricot
purée into two thirds of cream.
Put one meringue disc on serving plate.

Cover with apricot mixture, then top with
remaining meringue disc.
Decorate with remaining cream and grated
chocolate.

Strawberry Pavlova   V

Serves 6   Preparation 20 mins   Cooking 1 hr
Per meringue 382 kcals, 27g fat (15.1g saturated)

---

3 egg whites
175g (6oz) caster sugar
1 tsp cornflour
1 tsp white wine vinegar
300ml (½ pint) double cream
225g (8oz) strawberries, halved

Whisk egg whites until stiff.
Whisk in caster sugar 1 tsp at a time.
Mix cornflour and vinegar together and very
gently fold into egg whites.
Spoon mixture into a round on to a baking
sheet covered with non-stick baking paper.
Bake at 140°C (275°F) Mark 1 for 1 hour or
until crisp and dry.
Whip cream until softly stiff.
Pile cream into centre of Pavlova and
decorate with strawberries.

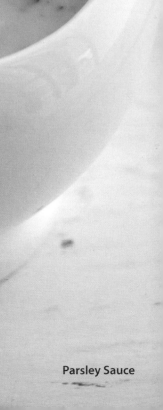

Sauces, Stuffings, Marinades & Butters

Parsley Sauce

Savoury Sauces

A pouring sauce will glaze the back of a wooden spoon and pours easily. Use for vegetables, pasta or serving separately or if you prefer a thin sauce.

A coating sauce will coat the back of a wooden spoon and will only just settle to its own level in the saucepan. Use for coating eggs, chicken, fish and vegetables.

Basic White Pouring Sauce ❄ V

Serves 4 Preparation 2 mins Cooking 15 mins
Per portion 76 kcals, 4g fat (2.7g saturated)

15g (½oz) butter
15g (½oz) plain flour
300ml (½ pint) milk
Salt and freshly ground black pepper

Melt butter in a saucepan.
Add flour and cook over a low heat, stirring, for 2 minutes. Do not allow mixture (roux) to brown.
Gradually blend in milk.
Cook, stirring, until sauce thickens, boils and is smooth.
Simmer gently for 3 minutes.
Season to taste.

Variations

Basic White Coating Sauce ❄ V

Follow recipe and method for Basic White Pouring Sauce. Increase butter and flour to 25g (1oz) each.

Easy White Sauce ❄ V

Follow recipe for Basic White Pouring Sauce. Put butter, flour and milk into a saucepan. Heat, whisking continuously, until sauce thickens, boils and is smooth. Add seasoning to taste.

Parsley Sauce ❄ V

For bacon, ham and fish dishes.
Follow recipe and method for either Basic White Pouring Sauce or Basic White Coating Sauce. After seasoning, stir in 2 tbsp chopped parsley.

Cheese Sauce ❄ V

For fish, poultry, ham, bacon, egg and vegetable dishes.

Follow recipe and method for either Basic White Pouring Sauce or Basic White Coating Sauce. Before seasoning, stir in 50g (2oz) finely grated Cheddar cheese or 50g (2oz) crumbled Lancashire cheese. Then add ½–1 tsp mustard and a pinch of cayenne pepper.

Mustard Sauce ❄ V

For herring, mackerel, cheese, ham and bacon dishes.

Follow recipe and method for either Basic White Pouring Sauce or Basic White Coating Sauce. Before seasoning, stir in 2 tsp mustard powder mixed with 2 tsp white wine vinegar. Reheat gently before using.

Mushroom Sauce ❄ V

For fish, poultry, veal, egg and cheese dishes.
Follow recipe and method for either Basic White Pouring Sauce or Basic White Coating Sauce.
Before seasoning, stir in 50–75g (2–3oz) mushrooms that have been finely chopped and lightly fried in butter. Reheat gently before using.

Prawn Sauce ❄

For fish dishes.
Follow recipe and method for either Basic White Pouring Sauce or Basic White Coating Sauce.
Before seasoning, stir in 50g (2oz) finely chopped, cooked peeled prawns, ½ tsp mustard powder mixed with 2 tsp lemon juice and ½ tsp anchovy essence. Reheat gently before using.

Onion Sauce ❄ V

For grilled and roast lamb.
Follow recipe and method for either Basic White Pouring Sauce or Basic White Coating Sauce. Before seasoning, stir in 1 large onion, boiled and finely chopped. Reheat gently before using.

Lemon Sauce ❄ V

For fish, poultry, egg and veal dishes.
Follow recipe and method for either Basic White Pouring Sauce or Basic White Coating Sauce. Before seasoning, stir in the grated rind of 1 small lemon and 1 tbsp lemon juice. Reheat gently before using.

Béchamel Sauce ❄ V

Serves 4 Preparation 15 mins plus standing Cooking 25 mins Per portion 140 kcals, 11g fat (6.3g saturated)

For fish, poultry, egg and vegetable dishes.
300ml (½ pint) milk
1 small onion, peeled and quartered
1 small carrot, peeled and sliced
½ small celery stick, sliced
2 cloves
6 peppercorns
1 blade of mace
1 sprig of parsley
25g (1oz) butter
25g (1oz) plain flour
Salt and freshly ground black pepper
2 tbsp double cream

Put milk into a saucepan. Add onion, carrot, celery, cloves, peppercorns, mace and parsley. Slowly bring just to the boil.
Remove from heat and cover. Leave to stand for 30 minutes.
Strain and reserve flavoured milk.
Melt butter in pan, add flour and cook over a low heat, stirring, for 2 minutes. Do not allow mixture (or roux) to brown.
Gradually blend in flavoured milk.
Cook, stirring, until sauce thickens, boils and is smooth. Simmer gently for 3 minutes.
Remove from heat, season and stir in cream.

Variations

Mock Hollandaise V

For poultry and fish dishes.
Follow recipe and method for Béchamel Sauce. Before seasoning, stir in 1 egg yolk mixed with 2 tbsp double cream and 2 tsp lemon juice. Reheat. Do not allow to boil.

Aurore Sauce ❄ V

For fish, egg and chicken dishes.
Follow recipe and method for Béchamel Sauce. Before seasoning, stir in 2 tbsp tomato purée and ½ tsp sugar. Reheat gently. Do not boil.

Mornay Sauce ❄ V

For poultry, fish, shellfish and egg dishes.
Follow recipe and method for Béchamel Sauce. Before seasoning, stir in an extra 2 tbsp double cream and 50g (2oz) grated

Cheddar cheese. Stand over a low heat. Whisk until smooth. Do not allow to boil.

Blender Hollandaise V

Serves 4 Preparation 10 mins Cooking 5 mins
Per portion 230 kcals, 25g fat (14.8g saturated)

3 egg yolks
1 tbsp lemon juice
Salt and freshly ground black pepper
110g (4oz) butter, melted

Place egg yolks, lemon juice and seasoning in a blender or food processor.
Cover and blend for a few seconds to mix.
Gradually pour hot, melted butter into blender while processing at high speed.
Blend until thick and light, and serve.

Hollandaise Sauce V

Serves 6 Preparation 5 mins Cooking 15 mins
Per portion 329 kcals, 35g fat (20.8g saturated)

For asparagus, broccoli, poached fish, egg and chicken dishes.
1 tsp lemon juice
1 tsp white wine vinegar
3 peppercorns
½ small bay leaf
4 egg yolks
225g (8oz) butter, softened
Salt and freshly ground black pepper

Put lemon juice, vinegar, 1 tbsp cold water, peppercorns and bay leaf into a saucepan. Boil gently until liquor is reduced by half.
Leave until cold and strain.
Put egg yolks and reduced vinegar liquor into a basin standing over a pan of gently simmering water.
Whisk until thick and foamy.
Gradually add butter, a tiny piece at a time. Continue whisking until each piece has been absorbed by the sauce.
Season to taste and serve.

Variation

Mousseline Sauce V

For asparagus, broccoli, poached fish, egg and chicken dishes.
Follow recipe and method for Hollandaise Sauce. Stir in 3 tbsp lightly whipped double cream just before serving.

Velouté Sauce

Serves 4–6   Preparation 5 mins   Cooking 50 mins
Per portion 69 kcals, 6g fat (5.2g saturated)

For poultry and veal, or poached, grilled and steamed fish dishes.

25g (1oz) butter
25g (1oz) mushrooms, wiped and finely chopped
2 or 3 parsley sprigs
25g (1oz) plain flour
300ml (½ pint) poultry, veal or fish stock (depending on dish)
2 peppercorns
2 tsp lemon juice
4 tbsp double cream or soured cream
Salt and freshly ground black pepper

Melt butter in a heavy saucepan. Add mushrooms and parsley and fry gently for 5 minutes.
Stir in flour. Gradually blend in stock. Add peppercorns.
Cook, stirring, until sauce comes to the boil and thickens.
Reduce heat, then cover pan. Simmer very gently for 30 minutes.
Strain, then stir in lemon juice and cream. Season to taste.
Reheat gently before using. Do not allow to boil.

Béarnaise Sauce   V

Serves 4   Preparation 5 mins   Cooking 20 mins
Per portion 244 kcals, 26g fat (15.2g saturated)

For meat grills and roasts or grilled fish.

2 tbsp tarragon wine vinegar (or ½ tsp dried tarragon with 2 tbsp white wine vinegar)
3 tbsp white wine vinegar
1 tbsp finely chopped onion
2 egg yolks
110g (4oz) butter, softened
Salt and freshly ground black pepper
1 tbsp chopped parsley

Put both vinegars and onion into a saucepan. Boil gently until liquid is reduced by about one third.
Leave until cold and strain.
Put egg yolks, reduced vinegar liquor and 2 tsp cold water into a basin standing over a pan of simmering water. Whisk until thick and fluffy.

Gradually add butter, a tiny piece at a time. Continue whisking until each piece has been absorbed by the sauce and it has thickened.
Season to taste and stir in parsley.

Meat or Poultry Gravy

Serves 4–6   Preparation 5 mins   Cooking 15 mins
Per portion 23 kcals, 1g fat (0.6g saturated)

Fat and sediment from roasting tin
1 tbsp cornflour
300ml (½ pint) meat stock or vegetable water

Pour off all but 1 tbsp fat from roasting tin.
Add cornflour and mix with fat and sediment.
Stand tin over a low heat. Gradually blend in stock or vegetable water.
Cook, stirring, until gravy comes to the boil and thickens.
Lower heat. Simmer for 3 minutes.

Cranberry Sauce   V

Serves 6   Preparation 3 mins   Cooking 25 mins
Per portion 121 kcals, 0g fat (0g saturated)

For duck, goose, game, turkey and lamb.

175g (6oz) granulated sugar
225g (8oz) cranberries

Put 300ml (½ pint) water and sugar into a saucepan. Heat slowly until sugar dissolves.
Add cranberries. Cook fairly quickly for 2–3 minutes or until skins pop open.
Reduce heat. Simmer gently for 10 minutes.

Cumberland Sauce   ❄ V

Serves 4   Preparation 10 mins plus standing   Cooking 10 mins   Per portion 66 kcals, 0g fat (0g saturated)

For ham and game dishes.

150ml (¼ pint) red wine or port
4 tbsp redcurrant jelly
Grated rind and juice of 1 lemon and 1 orange
2 tsp finely grated onion
1 tsp English mustard
¼ tsp ground ginger
Salt and freshly ground black pepper

Put all ingredients into a saucepan. Slowly bring just up to the boil, stirring occasionally.
Remove from heat. Cover and leave for 10 minutes.
Leave unstrained and serve hot or strain and serve cold.

Apple Sauce ❄ V

Serves 6   Preparation 10 mins   Cooking 15 mins
Per portion 32 kcals, 0g fat (0g saturated)

For grilled or roast pork, duck and goose dishes.

450g (1lb) cooking apples, peeled, cored and sliced

2 tsp caster sugar (optional)

Put apples into a saucepan with 3 tbsp water and cook until soft and pulpy.
Either rub through a sieve or liquidise.
Return to pan, then add sugar, if using.
Reheat gently.

Mint Sauce ❄ V

Serves 4–6   Preparation 10 mins
Per portion 11 kcals, 0g fat (0g saturated)

For roast lamb.

4 tbsp finely chopped mint

1 tbsp caster sugar

¼ tsp salt

3 tbsp white wine vinegar

Stir mint into 3 tbsp boiling water.
Add sugar and salt.
Leave until cold.
Add vinegar and mix well.

Tomato Sauce ❄ V

Serves 4–6   Preparation 10 mins   Cooking 25 mins
Per portion 41 kcals, 2.2g fat (0.3g saturated)

For meat, fish, eggs and pasta dishes.

1 tbsp olive oil

1 onion, peeled and chopped

1 garlic clove, peeled and crushed

400g can chopped tomatoes

1 tbsp tomato purée

300ml (½ pint) vegetable stock

Pinch of ground mace

2 tsp dried mixed herbs

Freshly ground black pepper

Heat oil in a saucepan. Add onion and garlic and fry until golden.
Stir in tomatoes, tomato purée, stock, mace and herbs. Season to taste.
Bring to the boil, stirring. Reduce heat and cover.
Simmer gently for 20 minutes.
Purée with hand-held blender (optional).

Curry Sauce ❄ V

Serves 4   Preparation 10 mins   Cooking 1¼ hrs
Per portion 182 kcals, 14g fat (6.8g saturated)

For pouring over hard-boiled eggs or mixing with cooked fish, chicken, meat or vegetables.

50g (2oz) butter

2 tsp olive oil

2 large onions, peeled and finely chopped

1 garlic clove, peeled and crushed

2 tbsp curry powder

1 tbsp plain flour

2 cloves

1 tbsp tomato purée

¼ tsp ground ginger

¼ tsp cinnamon

2 tbsp sweet pickle or chutney

1 tbsp lemon juice

450ml (¾ pint) vegetable stock

Put butter and oil into a saucepan. Heat until both are sizzling. Add onions and garlic. Fry gently until pale gold.
Stir in curry powder and flour. Add cloves, tomato purée, ginger and cinnamon, sweet pickle or chutney and lemon juice.
Gradually blend in stock. Slowly bring to the boil, stirring.
Lower heat and cover pan. Simmer slowly for 45 minutes–1 hour.
The sauce may be strained and reheated before using.

Sweet & Sour Sauce

Serves 4–6   Preparation 5 mins   Cooking 30 mins
Per portion 172 kcals, 10g fat (6.5g saturated)

For meats or poultry.

50g (2oz) butter

2 onions, peeled and finely chopped

2 tbsp tomato purée

300ml (½ pint) cider

150ml (¼ pint) water

1 tbsp demerara sugar

Salt and freshly ground black pepper

2 tbsp Worcestershire sauce

2 tbsp mango chutney

Melt butter in a saucepan and fry onions until soft. Add remaining ingredients.
Bring to the boil, stirring, and simmer for 15–20 minutes uncovered.

Bread Sauce ❄ V

Serves 4`–6 Preparation 5 mins Cooking 30 mins
Per portion 163 kcals, 11g fat (6.3g saturated)

For roast poultry.
4 cloves
1 small onion, peeled
6 peppercorns
1 blade of mace or large pinch of nutmeg
½ small bay leaf
300ml (½ pint) milk
50g (2oz) white breadcrumbs
Salt and freshly ground black pepper
25g (1oz) butter
2 tbsp single cream

Press cloves into onion and put into a saucepan. Add peppercorns, mace or nutmeg, bay leaf and milk.
Slowly bring to the boil. Reduce heat, cover pan and simmer for 15 minutes.
Strain. Combine hot milk with breadcrumbs. Simmer gently for 10–15 minutes. Stir occasionally.
Season to taste, then stir in butter and cream. Reheat gently.

Brown or Espagnole Sauce ❄

Serves 4 Preparation 20 mins Cooking 1 hr
Per portion 90 kcals, 6g fat (3.4g saturated)

25g (1oz) butter
1 tsp olive oil
25g (1oz) lean ham or bacon, chopped
½ small onion, peeled and chopped
½ small celery stick, chopped
25g (1oz) mushrooms, wiped and sliced
½ small carrot, peeled and sliced
25g (1oz) plain flour
450ml (¾ pint) beef stock
2 tsp tomato purée or 1 small chopped tomato
1 small bay leaf
2 sprigs of parsley
Salt and freshly ground black pepper

Put butter and oil into saucepan. Heat until both are sizzling.
Add ham or bacon, onion, celery, mushrooms and carrot.
Fry gently for 7–10 minutes or until golden.
Add flour and cook, stirring, until it turns light brown.

Gradually blend in stock. Cook, stirring, until sauce comes to the boil and thickens.
Add purée or chopped tomato, bay leaf and parsley. Cover pan.
Simmer gently for 30 minutes.
Strain, then season to taste.
Reheat before using.

Satay Sauce V

Serves 4 Preparation 5 mins Cooking 10 mins
Per portion 432 kcals, 41g fat (22g saturated)

25g (1oz) butter
50g (2oz) creamed coconut
110g (4oz) unsalted peanuts, ground
300ml (½ pint) single cream
1 tbsp soy sauce

Put butter and coconut into a saucepan with 125ml (4fl oz) water and heat until butter has melted.
Add remaining ingredients and heat through, stirring.
Cook on a low heat until slightly thickened.

Clarified Butter ❄ V

Clarifying butter raises the temperature at which butter browns and burns and also allows you to store it for a longer period of time. It can be used for cooking, melted as a sauce or for sealing foods such as pâté.
Place butter in a saucepan and melt over a low heat.
Leave to stand for a few minutes then strain through muslin into a clean bowl.
Discard milky sediment in base of saucepan.
Store in refrigerator.
Melt required amount of clarified butter when ready to use.

Lemon Butter Sauce ❄ V

Serves 4 Preparation 5 mins Cooking 5 mins
Per portion 169 kcals, 19g fat (12g saturated)

For poached and steamed fish dishes.
75g (3oz) clarified butter
1 tbsp chopped parsley
1 tsp lemon juice

Place butter in a saucepan. Heat gently until it turns light brown.
Stir in remaining ingredients. Serve immediately.

Pesto Sauce

Pesto Sauce

Serves 4   Preparation 20 mins
Per portion 257 kcals, 27g fat (4.5g saturated)

For pasta and chicken or fish.
25g (1oz) basil leaves
25g (1oz) pine nuts
1 garlic clove, peeled
25g (1oz) Parmesan cheese, finely grated
90ml (3fl oz) extra virgin olive oil
Salt and freshly ground black pepper

Place basil, pine nuts, garlic and cheese in a food processor and blend until smooth.
Very gradually add olive oil with food processor running; do not add too quickly.
Season to taste and serve or chill until using.

Variations

Vegetarian Pesto Sauce   V

Follow recipe and method for Pesto Sauce but use a vegetarian Italian hard cheese in place of the Parmesan.

Parsley Pesto Sauce

Follow recipe and method for Pesto Sauce but use parsley instead of basil and walnuts instead of pine nuts.

Barbeque Sauce   ❄ V

Serves 4–6   Preparation 3 mins   Cooking 25 mins
Per portion 93 kcals, 4g fat (2.2g saturated)

For meat, poultry or fish.
300ml (½ pint) tomato ketchup
25g (1oz) butter
3 tbsp white wine vinegar
¼ tsp chilli powder
1 tsp brown sugar
½ tsp celery salt
½ tsp dried mixed herbs

Put all ingredients into a saucepan.
Bring slowly to the boil, stirring.
Cover saucepan, simmer gently for 15 minutes and then serve.

Sweet Sauces

Sweet White Sauce ❄ V

Serves 4–6   Preparation 5 mins   Cooking 15 mins
Per portion 55 kcals, 2g fat (1.4g saturated)

For steamed and baked puddings.
15g (½oz) cornflour
300ml (½ pint) milk
Knob of butter
1 tbsp caster sugar

Mix cornflour to a smooth paste with a little of the cold milk.
Warm remaining milk in a saucepan. Pour on to paste and mix well. Return to pan.
Cook stirring until sauce thickens, boils and is smooth. Simmer for 2 minutes.
Remove from heat. Stir in butter and sugar.

Variations

Brandy Sauce V

For Christmas puddings, baked and steamed fruit puddings.
Follow recipe and method for Sweet White Sauce. Add 2 tbsp brandy with the butter and sugar.

Vanilla Sauce V

For steamed and baked puddings.
Follow recipe and method for Sweet White Sauce. Add 1 tsp vanilla extract with the butter and sugar.

Cocoa Sauce V

Follow recipe and method for Sweet White Sauce. Add 15g (½oz) cocoa powder with the cornflour.

Ruby Red Sauce V

Serves 6   Preparation 10 mins   Cooking 7 mins
Per portion 95 kcals, 0.1g fat (0g saturated)

For ice cream or steamed puddings.
225g (8oz) frozen summer fruits, thawed
175g (6oz) redcurrant jelly
50ml (2fl oz) port

Place fruit in a blender or food processor and purée. Pass through a sieve to remove seeds.
Place purée in a saucepan with jelly and port.
Heat until jelly has melted.

Raspberry Sauce V

Serves 6   Preparation 10 mins
Per portion 19 kcals, 0.1g fat (0g saturated)

For fresh fruit, ice cream and mousses.
225g (8oz) raspberries
Icing sugar, sifted

Place raspberries in a blender or food processor and purée.
Pass purée through a sieve into a bowl to remove seeds.
Stir sufficient icing sugar into fruit purée to sweeten to taste.
Serve, or store in refrigerator.

Jam or Marmalade Sauce V

Serves 4–6   Preparation 5 mins   Cooking 15 mins
Per portion 46 kcals, 0g fat (0g saturated)

For steamed and baked puddings.
2 tsp cornflour
4 tbsp jam or marmalade
2 tsp lemon juice

Mix cornflour to a smooth paste with a little cold water.
Put 150ml (¼ pint) water into a saucepan. Add jam or marmalade and lemon juice.
Heat gently, stirring, until jam has dissolved. Blend with cornflour paste.
Return to saucepan. Cook, stirring, until sauce boils, thickens and clears.
Simmer for 2 minutes.

Caramel Sauce V

Serves 4   Preparation 5 mins   Cooking 20 mins
Per portion 556 kcals, 34g fat (18.8g saturated)

250g (9oz) caster sugar
250ml (9fl oz) double cream

Put sugar in a saucepan with 150ml (¼ pint) water.
Stir over a low heat until dissolved.
Boil for 10 minutes, brushing any crystallised sugar from the sides with a damp pastry brush.
Warm cream in a separate saucepan.
Remove caramel from heat and plunge base of saucepan into iced water. Leave to cool slightly.
Slowly stir cream into caramel. Return to heat and simmer for 5 minutes.
Strain through a sieve.

Butterscotch Sauce   V

Serves 4–6 Preparation 2 mins Cooking 15 mins
Per portion 235 kcals, 20g fat (11.9g saturated)

For steamed and baked puddings, sliced bananas, or ice cream.

150ml (¼ pint) double cream
50g (2oz) unsalted butter
75g (3oz) light soft brown sugar
½ tsp vanilla extract

Place cream, butter and sugar in a saucepan. Heat gently, stirring continuously, until sugar has dissolved.
Boil for 2 minutes until syrupy.
Stir in vanilla and serve warm.

Chocolate Sauce   V

Serves 4–6 Preparation 10 mins Cooking 15 mins
Per portion 101 kcals, 5g fat (3.1g saturated)

For steamed and baked puddings.

1 tbsp cornflour
300ml (½ pint) milk
50g (2oz) plain chocolate, grated
½ tsp vanilla extract
15g (½oz) butter
1 tbsp caster sugar

Mix cornflour to a smooth paste with a little of the cold milk.
Put remaining milk into a saucepan and add chocolate. Heat very slowly until chocolate melts.
Pour chocolate on to cornflour paste and mix well.
Return to saucepan.
Cook, stirring, until sauce comes to the boil and thickens.
Add vanilla, butter and sugar. Simmer for 3 minutes.

Luxury Chocolate Sauce   V

Serves 4–6 Preparation 5 mins Cooking 5 mins
Per portion 198 kcals, 11g fat (6.4g saturated)

For ice cream or profiteroles.

175g (6oz) plain chocolate
20g (¾oz) butter
3 tbsp golden syrup
1 tsp vanilla extract

Break chocolate into small pieces.
Place in a small saucepan with butter, 3 tbsp water and golden syrup.

Heat gently until chocolate and butter have melted.
Remove from heat.
Add vanilla extract and stir to mix. Serve warm.

Real Custard   V

Serves 4–6 Preparation 5 mins plus standing Cooking 15 mins Per portion 90 kcals, 5g fat (1.7g saturated)

For steamed and baked puddings, fruit and mince pies and stewed fruit, as well as trifles and fools.

300ml (½ pint) milk
1 vanilla pod
4 egg yolks
25g (1oz) sugar

Reserve 3 tbsp milk.
Place remaining milk and vanilla pod in a saucepan. Gently heat until milk is almost boiling.
Remove from heat and leave to stand for 15 minutes.
Place egg yolks, sugar and reserved milk in a bowl. Beat until thick and creamy.
Remove vanilla pod from milk and pour milk on to egg mixture.
Strain mixture into a heavy based saucepan and cook, stirring, until custard thinly coats the back of a spoon (about the thickness of single cream).
Pour into a cold jug.
Serve hot or cold. The sauce thickens on cooling.

Variations

Coffee Custard   V

Follow recipe and method for Real Custard. Omit vanilla and add 1 tsp instant coffee granules to warm milk.

Orange Custard   V

Follow recipe and method for Real Custard. Omit vanilla and add 1 tsp grated orange rind before heating milk.

Chocolate Custard   V

Follow recipe and method for Real Custard. Omit vanilla and add 50g (2oz) finely grated plain chocolate.

Fudge Sauce

Serves 4   Preparation 10 mins   Cooking 15 mins
Per portion 180 kcals, 5g fat (3g saturated)

For ice cream, steamed and baked puddings.

25g (1oz) plain chocolate
15g (½oz) butter
2 tbsp milk, warmed
110g (4oz) soft brown sugar
1 tbsp golden syrup
½ tsp vanilla extract

Break up chocolate.

Put into a basin standing over a saucepan of hot water. Add butter.

Leave until chocolate and butter have melted, stirring once or twice.

Blend in milk. Transfer to a saucepan. Add sugar and golden syrup.

Stand over a low heat. Stir until sugar has dissolved.

Bring to the boil. Boil steadily without stirring for 5 minutes.

Remove from heat. Add vanilla and mix well.

Serve hot.

Brandy Butter ❄ V

Serves 6–8   Preparation 20 mins
Per portion 151 kcals, 4g fat (0g saturated)

For Christmas puddings, mince pies, baked and steamed fruit puddings.

110g (4oz) butter, softened
110g (4oz) icing sugar, sifted
110g (4oz) caster sugar
1 tbsp milk
1 tbsp brandy
50g (2oz) ground almonds
Ground cinnamon

Beat butter until creamy. Gradually beat in icing and caster sugars alternately with milk and brandy.

Cream until light and fluffy. Add almonds and mix well.

Pile into small dish. Sprinkle lightly with cinnamon.

Variation

Rum Butter ❄ V

Follow recipe and method for Brandy Butter but use rum in place of brandy.

Stuffings

When stuffing a bird only place it in the neck end, not in the body cavity unless it is boned. Do not stuff until just before cook time. Do not pack stuffing too tightly as it will expand on cooking. Cook any surplus stuffing in an ovenproof dish. If cooking on its own, bake for 25–30 minutes at 200°C (400°F) Mark 6.

Sausagemeat Stuffing ❄

Preparation 10 mins

225g (8oz) pork sausagemeat
110g (4oz) breadcrumbs
½ tsp dried thyme
¼ tsp nutmeg
2 tsp chopped parsley
Salt and freshly ground black pepper
3 tbsp milk

Put all ingredients into a bowl.
Knead well together. Use as required.

Sage & Onion Stuffing ❄ V

Preparation 20 mins   Cooking 20 mins

225g (8oz) onions, peeled and quartered
110g (4oz) breadcrumbs
½ tsp dried sage
Salt and freshly ground black pepper
25g (1oz) butter, melted
Milk

Cook onions in boiling water until tender.
Drain and chop finely.
Mix with breadcrumbs, sage and seasoning.
Bind loosely with melted butter and milk.
Use as required.

Lemon & Herb Stuffing ❄ V

Preparation 25 mins

110g (4oz) breadcrumbs
1 tbsp chopped parsley
½ tsp grated lemon rind
½ tsp dried thyme
Salt and freshly ground black pepper
25g (1oz) butter, melted
Milk

Mix breadcrumbs with parsley, lemon rind, thyme and seasoning.
Bind loosely with melted butter and milk.
Use as required.

Prawn Stuffing

Preparation 25 mins

110g (4oz) breadcrumbs
2 tsp chopped parsley
½ tsp grated lemon rind
50g (2oz) cooked peeled prawns, chopped
Salt and freshly ground black pepper
25g (1oz) butter, melted
Milk

Mix breadcrumbs with parsley, lemon rind, prawns and seasoning.
Bind loosely with melted butter and milk. Use as required.

Chestnut Stuffing ❄ V

Preparation 15 mins plus soaking overnight
Cooking 30 mins

110g (4oz) dried chestnuts, soaked overnight
110g (4oz) breadcrumbs
2 tsp finely grated onion
¼ tsp nutmeg
2 tbsp chopped parsley
Salt and freshly ground black pepper
50g (2oz) butter, melted
Single cream

Drain chestnuts. Cook in boiling water for 20–30 minutes or until tender.
Drain and chop chestnuts.
Mix with onion, breadcrumbs, nutmeg, parsley and seasoning.
Bind with butter and cream. Use as required.

Apple & Walnut Stuffing ❄ V

Preparation 35 mins

450g (1lb) cooking apples, peeled, cored and chopped
1 tbsp caster sugar
110g (4oz) breadcrumbs
25g (1oz) walnut halves, chopped
2 tsp finely grated onion (optional)
Salt and freshly ground black pepper
50g (2oz) butter, melted
Beaten egg

Mix apples with sugar, breadcrumbs, walnuts and onion, if using.
Season to taste. Mix loosely with melted butter and beaten egg if necessary. Use as required.

Marinades

Wine Marinade ❄
Preparation 10 mins plus 8–12 hrs marinating

For large legs and shoulders of lamb and game.

6 tbsp red wine
3 tbsp wine vinegar
3 tbsp olive oil
1 sprig each of parsley and thyme
2 small bay leaves, crumbled
1 garlic clove, peeled and crushed
1 small onion, peeled and sliced
¼ tsp nutmeg
1 tbsp caster sugar
Shake of cayenne pepper

Combine ingredients well together in a shallow container.

Add meat and toss in marinade until well coated.

Cover and chill for 8–12 hours, turning at least twice.

Yogurt Marinade
Preparation 10 mins plus 3 hrs marinating

For cubes of lamb.

275g (10oz) natural yogurt
2 tbsp lemon juice
2 tbsp grated onion
1 tsp salt
2 garlic cloves, peeled and crushed

Combine ingredients well together in a shallow container.

Add cubes of lamb and toss in marinade until well coated.

Cover and chill for at least 3 hours, turning frequently.

Spice Marinade ❄
Preparation 5 mins plus 5 hrs marinating

For cubes or small fillets of fish; cubes or cutlets of lamb.

2 tsp grated lemon rind
2 tsp turmeric
2 tsp ground ginger
2 garlic cloves, peeled and crushed
4 tbsp lemon juice
1 tsp salt

Combine ingredients well together in a shallow container.

Add fish or meat and toss in marinade until well coated.

Cover and chill for 5 hours, turning frequently.

Fiery Marinade
Preparation 10 mins plus 2–3 hrs marinating

For pork fillets and chops.

2 tsp cayenne pepper
4 tbsp lemon juice
1 small onion, peeled and finely grated
½ tsp mustard powder
4 tsp Worcestershire sauce
1 tsp salt

Combine ingredients well together in a shallow container.

Add meat and toss in marinade until well coated.

Cover and chill for 2–3 hours, turning frequently.

Caribbean Marinade
Preparation 10 mins plus 2 hrs marinating

For slices of duck breast.

2 tbsp rum
Grated rind and juice of 1 lime
Grated rind and juice of 1 orange
2 tbsp soy sauce
150ml (¼ pint) pineapple juice

Combine ingredients well together in a shallow container.

Add slices of duck and toss in marinade until well coated.

Cover and chill for at least 2 hours, turning frequently.

Marination
A marinade makes meat, fish or seafood taste even better as it adds moisture and flavour, especially if you are barbecuing or grilling your food. A marinade not only keeps the food moist, the acidic ingredient (often lemon juice, vinegar or wine) also tenderises it.

Experiment with different marinades and try adding your own flavourings.

Lemon Marinade

Lemon Marinade ✳

Preparation 10 mins plus 3 hrs marinating

For cubes or small fillets of fish of lamb.

2 tbsp lemon juice

3 tbsp olive oil

2 sprigs of rosemary or thyme, chopped

Salt and freshly ground black pepper

Combine ingredients in a shallow container.

Add fish or meat and toss in marinade.

Cover and chill for at least 3 hours, turning frequently.

Beer Marinade ✳

Preparation 10 mins plus 4–5 hrs marinating

For joints of beef and thick steaks.

6 tbsp olive oil

300ml (½ pint) beer

1 garlic clove, peeled and crushed

2 tbsp lemon juice

1 tbsp caster sugar

½ tsp salt

Gradually beat oil into beer then stir in remaining ingredients. Pour over meat.

Cover and chill for 4–5 hours, turning at least twice.

Chicken Marinade ✳

Preparation 15 mins plus 2–3 hrs marinating

For portions of chicken or turkey.

3 tbsp olive oil

6 tbsp dry white wine or cider

1 garlic clove, peeled and crushed

1 small onion, peeled and finely chopped

½ tsp celery salt

Freshly ground black pepper

½ tsp dried thyme or rosemary

Gradually beat oil into wine or cider. Stir in remaining ingredients.

Add chicken portions. Coat all over with marinade mixture.

Cover and chill for 2–3 hours, turning at least twice.

Butters

Highly seasoned butters add piquancy and flavour to grilled or fried meat and fish. After making, they should be well chilled and can be cut into small round shapes and put on to the hot food immediately before serving. All quantities are for 4

Lemon Butter ❄

Preparation 10 mins plus chilling

For fish, veal and chicken.
50g (2oz) butter
1 tsp grated lemon rind
1 tsp lemon juice

Cream butter until soft.
Gradually beat in lemon rind and juice.
Chill and use as required.

Garlic Butter ❄ V

Preparation 10 mins plus chilling

For steaks or bread.
50g (2oz) butter
2 garlic cloves, peeled and crushed

Cream butter until soft. Beat in garlic.
Chill and use as required.

Tomato Butter ❄

Preparation 5 mins plus chilling

For veal, lamb, bacon, ham and shellfish.
50g (2oz) butter
2 tsp tomato purée
¼ tsp caster sugar
¼ tsp Worcestershire sauce

Cream butter until soft.
Beat in remaining ingredients. Chill.

Mustard Butter ❄

Preparation 10 mins plus chilling

For beef, lamb, bacon, ham, shellfish, herrings and mackerel.
50g (2oz) butter
2 tsp French or wholegrain mustard

Cream butter until soft.
Gradually beat in mustard.
Chill and use as required.

Devilled Butter ❄

Preparation 10 mins plus chilling

For shellfish, ham, bacon and pork.
50g (2oz) butter
½ tsp mustard powder
1 tsp Worcestershire sauce
1 tsp lemon juice
Pinch of cayenne pepper

Cream butter until soft.
Beat in remaining ingredients.
Chill and use as required.

Herb Butter ❄

Preparation 15 mins plus chilling

For fish.
1 tbsp finely chopped tarragon
1 tbsp finely chopped chervil
1 tbsp finely chopped parsley
50g (2oz) butter
1 spring onion, trimmed and finely chopped

Cream butter until soft.
Gradually beat in herbs and onion.
Chill and use as required.

Horseradish Butter ❄

Preparation 5 mins plus chilling

For beef, herrings and mackerel.
50g (2oz) butter
1 tbsp horseradish sauce

Cream butter until soft.
Gradually beat in horseradish sauce.
Chill and use as required.

Christmas Butters ❄

Preparation 35 mins plus chilling

For turkey and cold meat sandwiches.
225g (8oz) butter, at room temperature
1 red pepper, grilled, deseeded and chopped
4–5 tbsp shredded basil
25g (1oz) sundried tomatoes in oil
1–2 tbsp capers, drained

Halve butter and place in separate bowls.
To one, add pepper and basil; to the other, tomatoes and capers. Blend each well.
Place each butter in centre of cling film and shape into a log, about 2.5cm (1in) in diameter. Chill and use as required.

Desserts & Puddings

Honey Blancmange

POACHED PEARS

The juicy pears in this dish absorb the flavour of the port
and spices they're cooked in and make a rich, warming dessert.
Special vanilla cream adds the finishing touch.

℘OACHED PEARS

 Preparation:
**

 Cost:
££

Timing:
Preparation 20 mins
Cooking 25 mins

For 4 servings:
- 150ml (¼pt) port
- 75g (3oz) caster sugar
- rind and juice of 1 lemon
- 1 cinnamon stick
- 3 cloves
- 4 large ripe pears
- 3 tbsp morello cherry jam

Vanilla cream:
- 150ml (¼pt) double cream
- ½ tsp vanilla essence
- 25g (1oz) caster sugar
- ½ tsp grated nutmeg

Preparation

1. Put port, sugar, lemon rind and juice, cinnamon and cloves in a saucepan with 150ml (¼pt) water. Heat gently until sugar dissolves. Bring to boil.

2. Meanwhile, peel pears, leaving stalks attached. Add to syrup, cover and simmer gently for 10–15 mins, or until just tender.

3. Meanwhile, whip together the cream, vanilla, sugar and nutmeg until it just forms soft peaks. Put in a serving dish and chill.

4. With a slotted spoon, transfer the pears to a serving dish and keep warm. Strain syrup into a small saucepan, add jam and boil rapidly, stirring, for 5 mins, to reduce.

5. Pour sauce over pears and serve warm or cold, with vanilla cream.

Nutritional information		
Calories	Fat	Fibre
1543 total (serves 4) 386 per serving	Low	Low

TIPS

One of the best kinds of pears to use for this recipe is the Comice pear.

Cold Desserts

Blancmange V

Serves 4   Preparation 15 mins plus chilling   Cooking 5 mins   Per portion 166 kcals, 6g fat (3.5g saturated)

40g (1½oz) cornflour
600ml (1 pint) milk
40g (1½oz) sugar
1 tsp vanilla extract
15g (½oz) butter

Blend cornflour to a smooth paste with a little milk.
Warm remaining milk and combine with cornflour paste, then return to saucepan.
Cook, stirring, until mixture comes to the boil and thickens. Reduce heat to low and simmer for 3 minutes.
Remove from heat and stir in remaining ingredients. Pour into a 600ml (1 pint) mould, first rinsed with cold water, then cool.
Chill until cold.
Turn out on to a plate.

Variations

Chocolate Blancmange V

Follow recipe and method for Blancmange but add 50g (2oz) melted chocolate to cooked mixture.

Honey Blancmange V

Follow recipe and method for Blancmange but use 3 tbsp honey in place of sugar.

Coffee Blancmange V

Follow recipe and method for Blancmange but add 2 tsp instant coffee granules to milk while it is warming.

Lemon Milk Jelly

Serves 4   Preparation 10 mins plus chilling Cooking 10 mins   Per portion 133 kcals, 2.6g fat (1.5g saturated)

4 tsp powdered gelatine
50g (2oz) caster sugar
1 tsp grated lemon rind
600ml (1 pint) milk

Sprinkle gelatine over 3 tbsp cold water in a small bowl. Leave to stand for 10 minutes.
Dissolve gelatine over a saucepan of hot water and cool slightly.

Put sugar, lemon rind and milk into a saucepan. Stand over a very low heat until sugar dissolves.
When gelatine and milk are both lukewarm, pour milk gently on to gelatine. Stir well.
Pour into a 900ml (1½ pint) mould, rinsed with cold water. Chill until set.

Variations

Orange Milk Jelly

Follow recipe and method for Lemon Milk Jelly but use grated orange rind instead of lemon rind.

Coffee Milk Jelly

Follow recipe and method for Lemon Milk Jelly but omit lemon rind. Instead, add 2 tsp instant coffee granules to milk.

Creamy Fruit Jelly

Serves 4   Preparation 30 mins plus chilling
Per portion 144 kcals, 1g fat (0.7g saturated)

135g lemon jelly
150ml (¼ pint) fairly thick apricot purée, made from stewed or canned fruit
2 tsp grated lemon rind
150g (5oz) natural yogurt

Put jelly and 5 tbsp boiling water into a saucepan and dissolve over a very low heat.
Pour into a measuring jug and make up to 300ml (½ pint) with cold water. Stir in fruit purée and lemon rind.
Leave until cold but still liquid, then gradually beat into yogurt.
Transfer to a 600ml (1 pint) jelly mould, rinsed with cold water. Chill until set.

Creamy Strawberry Jelly

Serves 4   Preparation 20 mins plus chilling
Per portion 161 kcals, 3g fat (1.6g saturated)

135g strawberry jelly
275g (10oz) strawberry yogurt
110g (4oz) strawberries, hulled and sliced

Dissolve jelly in 150ml (¼ pint) boiling water. Make up to 300ml (½ pint) with cold water.
Chill until almost set (about 1 hour). Whisk in yogurt until light and fluffy.
Reserve 4 slices of strawberry and divide rest between 4 glasses. Pour jelly over and chill.
Decorate with reserved strawberries.

Vanilla Honeycomb Mould

Serves 4–6   Preparation 30 mins plus chilling Cooking 15 mins Per portion 158 kcals, 8g fat (2.7g saturated)

4 tsp powdered gelatine

2 eggs, separated

50g (2oz) caster sugar

600ml (1 pint) milk

1 tsp vanilla extract

Sprinkle gelatine over 4 tbsp hot water in a small bowl. Leave to stand for 10 minutes.

Dissolve gelatine over a pan of hot water and cool slightly.

Beat egg yolks and sugar together until thick. Transfer to a basin standing over a saucepan of simmering water.

Add milk. Cook, stirring, until custard thickens and coats back of a spoon thinly. (Do not boil or mixture will curdle.)

Remove from heat and add vanilla and dissolved gelatine.

Whisk egg whites to a stiff snow and fold into custard mixture. Pour into a 1.25 litre (2 pint) mould, first rinsed with cold water.

Chill until firm and set. Turn out on to a plate.

Pashka ❄ V

Serves 8   Preparation 25 mins plus chilling overnight Per portion 279 kcals, 17g fat (7.9g saturated)

450g (1lb) curd cheese or quark

75g (3oz) caster sugar

½ tsp vanilla extract

90ml (3fl oz) double cream

50g (2oz) blanched almonds, chopped

50g (2oz) raisins

50g (2oz) glacé fruits, chopped

1 piece preserved stem ginger, chopped

Glacé fruit and almonds to decorate

Line a 900ml (1½ pint) basin with a double thickness of scalded muslin (or J-cloth).

Beat cheese or quark, sugar and vanilla extract together until smooth.

Lightly whip cream and fold into cheese mixture with almonds, fruit and ginger.

Spoon into prepared bowl and fold cloth over. Cover with a saucer and place a weight on top. Chill overnight.

Remove weight and plate, unfold cloth and invert pudding on to a plate. Peel off muslin. Decorate with glacé fruit and nuts.

Easy Fruit Brûlée V

Serves 4   Preparation 10 mins plus chilling Cooking 5 mins   Per portion 380 kcals, 28g fat (16g saturated)

350g (12oz) mixed summer fruits, thawed if frozen

200ml (7fl oz) double cream

200g (7oz) natural yogurt

65g (2½oz) demerara sugar

Reserve some fruit for decoration. Place remainder in base of a flameproof dish.

Whip cream until softly stiff; fold in yogurt.

Spread cream mixture over fruit and chill for 2 hours.

Sprinkle sugar over cream and place under a hot grill for a few minutes until sugar melts and caramelises.

Serve decorated with reserved fruit.

Gooseberry Cream

Serves 4   Preparation 25 mins plus chilling Cooking 10 mins   Per portion 202 kcals, 17g fat (9.4g saturated)

225g (8oz) gooseberries

25–50g (1–2oz) granulated sugar

2 tsp powdered gelatine

½ tsp grated lemon rind

125ml (4fl oz) double cream

2 tsp milk

1 egg white

Top and tail gooseberries. Put into a saucepan with 3 tbsp cold water.

Bring slowly to the boil. Cover saucepan with a lid and simmer until fruit is soft.

Remove from heat. Sweeten gooseperries to taste with sugar. Either rub through a sieve or liquidise.

Sprinkle gelatine over 4 tbsp hot water in a small basin. Leave to stand for 10 minutes.

Dissolve gelatine over a pan of hot water. Leave to cool.

Add cooled gelatine to gooseberry mixture with lemon rind. Leave until just beginning to thicken.

Whip 50ml (2fl oz) cream and milk together until softly stiff. Gradually stir in fruit mixture.

Beat egg white to a stiff snow and fold in.

Turn into a large serving bowl and chill until firm and set.

Just before serving, whip remaining cream until softly stiff and use to decorate.

Lemon Syllabub

Lemon Syllabub V

Serves 6 Preparation 15 mins plus standing and chilling
Per portion 314 kcals, 27g fat (15.1g saturated)

150ml (¼ pint) white wine
2 tbsp lemon juice
2 tsp grated lemon rind
75g (3oz) caster sugar
300ml (½ pint) double cream
Grated lemon rind to decorate

Put wine, lemon juice, rind and sugar into a bowl. Leave for a minimum of 3 hours.

Add cream and whip until mixture stands in soft peaks.

Transfer to 6 wine glasses and decorate with grated lemon rind.

Chill for several hours before serving.

Orange Syllabub V

Serves 4 Preparation 15 mins plus chilling
Per portion 296 kcals, x22g fat (12.5g saturated)

Rind and juice of 1 orange
2 tbsp Grand Marnier (orange liqueur)
50g (2oz) caster sugar
110g (4oz) fromage frais
150ml (¼ pint) double cream
Orange rind to decorate
Biscuits to serve

Stir orange rind, juice, liqueur and sugar into fromage frais.

Whip cream until softly stiff and fold into orange mixture.

Spoon into 4 wine glasses and chill. (This dessert separates into two layers when chilled.)

Decorate with orange rind and serve with biscuits.

Crème Monte Carlo V

Serves 4 Preparation 20 mins plus chilling
Per portion 466 kcals, 40g fat (22.7g saturated)

298g can mandarin segments in natural juice
300ml (½ pint) double cream
2 tbsp milk
2 tbsp icing sugar, sifted
6 meringue halves

Reserve 8 mandarin segments for decoration.

Divide remainder, with some juice, between 4 sundae glasses.

Whip cream and milk together until mixture stands in soft peaks then stir in sugar.

Break up meringue into small pieces and fold into cream mixture.

Pile over fruit in glasses. Decorate each with 2 mandarin segments.

Chill well before serving.

Rich Fruit Fool   V

Serves 4   Preparation 30 mins plus cooling   Cooking
15 mins   Per portion 550 kcals, 49g fat (26.6g saturated)

450g (1lb) gooseberries, apples, black
or redcurrants, rhubarb, blackberries or
raspberries
75–175g (3–6oz) caster sugar, to sweeten
depending on sharpness of fruit
350ml (12fl oz) double cream
2 tbsp milk
Chopped walnuts or chopped toasted
almonds for decoration

Prepare fruit according to type. Put into a
saucepan with 3 tbsp water.
Bring slowly to the boil, cover with lid and
simmer until fruit is soft.
Remove from heat. Add sugar to taste. Either
rub through a sieve or liquidise. Leave until
completely cold.
Whip 300ml (½ pint) cream and milk
together until lightly stiff, then fold in fruit
purée.
Transfer to 4 sundae glasses and chill.
Before serving, whip remaining cream until
thick, pipe whirls on top of each fool, then
decorate with nuts.

Variations

Custard Fruit Fool   V

Follow recipe and method for Rich Fruit Fool
but instead of cream and milk, combine
300ml (½ pint) fairly thick cold Real Custard
(page 186) with fruit purée.

Custard & Cream Fruit Fool   V

Follow recipe and method for Rich Fruit Fool
but use half the cream and milk and 150ml
(¼ pint) cold Real Custard (page 186). Mix
custard with fruit purée then fold in whipped
cream and milk.

Fruity Yogurt Pots

Serves 4   Preparation 20 mins plus chilling   Cooking
3 mins   Per portion 139 kcals, 3g fat (2g saturated)

1½ tsp powdered gelatine
3 tbsp orange juice
1 tbsp clear honey
425g (15oz) natural yogurt
50g (2oz) ready-to-eat dried apricots, chopped
175g (6oz) seedless grapes, quartered

Sprinkle gelatine over orange juice in a small
bowl. Leave to stand for 10 minutes.
Dissolve gelatine over a pan of hot water.
Leave to cool.
Blend together honey and yogurt.
Reserve some fruit to decorate, then stir
remainder into yogurt with gelatine.
Divide between 4 individual dishes and
decorate with reserved fruit.
Chill until set.

Raspberry & Walnut Swirl   V

Serves 4   Preparation 20 mins
Per portion 217 kcals, 14g fat (4.1g saturated)

225g (8oz) raspberries
2 tbsp clear honey
150g (5oz) natural yogurt
225g (8oz) fromage frais
50g (2oz) walnuts, roughly chopped
Mint and raspberries for decoration

Lightly mash raspberries with a fork and mix
with half the quantities of honey, yogurt and
fromage frais.
In a separate bowl mix remaining honey,
yogurt, fromage frais and walnuts.
Place half of raspberry mixture into
4 individual dishes.
Spoon over most of walnut mixture and then
remaining raspberry mixture.
Top with remaining walnut mixture and swirl
mixtures together with a cocktail stick.
Decorate with whole raspberries and sprigs
of mint.

Black Cherry Crunch   V

Serves 6   Preparation 15 mins plus chilling
Per portion 257 kcals, 16g fat (8.7g saturated)

410g can black cherry pie filling
150g (5oz) fromage frais
150ml (¼ pint) double cream, whipped
2 tbsp clear honey
50g (2oz) Crunchy Nut Cornflakes

Divide pie filling between 6 small dishes.
In a bowl, mix fromage frais, cream and
honey together.
Spoon on top of pie filling.
Place cornflakes in a plastic bag and gently
crush.
Sprinkle over the desserts.
Chill if desired before serving.

Swiss Toffee Apple

Swiss Toffee Apple   V

Serves 6   Preparation 30 mins plus chilling Cooking
15 mins   Per portion 470 kcals, 25g fat (14.9g saturated)

900g (2lb) cooking apples, peeled, cored and
sliced
150g (5oz) caster sugar
150ml (¼ pint) double cream
150ml (¼ pint) single cream
50g (2oz) butter
2 tbsp golden syrup
110g (4oz) cornflakes

Place apples in a saucepan with 110g (4oz)
sugar and 2 tbsp water and cook until soft.
Strain off any juice from apples then liquidise
fruit in a blender or press through a sieve to
make a thick purée. Add a little of the juice if
necessary.
Place apples in a serving dish and leave until
cold.
Whip creams together until softly stiff, then
spread over apple.
Melt butter and golden syrup together.

Add remaining sugar and cornflakes and stir
quickly to coat flakes.
Scatter over cream and chill before serving.

Apple & Hazelnut Crunch   V

Serves 4   Preparation 20 mins plus chilling Cooking
10 mins   Per portion 200 kcals, 7g fat (2.3g saturated)

450g (1lb) apples, peeled, cored and halved
Caster sugar
150g (5oz) hazelnut yogurt
2 fruit and nut cereal bars
Slices of apple, dipped in lemon juice

Place apples in a saucepan with 3 tbsp water.
Simmer until tender.
Add sufficient sugar to sweeten to taste.
Leave until cold.
Stir yogurt into stewed apple.
Spoon into 4 glasses or individual dishes.
Crush fruit and nut bars and sprinkle over
apple.
Decorate with apple slices.

Chocolate Mousse Cups   V

Serves 6 Preparation 20 mins plus cooling Cooking
5 mins Per portion 259 kcals, 21g fat (12.6g saturated)

90g (3½oz) plain chocolate, broken up
50ml (2fl oz) milk
200ml (7fl oz) whipping cream
110g (4oz) strawberries, hulled and sliced
6 chocolate dessert cups

Melt chocolate in a bowl over a saucepan of hot water.

Heat milk until boiling, then whisk into chocolate. Leave to cool.

Whip 150ml (¼ pint) whipping cream until softly stiff and fold into cool chocolate mixture.

Reserve 6 strawberry slices, then place remainder in chocolate cups.

Spoon in chocolate cream and smooth over tops.

Whip remaining cream and use to decorate with reserved strawberries.

Pots au Chocolat   V

Serves 4 Preparation 15 mins plus chilling Cooking
5 mins Per portion 366 kcals, 30g fat (16g saturated)

75g (3oz) plain chocolate, broken up
25g (1oz) butter
3 eggs, separated
90ml (3fl oz) double cream
Chocolate flakes, crumbled to decorate

Place chocolate in a basin standing over a saucepan of hot water.

Add butter and leave until both have melted, stirring once or twice.

Beat in egg yolks. When smooth, remove from heat and stir in 1 tbsp warm water.

Beat egg whites to a stiff snow and gently fold into chocolate mixture.

Spoon into 4 individual dishes and chill.

Just before serving, decorate each with cream, whipped until lightly stiff, and chocolate flakes.

Variation

Boozy Pots au Chocolat   V

Follow recipe and method for Pots au Chocolat but omit water. Use instead 1 tbsp lukewarm brandy or rum.

Irish Coffee Mousse

Serves 4–6 Preparation 30 mins plus chilling Cooking
3 mins Per portion 538 kcals, 45g fat (24.3g saturated)

2 tsp powdered gelatine
2 eggs, separated
50g (2oz) caster sugar
2 tbsp coffee essence
2 tbsp Irish whiskey
300ml (½ pint) double cream
Chocolate coffee beans to decorate

Sprinkle gelatine over 3 tbsp water in a small bowl. Leave to stand for 10 minutes.

Dissolve gelatine over a pan of hot water. Leave to cool.

Whisk together egg yolks, sugar and coffee essence until thick, creamy and leaves a trail.

Fold in whiskey and gelatine.

Softly whip cream, then fold half into coffee mixture.

Whip egg whites until stiff, fold into mousse and spoon into a serving bowl or glasses.

Chill until set. Top with remaining cream and decorate with coffee beans.

Easy Tiramisu   V

Serves 4 Preparation 15 mins plus chilling
Per portion 531 kcals, 35g fat (20g saturated)

75g (6oz) sponge fingers, broken into small pieces
125ml (4fl oz) strong espresso coffee
4 tbsp Tia Maria (coffee liqueur)
3 egg yolks
75g (3oz) caster sugar
250g pot mascarpone
Cocoa powder to decorate

Place half the sponge fingers into the bottom of four tumbler glasses.

Mix together coffee and liqueur. Pour half over sponge.

Whisk together egg yolks and sugar until light, thick and fluffy.

Gradually whisk in mascarpone.

Spoon half of mascarpone mixture over sponge, then add remaining sponge fingers.

Pour on remaining coffee mixture, then remaining mascarpone.

Chill for at least an hour.

Sprinkle with cocoa powder before serving.

Crèmes Caramel

Crème Caramel V

Serves 4 Preparation 15 mins plus cooling Cooking
1¼ hrs Per portion 347 kcals, 16g fat (7.8g saturated)

125g (4½oz) caster sugar
600ml (1 pint) milk
4 eggs, lightly whisked
½ tsp vanilla extract

Put 110g (4oz) sugar and 150ml (¼ pint) cold
water into a heavy based saucepan. Stand
over a low heat and stir until sugar dissolves.
Bring liquor to the boil, then boil more
briskly – without stirring – until syrup turns a
deep gold.
Remove from heat and add 2 tbsp boiling
water (stand well back as it will spit), tilt to
mix and pour syrup into a greased 900ml (1½
pint) ovenproof dish.
Tilt dish quickly so that base is completely
covered with caramel.
Warm milk and pour on to lightly whisked
eggs, remaining sugar and vanilla.
Strain into dish and stand in a roasting tin
containing enough hot water to come half
way up sides of dish.
Bake at 170°C (325°F) Mark 3 for 1 hour or
until set.
Remove from oven and cool, preferably
overnight.
Turn crème caramel out on to a serving dish
when completely cold.
Serve chilled with single cream.

Variation

Crèmes Caramel V

Follow recipe and method for Crème
Caramel. Spoon equal amounts of hot
caramel into 6 individual, well greased
ramekin dishes. Strain in custard, then bake
for 30–40 minutes, or until set. Leave until
cold. Stand in boiling water for 5 minutes
before unmoulding.

Crème Brûlée V

Serves 4 Preparation 15 mins plus chilling Cooking
15 mins Per portion 543 kcals, 47g fat (24.5g saturated)

300ml (½ pint) double cream
4 egg yolks, beaten
3 tbsp icing sugar, sifted
1 tsp vanilla extract
Caster sugar

Heat cream until hot in a basin standing over
a saucepan of simmering water. Pour hot
cream on to yolks, beating all the time.
Return mixture to saucepan. Add sugar and
vanilla. Cook without boiling, stirring, until
mixture thickens and coats back of a spoon.
Remove from heat, pour into 600ml (1 pint)
greased, flameproof dish and chill overnight.
About 1 hour before serving, sprinkle a 5mm
(¼in) thick layer of caster sugar over the top.
Stand under a hot grill and leave until sugar
starts to turn deep gold and caramelise.
Remove from heat and chill again.

Summer Pudding

Summer Pudding ❄ V

Serves 4–6 Preparation 25 mins plus chilling Cooking
10 mins Per portion 306 kcals, 1g fat (0.2g saturated)

9 large slices of bread, crusts removed
110g (4oz) sugar
680g (1½lb) soft summer fruits (rhubarb,
raspberries, strawberries, gooseberries,
stoned cherries, black or redcurrants, or a
mixture of fruits)
Fruit and a sprig of mint to decorate

Cut bread into neat fingers.

Put sugar and 5 tbsp water into a saucepan
and heat slowly until sugar melts, stirring.

Add fruit and simmer gently for about 7–10
minutes (gooseberries and blackcurrants
may take a few minutes longer). Reserve a
few spoonfuls of the juice.

Line base and sides of a 1.25 litre (2 pint)
pudding basin with bread fingers.

Add half the hot fruit mixture. Cover with
more bread fingers.

Pour in remaining fruit mixture and top with
remaining bread fingers. Trim any excess.

Cover with a saucer or plate. Place a heavy
weight on top. Chill overnight.

Turn out on to a plate. If there are any white
patches, spoon reserved juice over them.

Decorate with fruit and mint.

Variation

Autumn Pudding ❄ V

Follow recipe and method for Summer
Pudding. In place of soft summer fruits,
use 680g (1½lb) prepared mixed autumn
fruit such as blackberries, apples, pears and
plums.

Chocolate Apricot Trifle V

Serves 4–6 Preparation 20 mins plus chilling
Per portion 383 kcals, 23g fat (11.9g saturated)

1 chocolate Swiss roll
411g can apricot halves in syrup
2 tbsp orange juice or brandy
150ml (¼ pint) double cream
2 tbsp icing sugar, sifted
50g (2oz) plain chocolate, grated to
decorate

Cut Swiss roll into about 10 slices. Arrange
over base of a shallow serving dish,
overlapping if necessary.

Moisten with 4 tbsp syrup from apricots
mixed with juice or brandy. Arrange drained
apricots on top.

Whip cream until softly stiff. Stir in sugar.

Pile over apricots and chill.

Just before serving, sprinkle with chocolate.

Raspberry Amaretto Trifle   V

Serves 8   Preparation 30 mins plus cooling   Cooking
5 mins   Per portion 442 kcals, 30g fat (13.4g saturated)

4 trifle sponges
4 tbsp raspberry jam
150ml (¼ pint) sherry
3 tbsp amaretto liqueur (optional)
50g (2oz) ground almonds
50g (2oz) amaretti biscuits, crumbled
225g (8oz) frozen raspberries, thawed
4 egg yolks
50g (2oz) caster sugar
15g (½oz) cornflour
450ml (¾ pint) milk
300ml (½ pint) double cream
Toasted almonds to decorate

Halve trifle sponges and sandwich with jam.
Cut each into 4 and arrange in a trifle dish.
Pour over sherry and 1 tbsp amaretto.
Sprinkle with 25g (1oz) ground almonds and
crumbled amaretti biscuits.
Reserve a few raspberries for decoration and
place remainder in dish.
Blend yolks, sugar and cornflour with 1 tbsp
milk. Heat remaining milk in a saucepan.
When hot, blend in cornflour mixture and
heat gently until thickened, stirring.
Remove from heat and stir in remaining
liqueur, ground almonds and 3 tbsp cream.
Pour over raspberries, then leave to cool.
Whip remaining cream until softly stiff.
Decorate with whirls of cream, almonds and
reserved raspberries.

Ginger Pear Trifle   V

Serves 6   Preparation 30 mins plus chilling   Cooking
5 mins   Per portion 279 kcals, 17g fat (8.7g saturated)

15g (½oz) custard powder
1 tbsp caster sugar
300ml (½ pint) milk
150g (5oz) ginger cake, sliced
410g can pears, drained and sliced
150ml (¼ pint) cider
150ml (¼ pint) whipping cream
25g (1oz) flaked almonds, toasted

Blend custard powder and sugar with a little
of the milk. Bring remaining milk to the boil
and pour on to custard mixture, stirring well.
Return to pan and bring to the boil, stirring.

Cook for 1 minute. Leave to cool.
Arrange ginger cake in a glass serving dish.
Cover with pears and pour over cider.
Pour over cooled custard and leave to set.
Whip cream until softly stiff.
Spoon cream on top and decorate with
almonds. Serve chilled.

Strawberry Sensation Trifle   V

Serves 6   Preparation 25 mins plus chilling
Per portion 449 kcals, 30g fat (15.6g saturated)

1 large jam Swiss roll
2 tbsp Kirsch liqueur
450g (1lb) strawberries, hulled and halved
150ml (¼ pint) white wine
2 tbsp lemon juice
75g (3oz) caster sugar
300ml (½ pint) double cream
Chopped pistachio nuts and sliced
strawberries to decorate

Slice Swiss roll and arrange in a glass bowl.
Pour over Kirsch. Place strawberries on top.
Put wine, lemon juice and sugar in a bowl.
Add cream and whip until mixture is softly
stiff and holds its shape.
Pour over strawberries, cover and refrigerate
for about 2 hours.
Decorate with nuts and strawberry slices.

Tropical Trifle   V

Serves 6   Preparation 45 mins
Per portion 287 kcals, 15g fat (8.7g saturated)

50g (2oz) strawberries, hulled and sliced
2 bananas, peeled and sliced
1 kiwi fruit, peeled and sliced
2 apples, cored and diced
1 mango, peeled, stoned and diced
225g (8oz) canned pineapple chunks, drained
Juice of ½ lemon
75g (3oz) amaretti biscuits
50ml (2fl oz) white wine, sherry or fruit juice
150ml (¼ pint) whipping cream
225g (8oz) Greek-style natural yogurt

Combine fruit in a bowl with lemon juice.
Place biscuits in base of a glass dish, pour
over wine and leave to soak for 5 minutes.
Spoon fruit over biscuits, reserving a few
pieces for decoration. Whip cream until softly
stiff, fold into yogurt and spoon over fruit.
Decorate with reserved fruit.

Chocolate Orange Charlotte

Serves 8   Preparation 1 hr plus chilling Cooking
10 mins   Per portion 454 kcals, 29g fat (15.9g saturated)

15g (½oz) powdered gelatine
175g (6oz) plain chocolate, broken up
300ml (½ pint) milk
2 tbsp Grand Marnier (orange liqueur)
2 eggs, separated
50g (2oz) light soft brown sugar
Grated rind and juice of 2 oranges
300ml (½ pint) double cream, whipped
30 Langues de Chat biscuits or sponge fingers
Grated orange rind to decorate

Sprinkle gelatine over 3 tbsp water in a small bowl. Leave to stand for 10 minutes.
Dissolve gelatine over a pan of hot water. Leave to cool.
Place chocolate in a small saucepan with milk. Gently heat until melted. Stir in liqueur.
Beat egg yolks and sugar together until creamy, then blend in chocolate mixture.
Return to saucepan and heat gently, stirring until thickened.
Stir in gelatine, orange rind and juice. Cool.
Fold in two-thirds of cream.
Whisk egg whites until stiff and fold into mixture.
Pour into a lightly greased loose-bottomed, deep 19cm (7½in) cake tin and chill until set.
Turn out on to a plate. Arrange biscuits around sides. Decorate with remaining cream and orange rind.

Piña Colada Cheesecake

Serves 8   Preparation 30 mins plus chilling
Per portion 318 kcals, 21g fat (12.9g saturated)

50g (2oz) butter, melted
110g (4oz) digestive biscuits, crushed
25g (1oz) desiccated coconut
135g packet orange or pineapple jelly
225g (8oz) light soft cheese, softened
150g (5oz) natural yogurt
2 tbsp coconut rum liqueur
150ml (¼ pint) whipping cream
Pineapple and kiwi slices to decorate

Mix butter, biscuit crumbs and coconut together. Press into base of a greased loose-bottomed 20cm (8in) cake tin and chill.
Dissolve jelly in 150ml (¼ pint) hot water,
then cool slightly.
Beat together cheese, yogurt and liqueur. Gradually stir in jelly and mix well.
Whip cream until softly stiff and fold into cheese mixture.
Pour on to biscuit base and chill until set.
Remove from tin and decorate with pineapple and kiwi fruit.

Variation

Peach Cheesecake

Follow recipe and method for Piña Colada Cheesecake but omit desiccated coconut and liqueur. Use a peach jelly and add 2 chopped peaches to cheese mixture. Decorate with sliced peaches.

Citrus Cheesecake

Serves 8   Preparation 45 mins plus chilling Cooking
5 mins   Per portion 587 kcals, 46g fat (25.8g saturated)

225g (8oz) plain chocolate digestive biscuits, crushed
40g (1½oz) butter, melted
15g (½oz) powdered gelatine
225g (8oz) full fat soft cheese
3 eggs, separated
50g (2oz) caster sugar
Grated rind and juice of 2 lemons
300ml (½ pint) whipping cream, whipped
110g (4oz) lemon curd
150ml (¼ pint) double cream, whipped
Lemon strips to decorate

Mix biscuit crumbs and butter and press into base of a greased loose-bottomed 20cm (8in) cake tin. Chill for 30 minutes until firm.
Sprinkle gelatine over 4 tbsp water in a small bowl. Leave to stand for 10 minutes.
Dissolve gelatine over a saucepan of hot water. Leave to cool.
In a large bowl, blend together soft cheese, egg yolks, sugar, lemon rind and juice.
Add gelatine to cheese mixture and fold in whipped cream.
Beat egg whites until stiff and fold into mixture.
Pour into prepared tin, spoon on lemon curd and swirl with a sharp knife. Chill until set.
Remove from tin and decorate with whipped double cream and lemon.

Baked Cream Cheesecake

Baked Cream Cheesecake   V

Serves 10   Preparation 30 mins plus chilling Cooking
1¼ hrs Per portion 351 kcals, 25g fat (14g saturated)

50g (2oz) butter, melted

150g (5oz) digestive biscuits, crushed

¼ tsp ground cinnamon

500g (1lb 2oz) full fat soft cheese

125g (4½oz) caster sugar

3 eggs, beaten

Grated rind of 1 lemon

2 tbsp lemon juice

1½ tsp vanilla extract

150ml (¼ pint) soured cream

Grated lemon and lime rind to decorate

Mix together melted butter, biscuits and
cinnamon.

Press into base of a greased loose-bottomed
20cm (8in) cake tin.

Cook at 180°C (350°F) Mark 4 for 10 minutes.

Beat together soft cheese and 110g (4oz)
caster sugar, then gradually beat in eggs.

Stir in lemon rind, lemon juice and vanilla
extract.

Pour into cake tin and bake for 1 hour or
until centre is firm to touch.

Remove from oven and allow cheesecake to
cool.

Mix together remaining sugar and soured
cream.

Spread soured cream over cheesecake.

Remove from tin and chill until ready to
serve. Decorate with lemon and lime rind.

Chocolate Ginger Roulade   ❄ V

Serves 6–8   Preparation 40 mins plus cooling Cooking
30 mins   Per portion 481 kcals, 34g fat (17.3g saturated)

4 tbsp cocoa powder

150ml (¼ pint) milk

5 eggs, separated

150g (5oz) caster sugar

300ml (½ pint) double cream, whipped

2 tbsp ginger preserve

Icing sugar and preserved stem ginger to
decorate

Mix cocoa powder and milk in a pan and
heat gently until cocoa has dissolved, then
leave to cool.

Whisk egg yolks and sugar together until
pale and fluffy.

Whisk in cooled milk mixture.

Whisk egg whites until stiff, then fold into
cocoa mixture.

Spoon into a greased and lined 33 x 23cm
(13 x 9in) Swiss roll tin

Bake at 180°C (350°F) Mark 4 for 20–25
minutes until risen and firm.

Turn out on to greaseproof paper and cover
with a warm, damp tea towel.

Leave to cool for 20 minutes. Cut off and
discard outside edges.

Reserve a third of the cream. Fold ginger
preserve into remainder, spread on to
sponge and roll up carefully.

Dust with icing sugar then decorate with
reserved cream and pieces of ginger.

Berry Tart

Berry Tart ❋ V

Serves 6   Preparation 40 mins plus chilling Cooking
35 mins   Per portion 472 kcals, 32g fat (17.6g saturated)

Sweet Flan Pastry made with 175g (6oz) flour
(page 228)
1 egg yolk
25g (1oz) caster sugar
15g (½oz) flour
½ tsp vanilla extract
150ml (¼ pint) milk
150ml (¼ pint) double cream, lightly whipped
2 tsp orange juice or sherry
450g (1lb) raspberries, strawberries or
loganberries
2 tbsp redcurrant jelly, melted

Roll out sweet pastry on a floured work
surface.
Use it to line an 18cm (7in) deep fluted flan
ring resting on a lightly greased baking
sheet. Prick well all over.
Line with foil (to prevent pastry rising as it
cooks).
Bake at 200°C (400°F) Mark 6 for 15 minutes.
Remove foil. Return flan to oven.

Bake for a further 15 minutes until crisp and
golden. Remove and cool.
Beat egg yolk and sugar together until
thick and light. Stir in flour and vanilla and
gradually blend in milk.
Pour into a small saucepan and cook, stirring,
until mixture comes to the boil and thickens.
Simmer for 3 minutes.
Remove from heat and cool.
When completely cold, fold cream and
orange juice or sherry into custard.
Spread custard mixture over base of flan
case.
Arrange raspberries, strawberries or
loganberries over custard.
Brush berries with melted redcurrant jelly.

Variation

Grape Tart ❋ V

Follow recipe and method for Berry Tart
but omit soft fruit and use halved seedless
grapes instead. Brush grapes with melted
apricot jam instead of redcurrant jelly.

Almond & Apricot Flan V

Serves 6   Preparation 35 mins plus cooling Cooking
45 mins   Per portion 537 kcals, 40g fat (20.9g saturated)

Shortcrust Pastry made with 110g (4oz) flour
(page 225) or 1 sheet of ready-rolled bought
shortcrust pastry
2 tbsp apricot jam
75g (3oz) butter
75g (3oz) caster sugar
1 egg, beaten
25g (1oz) cake crumbs (from plain cake)
50g (2oz) ground almonds
25g (1oz) self raising flour
1 tbsp milk
411g can apricot halves in juice, drained
150ml (¼ pint) double cream

Roll out shortcrust pastry on a floured work
surface.
Use to line a 15–18cm (6–7in) flan tin.
Spread base with jam.
Cream butter with sugar until light and
fluffy, then beat in egg.
Stir in cake crumbs and almonds.
Fold in flour alternately with milk.
Transfer to pastry case and smooth top with
a knife.
Bake flan at 220°C (425°F) Mark 7 for
15 minutes.
Reduce temperature to 180°C (350°F) Mark 4
and bake for a further 30 minutes.
Remove from flan tin.
Leave until cold.
Just before serving, cover top of cold flan
with apricot halves.
Whip cream until softly stiff and use to
decorate.

Lemon Meringue Pie V

Serves 4–6   Preparation 25 mins plus chilling Cooking
1 hr   Per portion 568 kcals, 28g fat (15g saturated)

Shortcrust Pastry made with 175g (6oz) flour
(page 225) or 1 sheet of ready-rolled bought
shortcrust pastry
2 tbsp cornflour
50g (2oz) sugar
Grated rind and juice of 2 large lemons
2 egg yolks
15g (½oz) butter
Meringue Topping made with 2 egg whites
(page 176)

Roll out pastry on a floured surface.
Use it to line a 20cm (8in) fluted flan ring
that is resting on a lightly greased baking
sheet.
Prick well all over and line with foil (to
prevent pastry rising as it cooks).
Bake pie at 200°C (400°F) Mark 6 for
15 minutes.
Remove foil. Return flan to oven. Bake for a
further 15 minutes or until crisp and golden.
Remove from oven.
To make filling, put cornflour, sugar and
lemon rind into a basin.
Mix together to a smooth paste with a little
cold water.
Heat 150ml (¼ pint) water with lemon juice.
Combine with paste then return to saucepan.
Cook, stirring, until mixture comes to the
boil and thickens.
Reduce the heat and let filling simmer for
3 minutes.
Beat in yolks and butter. Cook gently for a
further minute then pour into flan case.
Pile meringue on top. Bake as directed for
Meringue Topping (page 176).
Serve chilled.

Profiteroles ❄ V

Serves 4   Preparation 30 mins   Cooking 30 mins
Per portion 910 kcals, 71g fat (39.7g saturated)

Choux Pastry made with 65g (2½oz) flour
(page 231)
300ml (½ pint) double cream
2 tbsp milk
3 tbsp icing sugar, sifted
Luxury Chocolate Sauce (page 186)

Pipe or spoon 20 equal amounts of choux
pastry – well apart – on to greased baking
sheets.
Bake at 220°C (425°F) Mark 7 for 25 minutes
or until golden and well puffed.
Remove from oven. Make a small slit in side
of each one.
Return to oven (with heat switched off) for
a further 5 minutes for puffs to dry out. Cool
on a wire cooling rack.
About 1 hour before serving, whip cream
and milk together until softly stiff. Stir in
sugar.
Halve puffs and fill with cream.
Serve with warm Luxury Chocolate Sauce.

Frozen Desserts

Ice Cream

When making ice cream turn on the fast freeze/super button (if your freezer has one) an hour before placing mixture in the freezer. Ice cream will freeze faster in a shallow container and if the sides or base are in contact with the freezer.

If you are freezing the mixture in an ice cream maker, do not whip the cream before adding to the other ingredients. If the mixture has been heated, allow it to cool then chill for 30 minutes in the refrigerator before freezing.

Vanilla Ice Cream ❄ V

Serves 6   Preparation 15 mins plus freezing
Per portion 563 kcals, 54g fat (30.2g saturated)

600ml (1 pint) double cream
4 tbsp milk
90g (3½oz) icing sugar, sifted
2 tsp vanilla extract

Pour cream and milk into a well-chilled bowl and beat together until softly stiff.
Stir in icing sugar and vanilla extract. Pour into a freezer container.
Freeze for 45 minutes or until ice cream has frozen about 1cm (½in) around sides.
Transfer to a chilled bowl, break up with a fork and stir gently until smooth.
Return to a clean container and freeze for 2 hours or until firm.

Variations

Chocolate Chip Ice Cream ❄ V

Follow recipe and method for Vanilla Ice Cream but stir in 110g (4oz) coarsely grated plain chocolate before freezing.

Berry Ice Cream ❄ V

Follow recipe and method for Vanilla Ice Cream. Stir in 450g (1lb) puréed strawberries or raspberries before freezing.

Ginger Ice Cream ❄ V

Follow recipe and method for Vanilla Ice Cream but reduce sugar by 2 tbsp and omit vanilla. Stir in 75g (3oz) finely chopped preserved stem ginger and also 2 tbsp ginger syrup.

Coffee Ice Cream ❄ V

Follow recipe and method for Vanilla Ice Cream but add 2 tbsp instant coffee granules mixed with 2 tbsp hot water (then left to go cold) instead of vanilla.

Orange Ice Cream ❄ V

Follow recipe and method for Vanilla Ice Cream but reduce sugar by 2 tbsp and omit vanilla. Add 1 tbsp grated orange rind and 2 tbsp Grand Marnier (orange liqueur).

Almond Ice Cream ❄ V

Follow recipe and method for Vanilla Ice Cream but add 1 tsp of almond essence instead of vanilla. Before second freezing, stir in 25g (1oz) toasted, finely chopped almonds.

Instant Ice Cream ❄ V

Serves 4   Preparation 10 mins
Per portion 173 kcals, 13g fat (7.7g saturated)

The fruit must be frozen hard in small pieces to make this recipe.

225g (8oz) frozen raspberries or strawberries
40g (1½oz) icing sugar
125ml (4fl oz) whipping cream, chilled
Biscuits or meringue nests to serve

Place frozen fruit in a food processor and process until finely chopped.
Add icing sugar and process until mixed.
Add cream and process until soft and creamy.
Serve immediately with crisp biscuits or in a meringue nest.

Quick Summer Berry Sorbet ❄ V

Serves 4   Preparation 10 mins
Per portion 119 kcals, 1.6g fat (0.9g saturated)

500g (1lb 2oz) assorted frozen small summer berries such as raspberries, blueberries, blackcurrants, redcurrants
6 tbsp undiluted blackcurrant cordial
Mint leaves to decorate
Icing sugar to dust

Put frozen fruits in a food processor or blender with blackcurrant cordial.
Blend for a few seconds until well crushed.
Pile into serving glasses and decorate with mint. Dust lightly with icing sugar and serve.

Frozen Raspberry Mousse

Frozen Raspberry Mousse ❄ V

Serves 6   Preparation 30 mins plus freezing
Per portion 309 kcals, 27g fat (15g saturated)

**300ml (½ pint) raspberry purée, made from
350g (12oz) fresh or canned fruit**
4 tsp lemon juice
50g (2oz) icing sugar, sifted
300ml (½ pint) double cream
2 tbsp milk
4 egg whites
Raspberries and sprigs of mint to decorate

Prepare 6 ramekin dishes with paper collars
as for Cold Soufflés on page 174.
Sieve purée and discard seeds.
Stir in lemon juice and icing sugar.
Whip cream and milk until softly stiff.
Whisk egg whites to a stiff snow.
Fold cream and egg whites alternately into
fruit mixture.
Spoon into ramekins, then freeze until firm.
Remove from freezer 30 minutes before
serving.
To serve remove paper collars and decorate
with raspberries and mint.

Italian Ice Cream ❄ V

Serves 4   Preparation 20 mins plus freezing Cooking
3 mins Per portion 467 kcals, 44g fat (23.6g saturated)

2 egg yolks
50g (2oz) icing sugar, sifted
2 tsp vanilla extract
300ml (½ pint) double cream
2 tbsp milk

Put egg yolks and sugar into a basin standing
over a saucepan of gently simmering water.
Beat until thick and creamy.
Remove from heat. Continue beating until
cool, then stir in vanilla.
Pour cream and milk into a chilled bowl and
beat until softly stiff.
Gently fold into beaten egg yolks and sugar
then transfer to a freezer container.
Freeze for 45 minutes or until frozen about
1cm (½in) around sides.
Turn into a chilled bowl, break up gently
with a fork then stir until smooth.
Return to a clean container and freeze for
1½–2 hours or until firm.

Rich Chocolate Ice Cream

Snowdrift Ice Cream   ※ V

Serves 6 Preparation 20 mins plus freezing
Per portion 330 kcals, 23g fat (13.8g saturated)

2 egg whites
50g (2oz) caster sugar
¼ tsp cream of tartar
1 tsp golden syrup
1 tsp vanilla extract
150ml (¼ pint) double cream
300ml (½ pint) soured cream
2 tbsp Tia Maria (coffee liqueur)
110g (4oz) glacé cherries, chopped

Place egg whites, sugar, 5 tbsp water, cream of tartar, syrup and vanilla extract in a large bowl.

Whisk together until thick and smooth.

Whip double cream until softly stiff and fold into egg white mixture.

Carefully fold in soured cream, liqueur and cherries.

Pour into a freezer container and freeze until half frozen.

Stir with a fork, breaking up ice crystals.

Cover and freeze until firm.

Rich Chocolate Ice Cream   ※ V

Serves 4 Preparation 25 mins plus freezing Cooking
5 mins Per portion 612 kcals, 51g fat (27.9g saturated)

110g (4oz) plain chocolate, broken up
2 eggs
50g (2oz) caster sugar
2 tsp vanilla extract
300ml (½ pint) double cream

Melt chocolate in a basin standing over a saucepan of hot water. Cool.

Place eggs and sugar in a basin standing over a saucepan of hot water. Whisk until thick and creamy.

Remove from heat. Continue whisking until mixture is cool. Stir in chocolate and vanilla.

Whip cream until softly stiff and fold into chocolate mixture.

Pour into a freezer container and freeze for 45 minutes or until frozen 1cm (½in) around sides.

Turn into a chilled bowl, break up with a fork then stir until smooth.

Return to a clean container and freeze for 1½–2 hours or until firm.

Chocolate Orange Ice Cream ❄ V

Serves 4–6 Preparation 25 mins plus freezing Cooking
25 mins Per portion 473 kcals, 32g fat (18.5g saturated)

450ml (¾ pint) single cream
3 egg yolks
110g (4oz) caster sugar
150ml (¼ pint) whipping cream, whipped
110g (4oz) chocolate chips
6 tbsp Grand Marnier (orange liqueur)
Grated rind of 1 orange

Heat single cream to simmering point. Do
not boil.
Beat egg yolks and sugar in a large bowl
until thick and pale yellow in colour.
Pour on hot cream, stirring constantly.
Strain mixture into a saucepan and stir
over a low heat for about 20 minutes or
until custard thickens to coat the back of a
wooden spoon. Allow to cool.
Whip whipping cream until softly stiff. Fold
with chocolate chips, liqueur and orange rind
into custard.
Pour into a freezer container and freeze for
1 hour.
Stir with a fork, breaking up ice crystals.
Return to freezer and repeat after 1 hour.
Cover and freeze until firm.

Tangy Fruit Sorbet ❄ V

Serves 6 Preparation 15 mins plus freezing Cooking
5 mins Per portion 145 kcals, 0g fat (0g saturated)

175g (6oz) granulated sugar
6 mint leaves
Juice of 1 small lemon
Grated rind and juice of 1 orange
1 egg white
25g (1oz) caster sugar
Orange slices to decorate

Put granulated sugar, 150ml (¼ pint) water
and mint into a saucepan. Cook over a low
heat and stir until sugar dissolves.
Remove from heat and strain. Stir in 300ml
(½ pint) water, lemon juice and orange rind
and juice. Mix well.
Pour into a freezer container and chill until
cold. Freeze for 1 hour or until half frozen.
Beat egg white to a stiff snow. Add caster
sugar. Continue whisking until white is very
stiff and shiny.
Pour fruit mixture into a chilled bowl.

Whisk until smooth.
Gently fold in beaten egg white.
Return to a clean container. Freeze for
45 minutes and whisk again.
Pour back into container. Freeze for
1½–2 hours or until firm.
Spoon into small dishes and decorate with
orange slices. Serve immediately.

Variations

Lemon Sorbet ❄ V

Follow recipe and method for Tangy Fruit
Sorbet but omit mint, orange rind and juice.
Instead use the grated rind and juice of
4 lemons.

Strawberry Sorbet ❄ V

Follow recipe and method for Tangy Fruit
Sorbet. Omit mint, orange rind and juice. Use
450g (1lb) strawberries, puréed, instead.

Apple Ices ❄ V

Serves 4 Preparation 25 mins plus freezing Cooking
5 mins Per portion 284 kcals, 20g fat (11.3g saturated)

4 eating apples
Grated rind and juice of ½ lemon
2 tbsp brandy
25g (1oz) sugar
150ml (¼ pint) double cream
Mint leaves to decorate

Cut top off apples. Carefully hollow out flesh
leaving a 1cm (½in) shell.
Brush cut surfaces with lemon juice.
Place chopped apple in a saucepan with
lemon rind and 1 tbsp water. Cook until
tender.
Purée until smooth. Stir in brandy and sugar
and leave to cool.
Whip cream until softly stiff.
Fold cream into cooled purée, pour into a
container and freeze for 1 hour.
Beat mixture until smooth and freeze until
half frozen.
Spoon mixture into apple cups. Open freeze
until solid.
Place each apple in a plastic bag, seal and
freeze.
Remove from freezer 30 minutes before
serving.
Serve decorated with mint leaves.

Meringue Dessert ❄ V

Serves 6   Preparation 20 mins plus freezing
Per portion 357 kcals, 27g fat (15.1g saturated)

300ml (½ pint) double cream
2 tbsp Grand Marnier (orange liqueur)
(optional)
110g (4oz) meringue nests, crumbled
225g (8oz) raspberries
50g (2oz) icing sugar

Lightly oil a 1.25 litre (2 pint) pudding basin.
Whip cream with liqueur, if using, until softly stiff. Stir in meringues.
Spoon into basin. Cover with foil and freeze until firm.
Press raspberries through a sieve and mix with icing sugar.
Turn frozen meringue dessert out and leave for about 1 hour before serving so it is only lightly frozen.
Serve with raspberry sauce.

Kulfi ❄ V

Serves 4   Preparation 20 mins plus freezing Cooking 45 mins   Per portion 814 kcals, 78g fat (39.6g saturated)

600ml (1 pint) Channel Islands milk
3 cardamom pods
450ml (¾ pint) double cream
2 tbsp honey
50g (2oz) almonds, chopped
25g (1oz) pistachio nuts, chopped

Place milk and cardamom in a saucepan. Bring to the boil and simmer until reduced to 450ml (¾ pint).
Reduce heat and stir in cream. Continue to heat, stirring frequently until reduced to 600ml (1 pint).
Remove cardamom, then stir in honey, almonds and half the pistachios.
Pour into a freezer container and leave until cold.
Freeze for 1 hour or until frozen about 1cm (½in) around sides.
Turn into a chilled bowl and mash with a fork to break up ice crystals.
Either return to freezer container or divide between 4 small moulds.
Cover and freeze until firm.
Serve sprinkled with remaining chopped pistachios.

Tortoni ❄ V

Serves 4   Preparation 30 mins plus freezing
Per portion 449 kcals, 33g fat (17.9g saturated)

150ml (¼ pint) double cream
150ml (¼ pint) single cream
25g (1oz) icing sugar
50g (2oz) macaroons, finely chopped
40g (1½oz) ratafia or amaretti biscuits, crumbled
2 tbsp Marsala or sweet sherry
2 egg whites
Melted chocolate

Combine creams and sugar and whisk together until softly stiff.
Refrigerate for 1 hour.
Stir macaroons, half the ratafia or amarettis and Marsala or sweet sherry into chilled cream.
Whisk egg whites to a stiff snow and fold into cream mixture.
Turn mixture into a lightly oiled 1.25 litre (2¼ pint) mould or large loaf tin.
Freeze until firm.
Turn tortoni out of mould and sprinkle with remaining ratafia or amaretti crumbs to coat.
Decorate with melted chocolate drizzled over surface and serve immediately.

Baked Alaska V

Serves 4–6   Preparation 15 mins   Cooking 3 mins
Per portion 682 kcals, 44g fat (23.5g saturated)

18cm (7in) sponge flan case or a single layer of sponge cake
2 tbsp brandy or sherry
Meringue Topping, made with 3 egg whites (page 176)
Vanilla Ice Cream made with 300ml (½ pint) double cream (page 206)

Put flan or cake on to an ovenproof plate or dish.
Moisten with brandy or sherry.
Make meringue topping.
Spoon ice cream in a mound on top of cake.
Swirl meringue completely over cake and ice cream.
Bake at 230°C (450°F) Mark 8 for 1–3 minutes, until meringue just starts turning gold.
Serve immediately.

Peach Melba

Peach Melba   V

Serves 4 Preparation 10 mins
Per portion 517 kcals, 44g fat (23.6g saturated)

175g (6oz) raspberries
Icing sugar
4 scoops Italian Ice Cream (page 207)
2 peaches, sliced

Purée raspberries in a blender or food processor. Reserve a few for decoration.
Pass through sieve to remove seeds.
Add sufficient sifted icing sugar to sweeten to taste.
Place a scoop of ice cream into 4 sundae glasses.
Top each glass with peach slices, raspberries and raspberry sauce.
Serve immediately.

Banana Splits   V

Serves 4 Preparation 20 mins
Per portion 727 kcals, 54g fat (29.5g saturated)

150ml (¼ pint) double cream
4 large bananas, peeled
Vanilla Ice Cream made with 300ml (½ pint) double cream (page 206)
25g (1oz) walnuts, chopped
Hot Luxury Chocolate Sauce (page 186) or hot Fudge Sauce (page 187)

Whip cream until softly stiff.
Split bananas lengthways. Sandwich together with spoonfuls of ice cream.
Stand on 4 individual plates then top with whipped cream. Sprinkle with nuts.
Serve immediately with chocolate or fudge sauce.

Hot Puddings

Baked Apples with Syrup ❄ V

Serves 4   Preparation 25 mins   Cooking 50 mins
Per portion 140 kcals, 5g fat (3.3g saturated)

4 cooking apples
1 tbsp golden syrup
½ tsp grated lemon rind
25g (1oz) butter

Remove apple cores two-thirds of the way down each one.
With a sharp knife, score a line round each apple, about a third of the way down from the top.
Stand apples in an ovenproof dish.
Mix syrup and lemon rind together.
Carefully spoon equal amounts into apple cavities.
Top each with a knob of butter. Pour 3 tbsp water into dish.
Bake at 180°C (350°F) Mark 4 for about 50 minutes or until apples puff up and are tender.

Variation

Baked Apples with Mincemeat

Follow recipe and method for Baked Apples. Omit golden syrup and lemon rind. Stuff centre of the apples with mincemeat.

Semolina Pudding   V

Serves 4   Preparation 5 mins   Cooking 15 mins
Per portion 157 kcals, 5.8g fat (3.5g saturated)

600ml (1 pint) milk
40g (1½oz) semolina
25g (1oz) caster sugar
15g (½oz) butter

Put milk into a saucepan and heat until lukewarm.
Sprinkle in semolina.
Cook slowly, stirring, until mixture comes to the boil and thickens.
Add sugar and butter. Cook very gently for a further 5–7 minutes, stirring often.
Alternatively, turn the pudding into a 600ml (1 pint) greased ovenproof dish as soon as it has come to the boil and thickened. Sprinkle with ground nutmeg and bake at 170°C (325°F) Mark 3 for 30 minutes.

Variation

Sago Pudding   V

Follow recipe and method for Semolina Pudding. Use sago instead of semolina.

Rice Pudding   V

Serves 4   Preparation 10 mins   Cooking 2–2½ hrs
Per portion 164 kcals, 6g fat (3.5g saturated)

50g (2oz) pudding rice
600ml (1 pint) milk
25g (1oz) caster sugar
1 strip of lemon rind
Ground nutmeg
15g (½oz) butter

Wash rice and drain well. Put into a 900ml (1½ pint) greased ovenproof dish and stir in milk, sugar and lemon rind.
Sprinkle top with nutmeg.
Dot with butter.
Bake at 150°C (300°F) Mark 2 for 2–2½ hours.

Variations

Barley Pudding   V

Follow recipe and method for Rice Pudding. Use barley instead of pudding rice.

Tapioca Pudding   V

Follow recipe and method for Rice Pudding. Use tapioca instead of pudding rice.

Eastern Rice Pudding   V

Serves 4   Preparation 5 mins   Cooking 35 mins
Per portion 259 kcals, 11g fat (8.2g saturated)

900ml (1½ pints) milk
40g (1½oz) creamed coconut
½ tsp ground cinnamon
Pinch of ground cloves
75g (3oz) pudding rice
25g (1oz) brown sugar
Chopped pistachio nuts to serve
Chopped fruit to serve

Place milk, coconut and spices in a saucepan, then heat until coconut has dissolved.
Stir in rice and sugar.
Bring to the boil, then reduce heat and simmer for 30 minutes or until rice is tender. Stir regularly.
Serve hot with nuts and fruit.

Tapioca Orange Pudding   V

Serves 4   Preparation 15 mins plus standing Cooking
25 mins   Per portion 359 kcals, 22g fat (16g saturated)

2 large oranges
600ml (1 pint) milk
50g (2oz) tapioca
75g (3oz) desiccated coconut
Pinch of allspice
25g (1oz) caster sugar
150ml (¼ pint) single cream
2 tbsp Grand Marnier (orange liqueur)
(optional)

Pare zest from oranges and place in a
saucepan with milk.
Bring to the boil, remove from the heat and
stand for 30 minutes.
Remove and discard zest.
Add tapioca, 50g (2oz) desiccated coconut
and allspice.
Bring to the boil and simmer for 15 minutes,
until thick and creamy, stirring occasionally.
Remove pith from oranges and cut into
segments.
Reserve some segments whole for
decoration, then chop remainder.
Toast remaining coconut and reserve for
decoration.
Stir oranges into tapioca with sugar, cream
and liqueur, if using.
Pour into serving dishes.
Top with toasted coconut and orange
segments.

Macaroni Pudding   V

Serves 4   Preparation 15 mins   Cooking 15 mins
Per portion 364 kcals, 13g fat (7.6g saturated)

1½ tbsp custard powder
900ml (1½ pints) milk
40g (1½oz) butter
115g (4½oz) macaroni
25g (1oz) sultanas
25g (1oz) caster sugar
Ground nutmeg
2 tbsp demerara sugar

Blend custard powder with a little milk.
Place remaining milk in a saucepan with 25g
(1oz) butter and bring to the boil.
Add macaroni and sultanas. Simmer for 7
minutes, stirring occasionally.

Remove from heat and stir in blended
custard powder and caster sugar.
Bring to the boil and cook, continuously
stirring, for 2 minutes.
Carefully pour custard into a flameproof
dish.
Sprinkle with nutmeg and demerara sugar.
Dot with remaining butter.
Grill until sugar has melted.

Baked Rice Custard   V

Serves 6   Preparation 20 mins   Cooking 1¾ hrs
Per portion 171 kcals, 5g fat (1.9g saturated)

50g (2oz) pudding rice
3 eggs, beaten
50g (2oz) sugar
½ tsp vanilla extract
600ml (1 pint) milk
40g (1½oz) sultanas
Pinch of ground nutmeg

Cook rice in boiling water for 10 minutes,
drain well.
Beat eggs, sugar, vanilla extract and milk
together.
Stir in sultanas and rice.
Pour into an ovenproof dish and sprinkle
with nutmeg.
Stand dish in a roasting tin containing
enough hot water to come about half way up
sides of dish.
Bake at 170°C (325°F) Mark 3 for 1½ hours or
until just set.

Baked Egg Custard   V

Serves 4   Preparation 15 mins   Cooking 1 hr
Per portion 163 kcals, 8g fat (2.9g saturated)

3 eggs or 4 egg yolks
600ml (1 pint) milk
25g (1oz) caster sugar
Ground nutmeg

Beat whole eggs or egg yolks with milk.
Strain into a 900ml (1½ pint) greased,
ovenproof dish, then stir in sugar.
Sprinkle with nutmeg.
Stand dish in a roasting tin containing
enough hot water to come about half way up
sides of dish.
Bake the custard at 170°C (325°F) Mark 3 for
45 minutes–1 hour or until firm.

Custard Tart   V

Serves 4–6 Preparation 15 mins Cooking 1 hr
Per portion 287 kcals, 16g fat (8.9g saturated)

Shortcrust Pastry made with 175g (6oz) flour
(page 225) or sheet of ready-rolled bought
shortcrust pastry
300ml (½ pint) milk
2 eggs plus 1 egg yolk
25g (1oz) caster sugar
Ground nutmeg

Roll out pastry on a floured work surface.
Use pastry to line a 20cm (8in) greased flan
tin or pie plate.
Heat milk until warm.
Beat milk with eggs, egg yolk and sugar.
Strain into pastry case.
Sprinkle top with nutmeg.
Bake tart at 200°C (400°F) Mark 6 for
15 minutes.
Reduce temperature to 170°C (325°F) Mark 3
and bake for a further 30–45 minutes or until
custard has set.

Fruit Pie   ❄ V

Serves 4–6 Preparation 30 mins Cooking 1 hr
Per portion 349 kcals, 17g fat (9.9g saturated)

900g (2lb) apples, rhubarb, gooseberries,
plums, damsons, fresh apricots, cooking
cherries, blackberries or mixture of fruits
50–110g (2–4oz) caster sugar, depending on
sharpness of fruit
Shortcrust (page 225) or Flaky Pastry (page
228) made with 225g (8oz) flour, or sheet of
ready-rolled bought shortcrust pastry
Beaten egg or milk for brushing
Caster sugar to sprinkle

Prepare fruit according to type, cutting any
larger pieces into slices.
Fill a 1.1 litre (2 pint) pie dish with alternate
layers of fruit and sugar.
Begin and end with a layer of fruit and dome
fruit in centre of dish so that it supports
pastry.
Carefully roll out pastry on a floured work
surface.
Cut into an oval or round 4cm (1½in) wider
than top of dish.
Moisten edges of dish with water.
Line with a strip of pastry cut from
trimmings.

Moisten strip with water then cover with
pastry lid.
Press edges well together to seal. Trim away
surplus pastry.
Flake edges by cutting lightly with back of a
knife then 'ridge' with a fork all the way round
pie dish.
Brush with beaten egg or milk.
Make 2 slits in top of pie to allow steam to
escape.
Bake at 220°C (425°F) Mark 7 for 15 minutes.
Reduce to 180°C (350°F) Mark 4 and bake for
a further 30–45 minutes.
Remove from oven. Sprinkle lightly with
caster sugar.

Double Crust Fruit Pie   ❄ V

Serves 4–6 Preparation 20 mins Cooking 30 mins
Per portion 389 kcals, 20g fat (12g saturated)

Shortcrust Pastry made with 275g (10oz) flour
(page 225) or 2 sheets of ready-rolled bought
shortcrust pastry
450g (1lb) stewed, cooked fruit, such as
apples, rhubarb, gooseberries, plums,
damsons, apricots, cherries, blackberries or
mixture of fruits
Beaten egg or milk for brushing
Caster sugar to sprinkle

Cut pastry into 2 equal pieces.
Carefully roll out 1 piece on a floured work
surface.
Use to line a 20cm (8in) flat ovenproof plate
(or shallow ovenproof pie plate).
Cover pastry with fruit to within 2.5cm (1in)
of edges of pastry.
Moisten edges of pastry with water. Cover
with lid, rolled and shaped from remaining
pastry.
Press edges well together to seal. Trim away
surplus pastry.
Flake edges by cutting lightly with back of a
knife then 'ridge' with a fork all the way round
pie plate.
Brush with beaten egg or milk.
Make 2 slits in top of pie to allow steam to
escape.
Stand pie on a baking sheet.
Bake at 200°C (400°F) Mark 6 for 30 minutes.
Remove from oven. Sprinkle lightly with
caster sugar.

Fruit Crumble

Fruit Crumble ❄ V

Serves 6 Preparation 25 mins Cooking 1 hr
Per portion 307 kcals, 11g fat (6.6g saturated)

900g (2lb) **cooking apples, rhubarb,
gooseberries, damsons, plums, blackberries
or red or blackcurrants**
75–110g (3–4oz) **granulated sugar, depending
on sharpness of fruit**
175g (6oz) **plain flour**
75g (3oz) **butter**
50g (2oz) **caster sugar**

Prepare fruit, slicing any large pieces.
Put into a 1.25 litre (2 pint) ovenproof dish in
layers with granulated sugar.
Cover with foil and bake at 190°C (375°F)
Mark 5 for 15 minutes.
Sift flour into a bowl. Rub butter into flour
until mixture resembles fine breadcrumbs.
Stir in caster sugar.
Sprinkle crumble evenly over fruit. Press
down lightly, then smooth top with a knife.

Reduce oven to 180°C (350°F) Mark 4 and
bake for a further 45 minutes or until top is
light brown.

Variations

Oaty Fruit Crumble ❄ V

Follow recipe and method for Fruit Crumble.
For the crumble topping mix together
wholemeal flour, brown sugar and 25g (1oz)
porridge oats with the butter.

Ginger Fruit Crumble ❄ V

Follow recipe and method for Fruit Crumble.
For the crumble topping use demerara
sugar instead of caster sugar and add 1 tsp
ground ginger.

Crispy Lemon Crumble ❄ V

Follow recipe and method for Fruit Crumble.
Add grated rind of 1 lemon and 2 tbsp
crushed cornflakes to crumble topping.

Roly-Poly Pudding ❄

Serves 4   Preparation 25 mins   Cooking 1½ hrs
Per portion 382 kcals, 19g fat (8.7g saturated)

Suet Crust Pastry made with 175g (6oz) flour
(page 230) or sheet of ready-rolled bought
shortcrust pastry
5 tbsp golden syrup, treacle, or jam
1 tsp grated lemon rind

Roll out pastry into a 25 x 20cm (10 x 8in)
rectangle.
Spread with syrup, treacle, marmalade or
jam to within 2.5cm (1in) of edges. Sprinkle
with lemon rind.
Moisten edges of pastry with cold water. Roll
up loosely like a Swiss roll, starting from one
of the shorter sides.
Press edges together and join well to seal.
Wrap loosely in greased greaseproof paper,
then in foil.
Twist ends of foil so they stay closed. Steam
pudding for 1½ hours or bake uncovered at
180°C (350°F) Mark 4 for 30 minutes.

Steamed Suet Pudding ❄

Serves 4   Preparation 20 mins   Cooking 3 hrs
Per portion 455 kcals, 19g fat (8.2g saturated)

110g (4oz) plain flour
¼ tsp salt
1½ tsp baking powder
110g (4oz) breadcrumbs
75g (3oz) caster sugar
75g (3oz) shredded suet
1 egg, beaten
6–8 tbsp milk
Sweet sauce (page 185)

Sift flour, salt and baking powder into a
bowl.
Add breadcrumbs, sugar and suet. Mix to a
soft batter with beaten egg and milk.
Turn into a greased 1.25 litre (2 pint)
pudding basin and cover securely with
buttered greaseproof paper or foil.
Steam for 2½–3 hours.
Serve with a sweet sauce.

Variation

Fair Lady Pudding ❄

Follow recipe and method for Steamed Suet
Pudding. Add grated rind of 1 orange or
lemon with sugar.

Treacle Tart ❄ V

Serves 4   Preparation 25 mins   Cooking 30 mins
Per portion 519 kcals, 18g fat (11.1g saturated)

Shortcrust Pastry made with 175g (6oz) flour
(page 225) or sheet of ready-rolled bought
shortcrust pastry
50g (2oz) white breadcrumbs
225g (8oz) golden syrup
½ tsp grated lemon rind
2 tsp lemon juice

Roll out pastry on a floured work surface. Use
to line a 20cm (8in) pie plate. Trim surplus
pastry from edges.
Mix breadcrumbs with syrup, lemon rind
and juice. Spread over pastry to within
2.5cm (1in) of edges. Moisten edges with
cold water.
Cut remaining pastry into thin strips. Criss-
cross over treacle filling.
Press strips well on to pastry edges and put
plate on to a baking sheet.
Bake at 200°C (400°F) Mark 6 for 30 minutes
or until pastry is golden.

Monmouth Pudding V

Serves 6   Preparation 15 mins   Cooking 1 hr
Per portion 271 kcals, 5g fat (2.7g saturated)

300ml (½ pint) milk, heated to boiling
225g (8oz) white breadcrumbs
4 tbsp granulated sugar
25g (1oz) butter, cut into small pieces
¼ tsp grated nutmeg
2 large eggs, separated
6 tbsp raspberry jam

Pour boiling milk over crumbs in a heatproof
bowl. Cover; leave to stand for 10 minutes.
Break up with a fork and work in 2 tbsp of
sugar with butter, nutmeg and egg yolks.
In another bowl, whisk egg whites until stiff
and fold into bread mixture.
Spoon 2 tbsp of jam into bottom of a
greased 1.2 litre (2 pint) pudding basin and
spoon over half breadcrumb mixture.
Spread remaining jam over top and add rest
of crumb mixture. Cover with greased foil.
Bake at 180°C (350°F) Gas 4 for about 50
minutes until set and firm to the touch.
Sprinkle remaining sugar over top of
pudding and cook under hot grill for about 5
minutes until caramelised.

Queen of Puddings

Queen of Puddings V

Serves 4 Preparation 25 mins plus standing Cooking
1¼ hrs Per portion 358 kcals, 11g fat (5.3g saturated)

110g (4oz) white breadcrumbs
25g (1oz) caster sugar
Grated rind of 1 lemon
450ml (¾ pint) milk
25g (1oz) butter
3 egg yolks
2 tbsp raspberry jam
Warmed Meringue Topping made with 2 egg
whites (page 176)

Put breadcrumbs, sugar and rind into a
basin. Toss lightly together to mix.
Pour milk into a saucepan. Add butter and
heat gently until butter melts.
Pour on to breadcrumb mixture. Stir well and
leave to stand for 30 minutes.
Beat in egg yolks.
Pour in to a 900ml (1½ pint) greased
ovenproof dish.
Bake at 170°C (325°F) Mark 3 for 30 minutes
or until firm and set.
Remove from oven and spread with jam.

Cover with whirls of meringue.
Return to oven and bake for a further 30–40
minutes or until meringue is pale gold.

Apple Charlotte V

Serves 4 Preparation 25 mins Cooking 1 hr
Per portion 385 kcals, 16g fat (9.8g saturated)

110g (4oz) caster sugar
110g (4oz) breadcrumbs
Grated rind of 1 lemon
450g (1lb) cooking apples, peeled, cored
and sliced
75g (3oz) butter, melted

Combine sugar, breadcrumbs and lemon
rind.
Fill a 1.25 litre (2 pint) greased, ovenproof
dish with alternate layers of breadcrumb
mixture and apples. Begin and end with
breadcrumb mixture, sprinkling melted
butter between layers.
Bake at 190°C (375°F) Mark 5 for 45
minutes–1 hour or until apples are tender
and top is golden brown.

Rich Bread & Butter Pudding

Rich Bread & Butter Pudding V

Serves 4   Preparation 30 mins plus standing Cooking
1¼ hrs Per portion 580 kcals, 40g fat (20.6g saturated)

1 vanilla pod

300ml (½ pint) milk

40g (1½oz) sugar

8 slices of fruit bread (about 225g/8oz)

50g (2oz) butter, softened

3 eggs

150ml (¼ pint) double cream

Apricot jam to glaze

Toasted almonds to decorate

Slit vanilla pod in half and scrape out seeds.
Put pod and seeds into a saucepan with milk
and sugar. Gently heat until almost boiling.

Leave to stand for 15 minutes to cool.

Butter bread, cut into triangles and arrange
in a flameproof dish.

In a separate bowl, beat together eggs and
cream.

Remove vanilla pod from milk and gradually
stir milk into cream mixture.

Pour over bread and leave to stand for
30 minutes.

Place dish in a roasting tin containing
enough hot water to come half way up dish.

Bake at 170°C (325°F) Mark 3 for 1 hour, until
custard has set.

Toast lightly under a medium–hot grill for a
crisp top.

Glaze with sieved, warm jam and sprinkle
with toasted almonds.

Bread & Butter Pudding   V

Serves 4   Preparation 30 mins plus standing Cooking
50 mins   Per portion 422 kcals, 17g fat (9.2g saturated)

8 slices of bread, crusts removed
50g (2oz) butter, softened
50g (2oz) currants or sultanas (or mixture)
40g (1½oz) caster sugar
2 eggs
600ml (1 pint) milk

Spread bread thickly with butter. Cut into
small squares or triangles.
Place half into a greased 1.25 litre (2 pint)
ovenproof dish.
Sprinkle with fruit and half the sugar.
Top with remaining bread, buttered sides
uppermost. Sprinkle with remaining sugar.
Beat eggs and milk together. Strain into dish
over bread. Leave to stand for 30 minutes so
that bread absorbs some of the liquid.
Bake at 170°C (325°F) Mark 3 for about 50
minutes until pudding is set and top is crisp.

Cherry Bread Pudding   V

Makes 16 squares   Preparation 15 mins   Cooking
50 mins   Per square 228 kcals, 9.8g fat (5.6g saturated)

225g (8oz) white bread, crust removed, bread
torn into small pieces
375ml (13fl oz) milk
Grated rind of 2 oranges, plus juice of 1
1 tbsp mixed ground spice
175g (6oz) seedless raisins
150g (5oz) sultanas
50g (2oz) mixed chopped peel
75g (3oz) ready-to-eat prunes, chopped
75g (3oz) ready-to-eat dried apricots,
chopped
75g (3oz) glacé cherries, quartered
3 eggs, beaten
150g (5oz) butter, melted
1–2 tbsp black treacle
Granulated sugar

Soak bread in milk for 10 minutes. Add rest
of ingredients, except sugar. Mix well.
Transfer to greased 23cm (9in) square
shallow baking dish. Spread evenly.
Bake at 180°C (350°F) Mark 4 for 45–50
minutes until pudding is lightly browned and
set in the centre.
Sprinkle with granulated sugar.

Bread Pudding   ❄

Serves 10   Preparation 25 mins plus standing Cooking
1½ hrs   Per portion 412 kcals, 18g fat (7.8g saturated)

1 small loaf of bread, about 400g (14oz)
110g (4oz) caster sugar
175g (6oz) shredded suet or chopped butter
5 tbsp mixed spice
350g (12oz) dried mixed fruit
Juice and rind of 1 lemon and 1 orange
2 eggs, beaten
Milk to mix if required
Caster sugar to serve

Break bread up and place in a bowl.
Cover with cold water and leave to stand for
30 minutes.
Squeeze all water out of bread and crumble
into a bowl.
Add sugar, shredded suet or butter, mixed
spice, fruit, juice, rind and eggs. Mix. It should
be like the dropping consistency of a fruit
cake. Add a little milk if necessary.
Pour into a greased roasting tin.
Bake at 180°C (350°F) Mark 4 for 1½ hours
or until firm to the touch. Cover with
greaseproof paper if it starts to go too brown.
Sprinkle with caster sugar.

Apricot Bread Pudding   V

Serves 4   Preparation 25 mins plus standing Cooking
40 mins   Per portion 360 kcals, 8g fat (2.8g saturated)

8 slices of wholemeal bread
75g (3oz) ready-to-eat dried apricots, chopped
50g (2oz) sultanas
2 tbsp clear honey
2 eggs
600ml (1 pint) milk
Grated rind of ½ lemon
1 tsp mixed spice

Cut bread into triangles and place half in
base of an ovenproof dish.
Mix apricots and sultanas, then sprinkle half
over bread and drizzle with half of the honey.
Repeat layers.
Beat eggs with milk, rind and spice. Pour
over bread and leave to stand for 15 minutes.
Bake at 180°C (350°F) Mark 4 for 40 minutes
or until set.

Christmas Pudding

Christmas Pudding ❄

Makes 2; each pudding serves 8   Preparation 40 mins
Cooking 6 hours plus 2 hours before serving
Per portion 452 kcals, 20g fat (7.8g saturated)

110g (4oz) plain flour

½ tsp mixed spice

¼ tsp ground nutmeg

225g (8oz) breadcrumbs

200g (7oz) shredded suet

225g (8oz) dark soft brown sugar

350g (12oz) raisins

350g (12oz) sultanas

50g (2oz) chopped mixed peel

50g (2oz) walnut halves or blanched almonds, chopped

Grated rind of 1 small orange

4 eggs, beaten

50ml (2fl oz) brandy or dry sherry

½ tsp almond essence

150ml (¼ pint) milk

Sift flour, spice and nutmeg into a bowl.

Add breadcrumbs, suet, sugar, dried fruit, peel, nuts and rind and mix thoroughly.

Combine with eggs, brandy or sherry, almond essence and milk. Mix well.

Divide between two greased and base-lined 1.25 litre (2 pint) pudding basins.

Cover with buttered greaseproof paper or foil. Pleat once to allow pudding to rise.

Secure with string, using extra for a handle.

Place in a steamer over a saucepan of boiling water and cover.

Alternatively, place on a metal trivet in a large saucepan and add boiling water to come halfway up the sides of basin. Add pudding and cover.

Steam for 5-6 hours, replenishing water.

Remove from steamer, and leave until cold.

Cover with foil. Store in a cool place.

To serve, steam for 2 hours or replace foil with cling film (puncture film) and microwave on medium-high for 6-8 minutes (depending on wattage).

Apple Amber   V

Serves 4 Preparation 30 mins Cooking 40 mins
Per portion 290 kcals, 10g fat (5g saturated)

450g (1lb) cooking apples, peeled, cored and sliced
25g (1oz) butter
50g (2oz) caster sugar
3 tbsp stale cake crumbs (plain cake gives best results)
1 tsp cinnamon
2 egg yolks
Meringue Topping made with 2 egg whites (page 176)

Put apples into a saucepan with 1 tbsp water and butter.
Cook until soft and pulpy. Beat until smooth.
Add sugar, cake crumbs, cinnamon and egg yolks. Mix well.
Transfer to a 900ml (1½ pint) ovenproof dish and top with meringue.
Bake at 150°C (300°F) Mark 2 for 30 minutes or until meringue is light gold.

Sponge Pudding   ❄ V

Serves 4 Preparation 25 mins Cooking 2 hrs
Per portion 452 kcals, 26g fat (15.3g saturated)

110g (4oz) self raising flour
Pinch of salt
110g (4oz) butter
110g (4oz) caster sugar
2 eggs, beaten
2 tbsp milk
Cream or sweet sauce (page 185)

Sift flour and salt into a bowl.
Cream butter and sugar together until light and fluffy.
Add beaten eggs, a little at a time, with a spoonful of flour, beating well after each addition.
Fold in remaining flour alternating with tablespoons of milk.
Transfer to a greased and base-lined 900ml (1½ pint) pudding basin.
Cover with buttered greaseproof paper or foil. Pleat once to allow pudding to rise.
Secure with string. Use extra string to make a handle for ease of removal.
Place in a steamer over a saucepan of boiling water and cover.
Alternatively, place on a metal trivet in a large saucepan and add boiling water to come half way up the sides of basin. Add pudding and cover.
Steam steadily for 1½–2 hours or until well risen and firm.
Serve with cream or sweet sauce.

Variations

Chocolate Sponge Pudding ❄ V

Follow recipe and method for Sponge Pudding but use 75g (3oz) self-raising flour only. Sift into bowl with salt plus 25g (1oz) cocoa powder. Cream butter and sugar with ½ tsp vanilla extract.

Fruit Sponge Pudding   ❄ V

Follow recipe and method for Sponge Pudding. Stir in 50g (2oz) currants, sultanas or raisins after beating in eggs.

Jam Sponge Pudding   ❄ V

Follow recipe and method for Sponge Pudding. Put 3 tbsp jam into bottom of a greased and base-lined basin before adding pudding mixture.

Syrup Sponge Pudding   ❄ V

Follow recipe and method for Sponge Pudding. Put 3 tbsp golden syrup into bottom of a greased and base-lined basin before adding pudding mixture.

Cabinet Pudding   V

Serves 4 Preparation 20 mins plus standing Cooking 1 hr Per portion 284 kcals, 7g fat (2.5g saturated)

6 trifle sponges
50g (2oz) glacé cherries, chopped
25g (1oz) caster sugar
2 eggs
600ml (1 pint) milk
1 tsp vanilla extract

Cut each trifle sponge into 6 cubes.
Put sponge cubes and cherries into a basin. Add sugar and toss lightly together to mix.
Beat eggs, milk and vanilla well together. Gently stir into sponge cube mixture.
Leave to stand for 30 minutes.
Turn into a 900ml (1½ pint) well-greased pudding basin. Cover securely with buttered greaseproof paper or foil. Steam very gently for 1 hour.

Eve's Pudding

Eve's Pudding ❋ V

Serves 4–5 Preparation 20 mins Cooking 1¼ hrs
Per portion 452 kcals, 21g fat (12.2g saturated)

450g (1lb) cooking apples, peeled, cored and
sliced

75g (3oz) caster sugar

Sponge Pudding made with 110g (4oz) flour
(page 221)

Arrange apples in layers in a greased 1.5 litre
(2½ pint) ovenproof dish, sprinkling sugar
between layers.

Cover with sponge pudding mixture.

Bake at 180°C (350°F) Mark 4 for 1–1¼ hours
or until wooden cocktail stick, inserted into
centre of sponge mixture, comes out clean.

Alternatively, use gooseberries, rhubarb,
apple mixed with blackberries, plums or
damsons instead of apples.

Honey & Spice Pudding ❋ V

Serves 4 Preparation 20 mins Cooking 40 mins
Per portion 154 kcals, 4g fat (1g saturated)

410g can pears in natural juice, drained

2 eggs

25g (1oz) brown sugar

25g (1oz) clear honey

50g (2oz) plain flour

½ tsp mixed spice

Place pears in an ovenproof dish.

Whisk together eggs, sugar and honey until
thick and creamy.

Fold in flour and spice and carefully pour
over pears.

Bake at 180°C (350°F) Mark 4 for about 40
minutes or until risen and firm to touch.

Upside Down Pudding ※ V

Serves 4–6 Preparation 30 mins Cooking 1 hr
Per portion 419 kcals, 23g fat (13.7g saturated)

150g (5oz) butter
25g (1oz) soft brown sugar
227g can pineapple slices in natural juice, drained
4 glacé cherries, halved
110g (4oz) caster sugar
2 eggs, beaten
175g (6oz) self-raising flour

Melt 25g (1oz) butter and stir in brown sugar. Pour into a greased and base-lined 20cm (8in) round cake tin.
Place pineapple rings and glacé cherries on top of butter and sugar.
Cream remaining butter and caster sugar until pale and fluffy.
Gradually beat in eggs.
Fold in flour. Spread over pineapple rings.
Bake at 180°C (350°F) Mark 4 for 1 hour, or until centre springs back when lightly pressed with a finger.
Leave to stand for 5 minutes.

Variation

Pear Upside Down Pudding ※ V

Follow recipe and method for Upside Down Pudding. Use canned pear halves instead of pineapple and 25g (1oz) cocoa powder in place of 25g (1oz) flour in sponge mixture.

Lemon Layer Pudding V

Serves 4 Preparation 20 mins Cooking 45 mins
Per portion 324 kcals, 15g fat (8.2g saturated)

Grated rind and juice of 1 lemon
50g (2oz) butter
110g (4oz) caster sugar
2 eggs, separated
50g (2oz) self-raising flour
300ml (½ pint) milk

Add lemon rind to butter and sugar and whisk until pale and fluffy.
Add egg yolks and flour and beat well.
Stir in milk and 3 tbsp lemon juice.
Whisk egg whites until stiff, then fold into lemon mixture.
Pour into a greased ovenproof dish.
Stand in a shallow tin of water.

Bake at 200°C (400°F) Mark 6 for about 45 minutes or until top is set and spongy to touch.
This pudding will separate into a custard layer with a sponge topping.

Apricot & Ginger Pudding ※ V

Serves 4–6 Preparation 30 mins Cooking 55 mins
Per portion 335 kcals, 17g fat (10.2g saturated)

411g can apricot halves in natural juice, drained
110g (4oz) butter
110g (4oz) caster sugar
1 egg, beaten
75g (3oz) self-raising flour
75g (3oz) wholemeal self-raising flour
2 tsp ground ginger
150ml (¼ pint) milk

Place drained apricots in base of a greased ovenproof dish.
Melt butter and sugar in a small saucepan over a low heat, then cool for 4 minutes.
Add egg and beat well. Stir in flours and ginger, then gradually add milk.
Pour over apricots.
Bake at 180°C (350°F) Mark 4 for about 50 minutes or until risen and firm to touch.

Pinkerton Pear Sponge V

Serves 8 Preparation 15 mins Cooking 1¼ hrs
Per portion 268 kcals, 13g fat (7.6g saturated)

110g (4oz) butter, softened
110g (4oz) caster sugar, plus 1 tbsp
2 eggs
175g (6oz) self-raising flour, sifted
½ tsp baking powder
2 William or Conference pears

Cream together butter and sugar until light and fluffy.
Beat in eggs, then fold in flour and baking powder.
Spoon into a lightly buttered 20cm (8in) loose-based sandwich tin. Smooth the top.
Peel, halve and core pears and slice thinly lengthways. Fan slices out on top of sponge mixture. Sprinkle with extra sugar.
Bake at 180°C (350°F) Gas 4 for 1 hour, then for a further 10–15 minutes if sponge is not quite set in middle.

Leek & Bacon Quiche

Pastry

Home-Made Pastry

When a recipe calls for a certain weight of pastry, the weight refers to the amount of flour used and not to the total amount of pastry.

Bought Pastry

When a recipe calls for a certain weight of bought pastry, this does refer to total weight.

Cooking Pastry

When cooking flans or quiches place a baking sheet in the oven to preheat. Place the flan tin on the hot baking sheet to cook. This ensures a fully cooked pastry base. To bake blind, fill pastry case with greaseproof paper and fill with rice, coins or baking beans.

Shortcrust Pastry ※ V

Preparation 25 mins

For sweet and savoury flans, pies, tarts and tartlets, pasties, patties and turnovers.

225g (8oz) plain flour
¼ tsp salt
110g (4oz) butter
Cold water to mix – allow 1–1½ tsp per 25g (1oz) of flour

Sift flour and salt into a bowl.

Add butter. Cut into flour with a knife, then rub in with fingertips. The mixture should look like fine breadcrumbs.

Sprinkle water over crumbs. Mix to a stiff crumbly looking paste with a round-ended knife.

Draw together with fingertips, turn out on to a lightly floured work surface. Knead quickly until smooth and crack-free.

Roll out and use as required. If not to be used immediately, transfer to a polythene bag or wrap in foil and refrigerate.

The usual cooking temperature is 200–220°C (400–425°F) Mark 6–7.

Variations

Rich Shortcrust Pastry ※ V

For same dishes as shortcrust pastry. Follow recipe and method for Shortcrust Pastry but use 150g (5oz) butter and mix with 4–5 tsp cold water. Transfer to a polythene bag or wrap in foil and chill for at least 30 minutes before rolling out and using.

Nut Pastry ※ V

For flans, pies and turnovers, etc. Follow recipe and method for Shortcrust Pastry but stir in 25g (1oz) very finely chopped unsalted peanuts or cashew nuts before adding water.

Quiche Lorraine ※

Serves 4–5 Preparation 30 mins Cooking 55 mins
Per portion 411 kcals, 33g fat (18g saturated)

Shortcrust Pastry made with 225g (8oz) flour
110g (4oz) streaky bacon
150ml (¼ pint) milk
150ml (¼ pint) single cream
3 eggs, beaten
Salt and freshly ground black pepper
Large pinch of ground nutmeg

Roll out pastry on a floured work surface. Use to line a 20cm (8in) flan tin.

Cut bacon into strips. Fry lightly in its own fat until soft but not crisp. Drain on kitchen paper. Place in base of pastry case.

Heat milk and cream to just below boiling point. Combine with eggs. Season to taste.

Add nutmeg. Pour into pastry case. Bake at 200°C (400°F) Mark 6 for 10 minutes.

Reduce temperature to 170°C (325°F) Mark 3. Bake for a further 35–45 minutes until set.

Leek & Bacon Quiche ※

Serves 6 Preparation 30 mins Cooking 35 mins
Per portion 514 kcals, 35g fat (18g saturated)

Shortcrust Pastry made with 225g (8oz) flour
225g (8oz) smoked streaky bacon, chopped
4 leeks, washed, sliced and quartered
110g (4oz) Caerphilly cheese, crumbled
3 eggs
225ml (8fl oz) milk
Freshly ground black pepper

Roll out pastry on a floured surface and use to line a 30 x 20cm (12 x 8in) flan tin. Prick base and bake blind at 200°C (400°F) Mark 6 for 10 minutes.

Cook bacon in a frying pan until browned, then remove and add leeks. Cook until soft.

Place bacon, leeks and cheese in flan case.

Beat together eggs and milk, season and pour into flan.

Bake at 180°C (350°F) Mark 4 for 25 minutes or until set.

Cut into squares and serve either hot or cold.

Meat & Vegetable Pasties ❄

Serves 4 Preparation 30 mins Cooking 1 hr 5 mins
Per portion 548 kcals, 29g fat (16.6g saturated)

175g (6oz) rump steak
110g (4oz) lamb's kidneys
1 onion, peeled and chopped
1 large potato, peeled and diced
Salt and freshly ground black pepper
Shortcrust Pastry made with 225g (8oz) flour
Milk for brushing

Cut steak and kidney into very small pieces.
Combine with onion, potato, 1 tbsp water and seasoning.
Divide pastry into 4 equal-sized pieces.
On a floured surface, roll out each into a 15cm (6in) round. Moisten edges with water.
Put equal amounts of filling into centres of each. Fold rounds in half over filling to form semi-circles.
Press edges well together to seal. Ridge with a fork. Transfer to a lightly greased baking sheet. Brush with milk.
Bake at 220°C (425°F) Mark 7 for 20 minutes.
Reduce to 170°C (325°F) Mark 3. Bake for a further 45 minutes. Serve hot or cold.

West Country Flan ❄ V

Serves 8 Preparation 30 mins Cooking 50 mins
Per portion 331 kcals, 21g fat (12.9g saturated)

Shortcrust Pastry made with 225g (8oz) flour
110g (4oz) clotted cream
2 tbsp caster sugar
½ tsp ground cinnamon
1 egg, beaten
1 tbsp cornflour
2 eating apples, cored, sliced and dipped in lemon juice
25g (1oz) apricot jam, melted

Roll out pastry on a floured work surface and use to line a 23cm (9in) flan tin.
Bake blind at 180°C (350°F) Mark 4 for 15 minutes.
Blend together cream, sugar, cinnamon, egg and cornflour.
Pour into flan case.
Arrange sliced apples in flan case and bake for a further 35 minutes until set.
Remove from oven and brush with melted jam. Serve hot or cold.

Mince Pies ❄

Makes 12 Preparation 25 mins Cooking 25 mins
Per portion 227 kcals, 10g fat (5.6g saturated)

Shortcrust Pastry or Rich Shortcrust Pastry made with 225g (8oz) flour
350g (12oz) mincemeat (page 279)
Beaten egg for brushing
Icing sugar, sifted

Roll out pastry on a lightly floured work surface.
Cut 12 rounds with an 8.5cm (3½in) biscuit cutter and 12 rounds with a 6.5cm (2½in) biscuit cutter.
Use larger rounds to line deep bun tins.
Put equal amounts of mincemeat in each.
Top with remaining rounds and brush with beaten egg.
Bake at 220°C (425°F) Mark 7 for 20–25 minutes or until golden brown.
Remove from tins and dredge thickly with sifted icing sugar.

Almond Slices ❄ V

Makes 12 Preparation 30 mins Cooking 25 mins
Per portion 322 kcals, 18g fat (5.7g saturated)

Shortcrust Pastry made with 225g (8oz) flour
2 tbsp raspberry or apricot jam
110g (4oz) caster sugar
110g (4oz) icing sugar, sifted
175g (6oz) ground almonds
1 egg plus 1 egg white
½ tsp almond essence
25g (1oz) flaked almonds

Roll out pastry on a floured work surface to fit a 28 x 18cm (11 x 7in) cake tin.
Use to line tin.
Cover base with jam.
Combine sugars with ground almonds.
Mix to a paste with egg, egg white and almond essence.
Cover jam with almond mixture, spreading it evenly with a knife.
Decorate with flaked almonds.
Bake at 200°C (400°F) Mark 6 for about 25 minutes or until golden and cooked through.
Cool on a wire cooling rack. Cut into 12 slices when cold.

Wholemeal Shortcrust Pastry ❄ V

Preparation 30 mins plus chilling

110g (4oz) wholemeal flour
110g (4oz) self-raising wholemeal flour
Pinch of salt
110g (4oz) butter

Put flours and salt in a bowl.
Add butter, cut into flour with a knife, then rub in with fingertips until mixture resembles fine breadcrumbs.
Add 125ml (4fl oz) water.
Mix together with a round-ended knife to a soft dough.
Draw together with fingertips.
Leave dough in bowl and refrigerate for 5 minutes.
Roll out and use as required.
The usual cooking temperature is 200–220°C (400–425°F) Mark 6–7.

Mixed Pepper Quiche ❄ V

Serves 4–6   Preparation 30 mins   Cooking 45 mins
Per portion 397 kcals, 27g fat (15.5g saturated)

Wholemeal Shortcrust Pastry made with 225g (8oz) flour
25g (1oz) butter
1 onion, peeled and sliced
3 assorted peppers, deseeded and sliced
1 garlic clove, peeled and crushed
2 eggs
150ml (¼ pint) single cream
90ml (3fl oz) milk
Salt and freshly ground black pepper

Roll out pastry on a lightly floured work surface.
Use to line a 20cm (8in) flan tin.
Bake blind at 200°C (400°F) Mark 6 for 15 minutes.
Melt butter and fry onion, peppers and garlic until soft but not brown.
Spoon into pastry case.
Beat together eggs, cream and milk.
Season eggs and milk to taste and pour over vegetables.
Reduce temperature to 180°C (350°F) Mark 4 and cook for 30 minutes or until set. It will remain a little wobbly when hot.
Serve hot or cold.

Broccoli & Bean Quiche ❄ V

Serves 6   Preparation 35 mins   Cooking 45 mins
Per portion 465 kcals, 31g fat (17.7g saturated)

Wholemeal Shortcrust Pastry made with 225g (8oz) flour
110g (4oz) broccoli florets
220g can red kidney beans, drained
110g (4oz) Double Gloucester cheese, grated
3 eggs
150ml (¼ pint) single cream
150ml (¼ pint) milk

Roll out pastry on a floured work surface and use to line a 23cm (9in) flan tin.
Bake blind at 200°C (400°F) Mark 6 for 10 minutes.
Cook broccoli florets in boiling water for 2–3 minutes. Drain well.
Arrange in base of flan case with kidney beans and cheese.
Beat eggs, cream and milk together and pour into flan case.
Bake for a further 35 minutes or until set. It will remain a little wobbly when hot.
Serve hot or cold.

Cheese Pastry ❄ V

Preparation 25 mins plus chilling

For savoury biscuits, straws, pies and flans.
110g (4oz) plain flour
¼ tsp dry mustard
¼ tsp salt
Shake of cayenne pepper
65g (2½oz) butter
50g (2oz) Cheddar cheese, grated
1 egg yolk

Sift flour, mustard, salt and cayenne pepper into a bowl.
Cut butter into flour, and rub in until mixture resembles breadcrumbs.
Add cheese and mix ingredients together.
Mix to a stiff paste with egg yolk and 2–3 tsp cold water.
Turn out on to a floured work surface. Knead quickly until smooth and crack-free.
Wrap in a polythene bag or foil.
Chill for 30 minutes before using.
The usual cooking temperature is 200°C (400°F) Mark 6.

Sweet Flan Pastry ❄ V

Preparation 30 mins plus chilling

For sweet flans, tarts, tartlets, small and large pies.

1 egg yolk
2 tsp icing sugar, sifted
110g (4oz) plain flour
Pinch of salt
65g (2½oz) butter

Mix egg yolk and sugar well together.
Sift flour and salt into a bowl.
Add butter, cut into flour with a knife, then rub in with fingertips until mixture resembles fine breadcrumbs.
Mix to a stiff paste with yolk, sugar and 1–2 tsp cold water.
Turn out on to a lightly floured work surface. Knead quickly until smooth.
Wrap in a polythene bag or foil.
Chill for at least 30 minutes before rolling out and using.
The usual cooking temperature is 190°C (375°F) Mark 5.

Flaky Pastry ❄ V

Preparation 35 mins plus chilling and resting

For sweet and savoury pies, patties, turnovers and sausage rolls.

175g (6oz) butter
225g (8oz) plain flour
¼ tsp salt
1 tsp lemon juice

Divide butter into 4 equal portions. Chill 3 portions. Sift flour and salt into a bowl.
Rub in unchilled portion of butter.
Mix to a soft dough with 150ml (¼ pint) chilled water and lemon juice. Turn out on to a floured work surface. Knead thoroughly.
Put into a polythene bag or wrap in foil. Chill for 30 minutes.
Roll out on a floured work surface into a 5mm (¼in) thick rectangle, measuring about 45 x 15cm (18 x 6in).
Using tip of a knife, dot second portion of butter (in small flakes) over top and middle third of rectangle to within 2.5cm (1in) of edges. Dust lightly with flour.
Fold in three, envelope style, by bringing bottom third over middle third and folding top third over.

Seal open edges by pressing firmly together with a rolling pin. Wrap and chill for 15 minutes.
Remove from bag or unwrap. With folded edges to left and right, roll out again into a 45 x 15cm (18 x 6in) rectangle.
Cover with third portion of butter as before. Fold, seal and chill.
Repeat again, adding last portion of butter and chill.
Roll out one more time. Fold and seal as before, then return to polythene bag or wrap in foil.
Chill for at least 30 minutes before rolling out to 5mm (¼in) thickness and using.
After shaping, let dishes rest for 30 minutes in a cool place before baking.
The usual cooking temperature is 220°C (425°F) Mark 7.

Eccles Cakes ❄ V

Makes 8   Preparation 45 mins   Cooking 15 mins
Per portion 168 kcals, 11g fat (6.6g saturated)

15g (½oz) butter, softened
25g (1oz) currants
25g (1oz) chopped mixed peel
2 tsp soft brown sugar
¼ tsp mixed spice
Flaky pastry made with 110g (4oz) flour
Milk for brushing
Caster sugar

Mix softened butter with currants, peel, brown sugar and spice.
Roll out pastry on a lightly floured work surface.
Cut into 8 rounds with an 8.5cm (3½in) biscuit cutter.
Put a heaped teaspoon of fruit mixture on to centre of each one.
Moisten edges of pastry with water.
With fingertips, draw up edges of each round so they meet in the centre, completely enclosing filling.
Press well together to seal. Gently turn each cake over.
Roll out until fruit shows through.
Make 3 slits in top of each with a sharp knife.
Brush with milk. Sprinkle thickly with caster sugar.
Bake at 230°C (450°F) Mark 8 for 15 minutes.
Cool on a wire cooling rack.

Puff Pastry ❄ V

Preparation 50 mins plus chilling and resting

For vol-au-vents, pasties and tarts.
225g (8oz) butter
225g (8oz) plain flour
¼ tsp salt
1 tsp lemon juice

Shape butter into a 1.5cm (¾in) brick.

Sift flour and salt into a bowl. Mix to a soft paste with lemon juice and a little chilled water.

Knead paste well on a lightly floured work surface.

Roll out into a rectangle measuring 30 x 15cm (12 x 6in).

Stand butter on lower half of rectangle. Bring top half over so that butter is completely enclosed.

Press open edges firmly together with rolling pin. Put into a polythene bag or wrap in foil. Chill for 15 minutes.

Remove from bag. With fold on right, roll into 45 x 15cm (18 x 6in) rectangle.

Fold in three envelope style, by bringing bottom third over middle third and folding top third over. Seal edges, wrap and chill for 20 minutes.

Repeat, until pastry has been rolled, folded and chilled 7 times.

Return to polythene bag or wrap in foil.

Chill for at least 30 minutes before rolling out to 5mm (¼in) thickness and using.

After shaping, let dishes rest for 30 minutes in a cool place before baking.

The usual cooking temperature is 230°C (450°F) Mark 8.

Rough Puff Pastry ❄ V

Preparation 1 hr plus chilling

For same dishes as flaky pastry.
225g (8oz) plain flour
¼ tsp salt
175g (6oz) butter
1 tsp lemon juice

Sift flour and salt into a bowl.

Cut butter into tiny dice.

Mix together 150ml (¼ pint) chilled water and lemon juice.

Add butter to flour.

Using a knife, mix to a fairly soft crumbly paste with water and lemon juice. Take care not to cut or break down butter any further.

Draw together with fingertips. Turn out on to a floured work surface and shape into a block.

Roll into a 5mm (¼in) thick rectangle, measuring about 45 x 15cm (18 x 6in). Fold in three, envelope style, by bringing bottom third over middle third and folding top third over.

Seal open edges by pressing firmly together with rolling pin.

Give pastry a quarter turn so that folded edges are to right and left.

Roll out. Fold and turn three more times.

If possible, put folded pastry into a polythene bag or wrap in foil and chill for 15 minutes between rollings.

The usual cooking temperature is 220°C (425°F) Mark 7.

Sausage Rolls ❄

Makes 10 Preparation 30 mins Cooking 20 mins
Per portion 284 kcals, 21g fat (11.1g saturated)

Rough Puff Pastry made with 225g (8oz) flour
225g (8oz) sausagemeat or skinless sausages
Beaten egg for brushing

Roll out pastry on a lightly floured surface into a long strip about 10cm (4in) wide.

Roll sausagemeat into a roll as long as pastry. Place in centre of pastry.

Brush edges of pastry with water. Fold over pastry and seal longest edge well.

Cut into 10 pieces and place on baking sheets.

Make 2 cuts in top of each pastry piece and brush with beaten egg.

Bake at 230°C (450°F) Mark 8 for 20 minutes or until golden brown.

Variations

Sausage & Apple Rolls

Follow recipe and method for Sausage Rolls. Peel, core and grate 1 eating apple and mix with sausagemeat before using.

Tomato Sausage Rolls

Follow recipe and method for Sausage Rolls. Mix 2 tbsp tomato purée with sausagemeat before using.

229

Apple Turnovers ❄ V

Makes 6 Preparation 25 mins Cooking 40 mins
Per portion 392 kcals, 25g fat (15.2g saturated)

Rough Puff Pastry or Flaky Pastry made with
225g (8oz) flour
225g (8oz) cooking apples, peeled, cored and
sliced
50g (2oz) caster sugar plus extra for
sprinkling
Lightly beaten egg white

Roll out pastry on a floured surface and cut
into 6 x 10cm (4in) squares.
Mix apples with sugar. Put an equal amount
on to centre of each square.
Moisten edges of pastry with cold water.
Fold in half to form a triangle, enclosing fruit.
Press edges together to seal. Flake by cutting
lightly with back of a knife then 'ridge' with
a fork.
Transfer on to a baking sheet. Brush with
egg white and sprinkle with sugar.
Bake at 220°C (425°F) Mark 7 for 20 minutes.
Reduce to 180°C (350°F) Mark 4 and bake for
a further 20 minutes.

Suet Crust Pastry

Preparation 10 mins

For sweet and savoury roly-polys, boiled and
steamed puddings and dumplings.
225g (8oz) self-raising flour
½ tsp salt
110g (4oz) shredded suet

Sift flour and salt into a bowl. Add suet and
mix ingredients lightly together.
Mix to a soft dough with 150ml (¼ pint) cold
water.
Turn out dough on to a lightly floured work
surface.
Knead until smooth and roll out to about
25mm (⅛in) thickness.
Use immediately as required.
This pastry can be steamed or baked.

Variation

Dumplings

Follow recipe and method for Suet Crust
Pastry but use half the quantities. Divide
into 8 pieces and shape into small balls. Add
to soups, stews or casseroles and cook for
15–20 minutes.

Hot Water Crust Pastry

Preparation 30 mins plus standing

For raised pies such as pork, veal, veal and
ham and game.
350g (12oz) plain flour
½ tsp salt
1 egg yolk
4 tbsp milk
25g (1oz) butter
75g (3oz) lard

Sift flour and salt into a bowl and warm
slightly. Make a well in centre.
Beat yolk with 1 tbsp milk and pour into well.
Pour remaining milk and 4 tbsp water into a
saucepan. Add butter and lard. Heat slowly
until melted. Bring to a brisk boil.
Pour into well. Mix with a wooden spoon
until ingredients are well blended.
Turn out on to a floured work surface. Knead
quickly until smooth.
Put into a bowl standing over a pan of hot
water. Cover and leave to rest for 30 minutes.
Roll out pastry to 5mm (¼in) thickness.
When making pies, cut off a piece for lid first.
Cover and leave it in bowl over hot water.
The cooking temperature is 220°C (425°F)
Mark 7, reducing to 180°C (350°F) Mark 4.

Chicken & Ham Pie

Serves 6 Preparation 1 hr plus chilling Cooking
1½ hrs Per portion 582 kcals, 28g fat (7g saturated)

800g (1lb 12oz) chicken meat, cubed
2 thick smoked gammon slices, cubed
3 tbsp white wine
1 tbsp olive oil
1 tsp mixed dried herbs
3 tbsp chopped parsley
2–3 tsp green or pink peppercorns in brine
Hot Water Crust Pastry made with 225g (8oz)
flour
Salt and freshly ground black pepper
1 egg, beaten
2 tsp powdered gelatine
150ml (¼ pint) chicken stock

Place chicken and gammon in a large bowl
and add wine, oil, herbs and peppercorns.
Mix, cover and refrigerate for at least 2 hours.
Cut off a quarter of dough and set aside.
Roll remaining dough into a rectangle large

enough to cover base and sides of a loaf tin.
Season meat and spread evenly over pastry.
Roll out remaining pastry to cover pie. Seal edges, trim off excess and brush with egg.
Make 3 x 5mm (¼in) holes in centre of lid. Insert foil tubes into 2 outside holes. Place pie on a baking tray and bake at 200°C (400°F) Mark 6 for 30 minutes. Reduce heat to 180°C (350°F) Mark 4 and cook for 1–1½ hours or until a skewer, when inserted into centre, feels hot on the back of your hand.
Allow the pie to cool and chill overnight.
Next day, sprinkle gelatine over 3 tbsp of water in a small bowl and leave to swell. Stand bowl in a pan of simmering water until gelatine is melted and hot. Stir into stock.
Remove foil. With a funnel, pour stock into pie until jelly is level with top of each hole.
Cover and chill for another 24 hours.

Choux Pastry ※ V
Preparation 30 mins

For sweet and savoury buns and éclairs.
65g (2½oz) plain flour
Pinch of salt
50g (2oz) butter
2 eggs, beaten

Sift flour and salt twice.
Put 150ml (¼ pint) water and butter into a saucepan. Heat slowly until butter melts, then bring to a brisk boil.
Remove from heat and tip in all the flour.
Stir briskly until mixture forms a soft ball and leaves sides of saucepan clean.
Remove from heat and cool slightly. Add eggs gradually, beating hard until mixture is smooth, shiny and firm enough to stand in soft peaks when lifted with a spoon.
Use immediately or leave in saucepan and cover with a lid to prevent pastry drying out.
The usual cooking temperature is 200–220°C (400–425°F) Mark 6–7.

Stilton & Walnut Choux V
Makes 20 Preparation 30 mins Cooking 40 mins
Per portion 67 kcals, 5g fat (2.7g saturated)

Choux Pastry made with 65g (2½oz) flour
75g (3oz) soft cheese
50g (2oz) Blue Stilton cheese, crumbled
1 tbsp milk
25g (1oz) chopped walnuts

Using a teaspoon, place 20 equal amounts of pastry on to a greased and lightly floured baking sheet.
Bake at 200°C (400°F) Mark 6 for 20 minutes.
Reduce temperature to 170°C (325°F) Mark 3. Bake for a further 20 minutes.
Cool on a wire cooling rack.
Just before serving, beat together cheeses and milk. Stir in nuts. Cut pastry puffs in half. Fill with cheese mixture. Replace tops.
Serve immediately .

Variation

Cheese & Prawn Choux
Follow recipe and method for Stilton & Walnut Choux. Use 75g (3oz) chopped cooked peeled prawns instead of Stilton. Stir in ½ tsp grated lemon rind instead of walnuts.

Chocolate Éclairs ※ V
Makes 12 Preparation 15 mins Cooking 40 mins
Per portion 253 kcals, 18g fat (10.2g saturated)

Choux Pastry made with 65g (2½oz) flour
300ml (½ pint) double cream
2 tbsp milk
Cocoa Glacé Icing made with 175g (6oz) icing sugar (page 268)

Fit a piping bag with a 1cm (½in) plain tube.
Fill bag with pastry. Pipe 12 x 10cm (4in) lengths on to a greased baking sheet.
Bake at 200°C (400°F) Mark 6 for 10 minutes.
Reduce temperature to 180°C (350°F) Mark 4. Bake for a further 20–25 minutes or until éclairs are well puffed and golden.
Remove from oven and make a slit in the side of each one. Return to oven for further 5 minutes to dry out.
Cool on a wire cooling rack.
When completely cold slit each éclair along one side.
Whip cream with milk until softly stiff. Fill éclairs with cream.
Cover tops with icing and leave until icing has set.

Variation

Coffee Éclairs ※ V
Follow recipe and method for Chocolate Éclairs. Cover tops with Coffee Glacé Icing (page 268) instead of cocoa.

Breads & Savouries

Bread

All doughs must be kneaded thoroughly after mixing for a good rise and even texture. It must be risen at least once before baking. Cover or place in a lightly greased polythene bag during rising to prevent a skin forming. The rising time varies with temperature and type of dough – it will take about 1 hour in a warm place or 1½–2 hours at room temperature. To save time, the dough may be made up the night before and left to rise for 8–12 hours in a cold room or refrigerator. The dough should then be allowed to reach room temperature before shaping. Once risen, all mixtures must be kneaded quickly to make the dough firm and ready for shaping.

When cooked, bread shrinks slightly from the sides of the tin, sounds hollow when tapped underneath and has golden brown crusts.

White Bread

Makes 2 loaves   Preparation 25 mins plus rising Cooking 40 mins   Per slice 211 kcals, 2g fat (1.1g saturated)

450g (1lb) strong plain flour

2 tsp salt

15g (½oz) butter

1 tsp caster sugar

2 tsp dried yeast

Milk or beaten egg for brushing

Sift flour and salt into a bowl. Rub in butter.

Dissolve sugar in 300ml (½ pint) lukewarm water and sprinkle yeast on top. Leave for 10 minutes in a warm place until frothy.

Add all at once to dry ingredients. Mix to a firm dough, adding more flour if needed, until dough leaves sides of bowl clean.

Turn out on to a floured work surface. Knead for 10 minutes.

Cover with a greased polythene bag and leave until doubled in size.

Turn out on to a floured work surface. Knead until firm. Cut into 2 equal-sized pieces.

Shape each to fit a 450g (1lb) loaf tin. Grease tin, then put in dough. Cover and leave until dough doubles in size and reaches top of tin.

Brush with milk or beaten egg and milk. Bake at 230°C (450°F) Mark 8 for 30–40 minutes, or until loaf shrinks slightly from sides of tin and crust is golden brown. Cool on a wire rack.

Variation

White Bread Rolls ❄ V

Follow recipe and method for White Bread. After first rising, divide dough into 12 equal-sized pieces and shape into round rolls, miniature plaits, knots or tiny cottage loaves. Put on to greased baking sheets, cover and leave to rise until doubled in size. Brush with milk or beaten egg and milk. Sprinkle with poppy or sesame seeds if desired. Bake at 230°C (450°F) Mark 8 for 20–25 minutes or until brown and crisp. Cool on a wire rack.

Wholemeal Bread

Makes 2 loaves   Preparation 40 mins plus rising Cooking 45 mins   Per slice 202 kcals, 3g fat (1.4g saturated)

680g (1½lb) wholemeal flour

2 tsp salt

2½ tsp caster sugar

25g (1oz) butter

1 tbsp dried yeast

150ml (¼ pint) milk, lukewarm

Salted water

Place flour, salt and 1½ tsp sugar in a bowl and rub in butter.

Dissolve remaining sugar in 300ml (½ pint) lukewarm water and sprinkle yeast on top. Leave to stand for 10 minutes in a warm place until frothy.

Mix dry ingredients with yeast liquid and milk to make a firm dough that leaves sides of bowl clean.

Turn out on to a lightly floured work surface. Knead thoroughly for 10 minutes or until dough is smooth and elastic and no longer sticky.

Cover and leave until doubled in size.

Turn out on to a floured work surface.

Knead well and cut in half.

Shape each piece of dough to fit a 900g (2lb) loaf tin. Grease loaf tins and then put in dough.

Brush tops of loaves with salted water. Cover and leave to rise until dough reaches top of tins.

Bake at 230°C (450°F) Mark 8 for 40–45 minutes or until loaves shrink slightly from sides of tins.

Turn out and cool on a wire rack.

Variation

Coburg Rolls ❄ V

Follow recipe and method for Wholemeal Bread. After first rising, divide into 18 equal-sized pieces and shape into rolls. Place on to greased baking sheets and make 2 crossed cuts on top of each. Brush with salted water. Cover and leave until doubled in size. Bake at 220°C (425°F) Mark 7 for 20–25 minutes.

Quick Brown Bread ❄ V

Makes 2 loaves   Preparation 30 mins plus rising Cooking 40 mins   Per slice 219 kcals, 3g fat (1.3g saturated)

225g (8oz) wholemeal flour

225g (8oz) strong plain flour

2 tsp salt

3 tsp granulated sugar

15g (½oz) butter

2 tsp dried yeast

150ml (¼ pint) milk, lukewarm

Salted water

2 tbsp crushed cornflakes

Place flours, salt and 2 tsp sugar into a bowl.

Rub in butter until mixture resembles fine breadcrumbs.

Dissolve remaining sugar in 150ml (¼ pint) warm water and all of milk. Sprinkle yeast on top. Leave for 10 minutes in a warm place until frothy.

Add all at once to dry ingredients.

Mix to a fairly soft dough that leaves sides of bowl clean. Turn out on to a floured work surface.

Knead for 10 minutes, or until elastic.

Cut into 2 and shape each to fit a 450g (1lb) loaf tin. Grease tins. Put in dough.

Brush tops of loaves with salted water. Sprinkle with crushed cornflakes.

Cover and leave until loaves have doubled in size and spring back when pressed lightly.

Bake at 230°C (450°F) Mark 8 for 30–40 minutes.

Turn out and cool on a wire rack.

Soda Bread ❄ V

Makes 1 loaf   Preparation 20 mins   Cooking 50 mins Per slice 172 kcals, 5g fat (2.7g saturated)

350g (12oz) wholemeal flour

110g (4oz) flour

1 tsp salt

1 tsp bicarbonate of soda

50g (2oz) butter

225ml (8fl oz) milk

150g (5oz) natural yogurt

Flour to dust

Mix together flours, salt and bicarbonate of soda. Rub in butter until mixture resembles fine breadcrumbs.

Add milk and yogurt and mix to a soft dough. Knead lightly.

Shape into a round and place on a greased baking sheet.

Score bread with a deep cross and dust with flour. Bake at 220°C (425°F) Mark 7 for 50 minutes.

When cool, slice and serve. This bread is best eaten on the day it is made.

Milk Loaf V

Makes 2 loaves   Preparation 45mins plus rising   Cooking 50 mins   Per slice 266 kcals, 7g fat (3.9g saturated)

2 tsp dried yeast

1 tsp sugar

200ml (7fl oz) milk, lukewarm, plus extra for brushing

450g (1lb) strong plain flour

1 tsp salt

50g (2oz) butter

1 egg, beaten

Stir yeast and sugar into milk and leave to stand for 5 minutes.

Put one-third of flour into a large bowl. Add yeast liquid, mix well. Leave in a warm place for 20 minutes or until frothy.

Meanwhile, sift remaining flour and salt into a bowl. Rub in butter then add, with beaten egg, to yeast mixture. Mix well.

Turn out on to a lightly floured work surface. Knead for 10 minutes or until dough loses its stickiness.

Cover, then leave to rise until doubled in size.

Turn out on to a floured work surface. Knead lightly. Cut into 2.

Shape each to fit a 450g (1lb) loaf tin. Grease tins. Put in dough.

Cover and leave to rise until dough doubles in size and reaches top of tins.

Brush with milk. Bake at 190°C (375°F) Mark 5 for 45–50 minutes or until loaf shrinks slightly from sides of tin and crust is golden.

Cool on a wire rack.

English Muffins ❄ V

Makes 12   Preparation 40 mins plus rising Cooking
10 mins   Per portion 163 kcals, 3g fat (1.4g saturated)

450g (1lb) strong plain flour
1 tsp salt
1 tsp caster sugar
150ml (¼ pint) milk, lukewarm
4 tsp dried yeast
1 egg, beaten
25g (1oz) butter, melted
Flour or semolina to dust

Sift flour and salt into a bowl.
Dissolve sugar in milk and 6 tbsp lukewarm
water and sprinkle yeast on top. Stand for
10 minutes in a warm place until frothy.
Add to dry ingredients with beaten egg and
melted butter. Mix to a fairly soft dough.
Turn out on to a floured work surface.
Knead for 10 minutes or until dough is
smooth.
Cover and leave to rise until doubled in size.
Turn out on to a floured work surface. Knead
lightly and roll out to 1cm (½in) thickness.
Cut into 12 rounds with an 8.5cm (3½in)
cutter. Put on a floured baking sheet. Dust
with flour or semolina. Cover and leave until
doubled in size.
Either bake at 230°C (450°F) Mark 8 for 5
minutes each side or cook in a frying pan for
about 7 minutes each side until golden.
Remove from oven. Cool on a wire rack.

Chapattis ❄ V

Makes 8   Preparation 20 mins plus standing Cooking
25 mins   Per portion 95 kcals, 1g fat (0.1g saturated)

225g (8oz) wholemeal flour
175ml (6fl oz) lukewarm water
Extra flour for rolling

Place flour in a bowl and stir in water.
Knead dough on a floured work surface until
soft and pliable. Replace dough in a bowl
and cover. Leave to stand for 15–30 minutes.
Divide dough into 8 even-sized pieces.
Dip in flour, roll out to 25mm (⅛in) thick and
12.5cm (5in) diameter.
Cook in a preheated frying pan. When small
bubbles appear on surface, turn chapatti
over and repeat. Press edges down with a
palette knife. It is cooked when both sides
have brown spots on surface.

Naan Bread ❄ V

Makes 6   Preparation 35 mins plus rising Cooking
5 mins   Per portion 362 kcals, 10g fat (5.3g saturated)

1 egg, beaten
½ tsp salt
1 tsp baking powder
1 tsp caster sugar
1½ tsp dried yeast
4 tbsp natural yogurt
50g (2oz) butter, melted
450g (1lb) strong plain flour
200ml (7fl oz) milk, lukewarm

Beat egg with salt, baking powder, sugar,
yeast, yogurt and half of the butter.
Stir in flour and add milk gradually.
Knead until smooth, cover and leave in a
warm place until doubled in size.
Knead for a minute.
Divide into 6 balls. Flatten and roll balls into
tear-drop shapes about 5mm (¼in) thick.
Leave for 5–10 minutes.
Brush with remaining butter and grill for
2 minutes on each side, until cooked and
lightly brown.

Cheese & Onion Bread ❄ V

Makes 1 loaf   Preparation 25mins plus rising Cooking
40 mins   Per slice 172 kcals, 6g fat (3.1g saturated)

280g (10oz) packet of bread mix
25g (1oz) dried onions, crushed
110g (4oz) Lancashire cheese, grated
200ml (7fl oz) milk, lukewarm

Place bread mix in a bowl, then stir in dried
onions and cheese.
Stir in sufficient milk to make a soft dough.
Knead on a lightly floured work surface for
5 minutes until smooth and elastic.
Shape into a round and place on a greased
baking sheet.
Cut top of dough to make a criss-cross
pattern.
Cover with greased polythene and leave in a
warm place for 30 minutes or until doubled
in size.
Brush with a little milk and bake at 220°C
(425°F) Mark 7 for 30–40 minutes or until well
risen and golden brown.
Cool on a wire rack.

Onion Rolls

Onion Rolls ❋ V

Makes 8   Preparation 30 mins plus rising   Cooking
25 mins   Per portion 294 kcals, 9g fat (5.4g saturated)

450g (1lb) strong plain flour
2 tsp salt
75g (3oz) butter
1 tsp caster sugar
300ml (½ pint) milk, lukewarm
2 tsp dried yeast
3 tbsp dried onions

Sift flour and salt into a bowl and rub in
25g (1oz) butter.

Dissolve sugar in warm milk and sprinkle
yeast on top. Leave to stand for 10 minutes in
a warm place until frothy.

Stir into flour with dried onions. Knead for 10
minutes. Place dough in a clean bowl, cover
with greased polythene, then leave to rise in
a warm place until doubled.

Melt remaining butter. Pour into a 23cm
(9in) round cake tin.

Divide dough into 8. Shape into rolls and
turn in butter to coat. Arrange 7 around the
edge of tin to form a ring. Place remaining
roll in centre.

Cover and leave to rise until doubled in size.

Bake at 220°C (425°F) Mark 7 for 20–25
minutes. Cover with foil after 15 minutes.

Catherine Wheels ❋

Makes 9   Preparation 40 mins plus rising   Cooking
25 mins   Per portion 163 kcals, 7g fat (3.6g saturated)

175g (6oz) full fat soft cheese
6 spring onions, trimmed and chopped
4 bacon rashers, crisply grilled and
chopped
1 tbsp wholegrain mustard
275g packet of bread mix
200ml (7fl oz) milk, lukewarm

In a bowl, mix soft cheese with spring onions,
bacon pieces and mustard.

Place bread mix in a bowl, then stir in
sufficient milk to make a soft dough.

Knead on a lightly floured work surface for
5 minutes until smooth and elastic.

Roll dough out into a rectangle 30 x 23cm
(12 x 9in).

Spread cheese mixture over dough and roll
up like a Swiss roll from longest edge.

Cut into 9 thick slices and arrange in a
greased 18cm (7in) square tin.

Cover tin with greased polythene and leave
in a warm place for 30 minutes, until doubled
in size.

Bake at 220°C (425°F) Mark 7 for about
25 minutes until golden brown.

Wholemeal Scones ❄ V

Makes 7–8   Preparation 25 mins   Cooking 10 mins
Per portion 139 kcals, 5g fat (2.9g saturated)

110g (4oz) wholemeal flour
110g (4oz) plain flour
1 tbsp baking powder
½ tsp salt
40g (1½oz) butter
150ml (¼ pint) milk
Extra milk for brushing

Sift flours, baking powder and salt into a bowl.
Rub butter into flour until mixture resembles fine breadcrumbs.
Add milk all at once.
Mix to a soft, but not sticky, dough with a knife.
Turn on to a lightly floured work surface. Knead quickly until smooth.
Roll out to about 1cm (½in) thickness.
Cut into 7 or 8 rounds with a 6.5cm (2½in) biscuit cutter.
Transfer to a greased baking sheet. Brush tops with milk.
Bake at 230°C (450°F) Mark 8 for 7–10 minutes, or until well risen and golden.
Cool on a wire cooling rack.

Cheese Scones ❄ V

Makes 7–8   Preparation 25 mins   Cooking 10 mins
Per portion 178 kcals, 8g fat (4.9g saturated)

225g (8oz) self-raising flour
½ tsp salt
1 tsp mustard powder
Pinch of cayenne pepper
50g (2oz) butter
50g (2oz) Cheddar cheese
150ml (¼ pint) milk
Extra milk for brushing

Sift flour, salt, mustard and cayenne pepper into a bowl.
Rub butter into flour until mixture resembles fine breadcrumbs.
Stir in cheese.
Add milk all at once.
Mix to a soft, but not sticky, dough with a knife.
Turn on to a lightly floured work surface. Knead quickly until smooth.

Roll out to about 1cm (½in) thick.
Cut into 7 or 8 rounds with a 6.5cm (2½in) biscuit cutter.
Transfer to a greased baking sheet. Brush tops with milk.
Bake at 230°C (450°F) Mark 8 for 7–10 minutes or until well risen and golden.
Cool on a wire cooling rack.

Potato Scones ❄ V

Makes about 10   Preparation 35 mins   Cooking 10 mins
Per portion 108 kcals, 4g fat (2.6g saturated)

450g (1lb) potatoes, peeled and quartered
2 tsp salt
50g (2oz) butter
110g (4oz) plain flour

Cook potatoes in boiling water for about 20 minutes or until soft.
Drain and mash well.
Add salt and butter, then work in flour, to make a stiff mixture.
Turn on to a lightly floured work surface and knead lightly.
Roll out to 5mm (¼in) thickness.
Cut into circles with a 5cm (2in) cutter.
Cook on a greased frying pan for 4–5 minutes on each side until golden brown.
Serve hot.

Granary Herb Scones ❄ V

Makes 6   Preparation 25 mins   Cooking 10 mins
Per portion 199 kcals, 8g fat (4.7g saturated)

225g (8oz) granary flour
1 tbsp baking powder
½ tsp dried oregano
50g (2oz) butter
150ml (¼ pint) milk
Extra milk for brushing

Place flour, baking powder and oregano in a bowl.
Rub butter into flour until mixture resembles fine breadcrumbs.
Add milk and mix to a soft, but not sticky, dough.
Roll out on a floured surface to about 1.5cm (¾in) thick and cut out 6 triangles.
Place on a greased baking sheet and brush tops with milk.
Bake at 230°C (450°F) Mark 8 for 10 minutes, or until well risen and golden.

Cornish Splits ❄ V

Makes 14 Preparation 1¼ hrs plus rising Cooking
25 mins Per portion 157 kcals, 4g fat (2g saturated)

450g (1lb) strong plain flour

50g (2oz) caster sugar

150ml (¼ pint) milk, lukewarm

4 tsp dried yeast

1 tsp salt

50g (2oz) butter, melted and cooled

Sift 110g (4oz) flour into a bowl. Add 1 tsp
of the sugar.

Dissolve 1 tsp sugar in milk and 150ml (¼
pint) lukewarm water and sprinkle yeast on
top. Leave for 10 minutes in a warm place
until frothy.

Add to sifted flour and sugar. Mix well and
leave for 20–30 minutes or until frothy.

Meanwhile, sift remaining flour and salt into
another bowl. Add remaining sugar.

Add to yeast mixture with butter. Mix to a
soft dough that leaves sides of bowl clean.

Turn out on to a floured work surface. Knead
for 5 minutes or until dough is smooth.

Cover and leave to rise until doubled in size.

Turn out on to a floured work surface. Knead
lightly and divide into 14 equal-sized pieces.

Shape each into a round bun. Stand well
apart on a greased and floured baking sheet.

Cover and leave to rise for 30 minutes or
until dough feels springy when pressed
lightly with a floured finger.

Bake at 220°C (425°F) Mark 7 for 20–25
minutes.

Cool on a wire cooling rack.

Brioches ❄ V

Makes 8 Preparation 35 mins plus rising Cooking
10 mins Per portion 181 kcals, 8g fat (3.9g saturated)

225g (8oz) strong plain flour

½ tsp salt

15g (½oz) caster sugar plus 1 tsp

2 tsp dried yeast

2 eggs, beaten

50g (2oz) butter, melted and cooled

Extra beaten egg for brushing

Sift flour, salt and sugar into a bowl.

Dissolve 1 tsp sugar in 2 tbsp warm water
and sprinkle yeast on top. Leave to stand for
10 minutes in a warm place until frothy.

Add yeast and liquid to dry ingredients with
beaten eggs and butter. Mix to a soft dough.

Turn on to a floured work surface and knead
for 5 minutes or until dough is smooth.

Cover and leave to rise until doubled in size.

Turn out on to a floured work surface. Knead
lightly. Divide three-quarters of the dough
into 8 equal-sized pieces.

Shape into balls. Put into greased muffin tins
or into 8.5cm (3½in) fluted brioche tins. Press
a deep hole in centre of each one.

Divide remaining dough into 8 pieces. Roll
into small balls and stand on top of holes.

Cover and leave in a warm place for about 1
hour or until brioches are light and well risen.

Brush with beaten egg. Bake at 230°C (450°F)
Mark 8 for 10 minutes.

Transfer to a wire rack.

Currant Bread ❄ V

Makes 2 loaves Preparation 30 mins plus rising Cooking
40 mins Per slice 284 kcals, 4g fat (2g saturated)

450g (1lb) strong plain flour

1 tsp salt

25g (1oz) butter

25g (1oz) caster sugar, plus 1 tsp

110g (4oz) currants

150ml (¼ pint) milk, lukewarm

4 tsp dried yeast

Clear honey or golden syrup

Stir flour and salt into a bowl; rub in butter.

Add sugar and currants and mix together.

Dissolve 1 tsp sugar in 150ml (¼ pint)
lukewarm water and all of milk. Sprinkle
yeast on top. Leave for 10 minutes in a warm
place until frothy.

Add to dry ingredients.

Mix to a firm dough, adding a little extra
flour if necessary, until dough leaves sides of
bowl clean.

Turn out on to a floured work surface. Knead
for 10 minutes or until dough is smooth.

Cut into 2 equal-sized pieces. Shape each to
fit a 450g (1lb) loaf tin.

Grease tins and put in dough. Cover and
leave to rise until dough reaches tops of tins.

Bake at 220°C (425°F) Mark 7 for 30–40
minutes.

Turn out on to a wire cooling rack. Glaze tops
of hot loaves by brushing with a wet brush
dipped in clear honey or golden syrup.

Leave until cold before cutting.

Yorkshire Tea Cakes

Bara Brith ❄ V

Makes 1 loaf Preparation 45 mins plus rising Cooking
1¼ hrs Per slice 305 kcals, 7g fat (3.6g saturated)

1 tsp sugar
150ml (¼ pint) milk, lukewarm
1 tbsp dried yeast
400g (14oz) strong plain flour
1 tsp salt
1 tsp mixed spice
75g (3oz) butter
75g (3oz) demerara sugar
450g (1lb) mixed dried fruit
1 egg, beaten
Clear honey to glaze

Dissolve sugar in warm milk. Sprinkle on
yeast and leave for 10 minutes in a warm
place until frothy.

Sieve flour and salt into a bowl with spice.

Rub in butter, then stir in sugar and dried
fruit to the mixture.

Pour yeast liquid and egg into mixture. Mix
until dough leaves sides of bowl clean.

Knead on a floured work surface for about
10 minutes until smooth and elastic.

Place in a greased polythene bag, then leave
until doubled in size.

Knead dough for 2 minutes and then shape
to fit a greased 900g (2lb) loaf tin.

Cover and leave to rise above top of tin.

Bake at 180°C (350°F) Mark 4 for 1¼ hours.

Turn on to a wire rack and glaze with honey
while still warm.

Yorkshire Tea Cakes ❄ V

Makes 6 Preparation 40 mins plus rising   Cooking
20 mins Per portion 355 kcals, 5g fat (2.9g saturated)

450g (1lb) strong plain flour
1 tsp salt
25g (1oz) butter
25g (1oz) caster sugar, plus 1 tsp
50g (2oz) currants
300-350ml (10-12fl oz) milk, lukewarm
2 tsp dried yeast
Extra milk for brushing

Sift flour and salt into a bowl. Rub in butter.

Add sugar and currants. Toss lightly together.

Dissolve 1 tsp sugar in warm milk and
sprinkle yeast on top. Leave for 10 minutes in
a warm place until frothy.

Add all at once to dry ingredients.

Mix to a firm dough, adding a little extra
flour if necessary, until dough leaves sides of
bowl clean.

Turn out on to a floured work surface. Knead
for 10 minutes or until dough is elastic.

Cover and leave to rise until doubled in size.

Turn out on to a floured surface. Knead well
and divide into 6 equal-sized pieces.

Roll each one out into a round cake 1cm
(½in) thick. Transfer to a greased baking
sheet. Brush tops with milk.

Cover and leave to rise until almost doubled
in size.

Bake at 200°C (400°F) Mark 6 for 20 minutes.
Cover with foil if browning too quickly.

Cool on a wire cooling rack.

Hot Cross Buns ❄ V

Makes 12 Preparation 1¼ hrs plus rising Cooking
25 mins Per portion 244 kcals, 5g fat (2.6g saturated)

450g (1lb) strong plain flour

50g (2oz) caster sugar

150ml (¼ pint) milk, lukewarm, plus extra for
glaze

4 tsp dried yeast

1 tsp salt

1 tsp mixed spice

½ tsp ground cinnamon

110g (4oz) currants

50g (2oz) chopped mixed peel

50g (2oz) butter, melted and cooled

1 egg, beaten

50g (2oz) granulated sugar

Place 110g (4oz) flour into a bowl.

Add 1 tsp sugar.

Dissolve 1 tsp sugar in milk and 4 tbsp
lukewarm water and sprinkle yeast on top.
Leave to stand for 10 minutes in a warm
place until frothy.

Add to sifted flour and sugar. Mix well and
leave for 20–30 minutes or until frothy.

Meanwhile, sift remaining flour, salt and
spices into another bowl.

Add remaining caster sugar, currants and
peel. Toss lightly together.

Add to yeast mixture with butter and egg.

Mix to a fairly soft dough that leaves sides of
bowl clean.

Turn out on to a floured work surface and
knead for 5 minutes or until dough is smooth
and no longer sticky.

Cover and leave to rise until doubled in size.

Turn out on to a floured work surface. Knead
lightly and divide into 12 equal-sized pieces.

Shape each into a round bun. Stand well
apart on lightly greased and floured baking
sheet.

Cover and leave to rise for 30 minutes or
until dough feels springy when pressed
lightly with a floured finger.

Cut a cross on top of each with a sharp knife.
Bake at 220°C (425°F) Mark 7 for
20–25 minutes.

Make glaze by dissolving granulated sugar in
milk and boiling for 2 minutes.

Transfer buns to a wire cooling rack and
brush twice with glaze.

Bath Buns ❄ V

Makes 14 Preparation 1¼ hrs plus rising Cooking
25 mins Per portion 208 kcals, 5g fat (2.3g saturated)

450g (1lb) strong plain flour

25g (1oz) caster sugar

150ml (¼ pint) milk, lukewarm

4 tsp dried yeast

1 tsp salt

175g (6oz) sultanas

50g (2oz) chopped mixed peel

50g (2oz) butter, melted and cooled

2 eggs

Coarsely crushed cube sugar

Sift 110g (4oz) flour into a bowl.

Add 1 tsp sugar.

Dissolve 1 tsp sugar in milk and 4 tbsp
lukewarm water and sprinkle yeast on top.
Leave to stand for 10 minutes in a warm
place until frothy.

Add to sifted flour and sugar. Mix well and
leave for 20–30 minutes or until frothy.

Meanwhile, sift remaining flour and salt into
another bowl.

Add remaining sugar, sultanas and peel. Toss
lightly together.

Beat eggs in 2 separate bowls.

Add dry ingredients to yeast mixture with
butter and 1 beaten egg.

Mix to a fairly soft dough that leaves sides of
bowl clean.

Turn out on to a floured work surface and
knead for 5 minutes or until dough is smooth
and no longer sticky.

Cover and leave to rise until doubled in size.

Turn out on to a floured work surface. Knead
lightly.

Put 14 spoonfuls of dough on to a lightly
greased and floured baking sheet.

Cover and leave to rise for 20 minutes or
until dough feels springy when pressed
lightly with a floured finger.

Brush with second beaten egg mixed with a
little water.

Sprinkle with crushed sugar.

Bake at 220°C (425°F) Mark 7 for 20–25
minutes.

Transfer buns to a wire rack and leave to
cool.

Malt Loaves V

Makes 2 loaves   Preparation 40 mins plus rising Cooking 45 mins   Per slice 340 kcals, 4g fat (1.8g saturated)

75g (3oz) malt extract
2 tbsp black treacle
25g (1oz) butter
450g (1lb) strong plain flour
1 tsp salt
225g (8oz) sultanas
1 tsp caster sugar
4 tsp dried yeast
Clear honey

Put malt extract, treacle and butter into a saucepan. Heat gently.
Leave to cool.
Sift flour and salt into bowl. Add sultanas and toss lightly together.
Dissolve sugar in 175ml (6fl oz) lukewarm water and sprinkle yeast on top.
Leave for 10 minutes in a warm place until frothy.
Add to dry ingredients with cooled malt mixture. Work to a soft dough that leaves sides of bowl clean.
Turn out on to a floured work surface. Knead until dough is smooth and elastic.
Cut into 2 equal-sized pieces. Shape each to fit a 450g (1lb) loaf tin.
Grease tins and put in dough. Cover and leave until loaves double in size – up to 5 hours.
Bake at 200°C (400°F) Mark 6 for 40–45 minutes.
Turn out on to a wire rack.
Glaze tops of hot loaves with a wet brush dipped in honey. Leave until cold.

Chelsea Buns V

Makes 9   Preparation 1 hr plus rising Cooking 25 mins
Per portion 195 kcals, 5g fat (2.7g saturated)

2 tsp dried yeast
25g (1oz) sugar
90ml (3fl oz) milk, lukewarm
225g (8oz) strong plain flour
½ tsp salt
40g (1½oz) butter
1 egg, beaten
50g (2oz) soft brown sugar
75g (3oz) dried fruit
25g (1oz) mixed peel

Stir yeast and ½ tsp sugar into milk. Leave to stand for 5 minutes.
Mix in 50g (2oz) flour and leave in a warm place for about 20 minutes or until frothy.
Mix together remaining flour, salt and remaining sugar. Rub in 25g (1oz) butter.
Stir egg and yeast mixture into flour and mix to a soft dough. Turn on to a floured surface and knead until smooth.
Cover and leave until doubled in size – about 1 hour. On a floured work surface, roll out into a rectangle 30 x 23cm (12 x 9in).
Melt rest of butter and brush over dough. Sprinkle on brown sugar, fruit and peel.
Roll up dough, like a Swiss roll, starting from longest side. Cut roll into 9 equal slices.
Place close together, cut side down, in a greased 18cm (7in) square tin.
Cover and leave until doubled in size and buns have joined together – about 40 minutes.
Bake at 220°C (425°F) Mark 7 for 20–25 minutes or until golden brown.

Mock Chelsea Buns V

Makes 8   Preparation 35 mins   Cooking 20 mins
Per portion 285 kcals, 11g fat (6.8g saturated)

225g (8oz) self-raising flour
75g (3oz) butter
25g (1oz) caster sugar
150ml (¼ pint) milk
25g (1oz) butter, melted
110g (4oz) currants
50g (2oz) demerara sugar
25g (1oz) mixed peel
25g (1oz) glacé cherries, chopped
1 tsp mixed spice

Sieve flour into a bowl and rub in butter until mixture resembles fine breadcrumbs.
Add sugar and milk to give a soft dough.
Stir in butter, currants, demerara sugar, mixed peel, cherries and spice. Mix well.
Roll out dough on a floured surface to 25 x 30cm (10 x 12in).
Dampen edges of dough with water.
Starting from a longer edge, roll up and cut into 8. Place cut sides down in a greased 23cm (9in) round loose-bottomed tin to form a ring – with one round in centre.
Bake at 200°C (400°F) Mark 6 for 15–20 minutes.

Variation

Sugar & Spice Rings

Follow recipe and method for Mock Chelsea Buns. Omit filling ingredients. Instead brush 25g (1oz) melted butter over rolled-out dough. Mix together 50g (2oz) caster sugar, 1 tsp ground cinnamon and 50g (2oz) currants and sprinkle over dough.

Stollen

Serves 12   Preparation 35 mins   Cooking 52 mins
Per portion 360 kcals, 8g fat (3.9g saturated)

680g (1½lb) flour
25g (1oz) butter
7g (¼oz) sachet fast action dried yeast
65g (2½oz) caster sugar
Pinch of salt
Grated rind of 1 lemon
1 tsp ground cardamom
1 tsp ground mace
175g (6oz) dried mixed fruit
300ml (½ pint) milk, lukewarm
2 eggs, beaten
2 tbsp rum
50g (2oz) marzipan
50g (2oz) butter, melted
Icing sugar sieved to dust

Sift flour into a bowl and rub in butter.
Add yeast, sugar, salt, lemon rind, spices and fruit. Stir in milk, eggs and rum.
Mix to form a soft dough. Knead lightly on a lightly floured work surface.
Divide dough in half, then shape into 2 rectangles 18 x 7.5cm (7 x 3in).
Shape marzipan into a roll that is 18cm (7in) long. Place roll down centre of one rectangle of dough.
Fold dough over to encase marzipan. Seal edges and put sealed edge underneath.
Roll remaining dough into a roll the same length as the other one.
Place two rolls close together on a baking sheet.
Cover and leave to rise for 20–30 minutes or until doubled in size.
Bake at 240°C (475°F) Mark 9 for 2 minutes. Reduce temperature to 170°C (325°F) Mark 3 for 50 minutes.
Brush with melted butter and dust with icing sugar.

Swedish Tea Ring

Serves 12   Preparation 1 hr plus rising   Cooking 25 mins   Per portion 177 kcals, 5g fat (2.1g saturated)

2 tsp dried yeast
25g (1oz) caster sugar
90ml (3fl oz) milk, lukewarm
225g (8oz) strong plain flour
½ tsp salt
40g (1½oz) butter
1 egg, beaten
50g (2oz) soft light brown sugar
2 tsp cinnamon
Glacé Icing made with 110g (4oz) icing sugar (page 268)
Glacé cherries and walnuts to decorate

Sift yeast and ½ tsp caster sugar into milk. Leave to stand for 5 minutes.
Mix in 50g (2oz) flour and leave in a warm place for 20 minutes or until frothy.
Mix together remaining flour, salt and remaining caster sugar. Rub in 25g (1oz) butter.
Stir egg and yeast batter into flour and mix to a soft dough.
Turn on to a floured work surface and knead until smooth and no longer sticky.
Cover and leave to rise for about 1 hour until doubled in size.
On a floured work surface roll out dough into an oblong 23 x 38cm (9 x 15in).
Melt remaining butter and brush over dough. Sprinkle with brown sugar and cinnamon.
Roll up dough like a Swiss roll, starting from longest side.
Place on a greased baking sheet and form into a circle sealing ends together with a little milk or water.
Holding scissors at an angle of 45 degrees, cut almost completely through dough at 2.5cm (1in) intervals.
Turn cut sections on their sides so that pinwheel effect is seen.
Cover and leave to rise for about 45 minutes until dough is light and fluffy.
Bake at 200°C (400°F) Mark 6 for 25 minutes or until golden.
Cool on a wire cooling rack.
When cold, ice with Glacé Icing and decorate with glacé cherries and walnuts.

Biscuits & Bakes

Plain Biscuits ❄ V

Makes 30 Preparation 30 mins plus chilling Cooking
15 mins Per portion 78 kcals, 4g fat (2.6g saturated)

225g (8oz) self-raising flour
Pinch of salt
150g (5oz) butter
110g (4oz) caster or sifted icing sugar
Beaten egg to mix

Stir flour and salt into a bowl.
Rub in butter and add sugar.
Mix to a very stiff dough with beaten egg.
Turn out on to a lightly floured work surface.
Knead gently until smooth.
Put into a polythene bag or wrap in foil. Chill
for 30 minutes.
Roll out fairly thinly.
Cut into about 30 rounds with a 5cm (2in)
plain or fluted biscuit cutter.
Transfer to greased baking sheets. Prick
biscuits well with a fork.
Bake at 180°C (350°F) Mark 4 for 12–15
minutes, or until pale gold.
Leave to cool for 2–3 minutes. Transfer to a
wire cooling rack.
When cool, store in an airtight container for
up to a week.

Variations

Almond Biscuits ❄ V

Follow recipe and method for Plain Biscuits.
Add 50g (2oz) ground almonds with sugar,
and ½ tsp almond essence with egg.

Cherry Biscuits ❄ V

Follow recipe and method for Plain Biscuits.
Add 50g (2oz) finely chopped glacé cherries
with sugar.

Currant Biscuits ❄ V

Follow recipe and method for Plain Biscuits.
Add 50g (2oz) currants with sugar.

Walnut Biscuits ❄ V

Follow recipe and method for Plain Biscuits.
Add 40g (1½oz) finely chopped walnuts with
sugar and then add ½ tsp vanilla extract with
egg.

Spice Biscuits ❄ V

Follow recipe and method for Plain Biscuits.
Sift 1½ tsp mixed spice with flour and salt.

Vanilla Fridge Biscuits ❄ V

Makes 45 Preparation 30 mins plus chilling Cooking
12 mins Per portion 53 kcals, 2g fat (1.3g saturated)

225g (8oz) plain flour
1 tsp baking powder
110g (4oz) butter
175g (6oz) caster sugar
1 tsp vanilla extract
1 egg, beaten

Stir together flour and baking powder.
Rub in butter. Add sugar.
Mix to a dough with vanilla and beaten egg.
Shape into a long sausage. Transfer to a
length of foil.
Wrap foil round 'sausage' and twist ends.
Work backwards and forwards to form a roll
about 5cm (2in) in diameter.
Refrigerate for 1 hour.
Thinly slice as many biscuits as required from
roll (store remainder in the fridge for up to a
week).
Place on a greased baking sheet, well
apart, and bake at 190°C (375°F) Mark 5 for
10–12 minutes or until pale gold.

Variations

Coconut Fridge Biscuits ❄ V

Follow recipe and method for Vanilla Fridge
Biscuits. Add 50g (2oz) desiccated coconut
with sugar.

Chocolate Fridge Biscuits ❄ V

Follow recipe and method for Vanilla Fridge
Biscuits. Add 50g (2oz) finely grated plain
chocolate with sugar.

Ginger Fridge Biscuits ❄ V

Follow recipe and method for Vanilla Fridge
Biscuits. Omit vanilla. Sift 1½ tsp ground
ginger and ½ tsp mixed spice with flour and
baking powder.

Raisin Fridge Biscuits ❄ V

Follow recipe and method for Vanilla Fridge
Biscuits. Add 50g (2oz) chopped raisins with
sugar.

Butter Whirls

Butter Whirls ❄ V

Makes 16–18 Preparation 25 mins Cooking 15 mins
Per portion 120 kcals, 8g fat (5g saturated)

175g (6oz) butter, softened
50g (2oz) icing sugar, sifted
½ tsp vanilla extract
1 egg yolk
175g (6oz) plain flour
8 or 9 glacé cherries, quartered

Cream butter with sugar, vanilla and egg yolk until light and fluffy. Stir in flour.

Transfer mixture to a piping bag fitted with a star-shaped large piping tube.

Pipe 16–18 flat whirls on to greased baking sheets. Put half a cherry on each one.

Bake at 170°C (325°F) Mark 3 for 10–15 minutes, or until pale gold. Leave to cool for 5 minutes. Transfer to a wire cooling rack.

Chocolate Drops ❄ V

Makes 18–20 Preparation 20 mins Cooking 17 mins
Per portion 70 kcals, 5g fat (3g saturated)

110g (4oz) butter, softened
50g (2oz) caster sugar
½ tsp vanilla extract
90g (3½oz) plain flour
15g (½oz) cocoa powder

Cream butter with sugar and vanilla until light and fluffy.

Stir in flour sifted with cocoa powder.

Drop 18–20 tsp of mixture, well apart, on to a greased baking sheet.

Bake at 190°C (375°F) Mark 5 for 17 minutes.

Leave on sheet for 1–2 minutes before transferring to a wire cooling rack.

Store in an airtight container when cold.

243

Soft Apricot Cookies ❄ V

Makes 36   Preparation 25 mins   Cooking 10 mins
Per portion 107 kcals, 7g fat (3.7g saturated)

175g (6oz) butter
110g (4oz) caster sugar
175g (6oz) soft cheese
225g (8oz) self-raising flour
75g (3oz) ground almonds
75g (3oz) ready-to-eat dried apricots,
chopped
75g (3oz) chocolate chips

Beat together butter, sugar, cheese, flour
and almonds. Mix well.
Stir in apricots and chocolate chips.
Place spoonfuls of mixture on to baking
sheets covered with non-stick baking paper
and press down lightly with a fork.
Bake at 220°C (425°F) Mark 7 for 10 minutes.
Cool for 2 minutes on baking sheets then lift
off and cool on a wire rack.
Store in an airtight container.

Butter Digestive Biscuits ❄ V

Makes 12   Preparation 20 mins   Cooking 20 mins
Per portion 69 kcals, 3g fat (1.8g saturated)

75g (3oz) wholemeal flour
15g (½oz) plain flour
¼ tsp salt
½ tsp baking powder
15g (½oz) oatmeal
40g (1½oz) butter
40g (1½oz) caster sugar
3 tbsp milk

Sift flours, salt and baking powder into a
bowl.
Add oatmeal.
Rub in butter. Add sugar.
Mix to a stiff paste with milk.
Turn out on to a lightly floured work surface.
Knead well.
Roll out thinly.
Cut into 12 rounds with a 6.5cm (2½in) fluted
biscuit cutter.
Transfer to a greased baking sheet and prick
well all over.
Bake at 190°C (375°F) Mark 5 for 15–20
minutes, or until light gold.
Transfer to a wire cooling rack.
Store in an airtight container when cold.

Soured Cream Biscuits ❄ V

Makes 35   Preparation 30 mins plus chilling   Cooking
15 mins   Per portion 76 kcals, 4g fat (2.1g saturated)

110g (4oz) butter, softened
175g (6oz) caster sugar
50g (2oz) light soft brown sugar
½ tsp ground cinnamon
1 egg
125ml (4fl oz) soured cream
1 tsp grated lemon rind
175g (6oz) plain flour
½ tsp baking powder
¼ tsp bicarbonate of soda
¼ tsp salt
Ground cinnamon to decorate

Cream together butter, sugars, cinnamon
and egg until light and fluffy.
Add soured cream and lemon rind and beat
until well blended.
Gradually beat in dry ingredients.
Refrigerate for 1 hour, then drop spoonfuls
of mixture on to baking sheets covered with
non-stick baking paper, allowing room for
them to spread.
Sprinkle a little cinnamon on top of each
biscuit.
Bake at 190°C (375°F) Mark 5 for 10–15
minutes, or until lightly browned.
Cool on a wire cooling rack. Store in an
airtight container.

Flapjacks ❄ V

Makes 24   Preparation 20 mins   Cooking 30 mins
Per portion 93 kcals, 5g fat (2.5g saturated)

110g (4oz) butter
75g (3oz) golden syrup
75g (3oz) soft brown sugar
225g (8oz) rolled oats

Put butter, syrup and sugar into a saucepan
and stand over low heat until melted.
Stir in oats and mix well.
Spread into a greased 20 x 30cm (8 x 12in)
Swiss roll tin, and smooth top with a knife.
Bake at 180°C (350°F) Mark 4 for 30 minutes.
Leave in tin for 5 minutes, then cut into
24 fingers.
Remove from tin when cold.
Store in an airtight container.

Chocolate Cherry Cookies ❄ V

Makes 18–20 Preparation 25 mins Cooking 20 mins
Per portion 79 kcals, 5g fat (3.1g saturated)

110g (4oz) butter, softened
50g (2oz) caster sugar
½ tsp vanilla extract
25g (1oz) glacé cherries, finely chopped
25g (1oz) plain chocolate, finely chopped
110g (4oz) plain flour, sifted

Cream butter, sugar and vanilla until fluffy.
Add cherries and chocolate. Stir in flour.
Put 18–20 tsp of mixture, well apart, on to a
greased baking sheet.
Bake at 190°C (375°F) Mark 5 for 15–20
minutes.
Leave to cool for 1 or 2 minutes before
transferring to a wire cooling rack.
Store in an airtight container when cold.

Variation

Date Cookies ❄ V

Follow recipe and method for Chocolate
Cherry Cookies. Add 50g (2oz) very finely
chopped dates instead of chocolate and
cherries.

Oatie Biscuits ❄ V

Makes 30 Preparation 30 mins Cooking 20 mins
Per portion 116 kcals, 6g fat (3.2g saturated)

175g (6oz) butter
150g (5oz) soft brown sugar
1 egg
4 tbsp milk
40g (1½oz) raisins
25g (1oz) hazelnuts, chopped and toasted
275g (10oz) wholemeal self-raising flour
75g (3oz) rolled oats

Cream butter and sugar together until light
and fluffy. Beat in egg and milk.
Add raisins and hazelnuts.
Fold in flour to make a fairly stiff dough.
Form 30 balls and roll each one in oats.
Place on greased baking sheets, allowing
room for them to spread.
Flatten each biscuit slightly.
Bake at 180°C (350°F) Mark 4 for 15–20
minutes until golden brown.
Cool on a wire cooling rack.
Store in an airtight container.

Coffee Walnut Cookies ❄ V

Makes 18–20 Preparation 20 mins Cooking 20 mins
Per portion 86 kcals, 6g fat (3g saturated)

110g (4oz) butter, softened
50g (2oz) caster sugar
50g (2oz) walnuts, finely chopped
110g (4oz) plain flour, sifted
2 tsp instant coffee powder

Cream butter with sugar until light and fluffy.
Add walnuts.
Stir in flour with coffee powder.
Put 18–20 tsp of mixture, well apart, on to a
greased baking sheet.
Bake at 190°C (375°F) Mark 5 for 15–20
minutes.
Leave to cool for 1 or 2 minutes before
transferring to a wire cooling rack.
Store in an airtight container when cold.

Syrup Bites ❄ V

Makes 24 Preparation 35 mins plus standing Cooking
15 mins Per portion 93 kcals, 5g fat (3g saturated)

110g (4oz) self-raising flour
75g (3oz) rolled oats
25g (1oz) desiccated coconut
110g (4oz) butter
125g (5oz) caster sugar
2 tbsp golden syrup
1 tsp bicarbonate of soda
1 tbsp milk

Combine flour with oats and coconut.
Put butter, sugar and syrup into a saucepan.
Very slowly bring to the boil, stirring all the
time.
Remove from heat. Add bicarbonate of soda
dissolved in milk.
Pour hot mixture on to dry ingredients. Mix
thoroughly. Leave on one side for 30 minutes
or until firm.
Break off 24 pieces of mixture and roll into
marbles.
Transfer to greased baking sheets, leaving
room between each one to allow for
spreading.
Bake at 180°C (350°F) Mark 4 for 15 minutes.
Leave to cool for 1 or 2 minutes before
transferring to a wire cooling rack.
Store in an airtight container when cold.

Fruit Sesame Squares

Fruit Sesame Squares   V

Makes 18   Preparation 10 mins   Cooking 30 mins
Per portion 134 kcals, 8g fat (3.6g saturated)

50g (2oz) sesame seeds
175g (6oz) medium oatmeal
6 tbsp clear honey
110g (4oz) butter, melted
50g (2oz) soft brown sugar
50g (2oz) dried ready-to-eat apricots, chopped
25g (1oz) raisins

Place sesame seeds in a saucepan and gently heat for 2-3 minutes to 'toast'.

Add remaining ingredients and mix well.

Spoon into a greased 28 x 18cm (11 x 7in) Swiss roll tin. Press mixture down and smooth surface level.

Bake at 180°C (350°F) Mark 4 for about 20–25 minutes.

Cool in tin for a few minutes, then cut into squares.

Allow to cool completely before removing from tin and storing in an airtight container.

Peanut Crisps   ❄ V

Makes 24   Preparation 25 mins   Cooking 12 mins
Per portion 51 kcals, 3g fat (1.4g saturated)

50g (2oz) plain flour
¼ tsp bicarbonate of soda
50g (2oz) butter, softened
25g (1oz) caster sugar
50g (2oz) brown sugar
½ tsp vanilla extract
50g (2oz) peanut butter
1 egg

Sift together flour and bicarbonate of soda.

Cream together butter with sugars, vanilla and peanut butter until very light and fluffy.

Beat in egg then stir in dry ingredients.

Drop 24 teaspoons of mixture, 2.5cm (1in) apart, onto ungreased baking sheets.

Bake at 180°C (350°F) Mark 4 for 10–12 minutes.

Cool for 1 or 2 minutes before transferring to a wire cooling rack.

Allow to cool completely before storing in an airtight container.

Florentines V

Makes 12   Preparation 40 mins Cooking 10 mins
Per portion 211 kcals,12g fat (5.3g saturated)

82g (3¼oz) butter
4 tbsp milk
110g (4oz) icing sugar, sifted
40g (1½oz) plain flour
75g (3oz) chopped mixed peel
50g (2oz) glacé cherries, finely chopped
75g (3oz) flaked almonds
1 tsp lemon juice
110g (4oz) plain chocolate

Cover two large baking sheets with non-stick baking paper.

Put 75g (3oz) butter, milk and sugar into a saucepan. Stand over a low heat until butter melts.

Remove from heat. Stir in flour, peel, cherries, almonds and lemon juice.

Leave on one side until completely cold.

Spoon equal amounts of mixture (well apart to allow for spreading) on to baking sheets.

Bake at 190°C (375°F) Mark 5 for 10 minutes, or until pale gold.

Leave until lukewarm. Carefully lift off baking sheets.

Cool completely on a wire cooling rack.

Melt chocolate and remaining butter in a basin standing over a saucepan of hot water.

Put a heaped teaspoonful on to each florentine.

Spread evenly with a knife.

Mark wavy lines with a fork on each one. Leave until chocolate hardens before serving.

Store in an airtight container, layered between non-stick baking paper.

Almond Macaroons V

Makes 18   Preparation 25 mins Cooking 25 mins
Per portion 93 kcals, 4g fat (0.3g saturated)

2 egg whites
110g (4oz) ground almonds
225g (8oz) caster sugar
15g (½oz) ground rice
½ tsp vanilla extract
½ tsp almond flavouring
A little extra egg white
9 blanched almonds, split in half

Grease two baking sheets. Line with rice paper.

Beat egg whites until foamy but not stiff.

Add almonds, sugar, ground rice, vanilla and almond flavouring. Beat well.

Pipe or spoon 18 mounds of mixture, well apart, onto prepared baking sheets. Brush with egg white.

Put half an almond in middle of each one.

Bake at 170°C (325°F) Mark 3 for 20–25 minutes, or until pale gold.

Leave to cool for 5 minutes. Carefully lift off, then remove rice paper from edges.

Cool on a wire cooling rack. Store in an airtight container when cold.

Gingerbread Men V

Makes 26   Preparation 25 mins Cooking 15 mins
Per portion 268 kcals, 11g fat (6.6g saturated)

110g (4oz) plain flour
50g (2oz) soft brown sugar
1 tsp ground ginger
50g (2oz) butter
1 tbsp milk
2 tbsp black treacle
Currants to decorate

Place flour, sugar and ginger in a bowl and mix together. Make a well in centre of dry ingredients.

Put butter, milk and treacle into a small saucepan and heat gently until butter has melted. Remove from heat and cool for 2–3 minutes.

Pour butter mixture into dry ingredients and mix with a wooden spoon to a soft ball.

Leave mixture to cool until firm to touch.

Roll out on a floured work surface until 0.5cm (¼in) thick. Cut out with a gingerbread man cutter.

Transfer to a greased baking sheet using a palette knife or fish slice. Allow room for them to spread.

Decorate with currants for eyes, nose and buttons.

Bake at 180°C (350°F) Mark 4 for 10–15 minutes.

Leave to cool for 3 minutes. Transfer to a wire cooling rack and leave until cold.

Ginger Snaps ❄ V

Makes 26–30 Preparation 25 mins Cooking 10 mins
Per portion 32 kcals, 1g fat (0.9g saturated)

110g (4oz) self-raising flour
1 tsp ground ginger
¼ tsp mixed spice
50g (2oz) butter
40g (1½oz) caster sugar
1 tbsp black treacle, melted
Milk to mix

Sift flour, ginger and spice into a bowl.
Rub in butter finely. Add sugar.
Mix to very stiff paste with treacle and milk.
Roll out very thinly and cut into 26–30 rounds with a 5cm (2in) biscuit cutter.
Transfer to greased baking sheets.
Bake at 180°C (350°F) Mark 4 for 10 minutes.
Leave to cool for 1–2 minutes before transferring to a wire rack.

Brandy Snaps ❄ V

Makes 16 Preparation 30 mins Cooking 8 mins per batch Per portion 59 kcals, 3g fat (1.6g saturated)

50g (2oz) butter
50g (2oz) granulated sugar
65g (2½oz) golden syrup
50g (2oz) plain flour
1 tsp ground ginger
2 tsp lemon juice

Put butter, sugar and syrup into a saucepan. Stand over a low heat until melted.
Sift together flour and ginger.
Add to melted mixture with lemon juice.
Drop 4 tsp of mixture, well apart, on to a large greased baking sheet. Bake at 170°C (325°F) Mark 3 for 8 minutes.
Leave for 1 minute. Lift off with a palette knife.
Roll quickly and loosely around greased handle of a wooden spoon.
Leave until firm and slide off handle.
Repeat with remaining mixture.

Variation

Brandy Snaps with Cream ❄ V

Follow recipe and method for Brandy Snaps. When cold whip 150ml (¼ pint) double cream and pipe into snaps before serving.

Rich Shortbread ❄ V

Makes 8 Preparation 25 mins Cooking 40 mins
Per portion 206 kcals, 12g fat (7.2g saturated)

110g (4oz) butter, softened
50g (2oz) caster sugar
150g (5oz) plain flour
25g (1oz) semolina
Extra caster sugar

Cream butter and sugar together until light and fluffy. Stir in flour and semolina.
Draw mixture together with fingertips.
Press into a lightly greased 18cm (7in) sandwich tin. Prick well all over.
Pinch up edges with finger and thumb.
Bake at 170°C (325°F) Mark 3 for about 40 minutes, or until colour of pale straw.
Leave in tin for 5 minutes. Cut into 8 triangles. Dredge with extra caster sugar. Remove from tin when cold.

Variation

Shortbread Round ❄ V

Follow recipe and method for Rich Shortbread, but roll out dough and cut out rounds with a 5cm (2in) cutter. Place on a greased baking sheet and cook for about 15–20 minutes, or until colour of pale straw.

Almond Shortbread V

Makes 10 Preparation 20 mins Cooking 35 mins
Per portion 390 kcals, 28g fat (13g saturated)

200g (7oz) plain flour, sifted
Pinch of salt, sifted
50g (2oz) ground almonds
50g (2oz) caster sugar, plus extra for sifting
250g (9oz) unsalted butter
50g (2oz) whole almonds, blanched and skinned, to decorate
10 glacé cherries

Mix flour, salt, ground almonds and sugar in a bowl. Rub in butter, then work into a ball.
Lightly knead until smooth. Roll out into a round a little smaller than a 25cm (10in) fluted, loose-bottomed flan tin. Put in tin.
Press out into flutes and smooth. Arrange blanched almonds and cherries on top.
Bake at 150°C (300°F) Mark 2 for 30–35 minutes, until lightly browned. Remove from oven, sift over caster sugar and allow to cool in tin. Cut into wedges.

Raspberry Shortcakes ❋ V

Serves 4   Preparation 35 mins   Cooking 20 mins
Per portion 522 kcals, 32g fat (18.3g saturated)

225g (8oz) self-raising flour
½ tsp salt
50g (2oz) butter
25g (1oz) caster sugar
150ml (¼ pint) milk
Extra milk for brushing
150ml (¼ pint) double cream, softly whipped
225g (8oz) raspberries

Sift flour and salt into a bowl.
Rub butter into flour until mixture resembles fine breadcrumbs.
Stir in sugar, add milk and mix to a soft, but not sticky, dough with a knife.
Turn out on to a lightly floured work surface. Knead quickly until smooth.
Roll out to about 2.5cm (1in) thickness. Cut into 4 rounds with a 7.5cm (3in) cutter.
Stand on a greased baking sheet and brush tops with milk.
Bake at 220°C (425°F) Mark 7 for 15–20 minutes, until well risen and golden.
When cool, top with cream and raspberries.

Doughnuts ❋ V

Makes 8   Preparation 1¼ hrs plus rising   Cooking 8 mins   Per portion 245 kcals, 12g fat (2.4g saturated)

½ tsp caster sugar
6 tbsp milk, lukewarm
2 tsp dried yeast
225g (8oz) strong plain flour
¼ tsp salt
15g (½oz) butter, melted and cooled
1 egg, beaten
4 tsp strawberry jam
Oil for frying
4 tbsp caster sugar
1 tsp ground cinnamon

Dissolve sugar in milk and sprinkle yeast on top. Leave to stand for 10 minutes in a warm place until frothy.
Sift 50g (2oz) flour into a bowl then add yeast liquid. Mix well and leave for 20–30 minutes until frothy.
Sift remaining flour and salt together, then add to yeast mixture with butter and egg.
Mix to a soft dough, leaving bowl clean.

Turn out on to a floured work surface and knead for 5 minutes or until dough is smooth and no longer sticky.
Cover, then leave to rise until doubled in size.
Turn out on to a floured work surface, knead lightly and divide into 8 equal-sized pieces.
Shape into balls. Cover and leave to rise for 30 minutes or until dough feels springy when pressed lightly with a floured finger.
Press a hole in each ball with a finger. Put in about ½ tsp jam.
Pinch up edges of dough so that jam is completely enclosed.
Deep fry doughnuts in hot oil for 4 minutes.
Drain on absorbent kitchen paper.
Mix remaining sugar with cinnamon and coat doughnuts with it.

Ring Doughnuts ❋ V

Makes 20   Preparation 30 mins   Cooking 6 mins
Per portion 177 kcals, 11g fat (3.7g saturated)

350g (12oz) self-raising flour
¼ tsp salt
½ tsp ground cinnamon
½ tsp mixed spice
110g (4oz) butter
50g (2oz) caster sugar
1 egg
150ml (¼ pint) milk
Oil for frying
Extra caster sugar

Sift flour, salt, cinnamon and spice into a bowl.
Rub butter into flour until mixture resembles fine breadcrumbs. Add sugar.
Beat eggs with milk.
Add, all at once, to dry ingredients.
Mix to a soft, but not sticky, dough with a knife.
Turn out on to a lightly floured work surface. Knead quickly until smooth.
Roll out to 1cm (½in) thickness.
Cut into rounds with a 5cm (2in) biscuit cutter. Remove centres with a 2.5cm (1in) cutter. Re-roll and cut into more rings.
Fry, a few at a time, in hot oil for 2–3 minutes, turning once.
Remove from pan. Drain thoroughly on absorbent kitchen paper.
Toss in caster sugar. Serve warm.

Scones ❄ V

Makes 7–8   Preparation 25 mins   Cooking 10 mins
Per portion 149 kcals, 6g fat (3.5g saturated)

225g (8oz) self-raising flour
½ tsp salt
50g (2oz) butter
150ml (¼ pint) milk
Extra milk for brushing

Sift flour and salt into a bowl.
Rub butter into flour until mixture resembles fine breadcrumbs.
Add milk all at once. Mix to a soft, but not sticky, dough with a knife.
Turn on to a lightly floured work surface. Knead until smooth.
Roll out to about 1cm (½in) thick.
Cut into 7–8 rounds with a 6.5cm (2½in) biscuit cutter.
Transfer to a greased baking sheet. Brush tops with milk.
Bake at 230°C (450°F) Mark 8 for 7–10 minutes or until well risen and golden.
Cool on a wire cooling rack.

Variations

Sultana Scones ❄ V

Follow recipe and method for Scones. Add 50g (2oz) sultanas and 25g (1oz) caster sugar before adding milk.

Date & Walnut Scones ❄ V

Follow recipe and method for Scones. Add 25g (1oz) chopped dates, 15g (½oz) chopped walnuts and 25g (1oz) caster sugar before adding milk.

Honey Scones ❄ V

Follow recipe and method for Scones. Mix to a dough with 1 tbsp clear honey (slightly warmed) and 7 tbsp milk. Serve warm.

Soured Cream Scones ❄ V

Makes 7–8   Preparation 25 mins   Cooking 10 mins
Per portion 149 kcals, 6g fat (3.7g saturated)

225g (8oz) self-raising flour
½ tsp salt
40g (1½oz) butter
4 tbsp soured cream
4 tbsp milk
Extra milk for brushing

Sift flour and salt into a bowl.
Rub butter into flour until mixture resembles fine breadcrumbs.
Add cream and milk all at once. Mix to a soft, but not sticky, dough with a knife.
Turn out on to a lightly floured work surface. Knead quickly until smooth.
Roll out to about 1cm (½in) thick. Cut into 7–8 rounds with a 6.5cm (2½in) biscuit cutter.
Transfer to a greased baking sheet. Brush tops with milk.
Bake at 230°C (450°F) Mark 8 for 7–10 minutes or until well risen and golden.
Cool on a wire cooling rack.

Variations

Yogurt Scones ❄ V

Follow recipe and method for Soured Cream Scones but use 4 tbsp natural yogurt instead of soured cream.

Buttermilk Scones ❄ V

Follow recipe and method for Soured Cream Scones. Use 150ml (¼ pint) buttermilk instead of soured cream and milk.

Rum & Raisin Scones ❄ V

Makes 14   Preparation 20 mins   Cooking 15 mins
Per portion 255 kcals, 10g fat (5.9g saturated)

175g (6oz) raisins
3 tbsp rum
225g (8oz) self-raising flour
225g (8oz) wholemeal flour
4 tsp baking powder
50g (2oz) caster sugar
150g (5oz) butter
284ml carton buttermilk
1 egg, beaten
Milk

Soak raisins in rum for 10–15 minutes.
Sift flours and baking powder into a bowl.
Add sugar and rub in butter.
Make a well in centre and add soaked raisins with rum, buttermilk and egg. Mix to a soft, slightly sticky dough.
Knead lightly on a floured surface. Roll out to 2.5cm (1in) thick.
Cut out circles using a 6.5cm (2½in) cutter.
Brush with milk and bake at 220°C (425°F) Mark 7 for 12–15 minutes, until well risen.

Apple & Cinnamon Scones ❄ V

Makes 10   Preparation 30 mins plus cooling Cooking
30 mins   Per portion 230 kcals, 13g fat (7.3g saturated)

350g (12oz) cooking apples, peeled, cored
and chopped
225g (8oz) self-raising flour
½ tsp salt
1½ tsp ground cinnamon
50g (2oz) butter
25g (1oz) caster sugar
150ml (¼ pint) milk
Extra milk for brushing
25g (1oz) demerara sugar
150ml (¼ pint) double or whipping
cream

Cook apples in a little water until soft,
then mash well or purée.
Allow to cool.
Sieve flour, salt and 1 tsp cinnamon into a
bowl.
Rub in butter until mixture resembles fine
breadcrumbs.
Stir in sugar.
Make a well in centre, then add milk and
one-third of apple purée.
Mix together until mixture forms a fairly firm
dough.
Knead quickly on a floured work surface
then roll out to 1.5cm (¾in) thick.
Cut out scones with a 5cm (2in) cutter.
Place on a greased baking sheet.
Brush tops with milk.
Sprinkle with demerara sugar and
remaining cinnamon.
Bake at 230°C (450°F) Mark 8 for 30 minutes
until risen and golden brown.
Leave to cool and split in half.
Sandwich together with remaining apple
and whipped cream.

Drop Scones ❄ V

Serves 4   Preparation 10 mins   Cooking 10 mins
Per portion 304 kcals, 9g fat (4.5g saturated)

225g (8oz) self-raising flour
½ tsp salt
1 tbsp caster sugar
1 egg
300ml (½ pint) milk
25–50g (1–2oz) butter, melted

Sift flour and salt into a bowl.
Add sugar.
Mix to a smooth creamy batter with whole
egg and half the milk.
Stir in remaining milk.
Brush a large heavy frying pan with melted
butter.
Heat frying pan§.
Drop small rounds of scone mixture (about
12 in all), from a spoon, into frying pan.
Cook for 2½–3 minutes or until bubbles
show on surface.
Carefully turn over and cook for a further
2 minutes.
Pile scones in a clean, folded tea towel to
keep warm and moist.
Serve immediately.

Variation

Sultana Drop Scones ❄ V

Follow recipe and method for Drop Scones
but stir in 3 tbsp sultanas and rind of ½
lemon with remaining milk before frying.

Orkney Pancakes ❄ V

Makes 20   Preparation 20 mins plus standing Cooking
15 mins   Per portion 92 kcals, 4g fat (2.2g saturated)

175g (6oz) fine oatmeal
300ml (½ pint) soured cream
1 egg, beaten
2 tbsp golden syrup
75g (3oz) self-raising flour
Pinch of salt
1 tsp bicarbonate of soda
200ml (7fl oz) milk

Mix together oatmeal and soured cream,
then cover and stand for 2 hours.
Mix in egg, syrup, flour, salt and bicarbonate
of soda.
Stir in sufficient milk to give a thick batter
consistency.
Heat a griddle or frying pan until hot.
Drop large spoonfuls of pancake mixture on
to griddle.
Cook for 2–3 minutes or until bubbles show
on surface.
Carefully turn over and cook for a further
2 minutes.
Cook remaining mixture in batches.
Serve buttered with jam, if desired.

Cakes

Preparation of Cake Tins

Use greaseproof paper, brushed with melted butter or oil, or non-stick baking paper, which will not require greasing.

Sponge Cakes: Grease tins, dust with flour.

Sandwich Cakes: Grease tins then line bottoms of tins with a round of greaseproof paper and grease this.

Fruit Cakes and Rich Mixtures: Grease and line whole tin. For mixtures requiring a long cooking period, use double-thickness greaseproof paper to prevent any overcooking of the outside of the cake.

To Line a Swiss Roll Tin

Cut a piece of greaseproof paper 5cm (2in) larger all round than tin. Put tin on it and cut from each corner of paper to corner of tin.

Grease tin and put in paper so that it fits closely and overlaps at corners. Grease all paper surfaces.

To Line a Deep Tin

Place tin on a piece of greaseproof paper and draw round base. Cut piece of greaseproof paper just inside pencil mark.

Cut a strip of greaseproof paper to the size of the depth of the tin, plus 5cm (2in) longer and deeper. Then make a 2.5cm (1in) fold along length of strip and cut diagonally up to the fold at 1.5cm (½in) intervals.

Grease inside the tin with melted butter.

Insert the strip of greaseproof paper, ensuring the snipped part lies flat against the base of the tin. Place base circle in position.

Grease all paper surfaces.

Victoria Sandwich ❄ V

Serves 6   Preparation 25 mins   Cooking 30 mins
Per portion 319 kcals, 18g fat (10.2g saturated)

110g (4oz) butter, softened
110g (4oz) caster sugar
2 eggs
110g (4oz) self-raising flour, sifted
3 tbsp raspberry jam
Icing sugar, sifted (optional)

Grease and line two 18cm (7in) sandwich tins.

Cream butter and sugar together until very pale in colour, light in texture and fluffy.

Beat in eggs, one at a time, adding 1 tbsp flour with each one.

Gently fold in remaining flour with a metal spoon.

Transfer to prepared tins and smooth tops with a knife.

Bake at 180°C (350°F) Mark 4 for 25–30 minutes, or until well risen, golden brown and firm.

Leave in tins for 2–3 minutes. Turn out on to a wire cooling rack.

Strip off paper and leave until cold.

When cold sandwich together with jam.

Dust cake with icing sugar, if using.

Variations

Jam & Cream Sandwich ❄ V

Follow recipe and method for Victoria Sandwich. When cakes are cold, sandwich together with 3 tbsp jam and 4 tbsp double cream, whipped until thick. Dust with icing sugar.

Chocolate Sandwich ❄ V

Follow recipe and method for Victoria Sandwich, but replace 25g (1oz) flour with 25g (1oz) cocoa powder. Sandwich together with butter cream (page 269).

Coffee Sandwich ❄ V

Follow recipe and method for Victoria Sandwich, but add 2 tsp instant coffee granules dissolved in 1 tbsp warm water after beating in eggs. Sandwich together with butter cream (page 269).

Small Iced Cakes ❄ V

Follow recipe and method for Victoria Sandwich. Transfer equal amounts of mixture to 18 paper cases standing in 18 ungreased bun tins. Bake at 190°C (375°F) Mark 5 for 20–25 minutes, or until well risen and golden. Cool on a wire cooling rack. When completely cold cover tops with either Butter Cream or Glacé Icing (page 268). Decorate with nuts, dried fruit or cake decorations.

Butterfly Cakes ❄ V

Follow recipe and method for Small Iced Cakes but omit icing. To make butterflies, cut a slice off the top of each cake. Cut slices in halves, for wings. Place a little Butter Cream (page 269) on top of each cake. Put halved slices into icing at an angle to form wings. Dust lightly with sifted icing sugar.

Fairy Cakes   ❋ V

Follow recipe and method for Victoria Sandwich. Stir 50g (2oz) currants or sultanas into mixture after beating in eggs. Transfer equal amounts of mixture to 18 paper cases standing in 18 ungreased bun tins. Bake at 190°C (375°F) Mark 5 for 20–25 minutes, or until well risen and golden. Cool on a wire cooling rack.

Chocolate Chip Cakes   ❋ V

Follow recipe and method for Fairy Cakes. Stir in 50g (2oz) chocolate chips instead of currants or sultanas.

Swiss Roll   ❋ V

Serves 8–10   Preparation 35 mins   Cooking 12 mins
Per portion 99 kcals, 2g fat (0.6g saturated)

3 eggs
75g (3oz) caster sugar
75g (3oz) self-raising flour
4 tbsp jam or lemon curd, warmed

Grease and line a 30 x 20cm (12 x 8in) Swiss roll tin.
Put eggs into a large bowl standing over a saucepan of hand-hot water. Whisk for 2 minutes. (If you are using an electric mixer no heat is required during whisking.)
Add sugar and continue whisking for a further 8–10 minutes, or until mixture is very light in colour, thick in texture – consistency of softly whipped cream – and at least double its original volume.
Remove bowl from saucepan. Continue whisking until egg mixture is cool.
Gently fold in flour with a large metal spoon. Transfer to prepared tin.
Bake at 200°C (400°F) Mark 6 for 10–12 minutes, or until well risen and firm.
Turn out on to a sheet of greaseproof paper. Carefully peel off paper.
Cut away crisp edges with a sharp knife.
Spread quickly with warm jam or curd.
Roll up tightly and hold in position for 1 minute. Cool on a wire cooling rack.

Variations

Chocolate Swiss Roll   ❋ V

Follow recipe and method for Swiss Roll. Use 65g (2½oz) flour sifted twice with 15g (½oz) cocoa powder.

Cream-Filled Swiss Roll   ❋ V

Follow recipe and method for Swiss Roll. After trimming away crisp edges, roll up loosely with paper inside to prevent sticking. Cover with a damp tea towel and leave until cold. Unroll, remove paper and fill with 150ml (¼ pint) whipped double cream. Roll up again and hold in position for 1 minute.

Sponge Sandwich   ❋ V

Serves 6   Preparation 30 mins   Cooking 20 mins
Per portion 205 kcals, 9g fat (3.9g saturated)

3 eggs
75g (3oz) caster sugar
75g (3oz) self-raising flour, sifted twice
3 tbsp jam
4 tbsp double cream, whipped

Grease and line two 18cm (7in) sandwich tins. Dust sides of tins with flour.
Put eggs into a large bowl standing over a saucepan of hand-hot water. Whisk for 2 minutes. (If you are using an electric mixer, no heat is required during whisking.)
Add sugar. Continue whisking for 8–10 minutes or until mixture is light in colour, has consistency of softly whipped cream, and is at least double its original volume.
Remove bowl from saucepan. Continue whisking for a further 5 minutes or until egg mixture is cool.
Gently fold in flour with a metal spoon.
Transfer to prepared tins.
Bake at 180°C (350°F) Mark 4 for 20 minutes or until well risen and golden.
Turn out on to a sheet of sugared greaseproof paper.
Carefully peel off lining paper. Leave until completely cold. Sandwich together with jam and whipped cream.

Variation

Deep Sponge Cake   ❋ V

Follow recipe and method for Sponge Sandwich but use plain flour instead of self-raising. Transfer mixture to a greased and lined 18cm (7in) deep cake tin. Bake at 180°C (350°F) Mark 4 for 40–45 minutes or until a wooden cocktail stick, inserted into centre, comes out clean. Leave until cold. Slice into 1 or 2 layers. Sandwich together with jam and cream.

Rich Butter Cake ❄ V

Serves 8   Preparation 25 mins   Cooking 1¾ hrs
Per portion 382 kcals, 121g fat (12.1g saturated)

175g (6oz) butter, softened
175g (6oz) caster sugar
3 eggs
225g (8oz) plain flour
2 tbsp milk
1½ tsp baking powder

Grease and line a 20cm (8in) round cake tin.
Thoroughly cream butter with sugar, until very light and fluffy.
Beat in eggs, one at a time, adding 1 tbsp of flour with each. Beat in milk with 1 tbsp of flour.
Sieve remaining flour together with baking powder. Gently fold in with a large spoon.
Transfer to prepared tin and smooth top with a knife.
Bake at 170°C (325°F) Mark 3 for 1½-1¾ hrs, or until a wooden cocktail stick, inserted into centre of cake, comes out clean.
Leave in tin for 5 minutes. Turn out on to a cooling rack.
Store in an airtight container.

Variations

Dundee Cake ❄ V

Follow recipe and method for Rich Butter Cake. Cream butter and sugar with grated rind of 1 small orange. After beating in eggs, stir in 50g (2oz) ground almonds, 110g (4oz) each currants, sultanas and raisins and 50g (2oz) chopped mixed peel. Before baking cake, cover top of mixture with 25-50g (1-2oz) blanched and split almonds. Bake at 150°C (300°F) Mark 2 for 2½-3 hours, or until a wooden cocktail stick, inserted into centre, comes out clean.

Genoa Cake ❄ V

Follow recipe and method for Rich Butter Cake. Cream butter and sugar with 1 tsp grated lemon rind. After beating in eggs, stir in 110g (4oz) each currants, sultanas and chopped mixed peel, 50g (2oz) finely chopped glacé cherries and 25g (1oz) finely chopped almonds. Before baking cake, decorate top of mixture with 25–50g (1–2oz) blanched and split almonds. Bake as Dundee Cake.

Frosted Walnut Cake ❄ V

Follow recipe and method for Rich Butter Cake. Stir in 50g (2oz) finely chopped walnuts after beating eggs. When cake is cold, cut into 2 layers. Sandwich together with American Frosting (page 269). Quickly swirl remaining frosting over top and sides. Decorate with 25-50g (1–2oz) walnut halves.

Traditional Madeira Cake ❄ V

Follow recipe and method for Rich Butter Cake. Cream butter and sugar with grated rind of 1 lemon.

Ginger Cake ❄ V

Follow recipe and method for Rich Butter Cake. Sift in 1 tsp ground ginger. Add 75g (3oz) chopped preserved ginger after eggs.

Parkin ❄ V

Serves 10   Preparation 35 mins   Cooking 1 hr
Per portion 385 kcals, 16g fat (8.6g saturated)

225g (8oz) plain flour
½ tsp salt
1 tsp mixed spice
1 tsp ground cinnamon
1 tsp ground ginger
1 tsp bicarbonate of soda
225g (8oz) medium oatmeal
175g (6oz) black treacle
150g (5oz) butter
110g (4oz) soft brown sugar
150ml (¼ pint) milk
1 egg, beaten

Grease and line an 18cm (7in) square cake tin.
Sift flour, salt, spices and bicarbonate of soda into a bowl.
Add oatmeal and make a well in centre.
Put treacle, butter, sugar and milk into a saucepan. Stir over a low heat until butter has melted.
Pour into well and add egg. Stir mixture briskly, without beating, until smooth and evenly combined.
Transfer to prepared tin. Bake at 180°C (350°F) Mark 4 for 1 hour, or until a wooden cocktail stick, inserted into centre, comes out clean. Cool on a wire cooling rack.
Store, without removing paper, in an airtight container for about 1 week before cutting.

Chocolate Layer Cake

Gingerbread ❄ V

Serves 6 Preparation 30 mins Cooking 1 hr
Per portion 230 kcals, 5g fat (2.6g saturated)

175g (6oz) plain flour
2 tsp ground ginger
1 tsp mixed spice
½ tsp bicarbonate of soda
110g (4oz) golden syrup
25g (1oz) butter
25g (1oz) soft brown sugar
1 egg, beaten
1 tbsp black treacle
2 tbsp milk

Grease and line a 15cm (6in) cake tin.
Sift flour, ginger, spice and bicarbonate of soda into a bowl. Make a well in centre.
Put syrup, butter and brown sugar into a saucepan. Stir over a low heat until butter has melted.
Pour into well with egg, treacle and milk.
Stir briskly, without beating, until well combined.
Transfer to prepared tin. Bake at 180°C (350°F) Mark 4 for 1 hour, or until a wooden cocktail stick, inserted into centre, comes out clean.
Turn out on to a wire cooling rack.
Remove paper when gingerbread is cold.

Chocolate Layer Cake ❄ V

Serves 8 Preparation 30 mins Cooking 40 mins
Per portion 430 kcals, 34g fat (19.1g saturated)

110g (4oz) self-raising flour
2 tbsp cocoa powder
110g (4oz) butter
110g (4oz) caster sugar
25g (1oz) golden syrup
½ tsp vanilla extract
2 eggs
4 tsp milk
200ml (7fl oz) double cream, whipped
Grated chocolate to decorate

Grease and line a two 18cm (7in) round sandwich tins.
Sift flour twice with cocoa.
Cream butter, sugar, syrup and vanilla together until very pale, light and fluffy.
Beat in eggs, one at a time, adding 1 tbsp of sifted dry ingredients with each one.
Fold in milk and remaining dry ingredients.
Transfer to prepared tins and smooth top.
Bake at 180°C (350°F) Mark 4 for 20 minutes, or until springy to touch.
Turn out on to a wire rack, strip off paper and leave until cool.
Cut cake into 2 layers. Fill and cover top with whipped cream. Sprinkle with chocolate.

255

Chocolate Brownies ❄ V

Makes 8   Preparation 20 mins   Cooking 30 mins
Per portion 374 kcals, 19g fat (8.7g saturated)

110g (4oz) plain chocolate
75g (3oz) butter
175g (6oz) dark soft brown sugar
3 eggs, beaten
150g (5oz) self-raising flour
25g (1oz) cocoa powder
50g (2oz) chopped mixed nuts

Grease and line a 28 x 23cm (11 x 9in) tin.
Break chocolate up and melt 75g (3oz)
with butter in a bowl over a saucepan of
hot water.
Stir in sugar and gradually beat in eggs.
Sift flour and cocoa together and fold into
chocolate mixture with nuts.
Spoon into prepared tin.
Bake at 180°C (350°F) Mark 4 for 30 minutes.
Cool in tin, then turn out.
Melt remaining chocolate and drizzle on top.
Cut into 8 pieces.

Chocolate Truffle Cake ❄ V

Serves 12   Preparation 40 mins   Cooking 1¼ hrs plus
chilling   Per portion 467 kcals, 33g fat (17.8g saturated)

425g (15oz) plain chocolate
90g (3½oz) butter
150g (5oz) caster sugar
2 tsp instant coffee granules
4 eggs, separated
40g (1½oz) plain flour
25g (1oz) ground hazelnuts or almonds,
toasted
300ml (½ pint) double cream
Strawberries for decoration

Grease and line a 21.5cm (8½in) cake tin.
Break chocolate up and melt 150g (5oz) in a
bowl over a saucepan of hot water.
Cream together butter and sugar until pale
and fluffy.
Dissolve coffee granules in 2 tbsp hot
water. Beat into butter mixture with melted
chocolate and egg yolks.
Whisk egg whites until stiff, then fold in to
mixture.
Fold in flour and hazelnuts. Pour into
prepared cake tin.
Bake at 170°C (325°F) Mark 3 for 1¼ hours.

Cool in tin for 15 minutes, then on a rack.
Place cream in a saucepan, then heat until
bubbling around edges. Remove from heat
and stir in remaining broken up chocolate.
Stand covered until chocolate melts, mix
well then chill for about 1½ hours until firm
enough to hold a peak.
Cover top and sides with chocolate cream
and swirl. Decorate with strawberries.

Chocolate Marble Cake ❄ V

Serves 8   Preparation 25 mins   Cooking 1½ hrs
Per portion 527 kcals, 28g fat (16g saturated)

225g (8oz) butter
225g (8oz) caster sugar
3 eggs
350g (12oz) self-raising flour
Salt
200ml (7fl oz) milk
25g (1oz) cocoa powder

Grease and line a 20cm (8in) round cake tin.
Cream together butter and sugar.
Add eggs one at a time, beating well.
Fold in flour, salt and milk. Divide mixture
into two bowls. Add cocoa to one and mix.
Spoon mixtures alternately into cake tin.
Bake at 170°C (325°F) Mark 3 for 1½ hours, or
until well risen.
Cool and turn out on to a wire cooling rack.

Cider Cake ❄ V

Serves 16   Preparation 10 mins plus soaking   Cooking
45 mins   Per portion 179 kcals, 7g fat (3.9g saturated)

150ml (¼ pint) dry cider
225g (8oz) sultanas
110g (4oz) butter
110g (4oz) light soft brown sugar
2 eggs, beaten
225g (8oz) plain flour
1 tsp bicarbonate of soda

Grease and line an 18cm (7in) square cake tin.
Soak cider and sultanas in a bowl overnight.
Cream butter and sugar until pale and fluffy.
Gradually add eggs, beating well. Add half
flour and all bicarbonate of soda and mix.
Add cake mixture to cider and sultanas and
mix. Fold in remaining flour and pour into tin.
Bake at 180°C (350°F) Mark 4 for 45–60
minutes, until well risen.
Cool and turn out on to a wire cooling rack.

Carrot Cake ❄ V

Serves 8   Preparation 35 mins   Cooking 1½ hrs
Per portion 534 kcals, 32g fat (7.6g saturated)

225g (8oz) self-raising flour
1 tsp baking powder
150g (5oz) light soft brown sugar
50g (2oz) walnuts, chopped
50g (2oz) raisins
110g (4oz) carrots, peeled and grated
2 ripe bananas, peeled and mashed
2 eggs
150ml (¼ pint) sunflower oil
75ml (2½fl oz) double cream
50g (2oz) icing sugar, sifted
75g (3oz) full fat soft cheese, softened
½ tsp vanilla extract
Chopped walnuts to decorate

Grease and line a 20cm (8in) deep cake tin.
Sift together flour and baking powder into a bowl and stir in sugar. Add nuts, raisins, carrots and bananas and stir to mix.
Add eggs and oil and beat until well mixed.
Pour into prepared tin and bake at 180°C (350°F) Mark 4 for 1½ hours or until firm to the touch.
Remove from tin and cool on a wire rack.
Whip cream until softly stiff.
Cream icing sugar, cheese and vanilla extract together. Fold in cream.
Spread over top of cake and sprinkle with walnuts.

Lemon & Almond Ring ❄ V

Serves 8   Preparation 45 mins   Cooking 40 mins
Per portion 374 kcals, 17g fat (7.9g saturated)

110g (4oz) butter
110g (4oz) caster sugar
1 tsp grated lemon rind
2 eggs
110g (4oz) self-raising flour, sifted
50g (2oz) blanched and finely chopped almonds
Lemon Glacé Icing made with 225g (8oz) icing sugar (page 268)

Grease a 900ml (1½ pint) ring tin.
Cream butter with sugar and lemon rind until light and fluffy.
Beat in eggs, one at a time, adding 1 tbsp of sifted flour with each one.

Stir in almonds.
Fold in remaining flour with a metal spoon.
Transfer to prepared tin. Bake at 180°C (350°F) Mark 4 for 35–40 minutes, or until a wooden cocktail stick, inserted into centre of cake, comes out clean.
Cool and turn out on to a wire cooling rack.
Pour icing over top and allow to run down sides. Leave undisturbed until icing has set.

Variations

Coffee & Hazelnut Ring ❄ V

Follow recipe and method for Lemon and Almond Ring. Use hazelnuts instead of almonds. Coat ring with Coffee Glacé Icing (page 268) instead of lemon. When icing is set, decorate with about 12 whole hazelnuts.

Orange & Walnut Ring ❄ V

Follow recipe and method for Lemon and Almond Ring. Use walnuts instead of almonds. Coat ring with Orange Glacé Icing (page 268) instead of lemon. When icing is set, decorate with walnut halves.

Banana & Pecan Cake ❄ V

Serves 16   Preparation 30 mins   Cooking 1 hr
Per portion 258 kcals, 11g fat (4.3g saturated)

110g (4oz) butter
225g (8oz) caster sugar
3 eggs, separated
225g (8oz) peeled, ripe bananas, mashed
150g (5oz) buttermilk
225g (8oz) plain flour
2 tsp baking powder
175g (6oz) sultanas
90g (3½oz) pecan nuts

Grease and line a 20cm (8in) square cake tin.
Cream together butter and sugar until smooth.
Beat in egg yolks, mashed banana and buttermilk. Mix well.
Add flour, baking powder and sultanas, then beat until smooth.
Whisk egg whites until stiff and fold into cake batter.
Pour into prepared cake tin and arrange nuts on top.
Bake at 180°C (350°F) Mark 4 for 1 hour.
Cool in tin for 10 minutes before turning out on to a wire cooling rack.

Rich Fruit Cake ❄ V

Serves 8–10   Preparation 40 mins   Cooking 2½ hrs
Per portion 551 kcals, 27g fat (10.3g saturated)

225g (8oz) plain flour
1 tsp mixed spice
½ tsp ground cinnamon
½ tsp ground nutmeg
1 tsp cocoa powder
175g (6oz) butter
175g (6oz) soft brown sugar
1 tbsp black treacle
1 tsp each grated orange and lemon rind
4 eggs
550g (1¼lb) mixed dried fruits
110g (4oz) chopped mixed peel
50g (2oz) chopped walnuts or blanched almonds
50g (2oz) dates, chopped
50g (2oz) glacé cherries, chopped
1 tbsp milk

Grease and line a 20cm (8in) round or 18cm (7in) square cake tin.

Sift flour with spices and cocoa.

Cream butter with sugar, treacle and orange and lemon rind.

Beat in eggs, one at a time, adding 1 tbsp of sifted dry ingredients with each one.

Stir in mixed fruits, chopped peel, nuts, dates and cherries.

Fold in dry ingredients alternately with milk.

Transfer to prepared tin and smooth top.

Bake at 150°C (300°F) Mark 2 for 2½–3 hours, or until a skewer, inserted into centre of cake, comes out clean. Leave in tin for 15 minutes.

Turn out on to a wire cooling rack. When cold, wrap in foil and store in an airtight container until needed.

Iced Christmas Cake ❄ V

Serves 10–12   Preparation 1 hr plus setting
Per portion 932 kcals, 32g fat (10.1g saturated)

1 Rich Fruit Cake
4 tbsp apricot jam, melted
Almond Paste made with 275g (10oz) ground almonds (page 268)
Royal Icing made with 2 egg whites (page 268)
Christmas cake ornaments to decorate

Brush top and sides of cake with melted jam.

Turn almond paste on to a sugared surface (either sifted icing or caster). Roll out about half into a 20cm (8in) round or an 18cm (7in) square. Use to cover top of cake.

Roll out remaining paste into a strip – same depth as cake – and wrap round sides.

Press edges and joins well together with fingers dipped in caster sugar.

When almond paste has set (overnight), wrap cake loosely in foil. Leave at least 1 week before icing.

To ice cake, stand on a suitable silver board.

Spread royal icing thickly and evenly over top and sides.

Flick icing upwards with back of a teaspoon so that it stands in soft peaks.

Decorate with Christmas ornaments. Leave cake undisturbed overnight while icing hardens.

Variation

Iced Celebration Cake

Follow recipe and method for Iced Christmas Cake. To flat ice the cake follow directions to royal ice a celebration cake (page 266). Decorate according to the occasion to be celebrated.

Family Fruit Cake   ❄ V

Serves 8 Preparation 25 mins Cooking 1½ hrs
Per portion 302 kcals, 13g fat (7.5g saturated)

225g (8oz) self-raising flour
110g (4oz) butter
110g (4oz) caster sugar
110g (4oz) mixed dried fruits
1 tsp grated lemon rind
1 egg
5 tbsp milk

Grease and line a 15cm (6in) round cake tin or a 450g (1lb) loaf tin.
Sift flour into a bowl. Rub butter into flour until mixture resembles fine breadcrumbs.
Add sugar, fruit and lemon rind.
Mix to a batter with egg and milk.
Stir with a metal spoon until evenly combined. Do not beat.
Transfer to prepared tin.
Bake at 180°C (350°F) Mark 4 for 1¼–1½ hours, or until a wooden cocktail stick, inserted into centre of cake, comes out clean.
Leave in tin for 5 minutes. Turn out on to a wire cooling rack.
Peel off paper. Store cake in an airtight container when cold.

Variations

Sultana & Orange Cake   ❄ V

Follow recipe and method for Family Fruit Cake. Use 110g (4oz) sultanas instead of mixed fruit and orange rind instead of lemon.

Date & Walnut Cake   ❄ V

Follow recipe and method for Family Fruit Cake. Stir 1 tsp mixed spice with flour. Add 75g (3oz) chopped dates and 25g (1oz) chopped walnuts instead of mixed fruit. Omit lemon rind.

Cherry & Ginger Cake   ❄ V

Follow recipe and method for Family Fruit Cake. Use 50g (2oz) each chopped glacé cherries and chopped preserved ginger instead of mixed fruit.

Coconut & Lemon Cake

Follow recipe and method for Family Fruit Cake. Omit fruit. Add 50g (2oz) desiccated coconut with sugar and increase lemon rind to 2 tsp.

Cherry Cake   ❄ V

Serves 8 Preparation 35 mins Cooking 1 hr
Per portion 369 kcals, 18g fat (10.3g saturated)

110g (4oz) glacé cherries, rinsed and quartered
225g (8oz) self-raising flour
50g (2oz) semolina
150g (5oz) butter
110g (4oz) caster sugar
1 tsp grated lemon rind
½ tsp vanilla extract
2 eggs, well beaten
3 tbsp milk

Grease and line an 18cm (7in) round cake tin.
Mix cherries with 1 tbsp flour. Sift remaining flour and semolina into a bowl.
Rub butter into flour until mixture resembles fine breadcrumbs.
Add sugar, lemon rind and cherries.
Mix vanilla, eggs and milk to a stiff batter.
Mix everything together. Transfer to tin.
Bake at 180°C (350°F) Mark 4 for 1 hour, or until a wooden cocktail stick, inserted into centre of cake, comes out clean.
Leave in tin for 5 minutes. Turn out on to a wire cooling rack. Peel away paper.

Westmorland Pepper Cake   ❄ V

Serves 12 Preparation 20 mins Cooking 45 mins
Per portion 285 kcals, 9g fat (5.3g saturated)

75g (3oz) butter
75g (3oz) raisins
75g (3oz) currants
110g (4oz) caster sugar
225g (8oz) self-raising flour
½ tsp ground ginger
½ tsp ground cloves
½ tsp finely ground black pepper
4 tbsp milk
1 egg, beaten

Grease and line a deep 18cm (7in) cake tin.
Put butter, fruit, sugar and 150ml (¼ pint) water in a saucepan and bring to boil. Simmer for 10 minutes and leave to cool.
Mix flour, spices and pepper in bowl. Gently stir in fruit mixture, milk and egg and mix.
Pour mixture into prepared tin.
Bake at 180°C (350°F) Mark 4 for about 45 minutes, until firm and golden brown.
Cool and turn out on to a wire cooling rack.

Apricot & Prune Tea Bread ❄ V

Serves 12 Preparation 20 mins Cooking 1 hr
Per portion 222 kcals, 10g fat (4.2g saturated)

275g (10oz) granary flour
2½ tsp baking powder
1½ tsp mixed spice
75g (3oz) butter
110g (4oz) ready-to-eat prunes, chopped
75g (3oz) unsalted peanuts, roughly chopped
75g (3oz) soft brown sugar
110g (4oz) ready-to-eat dried apricots, chopped
200ml (7fl oz) milk
1 egg, beaten

Grease a 900g (2lb) loaf tin.
Place flour, baking powder and spice in a bowl. Rub butter into flour until mixture resembles fine breadcrumbs.
Stir in prunes, peanuts, sugar and apricots.
Add milk and egg and mix well.
Turn into prepared tin and bake at 180°C (350°F) Mark 4 for 1 hour until an inserted skewer comes out clean.
Leave to cool in tin.

Spiced Date Bake ❄ V

Makes 10 Preparation 25 mins plus standing Cooking 40 mins Per portion 141 kcals, 6g fat (3g saturated)

150ml (¼ pint) milk
110g (4oz) ready-to-eat dried dates, chopped
175g (6oz) wholemeal self-raising flour
½ tsp baking powder
½ tsp ground cinnamon
1 egg, beaten
50g (2oz) butter, melted
Grated rind and chopped flesh of 1 orange

Grease and line an 18cm (7in) square tin.
Warm milk in a small saucepan. Add dates to milk and stand for 15 minutes.
Mix together flour, baking powder and spice in a bowl.
Beat egg, butter and orange rind into milk.
Stir in dry ingredients with orange flesh and mix well. Spoon into prepared tin.
Bake at 180°C (350°F) Mark 4 for 40 minutes, until risen and golden brown.
Cool and turn out on to a wire cooling rack.
Serve cut into fingers.

Family Tray Bake ❄ V

Makes 16 Preparation 30 mins Cooking 35 mins
Per portion 162 kcals, 7g fat (3.9g saturated)

110g (4oz) butter
225g (8oz) plain flour
110g (4oz) caster sugar
110g (4oz) dried mixed fruit
1 tbsp baking powder
½ tsp ground nutmeg
2 eggs, beaten
150ml (¼ pint) milk

Grease a 28 x 18cm (11 x 7in) cake tin.
Rub butter into flour.
Add sugar, fruit, baking powder and nutmeg and stir in.
Mix in eggs and gradually stir in milk.
Turn into prepared cake tin.
Bake at 180°C (350°F) Mark 4 for 35 minutes, until lightly browned and firm.
Cool on a wire cooling rack.
Cut into fingers to serve.

Pecan & Banana Loaf ❄ V

Makes 12 Preparation 20 mins Cooking 1 hr
Per portion 288 kcals, 13g fat (6g saturated)

2–3 bananas, roughly chopped
1 tbsp maple syrup or honey
1 tbsp rum
110g (4oz) butter, softened
110g (4oz) dark soft brown sugar
2 eggs, beaten
225g (8oz) self-raising flour
75g (3oz) pecan nuts, roughly chopped
75g (3oz) raisins
110g (4oz) glacé cherries

Grease and line a 1.25 litre (2 pint) loaf tin.
Mash bananas with syrup or honey and rum.
In a separate bowl, beat butter and sugar together until light and fluffy.
Gradually beat in eggs.
Fold in flour and then mix in nuts, raisins, cherries and banana mixture.
Spoon mixture into prepared tin and spread evenly.
Bake at 180°C (350°F) Mark 4 for 50 minutes–1 hour or until a skewer inserted in centre comes out clean.
Cool and turn out on to a wire cooling rack.

Ripon Spice Loaf

Ripon Spice Loaf   ❄ V

Makes 2 loaves   Preparation 30 mins   Cooking 1¾ hrs
Per slice 358 kcals, 14g fat (7.1g saturated)

225g (8oz) butter
275g (10oz) caster sugar
3 eggs, beaten
50g (2oz) chopped mixed peel
50g (2oz) glacé cherries, chopped
225g (8oz) currants
225g (8oz) raisins
450g (1lb) plain flour
150ml (¼ pint) milk
50g (2oz) ground almonds
1 tbsp baking powder
1 tbsp mixed spice

Grease and line two 900g (2lb) loaf tins.
Cream together butter and sugar until pale and fluffy.
Add eggs gradually.
Toss fruit in a little flour and stir into mixture with milk and almonds.
Add remaining ingredients and fold in.
Divide mixture between prepared loaf tins and bake at 150°C (300°F) Mark 2 for 1½ –1¾ hours.
Cool in tins for 15 minutes, then turn out and cool on a wire cooling rack.

Spice Cake   ❄ V

Serves 6   Preparation 30 mins   Cooking 30 mins
Per portion 469 kcals, 20g fat (10.3g saturated)

110g (4oz) butter
110g (4oz) caster sugar
1 egg, beaten
200g (7oz) self-raising flour
1 tsp baking powder
½ tsp ground nutmeg
½ tsp ground cinnamon,
½ tsp ground cloves
½ tsp allspice
150ml (¼ pint) milk
1 tsp vanilla extract
110g (4oz) marzipan
75g (3oz) lemon curd
Icing sugar to decorate

Grease and line two 18cm (7in) sandwich tins.
Cream butter and sugar until pale and fluffy.
Gradually beat in eggs, then add dry ingredients alternately with milk and vanilla extract. Mix until smooth.
Divide between prepared tins and bake at 190°C (375°F) Mark 5 for 30 minutes.
Cool in tins before turning out.
Roll out marzipan into an 18cm (7in) circle.
Sandwich cakes together with marzipan and lemon curd. Dust top with icing sugar.

261

Black Forest Gâteau

Black Forest Gâteau ❊ V

Serves 8–10   Preparation 50 mins   Cooking 25 mins
Per portion 613 kcals, 44g fat (24.3g saturated)

150g (5oz) butter, melted

6 eggs

½ tsp vanilla extract

225g (8oz) caster sugar

50g (2oz) plain flour, sifted twice

50g (2oz) cocoa powder, sifted

4 tbsp Kirsch liqueur

450ml (¾ pint) double cream

410g can black cherry pie filling

Chocolate curls (made with vegetable peeler)

Grease and flour bases and sides of three 20cm (8in) sandwich tins.

Strain melted butter through muslin or use Clarified Butter (page 183).

Whisk together eggs, vanilla and sugar over a saucepan of hand-hot water for 8–10 minutes or until mixture is thick and texture of softly whipped cream.

Remove bowl from saucepan and continue whisking for a further 5 minutes.

Gently fold in flour, cocoa powder and melted butter, using a metal spoon.

Divide mixture between prepared tins.

Bake at 180°C (350°F) Mark 4 for 10–15 minutes.

Remove from oven and cool for 5 minutes in tins, then place on a wire cooling rack to cool thoroughly.

Prick cooled sponge cakes all over with a skewer.

Spoon Kirsch over cakes and allow to rest for 5 minutes.

Whip cream until softly stiff.

Sandwich cakes together with some of the whipped cream and pie filling.

Spread top with cream and spoon pie filling in the centre.

Decorate top with chocolate curls.

Serve at once.

262

Jammy Cakes ❄ V

Makes 16 Preparation 25 mins plus cooling Cooking
30 mins Per portion 166 kcals, 8g fat (4.5g saturated)

110g (4oz) butter
110g (4oz) caster sugar
1 egg, beaten
Grated rind and juice of ½ orange
200g (7oz) self-raising flour
125ml (4fl oz) milk
75g (3oz) apricot jam
75g (3oz) plain chocolate, melted

Melt butter and sugar in a saucepan over
a low heat.
Remove from heat and leave to cool for
2 minutes, stir occasionally.
Add egg and orange rind and beat well.
Fold in flour, gradually add milk and then
orange juice.
Spoon into paper bun cases and bake at
180°C (350°F) Mark 4 for 25–30 minutes, until
well risen and golden brown.
Cool on a wire cooling rack.
Scoop out centre of each bun when cool,
then place a spoonful of jam in hollow.
Replace lid and ice with melted chocolate.

Rock Cakes ❄ V

Makes 10 Preparation 20 mins Cooking 20 mins
Per portion 225 kcals, 10g fat (5.9g saturated)

225g (8oz) self-raising flour
110g (4oz) butter
75g (3oz) caster sugar
110g (4oz) mixed dried fruit
1 egg, beaten
2–4 tsp milk

Thoroughly grease a baking sheet.
Sift flour into a bowl.
Rub butter into flour until mixture resembles
fine breadcrumbs.
Add sugar and fruit.
Mix to a very stiff batter with beaten egg
and milk.
Place 10 spoonfuls of mixture, in rocky
mounds, on to prepared baking sheet
allowing room between each one as they
spread slightly.
Bake at 200°C (400°F) Mark 6 for 15–20
minutes. Cool on a wire cooling rack.

Cherry & Walnut Muffins ❄ V

Makes 12 Preparation 20 mins Cooking 25 mins
Per portion 190 kcals, 7g fat (2.9g saturated)

150g (5oz) plain flour
150g (5oz) wholemeal flour
2½ tsp baking powder
½ tsp salt
50g (2oz) brown sugar
75g (3oz) glacé cherries, chopped
50g (2oz) walnuts, chopped
1 egg
225ml (8fl oz) milk
50g (2oz) butter, melted

Grease 12 muffin tins or place 12 paper cases
in 12 ungreased bun tins.
Place flours, baking powder, salt, sugar,
cherries and walnuts in a bowl.
Mix together well.
Lightly whisk together egg, milk and butter.
Stir in dry ingredients and mix until evenly
blended.
Spoon into prepared tins or cases.
Bake at 200°C (400°F) Mark 6 for 25 minutes.
Cool in tins for 5 minutes before turning out.

Bran Muffins ❄ V

Makes 6 Preparation 30 mins Cooking 25 mins
Per portion 233 kcals, 10g fat (5.3g saturated)

50g (2oz) bran
300ml (½ pint) milk
50g (2oz) caster sugar
50g (2oz) butter
1 egg
50g (2oz) raisins
110g (4oz) wholemeal flour
½ tsp salt
1 tbsp baking powder

Grease 6 muffin tins or place 12 paper cases
in 12 ungreased bun tins.
Soak bran in milk for 10 minutes.
Cream together sugar and butter until light
and fluffy.
Beat in egg, raisins, bran and milk.
Lightly fold in wholemeal flour, salt and
baking powder.
Divide mixture between prepared tins or
cases.
Bake at 200°C (400°F) Mark 6 for 25 minutes.
Cool in tins for 5 minutes before turning out.

Marmalade Cake ❄ V

Serves 6–8   Preparation 20 mins   Cooking 1¼ hrs
Per portion 264 kcals, 13g fat (7.7g saturated)

225g (8oz) plain flour

Pinch of salt

1 tbsp baking powder

110g (4oz) butter

50g (2oz) caster sugar

½ tsp grated orange rind

2 eggs, beaten

3 tbsp orange marmalade

2–3 tbsp milk

Grease and line an 18cm (7in) round cake tin or a 450g (1lb) loaf tin.

Sift flour, salt and baking powder into a large bowl.

Rub in butter until mixture resembles fine breadcrumbs.

Add sugar and orange rind.

Mix to a fairly soft batter with eggs, marmalade and milk. Transfer to tin.

Bake at 180°C (350°F) Mark 4 for 1–1¼ hours or until a wooden cocktail stick, inserted into centre, comes out clean.

Leave in tin for 5 minutes. Turn out on to a wire cooling rack.

Peel off paper. Store cake in an airtight container when cold.

Variation

Marmalade & Walnut Cake ❄ V

Follow recipe and method for Marmalade Cake. Add 50g (2oz) chopped walnuts with sugar.

Fruit & Honey Cake ❄ V

Serves 6–8   Preparation 30 mins   Cooking 25 mins
Per portion 528 kcals, 37g fat (21.8g saturated)

225g (8oz) butter, softened
225g (8oz) clear honey
4 eggs
110g (4oz) wholemeal self-raising flour
110g (4oz) self-raising flour
150ml (¼ pint) whipping cream
225g (8oz) Greek-style yogurt
Fresh fruit to decorate

Grease and line two 20cm (8in) round sandwich tins.
Cream butter and honey together until pale. Beat in eggs gradually with a spoonful of flour.
Fold in remaining flours. Divide between tins.
Bake at 180°C (350°F) Mark 4 for 25 minutes, or until firm to the touch. Cool in tins for 5 minutes, then cool on a wire cooling rack.
Whip cream until softly stiff. Fold into yogurt and sandwich cakes together with half the mixture and half the fruit.
Decorate with remaining cream and fruit.

Cider Apple Cake ❄ V

Serves 9   Preparation 30 mins   Cooking 35 mins
Per portion 313 kcals, 16g fat (9.5g saturated)

110g (4oz) butter
110g (4oz) caster sugar
2 eggs, beaten
75g (3oz) wholemeal self-raising flour
75g (3oz) self-raising flour
3 tbsp medium dry cider
50g (2oz) sultanas
1 tsp ground cinnamon
110g (4oz) Cheddar cheese, grated
2 eating apples, peeled, cored and sliced
2 tbsp apricot jam, melted

Grease and line a 20cm (8in) square tin.
Cream butter and sugar together until pale and creamy. Beat in eggs gradually.
Fold in flours, cider, sultanas, cinnamon and 75g (3oz) cheese. Spoon into prepared tin.
Arrange apple slices in 3 lines, pressing down gently. Sprinkle over remaining cheese and bake at 180°C (350°F) Mark 4 for 35 minutes until well risen and firm to touch.
Transfer to a wire rack. Brush with apricot jam. Leave to cool, then cut into squares.

Streusel Cake ❄ V

Serves 15   Preparation 30 mins   Cooking 40 mins
Per portion 201 kcals, 9g fat (4.3g saturated)

110g (4oz) butter
175g (6oz) caster sugar
1 egg
150ml (¼ pint) milk
225g (8oz) self-raising flour
75g (3oz) soft brown sugar
1 tsp ground cinnamon
50g (2oz) chopped mixed nuts

Grease and base-line a 28 x 18cm (11 x 7in) cake tin.
Cream 75g (3oz) butter and all of sugar until light and fluffy. Beat in egg and milk. Fold in 200g (7oz) flour. Place half mixture in tin.
Rub remaining butter into brown sugar, cinnamon and remaining flour. Stir in nuts.
Sprinkle half over mixture in tin. Cover with remaining cake mixture, then rest of nuts.
Bake at 180°C (350°F) Mark 4 for 35–40 minutes. Cool in tin and cut into bars to serve.

Scottish Ginger Cake ❄ V

Makes 16 slices   Preparation 15 mins   Cooking 1¼ hrs
Per slice 242 kcals, 10.5g fat (6g saturated)

225g (8oz) plain flour, sifted
½ tsp salt, sifted
½ tsp bicarbonate of soda, sifted
1 tsp ground ginger, sifted
1 tsp mixed spice, sifted
25g (1oz) medium oatmeal
50g (2oz) sultanas
110g (4oz) chopped mixed peel
50g (2oz) preserved stem ginger, chopped
4 tbsp treacle
5 tbsp golden syrup
175g (6oz) unsalted butter
50g (2oz) dark soft brown sugar
150ml (¼ pint) milk
2 eggs

Grease and line an 18cm (7in) square cake tin.
Mix dry ingredients and ginger in a bowl.
Gently melt rest of ingredients, except eggs.
Make a well in dry ingredients and add eggs. Pour in treacle mixture and mix well.
Pour into cake tin and bake at 150°C (300°F) Mark 2 for 1–1¼ hours, until firm and well risen. Turn out onto a wire rack to cool.

How to Ice Cakes

To Almond Paste a Celebration Cake

The almond paste acts as a foundation for royal icing to prevent the rich fruit cake from staining the white surface. The cake should have a flat surface for the almond paste to go on.

Dredge the working surface with a little sifted icing sugar. Knead the almond paste into a ball and divide in half.

Roll out one half to fit the top of the cake and then brush the almond paste with a little warmed and sieved apricot jam.

Place the cake upside down on the almond paste, press firmly, trim edges and then carefully place the right way up.

Measure the circumference and depth of the cake with a piece of string. If the cake is round, cut remaining almond paste into two and roll out each to the correct shape to encircle the cake. If the cake is square, divide the almond paste into four.

Brush almond paste with sieved apricot jam and place on the cake as for top.

Use a rolling pin to ensure the sides and top have a neat finish.

Leave the cake for a week before icing.

To Royal Ice a Celebration Cake

Before icing the cake ensure the almond paste has been allowed to dry.

Stand the cake on a suitable silver board, 5cm (2in) larger than the base of the cake. Place on an icing turntable, upturned mixing bowl or cake tin. Spoon a little royal icing over the almond paste.

Spread with a palette knife evenly across the top of the cake and at the same time burst any air bubbles.

Draw a warm steel rule at an angle firmly across the cake to obtain a smooth surface. Remove surplus icing. Allow to dry for 24 hours.

Repeat this process for the sides of the cake, holding the steel rule vertically against the side of the cake.

For a square cake, the two opposite sides should be iced and allowed to dry before icing the other two sides. Apply two or three more thin layers of icing to the surface until a good finish is obtained.

Decorate according to the occasion to be celebrated.

To Fondant Ice a Celebration Cake

Fondant icing is also called sugar paste and can be used to cover sponge, madeira, light fruit or rich fruit cakes. It's soft and pliable. It can be rolled out like almond paste to cover cakes or moulded to make edible decorations. It gives a softer texture and appearance than royal icing to decorated cakes and it remains softer to cut. It is available as plain white in small blocks from supermarkets. Colour can be kneaded into fondant icing to colour it or it can be bought already coloured from specialist cake decorating shops.

The cake may be covered with almond paste or marzipan before covering with fondant icing. If not, the fondant icing should be 5mm (¼in) thick and any crevices padded with fondant first to ensure as smooth a surface as possible.

If unmarzipaned, use a dry pastry brush to brush away any crumbs on the surface of the cake. Place on a cake board.

Brush cake with boiled apricot jam (if marzipaned, use cold boiled water).

Using either a piece of string or a rolling pin, measure both sides and top of cake.

Roll out fondant icing on a work surface lightly dusted with sieved icing sugar to about the measured size of the cake. Keep turning the icing to prevent it sticking and do not use too much icing sugar or it will dry the icing. Never leave rolled fondant or it will dry out and crack.

Lift fondant with both hands underneath on to centre of cake. Gradually slide hands out, draping fondant over cake.

If it is a square cake, use the palm of your hand to fit and smooth corners before the sides, making sure the sides are flat and not pleated.

Dust ringless hands with icing sugar or cornflour and gently smooth over top and down sides of cake to smooth icing and ease out any air bubbles or creases.

Cut away any surplus icing from base of cake.

Finish by rolling a flat-sided jar around cake.

If decorating the cake with crimping, do it while the fondant is still soft, otherwise cover with a dry tea towel and leave until dry and firm for decoration.

DO NOT store in an airtight container or leave in a cold damp room or the icing will absorb moisture.

Icings and Buttercreams

Royal Icing   V
Preparation 25 mins

Sufficient to cover top and sides of an 18–20cm (7–8in) cake.

2 egg whites
450g (1lb) icing sugar, sifted
½ tsp lemon juice
2–3 drops of glycerine

Beat egg whites until foamy.
Gradually beat in sugar, lemon juice and glycerine.
Continue beating hard for 5–7 minutes, or until icing is snowy-white and firm enough to stand in straight points when spoon is lifted out of bowl.
If too stiff, add a little more egg white or lemon juice. If too soft, beat in a little more sifted icing sugar.
If coloured icing is required, beat in a few drops of food colouring.
It is best to use royal icing a day after it is made to give air bubbles time to disperse. Always keep icing in an airtight, rigid plastic container until ready for use.

Variation

Royal Icing for Piping
Follow recipe and method for Royal Icing. Omit glycerine and make up ¼–½ quantity only.

Almond Paste   V
Preparation 15 mins

Sufficient to cover top and sides of a 20–23cm (8–9in) rich fruit cake fairly thickly.

275g (10oz) ground almonds
225g (8oz) icing sugar, sifted
225g (8oz) caster sugar
1 egg plus 2 egg yolks
1 tsp lemon juice
½ tsp vanilla extract

Combine almonds with both sugars.
Mix to a fairly stiff paste with remaining ingredients.
Turn out on a board or table covered with sifted icing sugar. Knead with fingertips until smooth, crack-free and pliable.

Glacé Icing   V
Preparation 10 mins

Sufficient to cover top of an 18–20cm (7–8in) cake.

225g (8oz) icing sugar, sifted

Put sugar into a bowl. Gradually add 2 tbsp hot water.
Stir briskly until smooth and thick enough to coat back of spoon without running off.
If too thick, add a little more water; if too thin, stir in more sifted icing sugar. If coloured icing is required, beat in a few drops of food colouring. Use immediately.

Variations

Cocoa Glacé Icing   V
Follow recipe and method for Glacé Icing but omit 1 tbsp water. Mix 2 tbsp cocoa powder with 2 tbsp boiling water and stir into icing.

Orange or Lemon Glacé Icing   V
Follow recipe and method for Glacé Icing. Add 1 tsp finely grated orange or lemon rind to sugar. Mix with 2 tbsp strained and warmed orange or lemon juice instead of water.

Coffee Glacé Icing   V
Follow recipe and method for Glacé Icing. Dissolve 2 tsp instant coffee granules in hot water before adding to sugar.

Chocolate Glacé Icing   V
Preparation 10 mins   Cooking 5 mins

Sufficient to cover top and sides of an 18–20cm (7–8in) cake.

50g (2oz) plain chocolate
15g (½oz) butter
½ tsp vanilla extract
115g (4½oz) icing sugar, sifted

Break up chocolate and put, with butter and 2 tbsp warm water, into a basin standing over a saucepan of hot water.
Leave until melted, stirring once or twice.
Add vanilla. Gradually beat in icing sugar.

Variation

Mocha Glacé Icing   V
Follow recipe and method for Chocolate Glacé Icing. Add 2 tsp instant coffee granules to chocolate, butter and water in basin.

Chocolate Icing V

Preparation 15mins   Cooking 2 mins

Sufficient to fill and cover top of a 2-layer 18cm (7in) sandwich cake.

65g (2½oz) butter
3 tbsp milk
25g (1oz) cocoa powder, sieved
1 tsp vanilla extract
225g (8oz) icing sugar, sieved

Place butter and milk in a small saucepan. Heat until butter has melted.
Pour into a bowl and blend in cocoa and vanilla essence.
Stir in icing sugar and beat until smooth.
Either use immediately to give a smooth, glossy finish or allow to thicken for a butter cream-type finish.

American Frosting V

Preparation 10 mins   Cooking 10 mins

Sufficient to fill and cover top and sides of three 18cm (7in) sandwich cakes or one deep 18 20cm (7–8in) cake, cut into two layers.

450g (1lb) granulated sugar
2 egg whites
Pinch of cream of tartar
1 tsp vanilla essence

Put sugar and 150ml (¼ pint) water into a saucepan. Stir over a low heat until sugar dissolves.
Bring to the boil. Cover pan and boil for 1 minute.
Uncover. Continue to boil fairly briskly, without stirring, for a further 5 minutes (or until a small quantity of mixture, dropped into a cup of very cold water, forms a soft ball when gently rolled between finger and thumb). Temperature on a sugar thermometer should be 116°C (240°F).
Meanwhile, beat egg whites and cream of tartar to a very stiff snow.
When sugar and water have boiled for required amount of time, pour on to egg whites in a slow, steady stream, beating all the time.
Add vanilla.
Continue beating until frosting is cool and thick enough to spread.
Quickly use to fill cake. Swirl remainder over top and sides.

Seven Minutes Frosting V

Preparation 5 mins   Cooking 7 mins

Sufficient to fill and cover top and sides of a 2-layer 20cm (8in) sandwich cake.

165g (5½oz) granulated sugar
½ tsp cream of tartar
Pinch of salt
2 egg whites
1 tsp vanilla extract

Place sugar, cream of tartar, salt, egg whites and 90ml (3fl oz) water in a bowl.
Place over a pan of hot water and beat with a hand-held electric mixer for about 7 minutes, until mixture thickens and stands in peaks.
Remove from pan and add vanilla.
Continue beating for 2–3 minutes.
Use to fill and spread over cake. Swirl with a palette knife or back of a spoon.

Coffee Fudge Frosting V

Preparation 10 mins   Cooking 5 mins

Sufficient to fill and cover top and sides of a 2-layer 18cm (7in) sandwich cake.

50g (2oz) butter
110g (4oz) soft brown sugar
3 tbsp coffee essence
1 tbsp single cream
225g (8oz) icing sugar, sifted

Put butter, sugar, coffee essence and cream into a saucepan over a low heat. Stir until butter melts and sugar dissolves.
Boil briskly for 3 minutes only.
Remove from heat. Slowly stir in icing sugar.
Beat until smooth and beat for 5 minutes or until frosting has cooled and can be spread.

Butter Cream ❄ V

Preparation 10 mins

Sufficient to fill and cover top of a 2-layer 18cm (7in) sandwich cake.

110g (4oz) butter, softened
225g (8oz) icing sugar, sifted
2 tbsp milk
Few drops of vanilla extract

Beat butter until soft.
Gradually beat in sugar and milk.
Continue beating until light and fluffy.
Stir in vanilla, then chill until a little thicker.

Confectionery

Coconut Ice

Peppermint Creams V

Makes 20 Preparation 15 mins plus setting
Per portion 42 kcals, 0g fat (0g saturated)

225g (8oz) ready-to-roll fondant icing
Few drops of peppermint flavouring
Icing sugar

Gradually knead peppermint flavouring into fondant icing.
Roll out on a work surface dusted with icing sugar to 3mm (⅛in) thick.
Cut into rounds with a 2.5cm (1in) biscuit cutter.
Leave for 24 hours until firm.

Variation

Chocolate Peppermint Creams V

Follow recipe and method for Peppermint Creams. Half dip the rounds in melted plain chocolate and leave to set on non-stick baking paper.

Coconut Ice ❄ V

Makes 50 Preparation 15 mins plus setting Cooking 25 mins Per portion 52 kcals, 2g fat (1.3g saturated)

75ml (2½fl oz) milk
450g (1lb) granulated sugar
15g (½oz) butter
110g (4oz) desiccated coconut
½ tsp vanilla extract
Pink food colouring

Pour milk and 75ml (2½fl oz) water into a saucepan. Bring to the boil.
Add sugar and butter. Heat slowly, stirring, until sugar dissolves and butter melts.
Bring to the boil. Cover pan and boil gently for 2 minutes.
Uncover and continue to boil steadily, stirring occasionally, for 7–10 minutes or until a little of the mixture, dropped into a cup of cold water, forms a soft ball when rolled gently between finger and thumb. Temperature on sugar thermometer, if using, should be 116°C (240°F).
Remove from heat.
Add coconut and vanilla. Beat briskly until mixture is thick and creamy.
Pour half into an 18cm (7in) square tin lined with non-stick baking paper.
Quickly colour remainder pale pink with food colouring.

Spread over white layer.
Leave in the tin until firm and set.
Cut into squares.

Marshmallows

Makes 48 Preparation 30 mins Cooking 15 mins
Per portion 99 kcals, 0g fat (0g saturated)

350g (12oz) cornflour
650g (1½lb) icing sugar
225g (8oz) granulated sugar
1½ tsp glucose syrup
15g (½oz) powdered gelatine
1 egg white
Pink food colouring (optional)

Sift cornflour and icing sugar together and spoon into two Swiss roll tins.
Using 2 eggs, make 24 shallow dents in cornflour mixture in each tin, leaving 1 egg in mixture when making next hollow so that sides do not collapse.
Place granulated sugar, glucose and 210ml (7½fl oz) water in a large saucepan. Heat gently until sugar has dissolved.
Bring to the boil and continue boiling until a little of the mixture, dropped into a cup of cold water forms a hard ball when rolled between finger and thumb. Temperature on a sugar thermometer, if using, should be 121°C (250°F).
Meanwhile, sprinkle gelatine over 60ml (2fl oz) water in a small saucepan. Leave to stand for 5 minutes. Then heat gently until dissolved.
Whisk egg white until stiff.
Remove syrup from heat.
Slowly and carefully add gelatine – syrup will bubble up.
Pour syrup slowly on to egg white in a steady stream beating all the time until mixture becomes thick and stiff.
Add food colouring to half the mixture, if using.
Spoon mixture into a large piping bag fitted with a 1cm (½in) plain nozzle and carefully pipe into moulds.
Leave to stand for 1 hour until set. Sprinkle with a little cornflour mixture.
Remove from tin and dust off excess.
Store in an airtight container, not touching.

Fruity Candies   V

Makes about 16 pieces Preparation 30 mins
Per candy 102 kcals, 5g fat (12.1g saturated)

75g (3oz) ready-to-eat prunes
75g (3oz) ready-to-eat dried apricots
75g (3oz) ready-to-eat dried dates
75g (3oz) chopped roasted hazelnuts
2 tbsp maple syrup
16 glacé cherries
25g (1oz) chocolate strands
4 tbsp desiccated coconut
Icing sugar

Blend dried fruits to a semi-smooth paste in a food processor.
Divide mixture into 16.
Place a cherry in centre of each fruit paste and roll into a ball.
Coat 4 balls in chocolate strands, 4 in coconut and 4 in icing sugar.

Milk Fudge   ❄ V

Makes 50 Preparation 10 mins plus setting Cooking 30 mins Per portion 55 kcals, 2g fat (1.2g saturated)

300ml (½ pint) milk
450g (1lb) granulated sugar
110g (4oz) butter
½ tsp vanilla extract

Pour milk into a saucepan. Bring slowly to the boil.
Add sugar and butter.
Heat slowly, stirring all the time, until sugar dissolves and butter melts.
Bring to the boil. Cover pan with lid. Boil for 2 minutes.
Uncover and continue to boil steadily, stirring occasionally, for a further 10–15 minutes or until a little of the mixture, dropped into a cup of cold water, forms a soft ball when rolled gently between finger and thumb. Temperature on a sugar thermometer, if using, should be 116°C (240°F).
Remove from heat. Stir in vanilla. Leave mixture to cool for 5 minutes.
Beat fudge until it just begins to lose its gloss and is thick and creamy.
Transfer to a greased 18cm (7in) square tin.
Mark into squares when cool. Cut up with a sharp knife when firm and set.
Store in an airtight container.

Variations

Cherry Fudge   ❄ V

Follow recipe and method for Milk Fudge. Add 50g (2oz) chopped glacé cherries with vanilla.

Chocolate Fudge   ❄ V

Follow recipe and method for Milk Fudge. Melt 110g (4oz) grated plain chocolate in milk before adding sugar and butter.

Walnut Fudge   ❄ V

Follow recipe and method for Milk Fudge. Add 50g (2oz) chopped walnuts with vanilla.

White Chocolate Fudge   ❄ V

Follow recipe and method for Milk Fudge. Add 150g (5oz) grated good quality white chocolate to milk and stir until melted before adding other ingredients.

Rum & Raisin Fudge   ❄ V

Follow recipe and method for Milk Fudge. With the vanilla, add 175g (6oz) seedless raisins soaked in 3 tbsp rum.

Butterscotch   V

Serves 18 Preparation 5 mins plus setting Cooking 25 mins Per portion 119 kcals, 2g fat (1.4g saturated)

450g (1lb) demerara sugar
50g (2oz) butter

Pour 150ml (¼ pint) water into a saucepan and bring to the boil.
Add sugar and butter.
Heat slowly, stirring, until sugar dissolves and butter melts.
Bring to the boil. Cover pan and boil gently for 2 minutes.
Uncover and continue to boil, without stirring for 8–12 minutes or until a little of the mixture, dropped into a cup of cold water, separates into hard brittle threads. Temperature on sugar thermometer, if using, should be about 138°C (280°F).
Pour into a greased 15cm (6in) square tin.
Mark into squares or bars when almost set with a buttered knife.
Break up when hard.
Store in an airtight container.

Syrup Toffee v

Serves 22 Preparation 5 mins plus setting Cooking
30 mins Per portion 112 kcals, 2g fat (1.2g saturated)

110g (4oz) golden syrup
2 tsp white wine vinegar
450g (1lb) granulated sugar
50g (2oz) butter

Pour 5 tbsp water and syrup into a saucepan.
Bring to the boil.
Add vinegar, sugar and butter. Heat slowly,
stirring, until sugar dissolves and butter
melts.
Bring to the boil. Cover pan.
Boil gently for 2 minutes.
Uncover. Continue to boil, stirring
occasionally, for 8–10 minutes or until a little
of the mixture, dropped into a cup of cold
water, forms a very hard ball when rolled
between finger and thumb. Temperature
on a sugar thermometer, if using, should be
138°C (280°F).
Pour into a greased 15cm (6in) square tin.
Leave until hard.
Turn out on to a board.
Break up into bite-sized pieces with a small
hammer or rolling pin.
Store in an airtight container.

Variation

Nut Toffee v

Follow recipe and method for Syrup Toffee.
Cover base of a greased tin with 110g (4oz)
blanched almonds or 110g (4oz) sliced Brazil
nuts before pouring in toffee.

Treacle Toffee v

Serves 18 Preparation 5 mins plus setting Cooking
30 mins Per portion 129 kcals, 5g fat (3.2g saturated)

110g (4oz) butter
350g (12oz) demerara sugar
2 tbsp golden syrup
1 tbsp black treacle

Put all ingredients into a saucepan with
4 tbsp water.
Heat slowly, stirring, until butter melts and
sugar dissolves.
Bring to the boil. Cover pan. Boil gently for
2 minutes.
Uncover and continue to boil, stirring
occasionally, for 10–15 minutes or until a

little of the mixture, dropped into a cup
of cold water, separates into hard and
brittle threads. Temperature on a sugar
thermometer, if using, should be about
138°C (280°F).
Pour into a greased 15cm (6in) square tin.
Leave until hard.
Turn out on to a board.
Break up into bite-sized pieces with a small
hammer or rolling pin.
Store in an airtight container between
greaseproof paper.

Toffee Apples

Makes 6 Preparation 5 mins plus setting Cooking
10 mins Per portion 266 kcals, 4g fat (2.2g saturated)

6 wooden lolly sticks
6 small apples
250g (9oz) granulated sugar
2 tbsp golden syrup
1 tbsp white wine vinegar
25g (1oz) butter

Push a stick into the stalk end of each apple.
Pour 125ml (4fl oz) water into a saucepan
and add sugar, syrup and vinegar. Heat
gently until dissolved.
Turn up the heat and boil rapidly until a little
of the mixture, dropped into a cup of cold
water, separates into hard and brittle threads.
Temperature on a sugar thermometer, if
using, should be about 147°C (290°F).
Remove from the heat and stir in butter.
Cool the base of the pan in cold water to
prevent the syrup getting any hotter.
Dip each apple into syrup and place on
baking parchment with sticks upright (syrup
can be reheated gently if starting to set).
Dip twice for thicker toffee.
Wrap apples in cellophane.

Variation

Treacle Toffee Apples v

Follow the recipe and method for preparing
and dipping the apples in Toffee Apples
but in place of the syrup use the recipe and
method for Treacle Toffee. Dip each apple
in to the hot toffee mixture and place on
baking parchment to cool and set.

Fresh Cream Truffles

Fresh Cream Truffles ❄ V

Makes 36   Preparation 45 mins plus setting   Cooking
5 mins   Per portion 126 kcals, 8g fat (4.7g saturated)

150ml (¼ pint) double cream
300g (11oz) plain chocolate, broken up
2 tbsp liqueur of your choice
25g (1oz) unsalted butter
Cocoa powder
Grated white and plain chocolate

Heat cream in a small pan until boiling,
remove from heat and add 200g (7oz)
chocolate, stir until melted.
Stir in liqueur and butter, and mix until
butter has melted. Pour into a bowl.
Freeze for about 20 minutes or until firm
enough to hold its shape.
Using a melon baller, scoop out rounds,
place on to non-stick baking paper and chill
overnight.
Roll a third in cocoa powder and a third
in grated white chocolate. Dip a third into
remaining plain chocolate, melted.
Leave to set and then remelt any chocolate

remaining and drizzle over truffles.
Place truffles in foil cases and store in the
fridge.

Chocolate Orange Truffles   V

Makes 32   Preparation 30 mins plus setting Cooking
5 mins   Per portion 82 kcals, 5g fat (2.8g saturated)

225g (8oz) plain chocolate, broken up
75g (3oz) butter, cut into small pieces
50g (2oz) icing sugar, sifted
2 tbsp double cream
Grated rind of ½ orange
1 tbsp Grand Marnier (orange liqueur)
75g (3oz) biscuits, crushed
Drinking chocolate powder

Put chocolate in a bowl over a pan of hot
water and heat to melt. Add butter and melt.
Stir sugar, cream, orange rind, liqueur and
biscuit crumbs into melted chocolate.
Leave until firm, then roll spoonfuls of
mixture into balls.
Refrigerate until firm.
Roll in drinking chocolate powder to serve.

Chocolate Rum Truffles ❄ V

Makes 36 Preparation 30 mins plus setting Cooking
5 mins Per portion 59 kcals, 2g fat (1g saturated)

110g (4oz) plain chocolate, broken up

25g (2oz) butter

1 tbsp rum

25g (1oz) ground almonds

25g (1oz) stale cake crumbs

225g (8oz) icing sugar, sifted

Drinking chocolate

Put plain chocolate and butter into a basin standing over a saucepan of hot water.

Leave until both chocolate and butter have melted, stirring occasionally.

Add rum and mix well.

Work in rum, ground almonds, cake crumbs and icing sugar.

Transfer mixture to a dish. Chill until firm for about 1½ hours.

Roll equal amounts of rum truffle mixture into 36 balls.

Coat in drinking chocolate.

Transfer to small paper cases.

Variation

Mocha Truffles ❄ V

Follow recipe and method for Chocolate Rum Truffles. Omit rum and use 1–2 tsp coffee essence.

Chocolate Strawberries V

Makes 12 Preparation 15 mins plus setting Cooking
5 mins Per portion 37 kcals, 2g fat (1g saturated)

75g (3oz) plain chocolate, broken up

225g (8oz) strawberries

Cover a baking sheet with non-stick baking paper.

Place chocolate in a small bowl over a saucepan of hot water and heat, stirring, until melted.

Remove from the heat and stir.

Holding strawberries at hull end, dip into chocolate, leaving part of the fruit uncovered.

Place on non-stick baking paper and leave until the chocolate is dry and set.

These are best eaten on the same day as they are made.

Honeycomb V

Serves 14 Preparation 5 mins plus setting Cooking
20 mins Per portion 93 kcals, 2g fat (0.9g saturated)

3 tbsp clear honey

250g (9oz) caster sugar

25g (1oz) butter

1 tsp vinegar

1 tsp bicarbonate of soda

Put honey, sugar, 4 tbsp water, butter and vinegar into a saucepan.

Heat slowly, stirring, until sugar dissolves and butter melts.

Bring to the boil.

Cover pan and boil mixture gently for 2 minutes.

Uncover and continue to boil, without stirring, for about 5 minutes or until a little of the mixture, dropped into a cup of cold water, separates into hard and brittle threads. Temperature on a sugar thermometer, if using, should be about 149°C (300°F).

Remove pan from heat.

Stir in bicarbonate of soda – mixture will rise in saucepan.

Pour into a small greased tin.

Break up into pieces when set.

Eat on the day it is made.

Chocolate Nut Clusters V

Serves 18 Preparation 20 mins plus setting Cooking
5 mins Per portion 130 kcals, 11g fat (5g saturated)

175g (6oz) plain or milk chocolate, broken up

110g (4oz) unsalted peanuts

50g (2oz) flaked almonds

50g (2oz) hazelnuts

Cover a baking sheet with non-stick baking paper.

Place chocolate in a bowl over a saucepan of hot water and heat, stirring, until melted.

Remove from heat.

Stir in nuts and mix thoroughly until coated in chocolate.

Drop spoonfuls of the mixture on to non-stick baking paper

Leave until chocolate is dry and set.

Store in an airtight container.

Pickles & Preserves

Spicy Pickled Onions

Pickles

Pickled Shallots V

Makes 2 x 1 litre (1¾ pints)   Preparation 15 mins

1kg (2¼lb) shallots, peeled
20g (¾oz) pickling spice
1 litre (1¾ pints) malt vinegar
2 tsp soft brown sugar

Fill 2 large jars half full with shallots.
Sprinkle with 2 tsp pickling spice and 1 tsp sugar.
Fill almost to the top with remaining shallots, then add remaining spice and sugar.
Pour vinegar over shallots, covering completely.
Seal with a lid and store in a cool, dark place for 2 months before eating.

Pickled Beetroot V

Makes 1.25–1.5kg (2½–3lb)
Preparation 10 mins, plus infusing   Cooking 1½ hours

1.25–1.5kg (2½–3lb) uncooked beetroot
1 cinnamon stick
3 blades of mace
1 tsp allspice
1 tsp whole peppercorns
3 dried chillies
5 whole cloves
2 tbsp caster sugar
700ml (1¼ pints) distilled malt vinegar

Place beetroot in a large saucepan, cover with cold water and bring to the boil.
Reduce heat, partially cover and cook gently for 1–1½ hours until cooked.
Drain and leave to cool.
Meanwhile, place all spices in a saucepan, add sugar and 300ml (½ pint) vinegar and bring to the boil.
Remove from heat, cover and leave to infuse overnight.
Peel beetroot and slice.
Place in jars.
Stir remaining vinegar into spiced vinegar, then pour into jars with spices, covering completely.
Seal with lids and store in a cool, dry place. It will keep for at least 6 months.

Spicy Pickled Onions V

Makes 1 litre (1¾ pints)
Preparation 15 mins plus soaking   Cooking 10 mins

900g (2lb) pickling onions or shallots, peeled
450g (1lb) fine sea salt
568ml bottle of distilled malt vinegar
6 cloves
1 cinnamon stick
4 dried red chillies
1 tsp allspice berries
15g (½oz) mixed peppercorns
4 slices fresh root ginger
3 bay leaves
175g (6oz) soft light brown sugar

Place onions or shallots in a bowl (halving any large onions).
Sprinkle onions with salt, cover and leave overnight.
Pour 300ml (½ pint) vinegar into a saucepan and add all remaining ingredients. Bring to the boil.
Remove pan from heat. Cool.
Rinse and dry onions and place in a large jar.
Add vinegar, spices and bay leaves and remaining vinegar to jar.
Seal with a lid and store for 3 months before eating.

Cucumber Pickle V

Makes 2.4 litres (4¼ pints)
Preparation 15 mins, plus infusing   Cooking 5 mins

3 cucumbers, thinly sliced
4 large onions, peeled and thinly sliced
3 tbsp salt
450ml (¾ pint) distilled white vinegar
150g (5oz) caster sugar
1 tsp celery seeds
1 tsp mustard seeds

Layer cucumbers and onions in a large bowl, sprinkling each layer with salt.
Leave for 1 hour, then drain and rinse well.
Put vinegar, sugar, celery and mustard seeds in a saucepan and heat gently, stirring, until sugar has dissolved. Boil for 3 minutes.
Pack the vegetable slices into jars and cover with hot vinegar mixture. Cover immediately with airtight tops.
Store in a dark place for 2 months before eating.

Chutneys

Chutney is cooked when it has reduced and thickened, and when a spoon drawn through the mixture leaves a clear trail that is slow to close up. After filling jars, remove air bubbles by working a skewer from side to side. Press a waxed disc on the surface of the chutney in each jar and wipe the rim carefully with a hot, damp cloth. Label and date; store in a dry, dark, cool, ventilated cupboard.

Spicy Tomato Chutney   V

Makes approx. 800g (1lb 12oz)   Preparation 10 mins,
Cooking 2½ hours

1.6kg (3½lb) **ripe tomatoes**
350g (12oz) **onions, peeled and chopped**
400ml (14fl oz) **distilled malt vinegar**
1 tsp **paprika**
2 tbsp **coriander seeds**
½ tsp **dried chillies**
15g (½oz) **salt**
250g (9oz) **granulated sugar**

Place tomatoes in a bowl and cover with boiling water.
Leave for 10 minutes and then remove skins and cut into quarters.
Place tomatoes in a saucepan with onions, half of vinegar, all spices and salt.
Bring to the boil and cook gently for 2 hours, until mixture is a thick pulp.
Meanwhile, dissolve sugar in remaining vinegar.
Stir into tomatoes and continue cooking until thick, stirring frequently.
Leave to cool completely.
Fill jars with chutney, then cover with lids. Leave for 1 months before eating.

Mango Chutney   V

Makes approx. 1.6kg (3lb 8oz)   Preparation 10 mins
Cooking 3 hours

2.2kg (5lb) **mangoes**
2 large **onions, peeled and chopped**
Finely grated **rind and juice of 3 limes**
1 large **red pepper, deseeded and chopped**
250g (9oz) **sultanas**
225g (8oz) **soft light brown sugar**
1 tsp **salt**
1 tbsp **curry powder**
750ml (1¼ pints) **distilled malt vinegar**

Put all ingredients into a large saucepan and bring to the boil, stirring.
Reduce heat and cook gently for 2½ –3 hours, until reduced by about two-thirds, stirring frequently.
Remove pan from heat and leave to cool completely.
Fill jars with chutney, then cover with lids. Leave for 1 month before eating.

Apple Chutney   V

Makes approx. 2.3kg (5lb)   Preparation 20 mins
Cooking 3 hours

1.8kg (4lb) **cooking apples peeled, cored and chopped**
900g (2lb) **onions, peeled and sliced**
500ml (16fl oz) **dry cider**
175g (6oz) **sultanas**
175g (6oz) **raisins**
25g (1oz) **salt**
15g (½oz) **ground ginger**
1 tbsp **paprika**
225g (8oz) **clear honey**
110g (4oz) **soft brown sugar**
900ml (1½ pints) **distilled malt vinegar**

Place apples and onions in a large saucepan.
Add cider and cook for 20 minutes, until the apples and onions start to soften.
Add sultanas, raisins, salt, ginger, paprika, honey and sugar.
Stir in half of vinegar and cook for 20 minutes.
Stir in remaining vinegar and bring to the boil, stirring occasionally.
Cook gently, stirring frequently, until reduced by approximately two thirds.
Remove pan from heat and leave to cool completely.
Fill jars with chutney, then cover with lids. Leave for 2 months before eating.

Sterilising Jars

There are several ways to sterilise jars for pickles and preserves. Either wash the jars in soapy water and rinse in clean warm water before allowing them to drip-dry, upside down, on a rack in the oven set to 140°C (275°F) Mark 1 for at least 30 minutes. Or run them through a cycle in the dishwasher.

Apple & Beetroot Chutney

Apple & Beetroot Chutney V

Makes approx. 2.3kg (5lb) Preparation 1 hour
Cooking 2½ hours

1.3kg (3lb) raw beetroot, peeled and grated
900g (2lb) cooking apples, peeled, cored and chopped
680g (1½lb) onions, peeled and chopped
225g (8oz) sultanas
225g (8oz) raisins
1 tbsp salt
1 tbsp peppercorns, crushed
1 tsp ground allspice
2 tsp ground mixed spice
500g (1lb2oz) light soft brown sugar
250g (9oz) granulated sugar
50g (2oz) root ginger, peeled and grated
900ml (1½ pints) distilled malt vinegar

Place all ingredients in a large saucepan.
Cook, stirring occasionally, until sugar is dissolved.
Bring to the boil and simmer for 2 hours until reduced and thickened.
Fill jars with chutney, then cover with lids. Leave for 2 months before eating.

Mincemeat

Makes approx. 2.5kg (5½lb)
Preparation 30 mins plus standing

1.6kg (3½lb) dried mixed fruit
225g (8oz) cooking apples, peeled, cored and grated
110g (4oz) chopped almonds
450g (1lb) dark soft brown sugar
175g (6oz) shredded beef suet
1 tsp ground nutmeg
1 tsp ground cinnamon
Grated rind and juice of 1 lemon
Grated rind and juice of 1 orange
300ml (½ pint) brandy or sherry

Place all ingredients in a large bowl and mix well.
Cover and leave to stand for 2 days.
Fill jars with mincemeat, then cover with lids. Leave for at least 2 weeks before eating.

Tropical Fruit Mincemeat V

Makes approx. 2.7kg (6lb) Preparation 30 mins

150g (5oz) ready-to-eat dried apricots, finely chopped
150g (5oz) ready-to-eat dried figs, finely chopped
150g (5oz) ready-to-eat prunes, finely chopped
150g (5oz) glacé cherries, quartered
200g (7oz) sultanas
200g (7oz) raisins
Finely grated rind and juice of 1 orange
Finely grated rind and juice of 1 lemon
Finely grated rind and juice of 1 lime
1 pineapple, peeled, cored and chopped
400g (14oz) cooking apples, peeled and grated
70cl bottle light rum

Mix all ingredients together in a large bowl.
Transfer to a plastic container and cover surface closely with cling film, then with a tight fitting lid.
Store in fridge, stirring occasionally, for up to 1 year.

Jams

Fruit for jam making should be firm, under-ripe or only just ripe and fresh. To test for setting, pour a teaspoonful of jam on to a cold saucer and leave for 1 minute. Setting point has been reached if the surface sets and crinkles when pushed with the finger. Remove the jam from the heat while this test is being made, otherwise it may boil too rapidly and the setting point may be missed. A sugar thermometer will register about 105°C (210°F) once setting point has been reached.

After filling jam jars, press a well-fitted waxed disc on the surface of the jam in each jar and wipe the rim carefully with a hot, damp cloth. Cover either while it is still very hot or completely cold. Label and date; store in a dry, dark, cool, ventilated cupboard.

Strawberry Jam V

Makes about 2.3kg (5lb) Preparation 30 mins
Cooking 35 mins

1.6kg (3½lb) strawberries, hulled
Juice of 1 large lemon
1.4kg (3lb) granulated sugar
15g (½oz) butter

Put strawberries, lemon juice and sugar into a large saucepan.
Heat slowly, stirring all the time, until sugar dissolves.
Bring to the boil.
Boil briskly for 10–15 minutes or until setting point is reached.
Move saucepan from heat. Stir in butter to disperse scum.
Leave jam to cool in saucepan until skin forms on surface.
Stir gently, pot and cover.

Raspberry Jam V

Makes about 2.3kg (5lb) Preparation 10 mins
Cooking 20 mins

1.4kg (3lb) raspberries
1.4kg (3lb) granulated sugar
15g (½oz) butter

Put raspberries into a large saucepan and crush finely with back of a wooden spoon.
Simmer gently for 5 minutes. Add sugar and stir until dissolved. Bring to the boil.

Boil briskly for 5–7 minutes or until setting point is reached.
Move saucepan from heat. Stir in butter to disperse scum.
Pot and cover.

Plum Jam V

Makes about 2.3kg (5lb) Preparation 10 mins
Cooking 1 hr

1.4kg (3lb) plums
1.4kg (3lb) granulated sugar
15g (½oz) butter

Put plums into a saucepan and add 450ml (¾ pint) water.
Bring to the boil, cover and reduce heat.
Simmer gently for about 10–20 minutes until fruit is tender. Add sugar and stir until dissolved. Bring jam to the boil.
Boil briskly for 10–15 minutes or until setting point is reached.
Remove stones with a perforated spoon as they rise to the surface.
Move pan from heat. Stir in butter to disperse scum.
Pot and cover.

Mixed Fruit Jam V

Makes about 2.3kg (5lb) Preparation 10 mins
Cooking 1 hr

1.4kg (3lb) mixed soft fruit, such as raspberries, strawberries, gooseberries, rhubarb and redcurrants
1.4kg (3lb) granulated sugar
15g (½oz) butter

Place fruit in a saucepan with 150ml (¼ pint) water.
Bring to the boil, reduce heat and cover saucepan.
Simmer gently for 10–15 minutes, crushing fruit against sides of saucepan until it is soft and pulpy.
Add sugar and heat slowly, stirring all the time, until sugar dissolves.
Bring to the boil.
Boil briskly for 10–15 minutes or until setting point is reached.
Move saucepan from heat. Stir in butter to disperse scum.
Pot and cover.

Blackcurrant Jam   V

Makes about 2.3kg (5lb)   Preparation 30 mins
Cooking 55 mins

900g (2lb) stemmed blackcurrants
1.4kg (3lb) granulated sugar
15g (½oz) butter

Place blackcurrants into a large saucepan
and add 900ml (1½ pints) water.
Bring to the boil, cover and reduce heat.
Simmer gently for about 45 minutes or
until fruit is tender. Add sugar and stir until
dissolved. Bring to the boil.
Boil briskly for 5–10 minutes or until setting
point is reached.
Move saucepan from heat. Stir in butter to
disperse scum.
Pot and cover.

Variation

Gooseberry Jam   V

Follow recipe and method for Blackcurrant
Jam. Use gooseberries instead of
blackcurrants and halve the quantity of
water. Boil for 10–15 minutes or until setting
point is reached.

Dried Apricot Jam   V

Makes about 1.4kg (3lb)   Preparation 20 mins
plus soaking   Cooking 1 hr

450g (1lb) dried apricots
450g (1lb) granulated sugar
75g (3oz) blanched and split almonds
Juice of 1 large lemon
15g (½oz) butter

Snip apricots into smallish pieces with
kitchen scissors. Cover with cold water and
leave to soak overnight.
Drain, put into a saucepan and add 900ml
(1½ pints) water.
Bring to the boil, lower heat and cover pan.
Simmer gently for about 45 minutes or until
fruit is tender.
Add sugar, almonds and lemon juice. Heat
slowly, stirring all the time, until sugar
dissolves.
Bring to the boil.
Boil briskly until setting point is reached.
Move pan from heat. Stir in butter to
disperse scum.
Pot and cover.

Thick Orange Marmalade   V

Makes about 2.3kg (5lb)   Preparation 30 mins
plus standing   Cooking 2½ hrs

680g (1½lb) Seville (or bitter) oranges
Juice of 1 lemon
1.4kg (3lb) granulated sugar
15g (½oz) butter

Scrub oranges well.
Put, without slicing, into a large saucepan.
Pour in 1.7 litres (3 pints) water and bring to
the boil.
Reduce heat and cover pan. Simmer very
gently for 1½–2 hours or until skins of fruit
are soft and can be pierced easily with a fork.
Lift oranges out of pan. Cool slightly and
chop coarsely.
Collect pips and tie in a muslin bag.
Return chopped oranges to pan with lemon
juice and bag of pips.
Add sugar and heat slowly, stirring all the
time, until sugar dissolves.
Bring to the boil. Boil steadily until setting
point is reached.
Move pan from heat. Stir in butter to
disperse scum. Leave in saucepan until a skin
forms on surface. Stir gently.
Pot and cover.

Lemon Curd   V

Makes about 550g (1¼lb)   Preparation 30 mins
Cooking 30 mins

110g (4oz) butter
225g (8oz) granulated sugar
3 eggs plus 1 yolk, beaten together
Grated rind and juice of 3 lemons

Melt butter in a basin standing over a
saucepan of gently simmering water.
Add sugar, eggs and extra yolk, and lemon
rind and juice.
Cook gently without boiling until curd
thickens sufficiently to coat back of a spoon.
(If overheated the mixture may curdle and
separate.)
Pot and cover.

Variation

Orange Curd   V

Follow recipe and method for Lemon Curd.
Instead of all lemons, use 2 oranges and
1 lemon.

Pink Grapefruit Crush

Cold Drinks

Pink Grapefruit Crush   V

Make 1 litre (1¾ pints)   Preparation 15 mins
Per glass 67 kcals, 0g fat (0g saturated)

50g (2oz) caster sugar
Handful of mint leaves
1 litre (1¾ pints) pink grapefruit juice
Crushed ice

Place sugar in a saucepan with 200ml (7fl oz) water. Bring to the boil and simmer for 3–4 minutes.
Add mint to sugar syrup. Cool.
Remove and discard mint leaves. Add juice and stir.
Divide ice between glasses and pour over juice.

Tropical Fruit Crush   V

Serves 4   Preparation 15 mins
Per portion 94 kcals, 0g fat (0g saturated)

1 large mango, peeled, stoned and chopped
4 large passion fruit, peeled and deseeded
300g (11oz) fresh pineapple, peeled, cored and chopped
Juice of 2 oranges
Juice of 2 limes
450ml (¾ pint) ice cubes

Place all ingredients in a blender or food processor. Blend until smooth.
Serve immediately.

Elderflower Cordial   V

Makes 1½ litres (2½ pints)   Preparation 10 mins plus infusing   Per portion 332 kcals, 0g fat (0g saturated)

1kg (2¼lb) caster sugar
50g (2oz) citric acid
20 elderflower heads
1 lemon, thinly sliced
4 limes, thinly sliced

Place sugar in a bowl with 900ml (1½ pints) boiling water and stir until dissolved.
Add remaining ingredients and stir.
Cover and store in a cool dry place for 6 days.
Strain through muslin or a clean J-cloth and discard fruit and flowers.
Pour into a bottle, seal and store in the fridge for up to a year.

Raspberry Cordial   V

Makes 500ml (18fl oz)   Preparation 5 mins   Cooking 10 mins   Per tbsp 32 kcals, 0g fat (0g saturated)

680g (1½lb) raspberries
225g (8oz) caster sugar

Place raspberries and sugar in a heatproof bowl. Place over a saucepan of simmering water and leave until fruit is very soft.
Strain through a sieve, pressing down on fruit to extract juice.
Pour syrup into a bottle and store in the fridge for up to 4 months.

Minty Lemon Sorbet Tea   V

Serves 4   Preparation 10 mins plus infusing and chilling
Per portion 70 kcals, 0g fat (0g saturated)

600ml (1 pint) hot Darjeeling tea
2 sprigs of fresh mint
Granulated sugar to taste
4 scoops lemon sorbet
1 lemon, sliced
Strawberries and mint sprigs to serve

Pour hot teat into a jug and add mint sprigs. Leave to infuse and cool. Then chill.
Remove mint and add sugar to taste.
Place sorbet into 4 tall glasses. Pour in tea.
Decorate with strawberries and mint.

Iced Tea Punch   V

Serves 8   Preparation 10 mins plus infusing and chilling
Per portion 214 kcals, 0g fat (0g saturated)

20g strong afternoon tea leaves
Rind and juice of 4 large oranges
Rind and juice of 2 lemons
175g (6oz) demerara sugar
1 mango, stoned, peeled and thinly sliced
1 dessert apple, cored and thinly sliced
12 ice cubes
600ml (1 pint) ginger ale
Small bunch of mint leaves

Put tea leaves in a bowl with lemon and orange rind and sugar.
Add 700ml (1½ pints) boiling water. Stir and leave to infuse for 20 minutes.
Strain through a sieve lined with kitchen paper.
Add orange and lemon juice and fruit slices. Chill until ready to serve. Just before serving, add ice cubes, ginger ale and mint.

Thick Strawberry Shake V

Serves 1 Preparation 10 mins
Per portion 151 kcals, 5g fat (2.7g saturated)

90ml (3fl oz) milk, chilled
2 scoops of strawberry ice cream

Place milk and ice cream in a blender and process until smooth.
Pour into a glass.
Serve immediately.

Nutty Banana Shake V

Serves 2 Preparation 10 mins
Per portion 321 kcals, 15g fat (6.4g saturated)

1 banana, peeled and sliced
150g (5oz) hazelnut yogurt
300ml (½ pint) milk, chilled
Banana chips, to decorate
Chopped hazelnuts, to decorate

Place banana, yogurt and milk in a blender and process until smooth and frothy.
Pour into a glass and decorate with banana chips and nuts.

Rhubarb & Ginger Shake V

Serves 2 Preparation 10 mins
Per portion 163 kcals, 6g fat (3.7g saturated)

300ml (½ pint) milk, chilled
65g (2½oz) rhubarb yogurt
1 tsp preserved stem ginger syrup
½ piece preserved stem ginger, chopped
1 scoop vanilla ice cream
Grated nutmeg to serve

Place all ingredients except nutmeg in a blender and process until smooth and frothy.
Pour into 2 glasses and decorate with a little ground nutmeg before serving.

Orange Yogurt Smoothie V

Serves 2 Preparation 10 mins
Per portion 378 kcals, 15g fat (9.2g saturated)

300ml (½ pint) milk, chilled
150g (5oz) orange yogurt
110ml (4fl oz) orange juice
Grated orange rind to decorate

Blend together milk, yogurt and orange juice.
Pour into 2 glasses and serve decorated with orange rind.

Strawberry Yogurt Smoothie V

Serves 2 Preparation 10 mins
Per portion 145 kcals, 5g fat (3.2g saturated)

150g (5oz) strawberry yogurt
300ml (½ pint) milk, chilled
Strawberries to decorate

Whisk yogurt and milk well together.
Pour into 2 glasses.
Decorate with strawberries.
Serve immediately.

Tropical Smoothie V

Serves 2 Preparation 10 mins
Per portion 81 kcals, 2g fat (1.3g saturated)

150ml (¼ pint) milk, chilled
65g (2½oz) peach yogurt
50ml (2fl oz) tropical fruit juice
Desiccated coconut to serve

Put the milk, yogurt and juice drink in a blender and process until smooth.
Pour into 2 glasses and top with desiccated coconut.
Serve immediately.

Pawpaw Smoothie V

Serves 2 Preparation 10 mins
Per portion 169 kcals, 4g fat (2.2g saturated)

150g (5oz) natural yogurt
2 tsp clear honey
75g (3oz) pawpaw, peeled, deseeded and chopped
1 banana, peeled and sliced
150ml (¼ pint) milk, chilled

Put all the ingredients in a blender and process until smooth and frothy.
Pour into 2 glasses.
Serve immediately.

Fruity Frais V

Serves 2 Preparation 10 mins
Per portion 122 kcals, 6g fat (3.4g saturated)

150ml (¼ pint) fromage frais
150ml (¼ pint) orange juice
1½ tsp clear honey

Put all the ingredients in a blender and process until smooth and frothy.
Pour into 2 glasses.
Serve immediately.

Iced Coffee V

Serves 3–4 Preparation 10 mins plus chilling
Per portion 99 kcals, 6g fat (3.4g saturated)

300ml (½ pint) espresso coffee
450ml (¾ pint) milk
Sugar to taste
2 tbsp double cream, whipped

Combine coffee with milk.
Sweeten to taste. Chill.
Pour into 3 or 4 tumblers just before serving.
Top each one with a swirl of lightly whipped cream.

Minty Chocolate Milk V

Serves 4 Preparation 15 mins plus chilling Cooking
5 mins Per portion 272 kcals, 13g fat (7.5g saturated)

75g (3oz) plain chocolate, grated
2 tbsp caster sugar
900ml (1½ pints) milk
1 tsp peppermint flavouring
2 tbsp double cream, whipped
Mint leaves

Slowly melt chocolate and sugar with 150ml (¼ pint) milk in a saucepan.
Stir in remaining milk with peppermint flavouring and chill.
Pour into 4 glasses just before serving.
Top each with cream and mint leaves.

Sloe Gin V

Serves 34 Preparation 45 mins plus infusing
Per portion 57 kcals, 0g fat (0g saturated)

500g (18oz) sloes
600ml (1 pint) gin
150g (5oz) soft brown sugar

Prick sloes all over with a pin and put into a large jar with a tight fitting lid.
Pour gin into jar and add sugar. Stir well.
Store in a cool, dark place for 3–4 months, shaking weekly.
Strain through muslin or a clean J-cloth. Discard fruit and pour into a bottle.

Variation

Plum Gin V

Follow recipe and method for Sloe Gin.
Replace sloes with sliced plums.

Whisky Cream Liqueur V

Serves 4 Preparation 15 mins plus chilling
Per portion 231 kcals, 14g fat (9g saturated)

1 tbsp light soft brown sugar
½ tsp vanilla extract
90ml (3fl oz) Drambuie
300ml (½ pint) single cream

Dissolve sugar in 2 tbsp hot water.
Allow to cool.
Stir in vanilla extract, Drambuie and single cream.
Chill before serving.
This will keep for 4 days in a refrigerator.

Variation

Coffee Cream Liqueur V

Follow recipe and method for Whisky Cream Liqueur. Omit Drambuie and use 90ml (3fl oz) Tia Maria (coffee liqueur).

Chocolate Ginger Frappé V

Serves 4 Preparation 15 mins
Per portion 218 kcals, 9g fat (5.2g saturated)

Crushed ice
6 tbsp drinking chocolate
900ml (1½ pints) milk, chilled
2 tbsp ginger wine
2 tbsp double cream, whipped

Cover base of 4 tumblers with crushed ice.
Mix drinking chocolate to a smooth liquid with 3 tbsp boiling water.
Whisk in milk and ginger wine.
Pour into glasses.
Top each with cream.
Serve immediately.

Pina Colada Cocktail V

Serves 4 Preparation 10 mins
Per portion 145 kcals, 7g fat (4.5g saturated)

4 tbsp white rum
4 tbsp coconut liqueur
4 tbsp pineapple juice
4 tbsp double cream
Ice cubes

Put all the ingredients in a blender and process until thick and frothy.
Pour into 4 glasses.
Serve immediately.

Hot Drinks

Winter Warmer   V

Serves 6   Preparation 5 mins   Cooking 30 mins
Per portion 217 kcals, 0g fat (0g saturated)

400g pack frozen summer fruits
175g (6oz) soft brown sugar
1 cinnamon stick
1 litre carton apple juice
1 apple, cored and sliced
1 orange, sliced

Place frozen fruit, sugar and cinnamon in a saucepan with 600ml (1 pint) water.
Heat gently for 20 minutes. Drain through a sieve, pressing down on fruit to extract juice.
Pour back into saucepan and add apple juice. Heat until hot.
Serve with sliced fruit.

Spiced Milk   V

Serves 1   Preparation 3 mins   Cooking 5 mins
Per portion 96 kcals, 4g fat (2g saturated)

200ml (7fl oz) milk
Pinch of ground cinnamon
Pinch of ground cardamom

Place milk and spices in a saucepan and heat until almost boiling, stirring occasionally.
Pour into a mug and serve sprinkled with a little extra spice.

Real Hot Chocolate   V

Serves 1   Preparation 10 mins   Cooking 5 mins
Per portion 223 kcals, 11g fat (6g saturated)

25g (1oz) plain chocolate
Pinch of ground nutmeg
200ml (7fl oz) milk
2 tbsp whipped double cream (optional)
Grated chocolate (optional)

Place chocolate, nutmeg and milk in a saucepan. Heat gently until chocolate dissolves. Do not boil.
Pour into a mug, spoon cream on top and sprinkle with a little grated chocolate if using.

Variation

Hot Chocolate Orange   V

Follow recipe for Real Hot Chocolate. Use orange chocolate instead of plain chocolate.

Malted Hot Choc   V

Serves 1   Preparation 5 mins   Cooking 5 mins
Per portion 271 kcals, 7g fat (4g saturated)

2 tbsp drinking chocolate
1 tbsp Ovaltine
300ml (½ pint) milk

Whisk together all ingredients in a small saucepan.
Heat until almost boiling.
Pour into a mug to serve.

Mocha   V

Serves 1   Preparation 3 mins   Cooking 3 mins
Per portion 124 kcals, 4g fat (2.3g saturated)

2 tsp drinking chocolate
2 tsp coffee granules
200ml (7fl oz) milk

Blend chocolate and coffee with a little cold milk. Add to remaining milk.
Heat in a saucepan, whisking until hot.
Pour into a mug and serve.

Spiced Orange & Cranberry   V

Serves 4   Preparation 5 mins   Cooking 10 mins
Per portion 115 kcals, 0g fat (0g saturated)

600ml (1 pint) cranberry juice
Rind and juice from 1 large orange
4 cloves
3 tbsp soft brown sugar

Pour juices into a saucepan.
Stud orange rind with cloves. Add to juice with sugar.
Heat gently until hot.
Discard rind and cloves and serve.

Hot Citrus Drink   V

Serves 3   Preparation 5 mins   Cooking 10 mins
Per portion 57 kcals, 0g fat (0g saturated)

Juice of 2 large lemons
Juice of 2 large limes
Juice of 4 large oranges
Caster sugar
Lemon slices to serve

Gently heat fruit juices in a saucepan, but do not boil.
Sweeten to taste with sugar.
Pour into heatproof glasses and serve with lemon slices.

Ginger White Chocolate V

Serves 1 Preparation 10 mins Cooking 5 mins
Per portion 323 kcals, 13g fat (7.6g saturated)

300ml (½ pint) milk
25g (1oz) white chocolate, broken up
1 tbsp ginger wine
1 tbsp rum
Ground nutmeg to serve

Place all ingredients except rum and nutmeg, in a small saucepan.
Heat, stirring until chocolate has melted and milk is hot.
Pour into a mug, stir in rum and sprinkle with nutmeg.

Cider Punch V

Serves 8 Preparation 10 mins Cooking 10 mins
Per portion 149 kcals, 0g fat (0g saturated)

1 apple
8 cloves
Rind and juice from 1 orange
Rind and juice from 1 lemon
1 cinnamon stick
50g (2oz) soft brown sugar
375ml (13fl oz) ginger wine
1¼ litres (2 pints) cider

Stud apple with cloves.
Place apple in a large saucepan with remaining ingredients.
Heat gently until hot.
Remove apple and serve.

Mulled Wine V

Serves 12 Preparation 10 mins Cooking 30 mins
Per glass 131 kcals, 0g fat (0g saturated)

2 x 75cl bottles red wine
600ml (1 pint) orange juice
900ml (1½ pints) water
2 oranges, sliced
1 lemon, sliced
4 tbsp clear honey
2 tsp ground ginger
1 cinnamon stick
4 cloves

Place all ingredients into a large saucepan and bring to the boil.
Simmer gently for 30 minutes.
Serve in heatproof glasses.

Cranberry & Wine Punch V

Serves 6 Preparation 20 mins Cooking 20 mins
Per portion 229 kcals, 0.3g fat (0g saturated)

1 litre carton cranberry juice
70cl bottle red wine
150ml (5fl oz) brandy, rum or whisky (optional)
2 large oranges, juice of 1, the other thinly sliced
2 lemons, juice of 1, the other thinly sliced
1 lime, thinly sliced
75g (3oz) granulated or caster sugar
12 cardamom pods
8 cloves studded into 2 slices of the orange
15cm (6in) piece cinnamon stick
1 vanilla pod
1 kiwi fruit, peeled and thinly sliced
1 star fruit, ribs trimmed with a vegetable peeler, then thinly sliced

Pour cranberry juice, wine and chosen spirit, if using, into large stainless steel saucepan.
Add prepared oranges, lemons, lime, sugar, spices and vanilla pod. Bring slowly to the boil, stirring until sugar dissolves.
Reduce heat and simmer for 15 minutes.
Just before serving, float kiwi fruit and star fruit slices on top of punch.

Irish Coffee V

Serves 1 Preparation 10 mins
Per portion 330 kcals, 24g fat (13.6g saturated)

2 tbsp Irish whiskey
2 tsp) brown sugar
Freshly made strong coffee
Double cream

Warm a coffee cup with hot water. Quickly wipe dry. Pour in whiskey, add sugar and fill with hot coffee to within 2cm (1in) of rim.
Stir briskly to dissolve sugar.
Top up with cream, by pouring it into cup over back of a teaspoon.

Variations

French Coffee V

Follow recipe and method for Irish Coffee. Use brandy instead of whiskey.

Jamaican Coffee V

Follow recipe and method for Irish Coffee. Use rum instead of whiskey.

Previous Books

Dairy Cookbooks are recognised as some of the most reliable recipe books ever written and have sold over 30 million copies. Each Dairy Cookbook is written around a topical theme and uses readily available ingredients. All recipes are triple-tested and have a full colour photograph.

The New Dairy Cookbook
(192 pages) was published in 2001 and features 150 delicious new recipes for all occasions.

Quick & Easy Dairy Cookbook
(192 pages) was published in 2003 and has 130 tasty recipes, which can be prepared in less than 30 minutes.

Year Round Dairy Cookbook
(192 pages), published in 2005 and features 130 seasonal recipes to give the taste buds a treat the whole year round.

Around Britain Dairy Cookbook
(192 pages) was published in 2006 and contains favourite regional recipes plus new ones with a contemporary twist.

Hearty & Healthy
(192 pages) was published in 2007 and contains recipes to help you eat well, keep well and enjoy good food.

Clever Cooking for One or Two
(192 pages) was published in 2008 and contains mouthwatering recipes for one or two that are simple to prepare with no waste.

Just One Pot
(176 pages) was published in 2009 and shows you how to cook great food with less fuss. All recipes use just one pot each.

Good Food, Fast
(176 pages) was published in 2010 and helps to make cooking a pleasure again even when you are short of time. Cook tasty meals in 30 minutes or less.

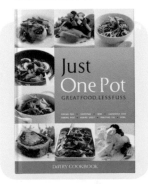

For more information and availability visit the Dairy Diary website at
www.dairydiary.co.uk